CONTENTS

EMPATH

SELF-DISCIPLINE

ANGER MANAGEMENT

DIALECTICAL BEHAVIOR THERAPY

HABIT

STOICISM

EMOTIONAL INTELLIGENCE

EMPATH

Master Your Emotions, Reduce Anxiety, Overcome
Negativity, Stop Worrying and Overthinking

RHONDA SWAN

Congratulations on purchasing *Empath,* and thank you for doing so.

The human connection is a remarkable ability. *What makes us connect and disconnect from the people around us?* Why do we feel so strongly about some relationships than we do about others? We may be different and unique individuals, but there are three things we all share in common: *We want to be seen. We want to be understood. We want to be heard.* That is the essence of empathy and what it means to be an empath. Now, most people understand empathy, but they're not quite sure what it means to be an empath. Even some empaths might not fully understand the gifts they possess.

What is an empath anyway? Well, an empath is simply an individual with a high ability to be able to hear information, gather it, assimilate it, and use this knowledge to understand the people around them better than most people can. An empath is an individual who is so sensitive to their surroundings that they are able to not only listen with their ears, but they can also feel the exact emotions someone might be experiencing, read body language, and absorb everything a person is telling them. Some empaths can understand a person better than that person understands themselves. They are highly-sensitive individuals, and if someone around them is displaying really intense energy, the empaths feel that energy but at a magnified level. For example, if someone was feeling sad, the empath would feel that sadness 10 times more. The emotional situation of others registers at a very high level for the empath.

If you've ever been told, *"You're very sensitive,"* you might have the qualities of an empath. If you feel the emotional pains of others so strongly, you might be an empath. Emotions are a part of who we are, and while everyone experiences emotions, empaths experience it on an entirely different level. The ability to be able to walk in someone else's shoes, to see things from their perspective and experience everything that they are feeling is a unique gift. If you're an empath in today's digital world, you possess a gift that is so rare and so overlooked that it is easily forgotten. Most people today are so consumed with what's going on in their own lives and what's happening in the online world that they have lost touch with the ability to connect on a human level. Yes, being an empath is a gift, but if you don't know how to manage this gift, it can quickly become a weight that feels like it's too much to bear.

By the time you get to the end of this book, you're going to have the tools and information you need to help you better manage your empathic abilities and restore balance in your life.

There are plenty of books on this subject on the market, thanks again for choosing this one! Every effort was made to ensure it is full of as much useful information as possible; please enjoy!

1 / THE EMPATH IN ME

WHAT DO WE MEAN BY "EMPATHY" or "compassion"? What makes us care about someone else's feelings? How do we even tell what they are feeling in the first place? Imagine walking down the street, and you come across a homeless person. You feel bad, even sorry for them partially stemming from your personal distress at the situation and nothing to do with their emotional state. Maybe you give them some money to take away some of the guilt you feel. In this scenario, one of two things can happen. If you're too focused on alleviating your own distress, you'll simply avoid the uncomfortable situation and not try to grasp the other person's mental state and how they must be feeling. In contrast, when you focus on their emotions, you're able to act altruistically and genuinely feel for them. The sympathy and compassion you feel don't necessarily mean you feel exactly what they are going through, but rather you feel *alongside* what they may be experiencing.

Suppose you want to find out exactly how someone else is feeling. How would you go about it? One approach would be to ask them directly how they feel, but then again, people can always hide their feelings. Sometimes they might not even understand how they truly feel in the first place and find it difficult to explain. The other approach is the logical approach. When you see someone smiling, you can deduce that they must be feeling happy, hence the reason for the smile. Then there is the other approach of putting yourself in the person's shoes, by imagining how you would feel if you were homeless. That's empathy.

Introduction to Empathy

Empathy. It is a word you've probably heard several times in your life, enough to get a general understanding of what it means. But the only way to truly understand empathy and what it means to be an empath is to *experience it.* This refers to the ability to recognize the emotions in others. *How does someone else feel in a situation? How do they respond to someone or something?* This is a skill that is going to take you far, especially professionally, because like self-awareness, having empathy is the key to helping you decipher the way someone else feels. This, in turn, will help you decide how you should respond and manage the situation. It will help you determine the best approach to use with them. Having empathy will help you anticipate the needs of another because you recognize the emotions that they are displaying. It helps you develop understanding and enhances your social skills. It is the tool that you need to help you develop good interpersonal skills, and effectively become an agent of change. It helps you become a better leader, communicate better, and even be able to exercise influential power over the people that you need to manage. It is the tool that is going to help you build and nurture meaningful bonds.

There's a difference between sympathy and empathy too, which is important to acknowledge before we dive deeper into the subject. *Sympathy* acknowledges someone's pain or difficulty. Sympathy might sound something like this:

"I'm so sorry this is happening to you."
"I can't believe that happened! I'm sorry to hear that."
"That must be really tough for you; I'm so sorry you're going through it."

Sympathy acknowledges that what the other person is going through is difficult and hard, and you are affected by that because you feel genuinely sorry they're going through a rough time. *Empathy*, however, takes it a step further. Empathy goes beyond the logical mind. It goes beyond the thinking and beyond the rational part of the mind too. Empathy envelopes the emotion and the state of being that the other person is in, and connects with them on their level. A lot of the time, empathy could be displayed without having to say much. There could be no explanation or the desire to "fix" the problem. Empathy creates a sense of "oneness" with the person you're experiencing it with. For example, let's say you just got the news that a very good friend of yours is diagnosed with a serious health problem. Your friend had this seemingly perfect life and everything going for them. All of a sudden, life hits the brakes, and their whole world is turned upside down by this news. Empathy allows you to feel exactly what they are going through. The shock at receiving such news, the questions that linger about where do you go from here, and probably every single emotion they must be experiencing. You find yourself crying, bawling your eyes out the way your friend must have done when they first got the news because you cannot believe this is happening. You experience all the same overwhelming emotions your friend did. You're in a state of grief and pain, just like they are.

Empathy can bring a real sense of comfort. Often, people who are going through a hard time need you to "be" with them, and this does not always mean help them fix a problem. There's a sense of comfort that comes from knowing someone completely and wholeheartedly understands what you are going through. When you find yourself in those moments where you don't always know what to say or how to act, pause for a minute. There is no "right way" to approach every emotional situation, and that is the beauty of empathy. It allows you to show your support by *being there* for them. Be the refuge that the other person needs.

Empathy is a necessity because life is built on relationships. Relationships are what life is all about. We've got a relationship with our families, friends, colleagues, partners, spouses, and various other people we may meet as we journey through life. Some relationships mean everything to us, and obviously, we would want to do everything that we can to keep the relationship healthy. Once a relationship has been damaged, it can often be hard to piece back together; sometimes, it can't be fixed at all. This is why empathy matters, because it provides you with the knowledge, tools, and skills that you need to foster and nurture these relationships, to keep them healthy and always thriving. Empathy helps you relate to the people closest to you and the people around you. It helps you to understand how you should react and respond to situations in the best possible manner. It helps you form deeper, more meaningful bonds because you can understand what the people around you may be feeling and see things from their perspective. The ability to empathize is going to benefit you in so many ways. It helps you resolve conflicts better and manage disagreements when you can empathize with others. It helps you accurately predict how others are going to react. It makes you more confident at expressing your point of view because you're attuned to your surroundings.

When you're attuned to the emotions and feelings of other people, they will view you as a source of comfort, sometimes even as someone you can heal them emotionally. It improves your motivation to become better and the ability to thrive in any social setting. You form better and stronger bonds with the relationships that you forge, even the new one. You will find it much easier to forgive others because you can see things from their perspective, reflect on why they reacted that way, and understand where you're coming from. It makes you more aware of your non-verbal body language and the way you come off to others. If you want to wield any kind of influence, you need to have empathy on your side. When you fail to sense the way that others around you feel, your social interactions will suffer as a result. You will find it very difficult to build effective rapports, and even to form solid bonds. People must be able to like you, trust you, and relate to you if they are going to allow themselves to be influenced by you.

Signs You Might Be an Empath

What springs to mind when you think of the word empath? Do you believe that empaths are people who have already been born with that gift? That's a common misconception, although true in some cases. But being an empath is a skill that you can learn. Becoming an empath is about training your mind, exercising it to become more attuned to empathy. It is about shifting your mindset, training it until empathy becomes second nature to you. It further enhances your ability to relate and understand those around you. Someone who is a skilled empath is someone who is effective at reading emotional cues. They are able to listen effectively to the voices of the people around them because they have a genuine understanding of where that person is coming from.

Empaths are compelled to help others because they are able to grasp the experience of another in a way not many people can. Abigail Marsh, a neuroscientist, and psychologist, wrote a book in 2017 called *The Fear Factor* in which she describes the evidence she has found. Marsh explains that there is a difference between the brains of people who are highly empathetic compared to everyone else. She refers to these groups of individuals as *altruists*. Empathy is no doubt a valuable skillset to have. It leads to stronger and more trusting connections with the people around you. It helps you figure out how to act appropriately in social situations. However, being an empath can also be a very draining experience. The intensity of the emotions that are felt by empaths is so powerful it can often leave them feeling drained as though they went through the emotional experience themselves, that is how vividly they experience these emotions. Being flooded with emotions is a difficult thing to go through, and it can negatively impact your mental health if you don't do something to take care of yourself. This is even more significant when the emotions you experience aren't yours.

Being an empath is not just a skill for someone who was born with that natural gift. It is something we all can learn. Empathy is not just about working on controlling and understanding emotions; it is about learning to act, be and care. These should slowly start to become part of your personality. By simply changing your attitude, displaying a little love and care, you would be surprised at what a world of difference it can make. With their highly sensitive nature, empaths are likely to feel over-whelmed by crowds and loud noises. They are also prone to feeling completely exhausted to the point of fatigue. Awareness is where it all begins, and it is important to know if you and empath before you can take the necessary steps needed to bring balance to the experience. Here are the signs you might be an empath:

- **You're Emotionally Intuitive -** Because of your empathetic nature, you can quickly tell what someone is feeling without really thinking about it. You're able to instinctively read a person's body language without them having to say a word. When you actively listen to someone tell their story, you're able to take on their pain, their anger, their happiness, or their excitement. You're like an emotional sponge that absorbs the feelings of everyone around you, whether you purposely want to or not.

- **You Immediately Jump At the Chance to Help Others -** Especially when you sense someone in distress. You instantly jump at the chance to help them if it means easing their pain or when you can clearly see how their struggles are impacting them. You relate to what they are going through because it's almost as though you are going through it too. You feel a strong desire to help them take away their pain, so you offer to help them in any way that you can. You give very little thought to the consequences of the emotional toll it takes on you when you're constantly reaching out to help others. The most common consequence is the neglect of your own emotional wellbeing.

- **You Think With Your Heart -** You tend to think with your heart rather than your head. As an empath, the way you do things might not always be logical, but it does tend to come from a place of care and concern. You're compelled to do the loving thing, even if it does not always work in your favor. Since the emotions you feel are so intense, you genuinely care about the other person, and you want to do everything in your power to help them, even at your own expense.

- **You're Sensitive -** Empaths are constantly engulfed in emotions, and it makes you vulnerable. A highly sensitive person is sensitive to many types of energies and reacts emotionally when they feel overstimulated. When a friend of yours is feeling enthusiastic, you share in their exuberance. When someone you care about is distraught, you cry along with them, feeling every bit as hurt and upset as they are. It takes a great deal of energy to feel these emotions, and naturally, they are overwhelming because empaths forget that they have to consider their state of emotions too. Over time, empaths become sensitive to even the slightest emotional change and stressors. Being an empath means you become more susceptible to extreme mood swings because you're so deeply affected by the emotions of others.

- **You Know How to Read People -** Empaths have an uncanny ability to read people and when it comes to understanding other people's motives. They can usually tell when someone is lying or not being authentic. Empaths are highly observant and notice the subtle messages that other people send through their body language and facial expression. They can read other people like an open book.

- **You Can Pickup the Vibe Of A Room -** If you're able to walk into a room and immediately pick up on the energy in that space, chances are you might be an empath. Whether the energy of the room is positive or negative, either way, you're picking up on its signals as soon as you walk through the door.

- **You're A Peacemaker -** Empaths don't like disharmony, for obvious reasons. In the face of conflict, an empath might do one of two things. They could either avoid the situation entirely or try to resolve the issue immediately. They are persistent in finding a solution, and some empaths won't rest until they make sure everyone is happy. They are very sensitive to any form of aggression, even the ones they see online or on the news. They could be moved to tears or feel physically ill watching violence on any kind of media platform.

- **You Are Quirky and Creative -** If you're an empath, you might be culturally creative. Maybe you enjoy painting, making music, singing, or inventing something new, you're inspired to do things that move society forward. Sometimes the ideas you have might not be understood by others or go against the grain, but that doesn't hold you back.

- **You Need Time to Recompose and Recharge Yourself -** Between juggling your own emotions and the emotions of others, you're bound to be emotionally exhausted. Empaths tend to attract people into their lives like magnets because of their gentle and compassionate nature. Being around people is both exhilarating and exhausting for an empath. Alone time becomes a necessity to refuel your emotional gas tank, reset yourself, and gain a sense of balance again. This alone time is necessary at helping to prevent burnout.

- **You Love Nature and Animals -** As an empath, you're more of a lover than a fighter. The love you feel doesn't stop at people alone but extends to animals and nature too. It is not unusual for an empath to feel a deep emotional connection to animals. They probably have a pet or two at home or feel the need to be outdoors often. This is their way of coping and neutralizing the effects of all the emotions they take on from other people. Some empaths prefer to be vegetarian because they connect to the emotions of the animals too.

- **You Tend to Daydream -** Empaths usually make great listeners, but they do have the tendency to daydream during small talk and less important conversations. If you're an empath, one minute you could be listening to a conversation about your friend telling you how their day was at work, and the next minute you'll be thinking about something another person might have said to you earlier. An empath might drift off if a conversation has no strong emotions involved.

- **You're Free-Spirited -** Do you find routines and rules debilitating? Are you free-spirited? Then there's a good chance you might be an empath after all. Even though overstimulation is not a good thing for an empath, you tend to get bored easily if you're not stimulated enough too. You're drawn to adventure, freedom, and travel, and those are the things that make you the happiest.

Is empathy a good thing? Absolutely. It has been proven to be useful in a number of jobs. One example would be if you're in a supervisory position and required to take on the perspectives of others. Actors who possess empathy will also find this skill helpful. Do you relate to any of the signs above? If yes, then chances are you might be an empath.

What Happens When You're an Empath

Is being an empath even a real thing? Or is all of this nothing more than spiritual mumbo-jumbo? It's easy to be dismissive about the whole thing, but the truth is being an empath simply means you're an individual who is highly empathetic. That's it. While other people talk about trying to cultivate the ability to walk a mile in someone else's shoes, empaths can do it for real. Empaths have the ability to go into such an emotional state that other people simply cannot fathom. Does being an empath make you better than a normal person? Not necessarily. An empath is like everyone else, except for the ability to be so highly tuned in to other people's emotions.

Empaths probably had a hard time growing up, or they were commonly misunderstood. Especially when you're growing up in a world today that repeatedly tells us it is *not okay* to be emotional. That it is *not okay* to show your emotions. That you need to bottle those emotions up and keep a stiff upper lip. It's hard to fine-tune your ability to manage your emotions, especially when you're a growing child or teenager who might not fully understand this gift that you possess just yet. It can feel isolating and lonely, and it can feel like no one understands you. When you're an empath:

- **You Connect With Yourself Better -** Before you can begin understanding others, you must first connect with yourself. An effective empath is someone who is centered, someone who is down to earth and grounded. When you are connected with yourself, you're less likely to become distracted easily by what's going on around you. You're able to focus on what matters at hand. It's easy to let our thoughts and emotions get the best of us. It is so easy to be consumed by negativity. Learning to become an empath begins within you, and you start by learning how to focus and gain control of what's happening internally. One of the best techniques you could apply to connect with yourself is through meditation. Meditation helps you find balance, calm, and inner peace, and it can be utilized in almost every aspect of your life whenever you feel anxious, worried or stressed. Learning to control our minds is one of the most difficult things we can do. But to become an empath, this is what is needed. Another method you could use to connect with yourself is spending a few minutes every day just being in your own company. We live in a society today that is far too attached to their mobile devices, and it is time we ditched them for a bit. You'll never connect with yourself if your eyes are constantly glued to a digital screen. Pause, take a breathe, slow down and just appreciate being with yourself. This can be done along with your meditational sessions. It gives you time to reflect on what matters to you, and more importantly, it gives you a few minutes to clear your head and think.

- **You're Focused on the Other Person More Than Yourself -** As an empath, life is less about yourself and more about the other people in it. When you're eating that delicious lunch you just bought from the store nearby, do you think about the people who worked hard to prepare it for you? The hours that they spent in the kitchen, so you didn't have to? When you're enjoying your delicious cup of coffee at the local coffee shop, do you think about the ones who went through all that trouble to gather the coffee beans that you're enjoying right now? The people who helped to ship and deliver that coffee to the local shop where you're sitting at this moment enjoying the fruits of their labor? These people do not necessarily have to be directly in front of you for you to make the connection. It is about taking a moment to think about these people and silently offer a quick thank you, to feel grateful for the people who have made it possible for you to enjoy the little luxuries you have. It is about connecting with humanity.

- **You Walk a Mile in Another's Shoes -** This is perhaps the most obvious thing that you can do, but it works. Being an empath will teach you to see beyond your own feelings and to be able to connect to someone else without prejudice or judgment. Whenever you're involved in a conversation with someone, always picture what it would be like to see things from their point of view, not just yours. This is one of the most basic, yet effective ways, which you can begin growing your empathy skills. We may not realize it, but rarely do we ever give proper thought to what someone else might be going through. We may listen to what they're telling us, and we may sympathize. But how often do we *attempt to feel* what they're currently dealing with? That's what happens when we lack the necessary empathy skills to respond appropriately. It may be silly or dramatic to us, but they to them it could be a very serious matter.

- **Your Curiosity Grows -** Empaths nurture their curiosity. They look for reasons to engage with people they normally wouldn't connect with. Strike up conversations with people who come from different backgrounds than you do. By socializing with a diverse group of individuals and casting your net far and wide, you develop a universal understanding of the world and the people around you. It helps you to see these individuals as humans and break down any further barriers which might have existed that prevented you from being more empathetic with them.

- **You Are No Longer Prejudice -** When someone of a different race, gender, or religion approaches you, how do you react if it is something you're unfamiliar with? Do you automatically set up a barrier? That's being prejudice. For some, being prejudice is already an innate part of who they are, but not for an empath. When you are an empath, you are going to have to challenge your prior beliefs, the prejudices you currently have. Work to get rid of them and start to view people, places, and situations with an open mind. Just because a person is different from you doesn't mean you should be wary. Everyone is still human at the end of the day. We're all equals on this earth and we should mutually respect one another. To help you with this, try to find something which you can connect on. Some common ground. When you can relate to them and connect on a shared interest, you'll have greater interactive experiences and eventually, boundaries will just slip away. This is when greater empathy occurs, by opening up to the people around you and welcoming them as part of your circle.

Empathy is a gift. There is always a reason for every reaction, and it is empathy that is going to help you see past the difficult behavior someone may be displaying towards you and take it a step further. There may be moments in your life when the emotions become so overwhelming you wish you didn't have this ability. That you wish you could be normal. Being an empath is not just about the passive receiving of emotion. Being an empath is not about being a hopelessly sensitive person who is battered by the emotions of others all the time. If you think about it, being an empath is almost like a *superpower*. Imagine being so connected to another human being beyond what others are capable of. Theoretically, if you know exactly what someone else is feeling, you should be able to know exactly how to comfort them, although admittedly, this does take practice. As an empath, you're in a powerful position of being able to relate to emotions and use them to your advantage. By developing an understanding of your emotions and the emotions of others, you are in a unique position to reach out and recognize that empathy is necessary for forming deep, meaningful relationships that are mutually beneficial. An empath knows how to appropriately respond and manage a situation because they are able to empathize with the people that they are speaking to. Empathy is a quality that is going to help you start developing even greater interpersonal and social skills, and this is how great leaders are able to influence change in the people that they manage under their care.

When empathy is combined with social skills, it will help transform the way that you relate to the people around you. For a leader to be able to forge good working relationships with their team members, they need to have good social skills about them. For you to maintain healthy, everyday relationships with the people who matter most in your life, you need empathy and good social skills to work with. Poor social skills have been known to be one of the main causes that arguments and misunderstandings happen because one or both parties have reacted poorly in the situation. As an empath, you can avoid all of this using your superpower. Instead of getting frustrated with the way that they are behaving, empathy will make you reach out towards them and ask them if they are really ok. Empathy will help you get to the root cause of the problem, and when you're able to anticipate someone else's needs because you can recognize the emotional symptoms that they're displaying, that's when you effectively become an agent of change. Walking a mile in someone else's shoes can do a lot to help you change your perspective.

Empathy and self-awareness will make you a much better person in a social setting. When you begin to develop an understanding of the emotions of those around you, you begin to find ways of relating to them on a more personal level. When you're viewed as someone who is easy to connect with, someone who is easy to talk to, people will automatically start to draw closer to you in a social setting because they feel comfortable being in your presence. Other people sometimes have painful emotions they need to deal with, and in times like these, they need someone to lean on. A shoulder to cry on. Someone who can listen to them without judgment and without prejudice. Someone who can make them feel better by just being *there*, even if that is all that they do. Displaying empathy towards others does not mean you're accepting of their less than desirable behavior, but rather empathy is there to serve as a reminder that everyone has their own troubles that they are dealing with. We often get so caught up in our own troubles and worries that we don't even consider the difficulties that someone else might be facing. If your colleague is going through a bad day and reacting harshly towards the rest of the team, empathy is the quality that helps you understand they have troubles too. Empathy will be the reason that you find some time to pull them aside and ask if everything is okay instead of getting worked up and irritated towards them because of the way that they're behaving. That is what it means to be an empath.

IN LIFE, we are faced with all sorts of challenges, and we desperately need each other to see things through. We need to be able to rely on each other, support each other, be there for each other, and empathize with each other during the most challenging moments of our lives. Challenges are never easy, but knowing that you're not going through it alone can make life a little more bearable and that's why being an empath makes you special. You're in a very unique position where your gift can prove to be a blessing in the lives of those who may need it. But is there more to empathy than just emotions? Is there actual science behind it?

The Science Behind Being an Empath

Empathy has been a part of our human emotional range for as long as we can remember. From the days of our early ancestors, in fact. We did not have survival abilities like claws are being able to leap from the tall branches of a tree to stay alive. We survived because we had this one, superpower on our side: *We had the ability to imagine what another person might be feeling*. This allowed us to work really well in groups and gave us the ability to form societies and empires. Humans are social creatures by nature, and without empathy, we would not have survived long as a species if we did not have this innate ability to feel someone else's emotions and genuinely want to help them.

Empathy may sound like a wishy-washy philosophy, but it is not. Far from it, in fact. Neuroscientists discovered what is known as the *Empathy Circuit*. This circuit was first discovered when the group of neuroscientists was working with patients who had dementia. These patients had a particular kind of dementia, which was referred to as *frontotemporal dementia* or FTD for short. One of the side effects of battling FTD was the patients started losing their ability to care. They don't care about their children, their lovers, their spouses, their family, their friends. Not caring about the significant people in your life is when the breakdown of every-thing that makes you human begins. The human connection is part of our unique makeup, and losing that ability to care and connect with others is like losing a part of ourselves. Patients dealing with FTD had certain parts of their brain shutting down, which indicated where in the brain empathy was supposed to be. That's how the empathy circuit was discovered.

Certain circuits in the brain are wired to help us detect emotions and then produce an appropriate emotional response to it. For example, certain parts of the *amygdala* and the *temporal pole* are important in helping us better understand the emotions and experiences that someone else might be going through. These experiences will then project to the *anterior cingulate cortex* of the brain, which generates this emotional reaction throughout the body through our autonomic nervous system and our face. This will, in turn, will trigger the *interior insula* portion of the brain, which is the part of the brain that helps us represent our internal states. It's not enough to have the brain working to produce the emotional reaction that we feel; our brain also needs to represent how the body has responded and monitor those internal cues.

The *Empathy Circuit* is powerful. Imagine for a minute that you're hanging out with a friend. Your friend is telling you about something terrible that happened to them this week and they are visibly distressed over the matter. As you're listening to them, your brain picks up on their emotions, and you begin to empathize. This feeling is triggered throughout your body by the brain, and the more you empathize with them, the more your entire body starts to get in sync with theirs. Your mirror their facial expressions, their posture, their heartbeat and even breathing. You start to take this a step further by reaching out and trying to comfort your friend and it works. Your friend starts to feel better as the two of you work on ideas and brainstorm solutions and suggestions about how to weather the storm, or you've helped by simply being the listening ear that your friend needed to vent their emotions. Now, can you imagine what would happen in this same situation if you *did not* empathize with your friend? Aside from probably causing your friend to feel more upset than they already did, you've probably done some damage to that friendship by not reacting in the appropriate manner expected. Especially when the two of you are supposed to be friends. The less empathetic you are, the more closed off you eventually start to become. Eventually, you'll reach a point where you're cold, distant, and aloof.

Relationships are a big part of who we are, even if you may be an introvert. Even introverts reach out to the people they trust and care about every now and then. It is *impossible* to survive this world without any kind of relationship or connection at all. Empathy is in our nature, and it is unfortunate that the world we live in today is weakening the internal empathy circuit we all have. We're so obsessed and distracted with what's happening in the digital world and social media that we forget to pay attention to what is happening right in front of us. The more connected we become to the digital world, the more disconnected we become to our fellow human beings. Being divided is only going to make it more difficult to come together to resolve problems and work together when we need to because we've lost the ability to do it. Unless it's behind a keyboard or computer screen, we've forgotten what it means to make a real connection because that part of our brain has shrunk from a lack of use. Yes, areas of the brain will shrink when they are underused. The activities we engage in creates changes in brain structure and rewires our neural circuits by eliminating the connections we don't use that often while simultaneously strengthening the ones we do.

The good news? If it can be shrunk, it can be *strengthened too.* Yes, our empathy circuits can be strengthened, and it begins with exercise. The exercise begins when you notice you're feeling negatively toward someone. Like when someone cuts you off in traffic as you're rushing to get home. This makes you angry and you notice this emotion. First, take a deep breath until you once again feel in control of your thoughts. Now, take the emotional state you fee a step further and try to understand *why* this person did what they did. Maybe they were rushing too. Maybe there's an emergency at home and they're in a hurry to get there. Maybe they've had a long day at work and they're distracted, not really thinking about the other people on the road. There could be a million reasons why they did what they did. You don't need to guess the right answer and you probably never will. But the act of trying to understand *why* the other person reacted the way they did is an exercise in strengthening your empathy circuit. You don't have to love everyone, but you can almost always empathize with them if you tried.

Empath Benefits

We all have the ability to empathize with others, but *empaths* take this to a whole new extreme level. Empaths can actually feel the emotions of others, whether they want to or not. It is something that happens so naturally that some empaths don't even realize when they're started to take on someone else's emotions. It just happens. Like a sponge that immediately soaks up what it comes into contact with. They don't have a choice in the emotions either, and whether what they pick up on is positive or negative, empaths are going to feel it as soon as they are within the space or in close contact with the person. That is some pretty powerful stuff. Yes, being an empath can be overwhelming, especially when you're flooded with multiple emotions at once. But there are benefits to this, and these benefits are the reason why empathy is a gift, even though sometimes it can feel like a curse.

Here's a mantra to start keeping in mind: *Empathy is your superpower.* Your highly sensitive state is going to allow you to be in a heightened state of awareness to other people and your surroundings. You have a greater capacity, capability, and awareness of yourself and others. It allows you to quickly shift and change the state that you're in too. This means if you're in a situation where you're feeling stressed, depressed, or anxious, you have the ability to shift your mental, emotional, and physical state if you want it to.

Empaths have an extremely reactive neurological system. They don't have the same filters that other people do to block out stimulation, which explains why they often feel overwhelmed by the energies and the emotions around them. Empaths are certainly a special group of people, although this ability does come with certain challenges, once you understand what a little more about your ability, the challenges become easier to deal with. Here are some other benefits that come with this superpower:

- **You Have the Makings Of A Good Leader -** Ambitious individuals stand to benefit the most from having empathy as a skill. In a leadership position, you will be responsible for several other individuals who are looking to you to set an example and to provide guidance. All eyes will be on you, and your relationships with those under your care are going to determine your success, your failure as a leader. Empathy-driven leaders use all five components of EI to help them build better bonds with people they work with; they use self- awareness, and self-regulation to tune in to what and how everyone else is feeling, and to assess the strengths and weakness of the team of people they're working with. They rely on their social skills and empathy to connect with these individuals and see things from their perspective. This is what separates a great leader from a mediocre one.

- **You Become Socially Adept -** Empathy will make you a much better person in a social setting. When you begin to develop an understanding of the emotions of those around you, you begin to find ways of relating to them on a more personal level. When

you're viewed as someone who is easy to connect wi
someone who is easy to talk to, people will
automatically start to draw closer to you in a social
setting because they feel comfortable being in your
presence.

- **Your Relationship Get Better -** Our life is all
  about relationships. The relationships that we have are
  what define us, what motivates us, and what can either
  drive us towards success or hold us back. Some
  relationships in our lives are more permanent, such as
  the ones we have with our families, friends, children,
  partners or spouses, and there are some relationships
  who may or may not be around for a certain period of
  time, like the ones we may have with our colleagues,
  roommates, and acquaintances. With every
  relationship, especially the ones that matter, you want
  to keep it as healthy as possible. Toxic relationships
  can quickly bring you down, and if you constantly let
  your emotions get in the way of your actions, you
  could be that toxic relationship. A damaged
  relationship is not always easy to repair, and to avoid
  damaging it at all in the first place, you need to have EI
  on your side.

- **You Treat Everyone with Kindness -** Empaths
  treat everyone with kindness because they have
  empathy and social skills. They are able to empathize

even with difficult people and try to see things from their perspective to understand the reason for their behavior. You're also a lot more respectful towards people. Respect is a vital habit towards cultivating happiness in your relationships that you seek. Each time that you show disrespect towards anyone, you are in a way letting them know that you don't accept them for the way that they are. Remember that people are unique individuals, just like you are, and part of cultivating relationships is accepting others and valuing them for who they are, not who you expect them to be.

- **You Have the Ability to Develop Connections -** Because you feel what others are experiencing, it gives you the ability to forge connections very quickly. Empaths also tend to exhibit their empathy in a subconscious way that promotes true, heartfelt connections. Sometimes without even saying a word. This encourages others to open up and share their vulnerabilities, maybe even confide in empaths in a way they would not feel comfortable doing with other people. Empaths are great at being such active listeners that people naturally gravitate towards them. This ability to forge deep connections could lead to stronger trust in the relationships that have been built, and this is an ability not everyone is privileged to have. Making any kind of real-life connection these days has become a challenge since social media and technology came into the picture, let alone a lasting, meaningful connection the way an empath can.

- **You Develop a Stronger Connection With Loved Ones -** You might say that your connection with your loved ones is almost telepathic. You understand the people you love the most in a way that no one else does. At times, you may experience a sudden emotion or pain, even if they are not right next to you at the time. That's how strong of a connection you can forge with them. Your intuition when it comes to your loved ones is strong and you tend to follow that implicitly, and as an empath, you pay attention to your intuition more than other people do.

- **You Tend to Be a Planner -** Being a planner can be a good thing since it stops you from rushing to make impulsive decisions. As an empath, you see deep meaning in certain situations, and you're able to assess what the emotional outcomes of each possible situation may be. You spend more time planning your next course of action to avoid rushing into a decision. Empaths prefer to choose the best course of action with the least resistance since they don't want to add to their emotional burden if they can avoid it.

- **You're More Forgiving -** Gandhi once said that *"forgiveness is something that is attributed to the strong."* He was right. That is exactly what empaths are. It takes great strength to take on someone else's emotions. It's not as easy as it might seem and neither is forgiveness. Forgiveness is one of the most powerful tools you could possess and coming from the perspective of an empath, it is much easier to forgive when you have the ability to see things from someone else's perspective. Not only will you eventually gain the ability to forgive others over time, but you'll also learn to forgive yourself. You'll learn acceptance, and you'll learn how to be much happier when you let go of all the unnecessary emotions that reside within you.

- **You Get Better at Naming Your Emotions -** Another great exercise that is going to enhance your self-awareness abilities is to name your feelings. Instead of just generalizing by saying I am feeling happy, define that emotion in greater detail. What level of happiness are you feeling? Cheerful? Joyful? You understand your emotions so well that you understand what triggered that reaction within you and then take a step back, assess the way you reacted at that moment, and think about how you might have reacted better in such a situation.

The Side Effects You Have to Live With As an Empath

One mistake many beginner empaths make when they are first learning to recognize their ability as a gift is that these beginner empaths believe they are less worthy than others might be. Especially in today's world where being overly emotional or sensitive is perceived negatively. Of course, this scenario could work both ways. Beginner empaths might start to believe that they are *better* than everyone else because they're got this gift. Either belief is common for many empaths who are starting to fully understand the unique perspective that comes with this ability. You might have experienced either one of these scenarios at some point or another. If you do notice either scenario might be the way you're feeling right now, don't judge yourself. Give yourself permission to notice it, acknowledge the way you feel. Remember this is part of the human experience. Right now, what you need to do is try not to tip the scales to either extreme. Feel too inferior, and you might impact your self-esteem while feeling too special or superior might lead you down the path of unhealthy narcissism.

Like everything else in life, being an empath has inevitable side effects. Like being constantly exhausted, for example, which is a side effect of being an empath that you might not have realized if you never noticed you had the gift. Empaths feel everything deeply and intensely, and that kind of intensity is not without its implications. Being an empath is something not many people can relate to. It's a feeling you get in your gut. If you've been able to relate to anything that has been talked about so far in this book, then your gut feeling is right, and you most likely have the gift. People rely on empaths for emotional healing, guidance, and support. But not many people think about the implications of what it means to bear the emotional burden of others. The darker side effects of being an empath can be both painful and harrowing to carry.

Here are some of the side effects of being an empath you might not have realized:

- **Sometimes It's Hard to Control Your Emotions -** If you find yourself losing control of your emotions far too often, getting emotionally carried away in situations that have no real cause for it, that's one of the side effects that come with being an empath. This can get better with emotional intelligence. Difficulty controlling emotions will make it hard for you to manage relationships too. Friendships, relationships with your family, colleagues, even your kids. Without the necessary social skills, empathy, and self-awareness, you're going to find it very hard to maintain any kind of lasting relationship in your life.

- **You Feel Tired and Demotivated -** You find yourself lacking the desire to do anything, even if it is something as small as checking and responding to your emails. You feel drained, tired, and demoralized all the time, especially after an encounter with anyone who might be harboring toxic emotions. Since empaths can understand people on a deeper emotional level, they feel it is their duty to listen and help others and when they fail to achieve that, they feel tired and demotivated.

- **You Feel the Need to Make the World A Better Place -** A lot of empaths believe that their purpose is to help make the world a better place. They feel an overwhelming desire to bring positive change, and this desire is second to none. Sure, other people may get the occasional thought of making a difference in the world, but empaths feel this desire within their very being and they are driven by it because they identify so deeply with the negativity around them.

- **You Feel Overwhelmed By What Others View As "Normal" -** Empaths are highly sensitive individuals, and because of their nature, what is considered normal to others might be overwhelming to them. Extreme sensitivity is not an exaggeration. Imagine an emotion that you're feeling right now, like sadness. Now, imagine feeling the intensity of that sadness by 10 times more. That intense feeling can cause a great deal of stress for someone who is deeply affected by it.

- **You Find It Difficult to Separate Yourself**

From Others - The hallmark of being an empath is your ability to feel and experience other people's emotions. As an empath, this awareness could result in a difficulty separating yourself from others because of the tendency to take on their burden and their pain as your own. Since an empath is an emotional sponge, if they're not careful, they can absorb the negative energies of others and take them on as their own. For a lot of empaths, joy and happiness come from helping others to heal. That's why they are referred to as emotional healers of the world. But the dark side of this desire is that they become so caught up in healing other people that they forget to heal themselves.

- **You Might Have Complex Emotions Yourself -** It's easy to think that empaths have their life together and forget that they have problems of their own too. A lot of empaths have complex emotions and issues that they are secretly dealing with too. They may have the gift of helping others go through difficult situations, but that does not mean the life of an empath is all sunshine and rainbows either. Some empaths struggle with problems like depression, anxiety, low self-esteem, and depression. They feel intense emotions daily, and this is bound to impact them in one way or another. If empaths are not careful, this high-intensity of emotions they feel every day can lead to self-destruction. Empaths who don't know how to deal with these challenges turn to addictive activities like smoking or consuming hard substances as a way to deal with the negative issues they are going through in their lives.

- **You Might Have Difficulty Falling In Love -** Most empaths have tried loving before, but their kind nature has left them hurt or preyed upon by others. Empaths are capable of loving to a fault, so much that they are sometimes exploited for their kindness. After a while, falling in love becomes difficult because it makes them wary of pain and disappointment. Like other people, they are afraid of being hurt again and may eventually have difficulty opening up to the idea of love. They hold back a piece of their heart and avoid falling in love too deeply to avoid putting themselves at risk of being hurt again.

- **You Neglect Yourself -** Empaths are givers rather than receivers. The challenge is that in doing so, they are prone to neglect themselves and their needs. They give up so much of themselves to make sure people around them are happy, but they receive nothing in return. Whenever value or energy is handed out without being replenished, sooner or later, the source is going to get dried up. In this case, the empath is the source. This is exactly what will happen if they neglect themselves for too long.

Being an empath is wonderful, but the painful dark side can sometimes feel like a burden that is too much to bear.

The Unforeseen Toxicity

Your desire to help others as an empath could leave you more open and vulnerable to being taken advantage of by toxic people. Unfortunately, these toxic personalities are only going to create more unnecessary drama in your life. This is the unforeseen toxicity, one that is going to leave you feeling miserable because toxic personalities are nothing more than a drain on your energy. Toxic personalities will never be truly happy, no matter what you do for them. There will always be a reason to complain, a reason why it is never good enough. They will hold you back and weigh you down in life, diminishing your confidence and belief in yourself. It can be difficult to leave once you've formed a bond with them, especially if you care about them. It is difficult to break free from the chain of narcissistic abuse that will be inflicted on you by these manipulators. Do you know why? Because they *don't* care about you. The only agenda they care about is their own.

But learning to recognize them at the beginning for who they are is how to learn to avoid them in the future. Have you ever been so frustrated or bothered by someone's behavior that even thinking about them is enough to get you worked up and exasperated? Even when they are not around? That' what a toxic personality can do to you. The most dangerous thing about them is how much power they have over your emotions, especially if you're an empath. A toxic person can be so powerful that they can inflict feelings of anger and frustration just by being themselves. If this is how you feel each time you encounter someone toxic, you are giving them power over your emotions. Each time they invoke a strong reaction from you, they have power over your life because you let them bother you to that extent. Replaying a toxic encounter in your mind is letting that toxic person have power over you. Even when they are not around, they are occupying your thoughts. The more you think about them, the more precious time you are giving them time, which they do not deserve. The more you try to help them, the more they will take advantage of you. It's in their nature. Letting a toxic person occupy your thoughts means you are letting them steal your valuable time, and this is precisely why they are so toxic and should be kept as far away as possible.

There is also a very real danger that empaths might get into relationships with toxic personalities, and this can be a real breeding ground for self-destruction. Narcissists and manipulative personalities love to prey on the benevolence and generosity of empaths. These narcissists know that empaths full of energy and positive vibes and this is what they prey on. Relationships like these are parasitic, where the narcissist ends up benefiting while the empath ends up feeling drained or hurt. Toxic people have a way of getting into people's heads and messing with their confidence. If you let them, they will hold you back because they prevent you from living your life to the fullest. Misery loves company, and so does a toxic person. They will do their best to make you feel as bad as they do, and they do it by making you feel like you are "stuck" without better options. Passive-aggressiveness could make an appearance here, where the toxic person would rely on this tactic to make you feel that you are incapable of moving forward and that you have no choice but to remain where you are with them.

It is crucial for empaths to acknowledge that narcissism is a disorder. By continuing to support the narcissist, you are either knowingly or unknowingly supporting a lie. The person you *think* you are helping does not exist. This can be a hard pill to swallow for the empath, and it is heartbreaking to know that there are unscrupulous individuals out there who will prey on their kindness in this manner. The narcissist is *not a tortured soul you need to help*. They don't need your special kind of love. They are demanding, judgemental, manipulative and ungrateful, always projecting their own selfish needs and feelings unto everyone else. They will have you trapped in an endless vicious cycle that will keep repeating on a loop unless you cut them out of your life once and for all. No matter how much you show them your deep, conditional love, they are never going to change for the better unless there is an internal motivation within them to do it. The sad truth is, narcissists are morally bankrupt individuals who will never appreciate the things other people do for them. Instead, they feel entitled to any love and devotion that is directed to them.

If only everyone in the world could be a little more like empaths, what a better utopian world it would be. Sadly, that is far from the truth. Most people today are so consumed with their own issues we have forgotten how to empathize with the people around us. To bring balance back into your life after an encounter with a toxic individual requires you to surround yourself with people who are the complete opposite. People who inspire you, you radiate positivity, you encourage you, and help you reach your full potential are the people you want to seek out. People who make you happy. Oprah Winfrey is a big advocate of this method, and she constantly reminds her followers to only surround themselves with people who are going to lift. them up higher. Dear empaths, if you have done everything in your power to help the people around you, then take comfort in that fact. Sometimes all you can do is your best and hope that it is good enough.

Is THIS A GIFT? Or a curse? If you're an empath, that thought has probably crossed your mind on more than one occasion. If you're struggling to find the balance between your emotions and that of others you take on, being an empath may seem like a curse. One of the emotions you're going to frequently feel from others is hurt. Maybe you've been labeled "hurt" or "overly emotional" by others who did not understand your abilities. In the beginning, you probably struggled with understanding yourself and why you feel emotions so strongly.

Reasons Why Being an Empath Is a Gift

You're a *healer*. As an empath, it is almost like you're bequeathed with a special mission to heal and help others, some of whom might not even realize they need help. Not a lot of people are walking this earth on a mission to heal other people emotionally and psychologically. You're one of the unique few with the power to make a genuine difference in someone's life. You could be the reason between hope and despair. You have a purpose in this world where so many others struggle to find purpose or even meaning to their lives. You have an ingenuity, skill, and a tireless ability to take on the energy of others, heal those that need, and still be a ray of hope for many who need a shoulder to cry on. Your gift is a *blessing. You are a blessing,* and it is time to start believing that. Like all gifts, not everything is going to be perfect and smooth sailing all the time. There will be moments when you experience highs and others when you feel so low you wish you never had this ability.

There's a reason why empathy is one of the core skills of emotional intelligence. It is the skill you need to comfort a grieving friend, understand someone else's point of view, persuade others to agree with you (in a non-manipulative way), diffuse tension, and find solutions to problems. In a complicated and stressful world, your gift is appreciated by the many lives you've helped to make a difference in, and you know this because you can *feel* their gratitude. Empathy is the glue that holds relationships together. While no doubt being an empath is overwhelming, it doesn't make it any less of a gift. No one understands the world and the people in it quite like you do.

For all these reasons and the reasons listed below, this is why your empathetic abilities should be considered a gift:

- **You See People As They Are -** You see the good, the bad, and everything in between. You see the emotions that they struggle to express. You see the pain they are so desperately trying to hide. Your ability to see beyond what's right in front of you means you see the potential in others where those who are not empaths might be quick to dismiss. You don't judge the person immediately, but instead, you try to understand the *reason* behind their emotions and actions. You question why they act the way they do and you try to find ways to help them. You know there is more to the story and you believe in the good in people. You're not quick to dismiss others without giving them the benefit of the doubt, and these are just some of the many reasons why the people you have helped love you so much. You're a unique spirit and the lives you touch are forever changed because you see people as they are.

- **You Don't Need Words to Be Expressive -** The accepted belief is that effective communication can only occur when two or more people are engaged in meaningful back and forth conversation. For an empath, communication can happen even without words. It is possible for an empath to merely sit with a friend and loved one, not say a word but somehow make them feel better. Some empaths can even read the minds of the people they are closest to, an ability that a lot of people would consider "weird" or "freaky." But it's not weird or freaky at all. It's because you are so attuned to the emotional vibrations of others. You think about them rather than focus on yourself.

- **You Have the Power to Heal -** Your ability to heal is your most significant attribute. It is a superpower that you have. Your ability to heal is so unique that in some cases, your presence alone is enough to bring a smile to someone's face when they are feeling down. Empaths also have this uncanny ability to actively listen, which is in itself a tremendous healing power. Active listening is an ability that requires you to be *fully present* in the conversation. When empaths actively listen, they are giving the other person their undivided attention. The easiest way to show someone you accept them, and you're open and willing to listen to what they have to say is to simply show them you're listening. How? Through non-verbal cues and make it apparent you're listening intently, like what an empath does. Encourage them to keep sharing their ideas without interrupting them or breaking the conversational flow by showing your support using non-verbal cues. Nod along in agreement when something they've said resonates with you. Maintain good eye contact throughout, have a friendly smile, or the appropriate emotional reaction on your face. These are all skills that come naturally to an empath and it is all part of their healing magic.

- **You Have the Ability to Read Auras -** Empaths that are extremely in tune with their gift have the ability to read auras. There are three types of people in the world: *The good buys, the bad guys, and the people who possess what can only be described as ugly personalities.* Some empaths have the power to see which category a person belongs too because they can read auras. An aura is described as the human energy field, and some believe that this energy field comes in different colors that emanate around a person. Sometimes not just a person, but it could also be present around an animal or even an inanimate object for that matter. Not everyone has the ability to see auras just like that on their own. Usually, it is psychics who claim to have that gift, and they are able to go as far as seeing the size, color, and the vibration intensity that is generated by a person's aura. Empaths can do it too. This ethereal radiation surrounds each living being, and it usually surrounds them within the space of two or three feet around the body. Most people are consumed by only believing and seeing what is directly in front of them that oftentimes they forget there is a whole other spiritual world out there that they are completely overlooking. But not you, because your empathic abilities give you the gift of being able to see a person's true intentions by reading their aura.

- **You Can Immediately Sense When Something Is Wrong -** Even with strangers. You don't have to be best friends with a person to know when something is not right. While other people are only able to develop a sixth sense about the people whom they consistently stay in contact with, you as an empath, have the ability to do this with *everyone*. Even complete strangers. Your ability to read others is not based on a relationship bias, but rather it is based on your gift of being able to immediately tune in to the emotions within your range.

- **You're Innate Creative Ability -** As an empath, you have a second gift of innate creativity. Most empaths are highly creative individuals who can transform plans and ideas and turn them into reality. There are certain industries in which empaths flourish well, such as fields of work that include art and design, marketing, and communication.

- **You Have the Powers of Persuasion -** The ability to read and sense the emotions of others puts you in a unique position. You have the ability to persuade others to see your point of view, believe in your ideas, and see things from your point of view when you're trying to reach an amicable agreement or diffuse an argument. Trying to convince, persuade, or change someone's mind is challenging. Perhaps the problem lies with the approach that we use. Most people tend to lead with their own point of view and their own perspectives and then proceed to point out what the other party needs to do to change. This approach hardly ever works the way we intend it to because it makes the other party defensive, even personally attacked when they're being told all the ways that they're "wrong" and why they need to "change" according to you. This is where your gift comes in handy. Being sensitive to your surroundings and the people in it means you're always going to be considerate of other people's feelings and you'll do your best to ensure all parties involved reach an agreement that everyone is happy with.

- **You Can Inspire Others -** Your empathetic nature can be used to inspire others to practice self-love and kindness towards themselves and others. You can inspire others by showing them how to be loving, caring, and giving, and treating everyone with kindness by being an example of what they should do. During hard times, your gift is going to be a beacon of hope for those who need to know that there is still love and kindness in the world. Among all the communication skills we can develop, empathic listening skills is one of the most valuable ones in our efforts to foster meaningful, deep connections with others. The ability to listen with compassion, demonstrate kindness for the plight of others, to be patient, loving, and accepting is a skill that not a lot of people possess these days. Therefore, to find someone with these rare attributes is like finding a diamond in the rough, and it is this very individual who is capable of becoming the master of both their professional and personal interactions. Simple acts of kindness will go a long way, and they will be remembered.

- **You're More Flexible in Relationships -** Successful relationships happen when there's an equal balance of give and take. Empaths are able to easily build connections and handle conversations effortlessly by being approachable, dependable, and caring. In most of the relationships that are formed, an empath's love and kindness are reciprocated equally unless they, unfortunately, encounter manipulative or toxic personalities.

- **You Can Expand Your Thoughts -** An empath is blessed with the ability to see beyond what other people can see. While others have a narrow, closed-off view of the world, empaths do not. You see beyond what is in front of you, and you make an effort to understand the perspectives and points of view of others. In doing so, you become intellectually and emotionally rich, which helps you take your communication abilities to the next level. No matter who you may be talking to, there is something to be learned from every encounter.

- **You Are Humble -** Stepping into someone else's shoes can be a very humbling experience. Most people believe their lives are hard until they encounter someone else who has it *much harder* than they do. Even then, they will not be able to fully comprehend the difficulty of the challenges that a person may be facing. They may sympathize, but they will never be able to empathize in a way the empath can. If you're an empath, this is why your gift is such a unique blessing. You understand others so well because you *literally* feel their pain, and this allows you to put away your judgments and assumptions. You're humbled by the emotions that you feel, and this trait is especially useful when you're dealing with difficult people. Difficult people want to be understood just as much as everyone else, and you have the power to do it. People open up to you when they see you're coming from a place of true intent to understand their perspective, rather than a malicious one.

Being an empath might make you feel like you are compelled to help everyone you meet, but that's not true. You *always* have a choice. You may get along well with a lot of people, but you still get to choose the kind of people you want to help and interact with at the end of the day. Whether you want to help them or not, it is still your choice; you don't have to feel forced into doing it because of your special ability. You still have a duty to protect your well-being and your emotions, and you need to take care of yourself first before you can take care of someone else. When necessary, you can always take a step back and disconnect from their energy so you don't have to feel overwhelmed

Identifying the Types of Empaths

Empaths are among the most beautiful souls around because of their naturally loving and caring personalities. The beauty of being human is how we are all unique and special in our own way, even empaths. Not all empaths are built equal. They come in all shapes, sizes, and with varying degrees of abilities. Understanding the type of empath you are can help you make the most of your ability. If you believe you have empathic abilities, you might resonate with one of the types of empath categories listed below:

- **Emotional Empaths -** These individuals are deeply affected by the emotions of others. They have an uncanny ability to connect with the people around them and feel what they are going through. Being very people-oriented individuals, it is not uncommon for the emotional empath to put the needs of others ahead of their own.

- **Spiritual Empaths -** Emotional empaths connect with people in the physical world, and spiritual empaths connect with the spiritual world. They are sometimes referred to as *Medium Empaths,* and have a deep connection with spirits, with the dead, and figures of the spiritual world. Although they may be present in the physical world, spiritual empaths have a mind that tends to wander because they relate with a world that is beyond this one. Some empaths serve as a medium between the spiritual and the physical world, sort of like what psychics do.

- **Physical Empaths -** They are like emotional empaths, with the ability to sense the emotional pain of others. Except that physical empaths can also sense *physical* pain, a person might be experiencing in their body. They thrive as natural healers since they have the ability to detect which areas of the body a person might be in need of healing.

- **Intuitive Empaths -** These empaths receive information from others by merely being around them. The more they connect with the person, the more they get to know the difficulties and challenges faced by the person without being told. They rely on intuition to decipher the hidden meaning and cues behind the body language and facial expressions exhibited.

- **Geometric Empaths -** They're also called environmental empaths. These empaths are deeply connected to the world around them, and they receive signals and energy about their physical environment. These empaths can read the energy and signals that are transmitted by rocks, soil, air, or water. Some empaths are even able to recognize when bad weather or some form of a natural disaster may be happening, an ability that is shared by animals. Animals always know before a natural disaster strikes and they run to higher ground and seek shelter even before it happens. Geometric empaths have the same ability. They're happiest when they are surrounded by nature, and find a deep connection to certain places that they feel most comfortable in. Geometric empaths love nature and they love to do what they can to preserve it. It's not uncommon to find in activist groups that advocate against anything that threatens to destroy nature.

- **Precognitive Empaths -** These empaths have the capacity to know what happens *before* it happens. Sometimes they see it in a dream, sometimes they see it in a vision. These visions of future events can be both good and bad. They can sometimes predict a situation or event before it has happened either through dreams or through a strong feeling or emotion they may receive. This strong sense of intuition can be a good thing that is useful in decision-making scenarios.

- **Animal Empaths -** Also sometimes referred to as *Fanna Empaths*. These individuals are drawn to animals so strongly it is almost as though they can communicate with these animals. Such a strong bond exists between these empaths and animals that at times, it almost seems as though the empaths and hear and speak the animal's language. To these empaths, the animals are their best friends, and they are firmly against animal cruelty or abuse of any kind. They are even against killing animals for food and opt to go down the vegan path instead. To them, hurting an animal is sacrilege. *Fanna* empaths thrive in animal-related occupations, and if this sounds like you, then you might be a Fanna empath.

- **Flora Empaths -** These are the floral empaths. You have the empaths who love animals, and you have the empaths you love plants and flowers, which are the *Flora Empaths.* They love greens, and they have the gift of the green thumb. They love spending time outdoors nurturing plants and flowers and planting seeds to grow new crops. They feel refreshed and full of life when they immerse themselves in gardens, parks, or any outdoor space with living things. These empaths are so tuned in to the plants they care for that like the *Fanna* empaths, they seem to hear and speak the language of the plants. They know exactly what a plant needs to grow and they are happiest when they are immersed in an occupation that pursues this course.

- ***Heyoka* Empaths -** The *Heyoka* empaths can sense things about others, know what is going to happen, and sometimes change or influence the course of events to a person's favor. Only a few empaths are considered *Heyoka's.* In Native America, the term *Heyoka* is used to refer to individuals who have the ability to mirror the emotions of others. *Heyoka* empaths see the world differently than other people do. These empaths feel unsettled if there is a problem that is unresolved. Even when they are sleeping, their mind is continually active.

- **Psychometric Empaths -** These empaths have the ability to draw meaning and impressions from objects. They can sense the energy, memories, and significant information from inanimate objects like photographs or jewelry. This information may be received in the form of images and sounds, tastes, aura, or emotions. These empaths are able to sense the past history of an object by touching it.

- **Claircognizant Empaths -** These empaths possess a high level of intuition that allows them to understand the true nature of any situation. These empaths are able to immediately detect when someone may be putting on an act or lying to them. Their intuition is so strong they can assess or read situations better than anyone else, which allows them to gauge exactly what needs to be done in such a situation. This makes them an excellent problem solver and the ones that others turn to when they need help solving a problem.

- **Telepathic Empath -** These empaths have the ability to transmit words, emotions, or images to someone else's mind without physical interaction. It is a form of communication in which thoughts are channeled or exchanged between a sender and receiver. If you are a telepathic empath, you're able to know what others are thinking when you look at them. It's a fantastic ability to have, but it does come with a price. Knowing someone else's thoughts is not always a good thing.

Being an empath can be a bittersweet experience. When you're in the presence of happy emotions, it empowers you and makes you feel happy too. At the same time, when you're in the presence of negative emotions, your ability won't allow you to simply tune out those feelings, and they affect you just as much as the positive ones do. Not all empath categories are also able to sense to see auras. The ability to read auras is a talent that not many people possess. If you are an empath who can, this is an added bonus to your existing gift. It is intriguing to find out things about the people around you that they wouldn't necessarily want to reveal on their own, and you can combine this information with what you're able to sense from their emotions. The ability to read auras is like having your very own personal in-built lie detector test. You will always be able to tell what the other person is thinking or feeling, even if they are pretending to cover it up or trying to hide it.

Being able to so acutely read people is going to be very beneficial to you because you will be able to take control of the situation at hand and guide it in the direction that you want it to go. Remember, auras reveal a person's intentions for what they really are, and having the ability to read auras will also put you in better control of your own body, your health, your emotions, everything you need to become a better version of yourself.

How to Make the Most Out of Your Gift

Once you've figured out you're an empath, the next question to think about would be what you can do to develop this ability so you can make the most out of your gift. To become a better, stronger, and more empowered empath, there are several things you need to do first:

Step 1: Avoid Judgment

When you judge the people that you perceive, you're not utilizing your empath abilities to the fullest. Judgment lowers your ability to be perceptive. Empaths need to listen with an open mind. Keep your judgments out of the picture because empathetic people are not judgmental. For true empathy to take place, you need to forget your point of view and put yourself in their shoes. When you do this, you may realize that the other person is just reacting to the experience or situation which they may be going through in the only way they know how to. They may not have made the right decision or reacted in the right way, but it was the only way they knew at that time.

Your ability to be perceptive is going to decrease based on the amount of judgment you have. Judgment causes you to measure people, and as soon as you engage in such an activity, you're falling out of tune with your intuition about others. To become a more empathic person, you're going to need to adopt a neutral attitude and avoid being too opinionated. For example, if you're who is judgmental and opinionated by nature, you're going to have to tone it down significantly if you want to improve your social skills. Strengthening your powers of empathy is about trying to understand the other person; it isn't about you. How do you minimize the judgment? By allowing people to be in the space of life, they are currently in and respect that for what it is. We naturally see things from our point of view first before anyone else's. Instead of trying to look at a situation through the eyes of another, we prefer to convince them why they should see things from our point of view instead. Instead of accepting their ideas and opinions, reject them if it is not something we want to hear. We have all been guilty of this, no question about it.

Only once you let go of your judgment and work on strengthening your empathic abilities can your relationships start to change. The world would get along much better if we could all learn to respect each other's differences. Conflicts would be minimized if we learned to exercise understanding rather than judgment. If we stopped to consider other people's point of view more, social interactions would be very different indeed.

Step 2: Don't Take It Personally

It's easy to feel like it's about you or confuse the emotions and feelings you're getting from others as something that is coming from you. If you do perceive someone's thoughts and emotions, and they happen to be about you, try to avoid taking it personally right from the start. This is *information*. When you take it personally, you're blocking your mind from being open and receptive. You're shutting out the powers of intuition that should get your senses tingling because your mind is defensive and rejecting the information that is coming your way.

. . .

Step 3: Create Dialogue

Another way to become stronger as an empath and make the best use of your gifts is to create dialogue. When you sense that someone has more to say, but they're holding back for one reason or another, *encourage them* to speak their mind by creating an opportunity to do so. Avoid questions that tend to end with a yes or a no, with no chance of prolonging the conversation. What you're after are open questions. The kind of questions that help you engage deeply with the person shows your interest and encourage the person to keep on talking.

Encouraging dialogue is easy enough when you pay close attention to the details. Not only does it show you've been listening to what they have to say, but they'll also be so delighted that you remember that they, in turn, will remember you as a great conversationalist. Paying attention to detail makes the speaker feel appreciated and valued, and in doing so, you build a much stronger bond and connection which them. Some empaths have already mastered the art of creating dialogue, and they're so in tune and perceptive that they can complete the sentences of their significant other, family member, or sometimes close friends too. Even before the other person has uttered a word.

Step 4: Try Not to "Fix" People

Not everyone needs to be "fixed." Sometimes people just want someone to listen to them. Someone to talk to where they can vent their feelings. Empaths are there to help, but help does not always mean "fix." To be effective as an empath, you need to be able to listen effectively and really pay attention to what someone else has to say. You are the one they will go to when they feel something needs to be improved, and when they feel you are taking their concerns seriously, no matter how small it may be, they will feel appreciated. Remember, empaths are not here to "fix." They are here to *guide,* and that's what you should be focusing on energy on if you want to use your gifts in a better way. You're here to support, to understand, to nurture, to let them know that their voice matters and they can be heard.

As an empath, you already have the gift of being more in tune with people than the common person can. But trying to "fix" everyone and everything is a common mistake that gets made by many empaths who have not fully understood their gifts yet. One way to strengthen your gift is to make yourself accessible to the people who need you. Let's imagine for a moment that you are an empath, and you also happen to be in a leadership-type role in your job. Making yourself accessible here means making yourself not just an approachable figure to your team who is willing and ready to listen to their complaints, but to be a successful leader, you need to make yourself open and accessible to receiving criticism too. It takes real courage for a leader to make themselves open to it because no one ever likes listening to negative things about themselves. When having a one-on-one conversation with a member of your team, listen to their voice inflections, the tone of their voice, which words they emphasize on, how do they sound when they are expressing what they feel.

These are valuable keys and skills that will enable you to really connect with your team, be emphatic towards them, be compassionate, be understanding, and nurturing in a way that they really need. Don't just listen to what they are saying, but listen to what they are trying to tell you and tune in to them in a way a lot of leaders fail to do today. *Listen* with an open mind and without trying to "fix" the situation right away. Let them pour their heart out to you first and then see what can be done from there.

4 / DEVELOPING EMOTIONAL
INTELLIGENCE

EMOTIONS ARE the breath of life. Our emotions are what make us so wonderfully human. Emotions color our world, and the one who can master their emotions can master actions. When you're aware of your emotions, you're better able to own it, claim it, and overcome it. This includes the emotions of others that you might have to deal with. Empathy is one of the five main components of emotional intelligence. An empath who has mastered emotional intelligence is an empath that is happier and more resilient because they have learned how to *control* emotions in themselves and others instead of letting *emotions control them.* If you have not mastered emotional intelligence, don't worry, it is a skill that can be learned.

For empaths in a leadership position, empathy is a critical component. There are three types of empathy that are essential for effective leadership, and each one of the three has strengths of their own. The empathy and social skills aspect of emotional intelligence means being equipped with the ability to attend to the emotions of others too. By adopting these methods to your communication style and approach, you'll find it easier to manage the way people respond and communicate with you in return. An angry customer, for example, could be appeased when you choose to greet them with a smile and respond in an empathetic manner to their complaints by chatting with them and being as under-standing as possible, you'll successfully manage your emotions and theirs without anyone doing or saying something they might regret.

Before we dive deeper into empathy as a key emotional intelli-gence component, let's talk about what the three types of empathy are:

- **Cognitive Empathy -** This gives you the ability to understand the way people think and to see things clearly from their point of view. This is helpful when it is time to give performance feedback or communication. It gives you the ability to communicate your points across in the way that the other party can understand and a way that makes sense for them.

- **Emotional Empathy -** This is the kind of empathy that resonates strongly with empaths. An empathic leader is someone who considers the emotions of others, and they go the extra mile to use this emotional knowledge to better understand the people they have to look after. Emotional empathy is critical for any kind of job where you need to relate to people. Client management, sales, teamwork and more because it is emotional empathy that creates chemistry between people and enables them to work well together. Emotional empathy creates a sense of rapport and simpatico, and empaths who have mastered this ability will go on to become effective leaders of the groups that they lead.

- **Empathic Concern -** Empaths with empathic concern spontaneously help out anyone whom they see might be struggling or in trouble. Without even thinking twice. Empathic concern is the quality that creates outstanding leaders. These are the leaders who take the time to listen and help their team develop their strengths. These are the leaders who take the time to give corrective feedback.

By now, you've probably determined that you're an empath. But the question you're asking yourself is, *what does empathy have to do with emotional intelligence?*

Understanding Empathy as a Core Emotional Intelligence Skill

We often hear about the need for more empathy in the world, and it's true. You've probably seen what a lack of empathy can do in one way or another. Friends who no longer see eye to eye. Colleagues who can no longer relate to the people they work with. Parents who have forgotten what it was like to be a teenager. Teenagers who can't understand why their parents do what they do (even though it is from a place of good intention and love). Most of us try to get others to understand our feelings and our point of view, *but do we put that same effort into trying to understand others?* Empathy is the ability to thoughtfully consider the feelings of others, along with other factors in the process of making an intelligent decision. Being an empath, you have the power to manage situations, to make people happy or do the opposite. To calm yourself and others around you. To regulate yourself especially when it matters the most, like in a professional setting for example.

Empathy is part of a bigger concept called emotional intelligence. That's why you often find emotionally intelligent people in the top leadership positions. Humans, by nature, are social creatures (yes, even introverts). Nobody can survive in isolation for long and be completely happy about it. We crave human companionship on a deeper level, which is why we often surround ourselves with others to avoid loneliness. But, being around others and being able to connect with them, are two different things entirely. You could be surrounded by a large group of people at any given time and still feel lonely because you have a hard time making a connection with anyone. Emotional intelligence can essentially be summed up in two ways - the ability to recognize, understand, and manage your own personal emotions, and the ability to influence the emotions of others. In Daniel Goleman's book, *Emotional Intelligence,* he divided emotional intelligence into 5 core principles:

- Self-awareness
- Self-regulation
- Motivation
- Empathy

- Social skills

Empathy helps emotionally intelligent individuals recognize and anticipate the needs of another individual, which is essentially what an empath does naturally. They then use this ability to work on fostering and building powerful relationships with a diverse group of people. Because they have the capacity to identify the needs and wants of another person, they are able to decipher the feelings of others, sometimes even preventing conflict before it happens because they can sense what's brewing underneath the surface. The more you can decipher the feelings of people, the better you can manage the thoughts and approaches you send them. Our emotions make up a large part of who we are. We are emotional, and sometimes we respond according to those emotions. We even make decisions based on those emotions. Having emotional intelligence is just as important to a person's success in life. For an empath, emotional intelligence is a way to find balance and to avoid being so overwhelmed by the emotional experiences you take on each day. Not only will you be able to manage and regulate your own emotions, but you can learn to influence the minds of the people around you too, as you learn to master and become better at.

Empathetic people excel at:

- Recognizing, anticipating and meeting a person's needs
- Developing the needs of other people and bolstering their individual abilities
- Taking advantage of diversity by cultivating opportunities among different people

- Developing political awareness by understanding the current emotional state of people and fostering powerful relationships
- Focusing on identifying feelings and wants of other people

Emotional intelligence is a learned skill, which means even if you're not an empath, you can still learn how to be an empathetic person by utilizing these practical tips below to increase empathy:

- **Learning to Listen Without Interruption -** This is easier said than done. If you've ever tried listening without saying a word or sharing an opinion you thought was brilliant, you'll know how hard it can be to hold your tongue at times. Listening intently can be a challenge. When we listen, most of us end up listening to give an answer instead of just listening. When you are the listener- do just that. Pay attention to what is being said and to empathize with your speaker.

- **Smiling Sincerely -** You know this, everyone knows this- a smile can light up the darkest days because it is contagious. You smile, they smile, everyone smiles. Thank the cingulate cortex for this amazing facial expression. Smiling releases all the feel-good chemicals from the brain, and it also activates all the happy neurons. It also increases your health and you'll be doing yourself a favor and the people around you just by smiling. It just brightens up everyone's day.

- **Using A Person's Name In the Conversation - A** simple nod while a person talks in a meeting shows that you are encouraging them and also agreeing to their ideas. This gesture, as simple as it is, makes a great impact on your relationship with your colleagues, team, and even with your boss. What's even better if you use their name along with the encouragement.

- **Empathize Regardless of Differences -** You may not share your beliefs with the people around you and vice versa. When these situations come up, you can approach your conversation with people just by saying simple things like 'That's interesting,' "Wow, I never knew that, tell me more.'

- **Being Present -** Simple gestures is all it takes to be fully present at the conversation or situation that is happening. You can start by putting your phone away, not connecting to any digital device that you have, and not answering calls or checking your email while you interact with someone. A study done by Albert Mehrabian, Professor Emeritus at UCLA, says that only seven percent of what is communicated is accounted for. The other 93 percent is contained in our body language and our tone of voice. If you are not present when someone is speaking, you will definitely miss the bulk of what the other person is saying.

- **Offer Genuine Praise and Recognition -** When giving recognition towards a colleague or a team member, move beyond just saying *"Well done"* or *"Good job."* Dig a little deeper and give constructive feedback and go along with feedback like *"You did really good research on this difficult topic."*

- **Encourage Deep Conversations -** When you want to empathize with someone, you want to understand a person's point of view or even the challenges they face, and this requires that you move the conversation beyond what the weather is like. This also doesn't mean you are asking them about their personal matters. You can start the conversation by talking about your own personal experiences on a certain topic and see if your colleague is comfortable talking about it. The above suggestions are just some of the ways you can empathize with someone and it is probably the safest and simplest way to jump into a situation that you are not familiar with. Just remember that when you speak to someone, use their name, smile at them and listen without interrupting them. All of this will lay the foundation for better rapport between you and them which will make way for a better relationship and help you in influencing them positively in the future.

The Art of Emotional Control

We don't give enough credit to just how powerful emotions can be. When you learn to control your emotions, you learn to control *your life and your destiny*. Think about it. The vast majority of people act out of impulse, and this is evident in moments of anger. We lash out when we're angry. We make impulsive decisions when we're emotional. We might do or say things in the heat of the emotional moment that we later come to regret. The thing is, no one admits that their reactions were a result of poor emotional control. There is always a reason or a justification as to why they behaved the way they did. But the truth is, poor reactions stem from a lack of emotional control. People let their emotions dictate their decisions and actions, and then look for excuses and reasons to justify their behavior, trying to make it seem okay. But it isn't okay.

Experiencing any emotion in excess is never a good thing, even for empaths. When something is experienced in excess, it makes it that much easier for you to feel overwhelmed and on the brink of losing control. Even excessive amounts of happiness is not a good thing, because that euphoria and happiness can result in you making decisions you normally would not. Too much empathy can be a bad thing too, especially when it starts to affect you more than it should. With empathy, you're trying to experience what the other person is going through, which means if they feel stressed, so do you. If they feel anxious or angry, you feel the same. Depending on your skills, you might even be able to feel their physical pain, not just the emotional pain alone, and if you absorb these emotions into your body and allow them to linger, they could start to emotionally hijack your body and mind. When you're an empath that taking on someone else's emotions, you become susceptible to feeling unhappy or miserable. Handling emotions can be a draining ordeal, and when you have to deal with the emotions of others on top of your own, your energy levels can quickly start to deplete. When left unbridled, empathy could potentially lead to a spike in your cortisol levels, which then makes it more difficult for you to manage your emotions. When you allow other people's emotions to affect you, you start to feel responsible for them, and you want to help them overcome their pain. You start feeling stressed about what you can do to help them feel better. But the thing is, if you try to help them too much, you might come off as intrusive, even if your intentions may be good.

When you control your emotions, you're less likely to let your emotions get the better of you. When you learn the art of emotional control, you're more likely to make a decision based on a rational decision-making process. In other words, you think carefully and weigh the pros and cons instead of reacting instinctively based on what you feel at the time. Emotional control is also crucial because it enables you to respond to others based on your values and character. As an empath, this is going to be of tremendous help in ensuring that you don't get swept up by both your emotions and that of the other person. A lack of emotional management is the reason so many people underperform, even the ones with high IQ. One of the first few things you must do for yourself in your efforts to become more emotionally intelligent is to make a personal commitment. Commit to yourself that from now on, you're no longer going to dwell on past emotional mistakes or failures. Commit to yourself that from now on, you're only going to look forwards, towards improvement. Commit to doing the things you know you must do to become better.

The art of emotional control first starts with your personal commitment to change. You have to want to see change, desire to make that change happen. That's the only way you're going to give this your 100% effort. When you make a commitment to change who you are, you're mentally preparing yourself to take the necessary action needed. You're dedicating f yourself to making this change for the better. If you ever struggled to control your emotions, you're not alone. But what a lot of people don't realize is that we *create* the emotions we feel. We *choose* the way we feel at any given time, empaths included. The art of emotional control then begins with the steps below:

- **Identifying Your Emotions -** Uncertainty about the type of emotion you're experiencing will leave you struggling to generate the appropriate response. Noticing your feelings alone is just one part of the process. Notice the way that they make you feel physically and give them a name so you can identify with them even better. *Friendly, happy, proud, nervous, angry, upset, disappointed.* These are just some of the names you could give the emotions that you're feeling. Put them in a sentence and say, *"This makes me feel proud"* or *"This makes me nervous."* Clearly defining your emotions is how you train yourself to focus on pulling your attention inwards, to where it matters the most.

- **Acknowledge and Appreciate Your Emotion** - Yes, even the negative ones because resisting emotions is not a healthy approach to take. Emotions are a part of who you are, and if you reject them, it's only going to make it harder to control. Resisting emotions causes uncertainty, and it may even stop you from using the emotion to your advantage. For example, something happened that caused you to feel frustrated. Instead of fighting the frustration, try to acknowledge it and the circumstances that made you feel that way.

- **Analyzing the Emotion** - Be curious about your emotions in this stage. Curiosity opens the door to new perspectives and opportunities. It provides unique insight into your emotions and the circumstances you find yourself in. Ask yourself, *"What is the true value of the emotion I'm feeling? In what way does this emotion serve me? What can I do to make things better?"*. Remember, emotions are felt for a reason, so you're probably feeling this emotion for a purpose. Emotions are capable of teaching us valuable lessons about ourselves and our circumstances, so don't be afraid to analyze them.

- **Formulating Multiple Responses -** There is more than one way to approach any emotional situation you face. Think about all the times in the past, where you may not have had the best reaction to certain situations because your judgment was impaired by your emotions. If faced with a similar situation again in the future, how would you handle things differently and why? Practice listing out all the different responses and reactions you would have, and ask yourself if this is what an emotionally intelligent person would do? How well are you regulating your reactions to these challenging emotional situations? You're not dwelling on the past, but rather using these past experiences as lessons which you can learn from. Observing what didn't work in the past so you don't repeat those same mistakes again in the future.

- **Reframe Your Perspective -** Your emotions have a lot to do with the way that you perceive certain situations and events. For example, if you're already feeling nervous and worried, getting an email from your boss saying that they want to see, you might aggravate your emotions even further. You may perceive it as bad news that you're about to be told off for a mistake that you made. Perhaps even fired. You'd probably be envisioning all the worst possible scenarios. Now, if you were to receive that same email from your boss but you were feeling happy or jubilant that day, you'd perceive the situation in an entirely different light. You might think that your boss wants to discuss a new opportunity, or give you some great feedback. Maybe even promote you. This is the perfect example to illustrate just how big of an influence our emotions can have on the way that we perceive things, and why it is important to start focusing on what's going on internally within you. Being able to identify your emotions makes it easier to reframe your thoughts by viewing situations from a realistic perspective.

How to Master Your Emotions

Let's look at the story of two different men named John and Jim. Two different individuals with different world views, two different goals, and two different paths in life.

John believes there are two kinds of people in the world. These are the conquerors and the ones who are conquered. To become someone great in the world, you need to be a conqueror. It's a harsh world out there, and you need to be bold and determined if you want to survive and succeed. You need to determine who is going to conquer the world with you. As a child, John read a lot and he loved stories of Greek heroes who displayed virtues like bravery and courage. He admired them because they were not followers. They were strong, powerful leaders, which were qualities he looked up to. John had to work hard from a young age for everything that he had because his family was not wealthy. This upbringing led John to believe that a person is responsible for the actions they take that shape the course of their life. One day, John encountered a homeless man who asked him if he had any change to spare. John realized that he was looking at a man who was conquered in life. John begins to wonder how this man had allowed himself to be conquered to this point. How many mistakes did the man make for him to end up where he is right now. Why is this man not taking responsibility for his life to change it or dig himself out of the hole? John believed this man was not trying hard enough and chose instead to take the easy way out by seeking help from those who had to work hard for everything they have. John believed if the man wanted to fish, then he had to be taught how to fish instead of having fish handed to him. John became annoyed by what he perceived to be the man's weakness and refused to give him a single penny. John believed that giving in to what the homeless man wanted would only enable his destructive attitude and poor lifestyle habits.

Jim believes there are two kinds of people in this world. The first are the people who can help, and the second is the people who need help. Growing up, Jim's father taught him that the highest good was when you served those who have nothing and to do what you can to lift them up. Life is full of hard knocks and challenges, and those who were in a position to help should lend a helping hand. Jim read a lot as a child, and the stories he was drawn to the most were those of spiritual leaders who dedicated their lives to helping others. Jim came from a wealthy family and felt indebted to help those who were not as fortunate and blessed as he was. One day, Jim came across a homeless man who asked him for some change. Jim knew he was looking at a man who was all alone and abandoned by society. A man who had no one else to turn to, no roof over his head, and no inkling of where his next meal was coming from. Jim felt like crying when he thought of this man's plight. Jim took out the money he had in his pocket and gave it to the man.

Both John and Jim have very unique world views that are

shaped by their past experiences. Both perceived the homeless man in a very different way. Where John saw someone who was weak, Jim saw someone who was forsaken and in need of help. Their emotions were heavily impacted by what they thought they were seeing. The truth was, both men had no idea of the circumstances that led the homeless man to this position. This same thing can be said in real life. From a young age, all of us are surrounded by an invisible force that is subtly shaping our perspectives and world views. This force is our environment and our culture, and the knowledge that we grab from this structure is what enables us to navigate the world. In John's world, for example, anger was a tool he used to help him grow stronger while Jim used compassion that led him to empathize strongly with others and become a giver. What if John and Jim had their roles reversed? What if their lives were reversed? Would they perceive the world differently? Would they feel any differently about the homeless man?

The master of emotions is the one who can change their perspectives and see the world around them differently, despite being brought up in a certain way by the invisible force. The ability to change the invisible force allows you to gather a diverse set of concepts so you can view one scenario from multiple perspectives. When you learn to master your emotions, you're not John or Jim. You become *both*, or you can be either one depending on your circumstances. Emotional mastery is about understanding perspectives from various angles. The better you understand your emotions and the emotions of people around, the more apt you will be at deciphering the way they feel and how you should respond to that. Conflicts, hurt feelings, and misunderstandings are minimized when you develop the ability to see things from someone else's point of view. When a friend has had a particularly rough week at work, and they happen to be short-tempered or snappish when you try to engage them in a conversation, emotional mastery is the skill that is going to give you the ability you need to put things into perspective. Instead of feeling hurt, possibly even angry with your friend for what they did, you'll be able to reflect on why they reacted that way and understand where they're coming from. Empathy is an important yet underrated skill, and it can make such a difference in the way you communicate once you know how to use it.

You experience dozens (if not hundreds) of emotions on a daily basis. Each emotion combines personality, context, and experience to create a mental state that is unique to you as an individual. Despite the emotional diversity possibilities, most of us group our emotions into a few simple categories that make it easy for us to understand. For example, you might say, *"I feel bad"* to describe nearly every negative emotion (don't forget you're supposed to specifically put a name to each emotion you feel). Being an empath, it is important you learn to master your emotions to avoid emotions getting the best of you, especially when you feel so much more of it than others do.

- **Focus on What Makes You Happy -** Learning to master your emotions is not just about getting it under control; it is about reconnecting with yourself too, and finding your happiness once more. The best way to do that is to do something that makes you happy. When you find yourself in an emotional situation and you're struggling to get a hold of yourself, walk away and choose instead to do something that makes you happy. As hard as it may be to ignore the compelling urge to help others, you can't help anyone if you're not in control of yourself. Each time you actively try to engage in an activity that brings you joy, you'll find your negative emotions ebbing away quicker with each effort you make. Harness the all-consuming power of happiness, because it's a good kind of emotion which will benefit you and everyone else around you. A happier state of mind also makes it much easier for you to think with clarity, and in doing so, gives you a much better handle at controlling your emotions.

- **Avoid Focusing on Your Worries -** Nothing good will ever come out of worrying. There's always going to be a reason to worry, but why worry about what you cannot change? Emotionally intelligent people don't do that. They know that worrying does nothing except waste your precious time, which could instead be spent devising strategies to help you get to the next phase of your mission to master your emotions. Successful people are mentally tough because they do not waste their energy on what is beyond their control. Instead, they shift their focus toward what needs to be done. If it works, it works; if it doesn't they find a way to make it work the next time they attempt it.

- **Pay More Attention To the Good -** Writing down your positive experiences can have a significant impact on your mood. It's easier to focus on what negative episodes may be taking place in our lives. If we go through the entire day experiencing 10 positive episodes and one negative episode, the negative episode is the one that is going to resonate the strongest. It's how our mind works. To make it easier to pay more attention to positive experiences, it helps to write it down, so there's something for you to refer to when you need it.

- **Maintain Realistic Expectations -** This is an important one for empaths in particular because as much as you want to change the world, there's only so much you can do, and you need to be realistic about your capabilities. If you don't, your emotions are always going to get the best of you when you can't help someone despite trying your very best. Unrealistic expectations will only kill your happiness. Learning how to master your emotions is something that is going to happen over time. You are essentially cultivating a better version of yourself. Building anything from scratch is always going to take time, but those who have been patient enough remain optimistic and happy throughout the process because they know that good things always take time.

IF YOU'RE an empath and highly sensitive, the kind of career you want to get involved in are the ones that connect you with emotions of joy. Being an empath is hard work as it is, and if you're in a profession that is draining you because there's such a high level of negativity and unhappiness you encounter on the job, that's not going to be good for your wellbeing. Empaths are driven to help people and a career that focuses on that passion for helping others.

The Best Career for Empaths

It is important for everyone to feel at peace and at least somewhat happy in their place of work. For an empath, this is even more of a necessity because of your highly sensitive nature. You may love what you do, but if there is too much in the job that is causing you to burn out, eventually, you're going to have to leave that job when you can no longer cope. Empaths have a lot of qualities that can be extremely beneficial in the workplace. For example:

- Empaths are loyal and dedicated
- Empaths are wonderful listeners
- Empaths are very detail-oriented
- Empaths are organized and fair
- Empaths are independent, and they don't require a lot of supervision
- Empaths are sensitive to the needs and emotions of others, which makes them great team players.

Are there certain kinds of jobs that an empath should avoid? Yes, there is. One of them being jobs that are sales focused and jobs that include a lot of confrontation. Jobs, where you're required to deal with people non-stop for several hours a day, is exhausting for an empath to handle. Cut-throat and competitive jobs are also not suited for empaths because it is simply not in their nature to betray or backstab another for their own personal gain. Any jobs that take place in a loud, hectic environment are the kind of jobs empaths should endeavor to stay away from.

Of course, not all work environments are the same. One empath might have an entirely different experience from another depending on the environment they find themselves in. Every empath is different, and the kind of job you would enjoy the most would be based on your principles, values, and what your interest or calling is. Here are some examples of the types of careers that might suit you best if you're an empath:

- **Counselor or Therapist -** This is probably one of the few jobs in which an empath can really thrive. It fulfills the calling of wanting to make a difference in the lives of others, you'll excel at this job because you're naturally a great listener, there are no crowd and no large groups of people at a time to deal with, and you get to focus on your goal of helping the person under your care.

- **Nurses -** Empaths are natural caregivers and healers, which makes them perfect for this job. Being a nurse allows you to put your natural empathic gifts to good use, helping patients stay calm when they feel unsettled and in pain. You're literally the support system for the patients who need it. The demand for quality nurses is never going to diminish, which means you'll always be assured of a job since nursing is an essential healthcare service.

- **Psychologists -** You're the nurse and the healer of the mental world for those who need someone to talk to about their mental health issues. Mental health is just as much of a concern these days as physical health, and these issues can be equally debilitating if not properly attended to. Since empaths have an innate talent for understanding emotions and the ability to listen actively, this makes them perfect for this job since they can have a soothing and calming effect on the people they talk to.

- **Veterinarians -** Empaths with the ability to connect with animals will love working in this role.

Some empaths are even able to form such a strong bond and connection with the animals that they have been referred to as "animal whisperers." An empath in this role has the ability to both calm and soothe the animals in their care as well as the frantic owners who might be worried about their pets. It gives the owners a little more peace of mind knowing their beloved pets are in good hands.

- **Graphic Designer -** The possible pros of this job is how it taps into your creative nature. It lets you explore your creative and imaginative side, and although you do come into contact with people, for the most part, you get to work independently and sometimes in a team. This minimizes the chances of you being emotionally drained on the job.

- **Accountant -** Being an accountant lets you tap into your analytical, problem-solving side if that is what you enjoy best from your empathic abilities. If solving problems makes you happy, this job might be something you enjoy.

- **Life Coach -** An empath's natural desire to want to help people better their lives is one reason why they will love their job as a life coach. Working one on one with your clients, you will help them be the best version of themselves that they can be. You'll always have their best interest at heart because it is in your nature. Encouraging others to meet their goals is one of the most fulfilling things that you can do.

- **Online Business Owner -** The advantage of this job is the minimal face to face interaction with your customers, which means minimal energy drain. There's also the independence and flexible hours that come with the job, which gives you the freedom to recharge and find your balance again when you feel the need for it.

- **Private Tutor -** If you love teaching but being in a room full of students is a strain on your emotions because of your empathic nature, the next best option would be to consider private tutoring. You still get to do what you love, helping, and teaching others, but dealing with one student at a time is not going to be as stressful and gives you a sense of control. You set your hours and in between, you get time to yourself to recuperate if needed.

- **Actor -** The ability to feel the emotions of others and to feel it so deeply that it becomes a part of you is what makes empaths such great actors. However, this job might not be for every empath because being an actor can put an immense strain on an empath's emotional state. Especially when they have to juggle multiple emotions all at once.

How to Thrive At Work

Empaths need to find ways to thrive at work without getting overwhelmed and drained. Being affected by emotions can be a real liability on the job, especially if it gets to a stage where it is impacting your ability to perform. Without the proper coping techniques to handle themselves, an empath can easily find themselves stressed and overwhelmed at the workplace, especially if you happen to be working with a lot of negative and toxic personalities. Here is how you make the most of your empathic nature and thrive at work without feeling drained or weighed down too heavily by the emotions of others:

- **Spend More Time Doing and Less Time Overthinking -** It's best to keep yourself busy when you're on the job. If you're always occupied handling one task after another, you don't have as much free time to dwell on emotions because you've got deadlines to meet. Since an empath tends to feel emotions so strongly, they're also prone to overthinking, trying to analyze what it all means.
- **Avoid Taking Everything Personally -** It's hard to feel like it's not about you when you feel emotions so intensely, but yes, not everything is a

personal attack against you. That is why it's important to learn how to identify emotions using emotional intelligence, so you can figure out which emotions are yours and separate yourself from confusing the emotions of others as things that you are feeling. Taking everything personally can result in a "me-against-the-world" thinking, which can be very lonely and isolating if you feel like no one understands you, and everything is a personal attack against you.

- **Learning to Let Things Go -** Empaths are individuals who easily feel overwhelmed because of how much they are taking on from other people. Once you learn to differentiate between the emotions that are yours and those that belong to someone else, it's time to let go of the emotions that aren't yours. You would also need to learn to let go of the guilt of not being able to help everyone. If you've tried your best, that's all you can hope for. After all, your capacity as a human being is limited. Push yourself too hard, and you'll only end up overwhelmed and exhausted, unable to help anyone.

- **Make Time to Be Alone -** Break times can also be alone times. Gather your thoughts and compose yourself by stepping away from everyone at work when it is your designated break time so you can spend some time alone quietly. During those few minutes alone, if it helps and the space permits, try meditating, visualization, or going for a quick walk in nature. Whatever you need to feel better so you can come back to work somewhat refreshed and ready to tackle the next half of the job until it's time for a break again.

- **Be Around Positive-Minded People -** Not all colleagues are alike. There are bound to be at least one, two, or several people at work who are positive-minded and, if you can, seek them out and actively spend time in their company. Surrounding yourself with positive people is the key for anyone to thrive and succeed in this world, not just empaths. You can learn a lot from these individuals and more importantly, they infuse you with the positive energy you need to feel better.

- **Be Clear About What Your Needs Are and Prioritize Them -** In rare cases, you might need to set aside your own needs to prioritize others. For example, if you were working as a counselor or a healer where your clients truly need your help. Where possible, avoid sacrificing your needs too much for the sake of others. Neglecting your own needs is the quickest way to burn out. To thrive at work, you need to make a list of what your needs and priorities are.

Keep that list with you on your desk at work to remind yourself that you need to make yourself a priority or risk burning out.

Protecting Yourself from Toxic People

Empaths are caring, compassionate, helpful, gentle, and nurturing. Because they are driven by such a strong desire to help, an empath is unlikely to immediately dismiss someone without valid cause. Unfortunately, this makes them easily susceptible to falling into unhealthy relationships with the wrong type of individuals. An empath can quickly become drained in the wrong type of environment surrounded by the wrong people, especially if they're around toxic people. Empaths are loyal and loving to a fault sometimes, and because of their nature, they want to see the good in everyone, even in toxic personalities.

Who are these toxic personalities? Narcissists, for one. Throughout our lifetime, we will engage in many relationships. Friendships that bring us joy, romantic relationships which are exhilarating and family relationships which can be supportive. Unfortunately, these relationships could also be destructive, which is usually the moment it becomes toxic. The kind of people that you surround yourself with can be one of two things: they can either be your greatest blessing, or they can be the negative force that drags you down. People get into unhealthy and destructive relationships all the time, that is not uncommon. For an empath though, this experience is going to be 10 times worse than it is for everyone else because of how sensitive they are to emotions. Emotional abuse is the worse thing that can happen to an empath. The union between an empath and a narcissist is a terrible idea. These two personalities are like two parallel lines that never get to meet. It is so important as an empath that you assess the kind of people you allow into your life. What kind of influence do they have over you? Are they inspiring you? Or are they draining you?

A narcissist will perceive an empath as an easy victim, someone who is weak because of their kind and benevolent nature. If the empath does not have a level of control over their emotions, they will end up becoming emotional sponges when a narcissist comes into the picture, absorbing the wrong energies of the exploitive and toxic personality. The reason why empaths and narcissists should never be together is that empaths are out there to heal the world and make it a better place, and they can't stand to see anyone in pain. A narcissist, however, is the kind of personality that capitalizes on someone else's misery. Why do these toxic individuals have such a powerful impact on our lives? Because they leech on your emotions. Being constantly surrounded by people who criticize you, complain and affect you both emotionally and physically is an exhausting affair. Negativity is a powerful force, and being around these individuals too much might make you tempted to get sucked into their cycle of misery. The narcissist is not someone who needs healing. They are someone who is there to exploit the goodness of others. They get into relationships with empaths and then manipulate, belittle, and use them. A toxic relationship is one that can be very damaging because of how it can chip away at your confidence. Being around the constant negativity which toxic people emit will eventually undermine your dignity, affect your self-esteem and perhaps even warp your personality depending on the relationship's impact.

Narcissists are among the most dangerous types of toxic personalities because they have exaggerated levels of self-esteem. They believe they are the picture of perfection, and to themselves, they are infallible. Depending on the individual in question, the strength of the narcissistic tendencies would vary in strength, with some people having a stronger disposition towards this personality than others. Narcissism is associated with grandiosity, a distinct lack of empathy, egotism, and pride. Confront a narcissist about their behavior and you'll immediately be met with denial. Yes, even if you were to present them with evidence about their narcissistic tendencies, they'll deny it point-blank and refuse to accept the truth, even if it is literally staring them in the face. Believe it or not, this is actually one way they continue to whole their victims captive, by denying any kind of wrongdoing and not owning up to their mistakes. They'll deny is so often that the victim will begin to question if they were the ones who were in the wrong after all. That perhaps they misjudged the narcissist. Bear in mind that the narcissist is a master manipulator, and they will gaslight their victims so much that the victims give in and be inclined to believe what the narcissist is telling them after all.

The side effects which result from the toxic relationship can either happen immediately or over time. In an empath's case, it can happen almost immediately. Narcissists crave attention. They need it to feed into their egos and belief about their own self-importance. If they can't get it from you through admiration, they will resort to another approach by getting you to feel sorry for them instead. They shift the focus of your attention towards them, their needs, and their so-called "misfortunes." They'll regale you with tales that make you feel sorry for them, and feel bad enough for them to shower all your time and attention is completely devoted to making them "feel better." They will go to any lengths to get the attention they seek, even if they must make up some stories along the way. Regardless, the consequential distress can leave an impact that will last a lifetime, especially if the wound is something that is difficult to heal. When an empath loves a narcissist, this is what happens:

- **It Starts Out Beautifully -** Almost all relationships start out wonderful during the honeymoon phase, and it's no different when an empath first begins a relationship with a narcissist. However, it won't take long before that quickly fades away into thin air. The common themes which occur in a toxic relationship are generally abuse, which can either be physical or emotional, and the other is co-dependency. Co-dependency is considered an unhealthy and toxic relationship because it starts off involving two people who were already not secure to begin with. These two people then seek each other out and form a relationship, trying to make themselves whole. They don't come into the relationship as independent and self-sufficient individuals. In this relationship dynamic, the empath will find it hard to accept the changes in their partner because the empath loves so completely and wholeheartedly. They believed with all their heart in the beginning that their partner was the same. One of the reasons why this relationship will start off so beautifully is that the empath naturally shows a lot of love right from the beginning, and they shower the narcissist with all the love and energy they have to give. This is exactly what the narcissist wants, and they will keep taking and taking until there is nothing left to give. Sure, the narcissist will put in some effort in the beginning (as everyone does with all new relationships), and once the empath is convinced they are being loved in return, that is when the tables start to turn. The narcissist will always capitalize on the naivety of the empath.

- **The Narcissist Is The One In Control -** The relationship with a toxic personality will never be one that is fair and balanced. It will always be one-sided, and in this case, the narcissist is the one who is going to be calling all the shots. By nature, the narcissist wants to have control over everyone in their lives, and the empath is in very real danger of losing themselves in the relationship. When you lose yourself in a toxic relationship, your judgment becomes clouded and it is harder to see what is best for yourself anymore. You forget who you are and what you want, and your happiness no longer becomes a priority. You start to get comfortable with it and make excuses for being in that toxic relationship because it feels better than having to deal with the pain of letting go of the person that you love or think you love. The narcissist will want the empath to be dependent on them for everything, and the narcissists try to make the empaths feel like they are fortunate to have them in their lives. That there is no one else out there who will love the empath quite like they can. It is easy to get consumed in a toxic relationship because those types of individuals are so overbearing. When people lose themselves in their relationships, they are no longer themselves anymore and everything becomes all about their partners. The empath is in danger of being loyal and submissive to a fault, feeling guilty at having to cut ties with someone they believe "loves them," even though there can never be any real love when a narcissist is involved.

- **Regular Conflicts -** A loving and gentle soul like the empath is going to eventually feel tired and fatigued when it keeps getting hurt. The narcissist will see an empath as someone they can walk all over because of how loving and accomodating they can be. But empaths are anything but pushovers. They have feelings too, and when they feel their partner is not meeting their needs, agitation and frustration tend to follow. You should never be willing to put up with a toxic relationship. It could end up hurting more than just your feelings. Relationships can be complicated. When it's good, it can be really great. But when it's bad, it could potentially impact your health physically and emotionally. Arguments, confrontation, and conflict are all things that drain an empath considerably, and being trapped in this kind of unhealthy dynamic is going to take its toll on the empath eventually.

- **Your Confidence Suffers A Blow -** Toxic relationships will erode your confidence slowly but surely. This is because you are constantly surrounded by a partner who makes you feel like you are never good enough. They make you feel bad about yourself, casting doubt on your abilities, and even make you question whether you are good enough. Being around this all the time will cause wear and tear on your confidence, stripping you of it until eventually, your self-esteem takes a nosedive. There is only so much an empath can handle before they finally cave under the constant pressure and emotional turmoil of being made to feel like they are never good enough no matter what they do. Nothing is a bigger energy drainer than spending all of your efforts making sure the other person is happy but not receiving the same kind of support in return. When you spend your time around toxic people, it is always "all about them," and you become secondary.

- **When the Relationship Ends, the Empath Feels Guilty -** Empaths are naturally kind, and they will try to make up for things that are not their fault sometimes. When in a relationship with this type of toxic behavior, you will often be made to feel "guilty" even when there is no reason for you to feel bad. This type of toxic relationship can occur amongst friends, co-workers, families, and couples. The toxic person will try to control and manipulate the situation to their benefit by inducing guilt upon you, sometimes subtly disguised. For example, the narcissist would appear to "support" your decision, but then subtly remind you of the things that you're neglecting to make you feel bad. Being around somebody who is toxic for too long will make you feel bad about yourself, insecure, drained, stressed, pressured and even emotionally scarred. Even though the breakup was for the best, the narcissist will have no problem throwing in words that makes the empath feel guilty and selfish for thinking about their own needs.

Narcissists are the complete opposite of empaths, that much is clear. These types of individuals are a bit tricky because they can be difficult to spot in the beginning, and they hide their true personalities so well. Narcissists tend to be manipulative and they will always push your buttons and subtly emotionally blackmail you until they get things done their way. They have an ulterior motive and will not hesitate to use information against you if it means they get what they want. Once the relationship is no longer beneficial to the manipulators, they have no qualms about discarding you without a second thought. Yet another reason why the relationship between an empath and a narcissist is so harmful is that the narcissist genuinely believes that the empath owes them a lot, and these are some examples of what these narcissists feel entitled to (even though you don't owe them anything):

- **They Believe You Owe Them Attention -** Narcissists are completely ignorant and oblivious to everyone else's feelings. All they ever think about is themselves, and if you don't give them the attention they think they deserve, they begin emotionally lashing out at you and making you feel like you're the worst partner in the world.

- **They Believe They Can Do Anything They Want -** A narcissist will have no problem violating your boundaries. There is no such thing as respecting boundaries in the eyes of the narcissist, simply because they don't care about anyone else except themselves. They enjoy pushing others to the limits, and they will go to any lengths to do it, including pushing past your boundaries or violating rules to do so. They may resort to behavior, which includes intruding on your personal space, taking or borrowing your things without returning them, taking someone else's work and passing it off as their own, breaking promises, appointments, and even negating on agreements that were made. In some extreme cases where you might be romantically involved with a narcissistic manipulator, they could even resort to tactics that include sexual abuse or harassment, domestic violence or abuse, and even verbal and emotional abuse. The worst part of it all is some narcissists even take pride in their behavior under the misguided notion of feeling "powerful" when they see someone else suffer at their hands.

- **They Believe You Owe Them Your Loyalty -** They lead you to believe that you have a "special connection," and thus, the two of you were meant to be together forever. They could deceive you into believing that you're special by using phrases such as *I've never loved anyone the way that I love you*, or *I never knew what love was until I met you*. This statement may be true for some people, but it rarely ever holds any truth if you're dealing with a narcissist. It is simply another tactic which they use to reel you in before inflicting even more emotional abuse on you later once you have been lulled into a false sense of security and lead you to believe you owe them your loyalty because they deign to be with you.

You need to protect yourself from these toxic personalities. You need to protect your energy and your emotions, and you have every right to do it without having to feel bad or selfish. Everyone (empath or not) should protect themselves from overbearingly toxic personalities. It is the only way to reclaim your life and your happiness again and put a stop to these energy vampires. These are several ways an empath can protect themselves from being hurt by the toxic relationships they encounter, and these measures include:

- **Decide What You Want -** Before taking any kind of action, you need to determine what you want from the relationship. No one else can do this step for you because unless they are an empath, they won't be able to fully comprehend what you're going through. You already know that you might not be able to change someone with a toxic personality, so you need to now ask yourself what can you take away from the relationship that you will be okay with. If you decide that you don't want a relationship with them at all, then that is okay too. If the relationship has no hope of changing, then there is only one thing left to do. Plan your exit strategy. Leading up to it, you need to start setting boundaries with your partner, be firm and decisive. They may push back and retaliate because toxic people always want to be in control of the situation, but you need to be just as firm and say no. Stand your ground and do not give in to their demands any longer.

- **Creating A Safe Emotional Space for Yourself -** One method of coping with toxic relationships is to create a space for your emotions. A place where you feel safe enough to express yourself without fear of being judged or ridiculed. You may not be able to find this in the home environment, but there are other outlets that you can utilize to help you find that safe space you need. You could journal about the way you feel and what you're going through, or maybe even blog about it. As long as you have something to release your pent up frustrations. Keeping your feelings bottled up deep inside is never a good move, and it can often lead to depression and feelings of loneliness and isolation.

- **Create A Support System for Yourself -** The support system can be in the form of friends or even other family members that you trust and can confide in. It can even be a counselor or a co-worker that you trust enough to talk to. Reach out to someone and find a support system because you're going to need it to help you through the process of cutting ties with a toxic relationship. It will help a lot in managing your emotions and the stress of dealing with what you may be going through until you feel better.

- **Set Boundaries for the Relationships That You Build -** With any future relationships that you encounter, you should set boundaries to avoid getting hurt again. Set boundaries for what you're willing to put up with and stick to it as best you can. Keeping and maintaining your distance is one of the best things you could do for yourself when it comes to coping with toxic relationships. The more space you put between you and them, the better you will feel. If you can't avoid these personalities entirely (for example, if the narcissist is not a romantic partner but a friend or family member), then keep the contact with them to a minimum. Find ways to keep yourself busy and always have something to do so you have an excuse not to be around them.

As WONDERFUL AS it can be to be an empath, it is also a tough gift to have. Not everyone is going to understand your abilities, some may mock you because they don't believe in it, and there will be many times in your life when you wish you did not have this ability at all. There are times when an empath can't help feeling overwhelmed because emotions can be such a powerful force to be reckoned with. It takes great inner strength and emotional intelligence to truly be in control of yourself and the way you feel every step of the way. If you let it, emotions will flood your mind and your being like a tidal wave, especially when you're not equipped with the necessary skills and techniques needed to survive your gift. This final chapter is going to focus on how to keep your gift under control while protecting yourself from getting overwhelmed and exhausted.

Why a Lot of People Can't Handle It

Like anyone else, an empath wants to love and to be loved in return. Although empaths tend to give their all without expecting anything in return, they're only human too. Of course, they would love to be treated with the same love and care that they shower upon other people. One common misconception is that empaths tend to struggle in life because they are *too sensitive* to the energy and emotions around them. But some people actually find it difficult to be around an empath, believe it not. Yes, the empath is not the only one who struggles with their gift. Other people do too. Maybe it's because of the empaths intensity and the way they feel emotions so deeply. A lot of people can't understand or process that because they're *sympathetic,* but not *empathetic.* Both the empath and the people around might also struggle with a fear of intimacy. An empath's friends, family, and even partners may be uncomfortable with the idea of knowing someone can sense the way they feel and what they might be thinking all the time, even if they haven't said a word about it themselves.

Here are some of the reasons why empaths and a lot of people close to them struggle with and find it difficult to handle this gift:

- **Difficulty Forming A Serious Relationship -** Some empaths might be afraid of getting into a serious relationship for fear of being hurt again. For the empath, there's a very good chance they have been through many failed and toxic relationships over the course of their life (and will continue to do so unless they start implementing measures to protect themselves). Eventually, the empaths will reach a point where they are afraid of getting involved in yet another serious relationship and risk getting their hearts broken again. For the one who is on the other side of the relationship with an empath, this wall that the empath puts up in an attempt to protect themselves might make it difficult to form a bond of intimacy. The empath's partner is always going to feel like the empath is holding back a part of themselves, and that might cause frustration and misunderstanding. It may take time before the empath is ready to open their heart again. Unfortunately, some partners either can't understand or are not willing to wait around for things to change.

- **Too Many Questions -** Because of the empath's desire to get to the root of the problem and to try and help others, they prone to asking a lot of questions. They can't help it since they feel everything more intensely than other people do. To them, everything has a deeper meaning. Sometimes they don't accept things at face value if they sense there might be more going on, but despite their genuine desire to help, some people might find this uncomfortable as they think the empath might be coming on too strong. Not everyone feels comfortable with being asked too many questions, especially in the initial stages of a relationship, and an empath's desire to help might end up backfiring on them.

- **Too Many Expectations About Honesty -** Most empaths are genuine, and their actions, motives, and intentions usually stem from a good place. The downside is, this expectation of honesty that they project onto others might be the cause of a lot of disappointment, especially in a romantic relationship. Part of an empath's ability is to be able to sense when someone is lying to them, and they will call you out on it. Not everyone is comfortable or necessarily happy with this approach. Even if a partner may be lying or holding back to protect the empath's feelings, it can cause a lot of friction (and possibly arguments) if an empath keeps pressing for honesty. That's why not everyone is able to handle being around an empath and why empath's themselves struggle with some of the relationships that they have.

- **They Sense Things Even Before You've Told Them -** Everyone is bound to encounter problems. Personal, professional, or relationship-wise. While most people do want to talk about it at some point, they might not want to do so right away. If they are in a relationship with an empath, the empath might immediately start asking what's wrong if they sense any kind of unhappiness. The empath might not know the actual problem, but they will be able to feel like you're hiding something from them. They'll keep pushing and pressing for an answer because it bothers them when something is wrong. Unfortunately, not everyone is going to be responsive right away, and the more you push them, the further they retreat from you emotionally.

- **Empaths Have Seen the Good and Bad -**
Empaths have seen it all. They've seen the beauty in people, and they've also seen the bad in people. With the emotional roller coaster that some relationships put them through, empaths will eventually reach a point when they realize some people are just not going to change (these would be the toxic personalities). No matter how much the empath may want to help, they can't do much if the person themselves refuses to change. It can be a very disappointing moment for an empath when they come to this realization, and they may find it difficult to accept, perhaps even difficult to handle. The empath could end up carrying that guilt around with them for a long time, even though it isn't their fault.

- **Empaths Might Freak Some People Out -**
Some people might get freaked out by the idea of what an empath is capable of. Not everyone likes their secrets revealed, and the idea that an empath knows things even though you've tried to hide it and never said anything about it can be extremely uncomfortable for some people. Empaths are also prone to expressing their thoughts and feelings a lot sooner than some people might be comfortable with. Especially when most people don't even know how to process or understand their own feelings. It can be a challenging thing, being around an empath. This whole experience might be a bit too much for some people to handle, and

they avoid being around empaths because of it, much
to the empath's hurt and dismay.

- **The Mood Swings -** For those who don't
understand what it's like to be an empath, they might
not be able to comprehend why empaths can swing
from one extreme mood to another. Empaths could be
happy one moment and then become extremely sad
the next. Since an empath feels every emotion 10
times more intensely, it is only natural that the way
they express these emotions or the mood swings they
experience may be heightened as well. An empath
who is struggling to get a handle on their emotions
might inadvertently lash out at the people who are
closest to them. Some people find this extremely
difficult to be around since there's no telling when the
empath's mood is going to shift or change just like
that.

The Habits of Highly Empathic People

Empaths are a gift to the world around them. No one else will
be able to come close to displaying the paragon of goodness and
selflessness the way an empath can if they don't have this ability.
Empaths are unique people with equally unique habits. They're
not the kind of people you meet every day. Empaths are as rare as
their abilities. Anyone can show empathy, which makes spotting a
genuine empath a real challenge. Once you are around an empath,
you'll start to notice that they have certain quirks and habits about

them. These are not habits or quirks you'll see often either. Here are some of the habits of highly empathic people:

- **Cultivating Curiosity -** Most empaths are extremely curious about the people around them. You might say their curiosity is almost insatiable, and they find other people a lot more interesting than themselves. They have no problems striking up a conversation with strangers, and it is their avid curiosity that makes others open up to them too. People want to be heard and they want someone to listen to them, and when an empath comes along with a genuine curiosity about how they are and what they do, it's hard not to warm up to them.

- **They're Good At Making Conversation -** Their natural curiosity enables them to be good conversationalists. They pay attention to what is being said, and this allows them to ask all the right questions to keep the conversation going. To encourage others to open up about their lives, empaths like to focus on open-ended questions and when the other person speaks, the empaths immerse themselves in the moment and listen without interruption. They make a real effort to be present and minimize distractions that take place during a conversation so they can give the other person their full, undivided attention.

- **They Seek Commonalities -** While most people let differences and prejudices be the wall that divides them others, empaths seek out the commonalities they can use to build a bond with others. Empaths focus on what they have in common with others rather than the differences. It is one of the ways they are able to see things from another's perspective because they focus on what they have in common rather than how different their lives or opinions may be. They immerse themselves in the lives of another, join in experiences, volunteer, travel to other countries to experience different cultures, all of which help to broaden their perspective on life.

- **They Tend to Avoid Being In A Crowd -** It's not because they are antisocial, but rather it is because they feel so overwhelmed by all the energy that is coming their way. Crowded environments will with both positive and negative emotions are not a comfortable environment for them, and they would rather avoid it if they can. Some extroverts might find this retreating habit of theirs difficult to understand.

- **They Put Other People's Needs Before Their Own -** Not necessarily the best habit to have since it puts the empath at risk of neglecting themselves (which admittedly tends to happen a lot). Friends, family, and partners of the empath might find this habit frustrating to deal with, especially when they see how emotionally exhausted the empath becomes from constantly placing the needs of others before their own. They spend far too much time being busy helping others and not enough time helping themselves.

- **The Attract People Who Want Their Help Rather Than Their Love -** Loving to a fault is both a blessing and a curse for the empath. Empaths have the habit of giving away too much of themselves and not getting enough love and care in return. Some people are more interested in what the empath can do for them rather than the love they can receive from them, which is one of the many reasons why empaths tend to fall into the trap of associating themselves with toxic individuals.

- **It's Hard to Say "No" -** This happens a lot to an empath. They *know* that they should be saying "no," but it's easier said than done when they sense someone in need. Even if their plate is full and they have no more time to spare, they still struggle with the idea of saying "no" if they sense someone needs their help. Again, this can be both a good and bad thing. If an empath does not know when to draw the line, they can easily find themselves burned out before they know it. No matter how much they may want to help others, if an empath keeps going with this habit and enforcing no boundaries, soon they will find themselves in a position where they are unable to help anyone. Including themselves.

Survival and Self-Care Tips

Empaths are gentle souls, and it is unfortunate that some people will take advantage of their loving and giving nature. More than anyone else, empaths are in need of survival and self-care tips to protect themselves from being taken advantage of, which can happen a lot if you're unaware. One of the most difficult challenges as an empath can be when people think you're the "strange" one for being so highly sensitive to the world around you. Those who don't have the empathic gift will not be able to comprehend or understand where you're coming from and why you react this way to your surroundings and to the emotions that you pick up from others. People may try to define who you are in an attempt to understand you. Sometimes the words or thoughts they may have about you can be hurtful (even if they don't say it out loud, you're able to sense the way they feel).

Most empaths have at one point, or another experienced an emotional or psychic attack at some point. It can be unbearable when you're not equipped with the safety tips to protect yourself and an immense drain on your energy. What is a psychic attack? Well, it is a discouraging message that is delivered from one individual to another. It often comes from dark thoughts that arise from anger, jealousy, envy, or other negative emotions. Even though empaths are exposed to this on a frequent basis, a lot of empaths who are only just beginning to understand their incredible gift don't know how to cope. It is even harder when the one who is inflicting these emotional and psychic attacks has a strong connection with the empath. They could be family members, friends, or partners and spouses. It's hard enough to balance your emotions without having to deal with the sometimes overbearing emotions of others.

Survival and self-care tips are the ways an empath survives, and if you're struggling to cope with your gift, this is what you can do:

- **Associate With Your Emotions -** The thing about empaths is that they tend to prioritize the emotions and needs of others before themselves. For an empath, it is important to associate with your emotions, understand your feelings, and fulfill your needs.

- **Taking Care of Your Mental and Physical Health -** It is impossible to protect yourself without a healthy mind and body. Get enough rest at night. Exercise for good health. Drink enough water each day. Make healthy food choices. These mantras have been repeated over and over as we scramble for the pursuit of better health. Good health matters because you can do so much more when you're healthy. Think of a time when you have been sick, or when you've injured a certain part of your body, and suddenly, life became a struggle because even the simplest things felt difficult. Do you see how important it is to be healthy? Good health is often taken for granted, and you don't fully learn to appreciate it until you need it most, which is something that needs to change, and that change is going to start with you. Start appreciating how healthy you are right at this moment, and every morning when you wake up, be grateful because you have your health.

- **Meditate Regularly -** Those who avidly do this find that their mind is peaceful and free from worries and mental discomfort, making it easier for them to achieve happiness compared to those who do not practice meditation at all. If you've never tried it, you may not fully understand how sitting quietly for a few minutes every day is going to make a difference in your life, but you would be surprised. By spending a few minutes each day training your mind and making meditation part of your routine, you will discover that your mind gradually is able to find peace a lot easier and finding happiness is something that doesn't seem so elusive anymore, even if you have certain challenges that you may be going through in your life. Even in the most difficult of circumstances, you will find that you're able to remain calm, steady, and still be able to look at the bright side of life. A calmer state of mind means you're in better control of your emotions and you're less likely to feel as overwhelmed.

- **Control Your Energy -** Avoid the circle of people who always give you nothing but negative vibes. That is one way of controlling the energy that you surround yourself with. These energy vampires are only going to drain you if you spend too much time around them. Limiting contact is one way of protecting your emotional and mental state. It is not your duty to continuously try and help those who will not help themselves.

- **Maintain a Positive Living Space -** This can be as simple as keeping your home neat and tidy, a happy sanctuary that you can look forward to coming home to at the end of a long day. Your home should be a place that infuses you with happiness the moment you walk through the door. Try crystals and aromatherapy to infuse your home with positive energy.

- **Practice Shielding Visualization -** This can be a very helpful technique when it comes to protecting yourself from surrounding energies. Fall back on this technique whenever you find yourself in an uncomfortable situation, like when you're in a crowded room, or you're in the presence of an energy vampire. Shielding visualization means you're trying to picture something else in your mind rather than focusing on yourself or any negative energy you might be picking up on. In a way, it is a distraction technique. Take a few deep, measured breathes, focus on your breathing, and then visualize an invisible shield around yourself that is protecting you from negative energy. This protective visualization technique gives your mind something to focus on other than the unwanted energy you might be at risk of absorbing.

- **Don't Be Afraid to Seek Help When You Need It -** Even empaths need someone to talk to and listen to them. Even the strongest people need a shoulder to cry on or someone to turn to when it all feels like too much. If the self-care and survival tips above don't work for you, there is no shame in seeking professional help when you need it. Professional help can be in the form of spiritual guidance, a guardian angel, family member, friend, or partner who genuinely cares for you and is someone you can count on. Professional help can also come in the form of counselors or therapists if you feel like these might work better for you. Seek out professional guidance anytime you feel like you need it because your mental health and wellbeing deserves it.

- **Keep Your Eyes Open -** Keep your eyes open and stay alert to the possibility of toxic personalities in your midst. As soon as you sense them, try to avoid them at all costs before they've had a chance to inflict their damage on you. This preventative action is crucial to preserving your mental and physical state.

- **Define Your Relationship Needs -** Remember how important it is to prioritize your needs? It cannot be stressed enough how vital it is that you learn to take care of yourself. You cannot hope to help others if you're not performing at your very best. Only when you understand what your needs and priorities are will you then be able to create a form of self-protection for yourself, especially when it comes to what you want from the relationships that you have. Each time you feel like you might be in danger of drowning, focus on what your priorities are, define them, and express them. Whenever you don't feel right, don't be afraid to raise the issue and speak up.

How to Thrive Without Feeling Overwhelmed

While being an empath is a wonderful thing, you need to be careful not to experience empathy overload. If you keep absorbing the stress or pain or others continuously, you're going to get overwhelmed in no time at all. Being overwhelmed, of course, makes it very difficult to thrive when you can't focus or think straight. Emotions have a way of sweeping you up and engulfing you, overpowering you until you feel like you're drowning.

Meditation is one way of calming the mind and protecting your sanity against the unending slew of emotions. Learning to control our minds is one of the most difficult things we can do. It's easy to let our thoughts get the best of us, which is why it is so easy to be consumed by negativity, and external circumstances can affect us to such an extent. The thing about this is, we don't even realize just how severely we are affected by it all because we're not really thinking too much about it. Fluctuations in our moods seem like a normal, everyday occurrence and we brush it off as being part of life and we can't control it. But that's where you're mistaken because you absolutely can do something about it. Meditation is one way of creating that inner space and clarity in your mind that will enable you to always be in firm control of your thoughts despite the circumstances you may be facing. Meditation is how you find that mental balance, so you're never at one extreme or the other. It's always about finding the right balance. You've always been told you need to live a balanced life, eat balanced meals, why not have a balanced mind too? Meditation is a way of bringing you mental clarity, and to change the way you look at the world around you. It is one of the best ways to bring about a sense of fullness and completion, and believe it or not; it is the only way to truly achieve tranquility that is easily accessible to everyone on this planet. True, there may be other temporary forms of serenity, but nothing will come close to bringing you the long-term peace that you seek no matter what you may be going through in your life the way meditation will.

Are there other measures that can be taken so you can thrive instead of feeling overwhelmed by your gift? Absolutely.

- **Set Energy Boundaries -** Healthy boundaries are your ultimate protection against absorbing too many emotions, especially when it comes to fending off toxic personalities. If a person does not respect your boundaries, they are generally toxic, and it is best to steer clear of them. These toxic individuals make it very difficult to have a normal, healthy and respectful relationship with anyone in their life because they will literally just push all your boundaries and they do not know when to stop. Avoid forming relationships with them because it is not worth it in any context. You must start setting up boundaries and be firm about it. Protecting yourself and your own self-worth comes first, and you should never allow yourself to be emotionally bullied by a toxic person, no matter who they are. Do not let someone else make you feel that you are unworthy or inferior; this kind of behavior pattern is dangerous. Setting boundaries helps to protect yourself from them because it helps to limit how much influence they will have over your life. Setting boundaries can be in the form of limiting your time with them or finding a support system to help you manage your emotions after each encounter. It would depend on the situation you may be in. By defining your boundaries, you will come to understand what your limits are when it comes to absorbing surrounding energies too.

- **Be Selfishly Protective of Your Time -** Even empaths deserve some alone time to recuperate from helping, listening, and absorbing the emotions of everyone else. To avoid being overwhelmed, you must be selfishly protective of your time or toxic people, and energy vampires will always have more control over you than they should. If the relationship cannot be fixed, then you need to focus on what can be changed, which is you and the time that you give them. Spend more time with people who bring out the best in you instead, and where possible avoid the toxic person as best that you can. You are not obligated to spend more time with the toxic person than you should, so don't feel guilty about making excuses not to be around them. For the sake of your emotional wellbeing, this is something that must be done.

- **Be Disciplined with Your Quiet Time -** Your quiet time is not something you should willingly compromise on. This is part of your healing process and a way to balance your mental and physical wellbeing. Retreating to your quiet time is the easiest way to keep yourself from feeling emotionally exhausted, and quiet time can be done anywhere, and whenever you feel it. Go for a walk, stretch your muscles, spend time alone until you feel better, taking short breaks throughout the day to step away from people. Your quiet time routine can be anything that works for you.

- **Stay Preoccupied with Your Hobbies -** Everyone has got things they love to do that brings out their skills and creativity. Playing an instrument, a sport, an activity you like to do, crafts that you like to indulge in to keep your hands and your mind busy, reading a good book in a quiet room by yourself, a hobby is something we all enjoy spending our time on. For an empath, it is important to indulge in these hobbies regularly since they tend to get stressed out very easily.

- **Take A Break from Social Media -** Or media in general, for that matter. Unplugging from the media is essential to avoid overwhelming your empathic senses. Media and social media can be full of negativity, shock value, sensationalism, and extremely traumatic or emotional moments. None of which are good if they're overloading your senses. It doesn't help that we all have minds that are biased toward being attracted to the negative in the first place, even for empaths. Continuously feeding your mind with this type of content is only going to make it harder for you to find peace and balance, so avoid it whenever you can and choose to spend some quiet time alone instead. This is an outstanding self-care and survival practice that is going to help you thrive without feeling overwhelmed.

- **Spend Time in Nature -** Most empaths feel refreshed when they're around nature. If you haven't spend a lot of time in nature lately, it might be time to revisit that again. Whenever you feel overwhelmed, choose to retreat to nature. Go to the beach and listen to the sound of the waves crashing against the shore. Go for a walk in the park and listen to the birds singing. Feel the breeze caress your skin and take in a deep breath as you lose yourself in your surroundings. Spend as much time in nature as you need until you feel refreshed again.

- **Don't Make Other People's Problems Your Own -** This is only going to make you feel pressured to help, even when you can't. Not everyone's problems can be fixed, and it is important not to take on their burden and make it your own. Help them as best you can, but don't make the problem a personal one. Your passion for wanting to help is one of your best qualities as an empath, but the truth is you simply cannot fix the world on your own. You need to know when to step back and say this is something you cannot help with.

CONCLUSION

Thank you for making it through to the end of *Empath by Rhonda Swan*, let's hope it was informative and able to provide you with all of the tools you need to achieve your goals whatever they may be.

Being an empath is wonderful. Not everyone has the ability to listen to another with their entire body, mind, and soul. Not everyone has the power to heal others and help them through their pain quite like the way an empath can. If you don't know you're an empath, it's easy to feel like there's something wrong with you. It's easy to struggle to comprehend why you feel so emotional and so sensitive. It's easy to believe when people tell you that you're over-reacting or you're too sensitive about something.

Being an empath is not without its challenges, but these can be managed when you know what you're dealing with. The important thing to remember is not to neglect yourself. Take care of your mind, body, and spirit because you need as much healing as everyone else does. If you need to take some time being on your own, recharging and replenishing your energy reserves, do it and don't feel guilty about it. Your ability to help others becomes diminished when you feel like you are burned out and running on empty yourself. Feeling discouraged, frustrated, upset, and really sad, and sometimes you can't explain why, then learn to take a step back and focus your energy on yourself. You can't help someone else if you are in need of healing too. You need to take that time to figure out what your emotions are and how to separate that from the emotions of others. Hopefully, now that you understand a little more about what it means to be an empath, you'll be able to better regulate your emotions and minimize the moments when you feel so overwhelmed by your gift.

Finally, if you found this book useful in any way, a review on Amazon is always appreciated!

SELF-DISCIPLINE

Mental Toughness Through Focus and Concentration

RHONDA SWAN

Do you have self-discipline? Most people would be inclined to say that they do, but there is one simple reality to this—many people struggle with it. A lot. And, unfortunately for those people, self-discipline is one of those critical aspects of one's personality and actions that they do not want to lose. Self-discipline is crucially important—it can impact the quality of life that someone lives. It can impact how likely someone is to be in a relationship that they know is going to succeed. It can determine how healthy someone is and how well they do at work. Self-discipline can touch nearly each and every single aspect of someone else's life—and many people do not realize that they are lacking it.

When you lack self-discipline, you run the risk of a very serious problem: You run the risk of not being able to succeed, and even worse, you probably will not realize that the problem is there in the first place. You may not realize that all of your problems that you have in life likely stem right back to that poor self-discipline, and that is a major problem for you.

Self-discipline is about so much more than simply being able to resist temptation. Just because you did not reach for that bowl of ice cream today does not necessarily make you self-disciplined. Self-discipline as a trait is a lifestyle choice—it is choosing to lead a life in a very specific manner that you know will benefit you. If you can ensure that you are self-disciplined, your life will improve drastically, and this book is here to do that for you.

When you read through this book, you will be introduced to what it means to develop self-discipline. You will learn all about how so many people actually do lack it—and how to tell if you are currently one of the people struggling with it. You will learn to see whether there is a self-control problem in your life that, if you eliminated it, would actually save you an awful lot of unhappiness in your life.

You will be introduced to the lifestyle choices that go along with self-discipline. You will learn to recognize what it means to resist those temptations that you have at any point in time. You will learn what it means to be able to stay true to what you know is good and what you know is right. However, in order to get that benefit, you must first learn how to recognize the lifestyle itself.

You will be guided through recognizing the power of self-discipline as well as how you can develop it yourself. Then, the last half of this book will be all about ensuring that you can deal with varying tasks and tools related to the particular skills that self-discipline usually entails. You will get tools designed to help you learn how to concentrate or to delay gratification. You will learn about the importance of perseverance and endurance. You will learn about fending off negativity and difficult feelings such as temptation.

Ultimately, all of this will come together to produce something that you will be able to put together and use. You will come to recognize that, ultimately, this lifestyle is not something that you should be afraid of, nor is it something that you should be bothered by. It is something that you can embrace, and in embracing it, you will be able to make it work for you. You will be able to ensure that, at the end of the day, you are happier and you are more successful, all because you were able to embrace the self-disciplined lifestyle and that matters greatly.

1 / THE SELF-DISCIPLINE PROBLEM

IF SOMEONE ASKED you what it meant to be self-disciplined, what would you tell them? Would you say that it meant that you were able to sleep for 30 minutes a day and resisting the desire to eat more than precisely 1000 calories per day while still training for a marathon? Would you say that it had to do with being able to sit underneath a rushing waterfall with the water crashing atop your head? Is it about meditation? Is it about perfect obedience that you would only see in the barracks of militaries?

Many people have a skewed idea of what it means to be disciplined. They may assume that it means that they can never splurge on that ice cream after dinner, or decide that they cannot decide that they are going to stay up just a little bit later than usual so they can finish that movie that they began watching. They assume that self-discipline is all about being perfectly draconian over each and every aspect of their lives—and that makes it something undesirable. They do not want to live a life that is bound to specific rules and norms that they do not want to follow—they want to be able to enjoy themselves!

However, that is not self-discipline. Self-discipline is not meant to be something that makes you miserable. It is not something that should deprive you of any of your basic needs. It should not force you to give up something that you need, or even something that you desperately want on occasion, because you deserve to be happiness. And yet, so many people assume that to be self-disciplined, they must be miserable.

Sometimes, people are perfectly happy in their rigid, draconian schedules. Sometimes, people love to get up at 4:30 AM on a Sunday, beating the sun, because they want to go for a 10 mile run before they get ready for their day. They are totally happy to have a smoothie made entirely of vegetables and then work out for three hours—because they enjoy it.

What some people may enjoy to do is something that could make other people panic, shake their heads no, and run away. You may see someone else clearly torturing themselves as they put themselves through all of that hardship—only to find out that, to them, it is not hardship at all.

The problem here is that so many people conflate doing something that took plenty of willpower with something that is inherently unenjoyable—and then they decide that self-discipline is not for them. These people may decide that they are uninterested in ever developing it because of that idea that it will be so miserable, or they will simply be unaware that they are lacking self-discipline in the first place.

However, lacking self-discipline, either willingly or because you are unaware that you are, in fact, lacking it in the first place, are both major problems. They can both come with all sorts of other problems. Self-discipline is necessary, and yet so many people instead decide to focus on their own hedonistic pleasures, even when they know that they will be harmful. Think about it—some people are totally happy to spend their days doing nothing. They are perfectly content eating unhealthily and not working to better themselves. Within this chapter, we are going to address this problem—we are going to take a look at what a lack of self-discipline can do to an individual so you can then begin to recognize why it matters. This chapter is all about showing you precisely why you need self-discipline and precisely how you can make it happen.

Lacking Self-Discipline

Have you ever sat down, stared at your computer at work, and then wondered what happened? Maybe you suddenly realized that your deadline is 30 minutes away and you have three hours of work left—and you do not know where that time went. Perhaps you run into the problem of not being able to manage your time. Maybe you try to begin fixing your problems, only to realize that you are struggling to actually make those changes that you need.

Oftentimes, when people are asked why they failed at something, the answer is simple—they blame it on a lack of self-discipline. Is it true? Perhaps—but ultimately, that is something that will need to be fixed. You may be trying desperately to make the chances that you need to see, but when push comes to shove and things get rough, you realize something: You do not actually want to make it happen. If this sounds familiar, you may already recognize that you lack self-discipline, and that could be precisely why you are here right now.

Ultimately, self-discipline requires willpower. However, in almost a cruel sort of trick of fate, you cannot develop willpower without discipline. So, which comes first, then? How do you develop the willpower that you need for discipline if you do not have the discipline for willpower? It is a very difficult conundrum that plagues people. However, if that sounds like you, there is good news—you have a way to develop both at the same time. It may be difficult, but you can make it happen. All you have to do is make sure that you work on them both at the same time, and we will be addressing this soon.

For now, we are going to look at what a lack of self-discipline looks like. Keep in mind here that people are not born with self-discipline already in place. It is something that needs to be cultivated and fostered. One look at a toddler can tell you that much—have you ever seen a toddler doing something that you know is ridiculous, but you cannot convince them that they should not do it? Their lack of any sort of self-discipline is their problem. They get so caught up in the hedonistic aspect of what they are doing that they fail to succeed.

. . .

Of course, with toddlers, that often happens because they are not yet developed enough mentally to recognize that they are simply giving in to what will give them the most instant gratification. So, then, what's your excuse?

A lack of self-discipline usually comes with some very serious signs and some very serious detriments that must be eliminated if you want to be able to succeed in life. However, to do that, you must first begin to understand what it looks like.

What Happens Without Discipline?

When you do not have discipline, you oftentimes fall into complacency. You do not care about how you can succeed—that takes effort. Much like the fabled fox that cannot reach the grapes and then declares them sour, when you lack discipline, you may decide that ultimately, your laziness is comfortable. You may decide that you are fine with the lack of effort because you know that ultimately, it is going to be more enjoyable than any sort of effort that you would otherwise have to engage it. That extra effort can be a huge detriment to many different people and because of that, they do everything in their power to avoid it altogether.

Without discipline, then, you are weak-willed. You are not going to make decisions because they are the right ones to make. You will not make decisions because you believe that they are better than other ones. You will not be able to stop yourself from doing something that is impulsive because ultimately, the impulse probably sounds pleasant. There is a word for this kind of person: Hedonistic.

· · ·

Those that are hedonistic do not care about what they should be doing or what they should be wanting. Rather, they focus entirely on what they will enjoy and what will bring them the most possible pleasure. It does not matter what they are doing—they will always side on the side of self-indulgence.

The idea behind hedonism, believed to have been started by a student of Socrates in ancient Greece, named Aristippus of Cyrene, was that ultimately, pleasure was the greatest good that people would ever achieve. He argued that ultimately, the only aspect of life that mattered was that they needed to reduce suffering. In reducing suffering and therefore increasing pleasure, they are doing what they believe is right.

However, is it right to eat ice cream for breakfast, lunch, and dinner, for three weeks? You may think that it is pretty great after the first day. It may have been enjoyable days 2 and 3, too, but most people would very quickly begin to tire of their ice cream diet. They may find that their stomachs, or even their teeth, are beginning to hurt, because the human body is not designed to subsist on just ice cream and nothing else.

Ultimately, then, the problem with this sort of hedonistic lifestyle is that it is incredibly unclear. It is very nonspecific—are you doing the right thing when you are enjoying yourself? What if you are enjoying yourself while you do not go to work, ultimately losing your job? Is that still the right thing to do, morally speaking?

· · ·

This is precisely what happens when you fall into a life without self-discipline. You are too indulgent. You are too swayed by your current whims to stop and look at what happens in the future. The future consequences do not matter to you so long as you enjoyed what you were doing in the moment. You do not care if you are going to do something that could have a devastating effect later on —all because you think that the joy that you would get right then would be worth it to you, and that is a huge problem.

Now, with the idea of what a lack of self-discipline is, let's take a look at what having self-discipline will look like. Again, consider what you would assume self-discipline would look lie. What is it about someone that you would consider self-disciplined? Answer this question for yourself before you continue reading on. Would you consider yourself self-disciplined by that definition?

Before moving forward, let's get one thing straight—self-discipline is not about punishment. It is not about pain. It is not about sacrifice. While sacrifice can be a part of it to some degree at some points in time, you are going to find that it is not always about sacrifice. In fact, if you want to be self-disciplined, the goal is to get to a point where you do not feel like you are being punished, you do not feel hurt by your choices, and you do not feel like you had to make sacrifices.

. . .

Oftentimes, because we use the word, "discipline" so much in regard to punishment, it is very easy to get caught up in it. It is very easy to believe that you cannot be disciplined if you are not giving yourself 100 lashes on your back by yourself every day just because you want to teach yourself a lesson. That is a very unnecessary part of discipline and it does not have a place in it.

Discipline and punishment could not be further apart from each other. Think about it this way—disciples are students of leaders. They are people that are dedicated to learning what someone else is teaching. They are not being punished—they are being taught. Likewise, when it comes to discipline, you are not going to be punishing people—you are meant to be teaching them.

This clear distinction shows you that self-discipline should not be associated with punishment at all. In fact, that association could be a major reason for failure later on if you assume that you have to punish yourself in some way to be deemed disciplined. Rather, you are trying to teach yourself. You are teaching yourself how to make good judgment calls. You are learning what matters to you most and you are sticking to it, no matter how difficult that it might be at that point in time.

Within this chapter, we are going to go over self-discipline. We are going to see precisely how it works and why it matters. We are going to see what goes into self-discipline as well, and hopefully, by the time that you get to the end of this chapter, you will have a pretty solid idea of what self-discipline is, because at this point in time, it has been a whole lot of determining what it is not.

Defining Self-Discipline

To begin, let's go over what self-discipline really is. Let's get one thing straight right here: There is no one specific form of self-discipline. Rather, there are several different traits that come together to allow you to become self-disciplined. The self-discipline itself is not something that is its own sort of trait. Rather, it is a sort of amalgamation of lots of different traits that all come together. Instead of just being on its own, it is being able to meet several different requirements.

To be self-disciplined, you must be willing to think first. You must be able to control yourself. It is, ultimately, the ability to do one thing: It is the ability to control yourself when it comes down to avoiding something that will be unhealthy or problematic for you. When you are self-disciplined, you are able to reject or turn down something that, as much fun as it sounds, would be a big problem at the end of the day.

For example, imagine that you are given two choices: You can have $50,000 today, or if you wait three months, you can have $500,000, what would you do? There is no doubt that ultimately, that $500,000 is going to last longer. That $500,000 will be able to be used many different ways, and yet so many people would be so much quicker to take the $50,000 in front of them because they know that they can have it right that moment. They cannot forego that instant gratification, and so, instead of having a bit of patience and therefore getting what really mattered the most to them, they make the mistake of doing something what will bring them some joy sooner.

· · ·

Think about the problem with this- if you cannot wait a little bit to get more, what is going to happen? You will constantly be working on that sort of instant gratification scale that will ultimately bring you down and make it impossible for you to succeed at all.

The Factors of Self-Discipline

Really, at the end of the day, self-discipline is nothing but habits. It is nothing but being able to make the same beneficial choices for yourself consistently and repeatedly, no matter what is happening. You are essentially able to figure out what matters to you and you are able to remain steadfast even when you are in the face of crisis or you feel like there is no better way to succeed. Self-discipline ultimately requires you to have several habits and bits of knowledge understood so you can, in fact, succeed. If you can develop those factors, you know that you can succeed because the more you use them, the better they work.

Think of self-discipline as a muscle for a moment. When you first start to work it, it is very weak. It is not really able to do much at all. The muscle just sits there because it is so hard to use. You cannot do much with it if you have never been able to strengthen it at all—so you stop trying altogether.

However, what you could do is start to use it. You can start to exercise it and work with it and little by little, it will get more powerful. Little by little, you start to find that ultimately, self-discipline is not so bad. You recognize that it can be used more often, so you start to use it more. Over time, you eventually realize that self-discipline is actually entirely beneficial and you decide that it is something that you should live by. Perfect! All of that happened because you made a change, liked the change, and then kept that same change rolling constantly. You were able to essentially make sure that those changes occurred and remained there for you, meaning that you would then turn those changes into habits.

To habituate your own self-discipline and therefore get all of those benefits that you are looking for, there are a few factors that must be considered. These factors must come into play somehow if you hope to ever truly develop that self-discipline in the first place.

Your purpose

Perhaps one of the most basic parts of developing your own self-discipline is recognizing that you need to have some sort of push. There has to be some sort of reason that you are doing everything that you are. You need to figure out what that purpose is so you can properly tap into it. If you know that you are driven to do something because you genuinely think that it is the best thing that you can do, then you are going to find it much easier to stick to it than if it is something that was decided upon on a whim.

Think about it this way—would you be more driven to lose 20 lbs. if you knew that it would save your life than you would be driven if you simply thought that losing a bit of weight would be nice? When you put a purpose onto something that is inherently valuable motivation skyrockets—and for good reason.

. . .

Your reason why will likely either be an inspiration for you—you have something that you want and you are inspired by that want. Alternatively, you could have the motivation and drive necessary to push yourself to focus for longer terms. If you have that sort of motivation to keep pushing yourself forward, you will find that it becomes so much easier to remain true to what you need to do.

Your commitment

Next, you must consider the fact that you need to be unwavering in what you are doing. If you really want to succeed at something that requires long hours of hard work, you must be committed to it. You must ensure that you are entirely dedicated to ensuring that your goal succeeds and because of that, you need commitment. It could be commitment due to obligation—such as feeling obligated to feed your children or ensure that your dog goes out on a regular basis. It could be commitment because you are genuinely passionate about something. Either way, so long as that commitment to doing what you need to do is there in some way, shape, or form.

This can be very difficult—it can be hard to remain committed to something in order to build discipline just due to the fact that commitment itself requires some degree of discipline. People are not usually very good at deciding that they want to do something on their own without something holding them accountable.

. . .

Keep in mind that your commitment will require you to hold your-self accountable for what you are doing. If you cannot remain accountable for your actions, you may find that you actually need to change what you are doing somehow. You may need to find someone else to hold you accountable or you may need to find new tactics altogether. No matter whether you can hold yourself accountable or you can get someone else to hold you accountable, you will be able to essentially allow yourself to begin developing those necessary tendencies and habits that will drive your own self-discipline so long as the accountability is there somewhere in the first place.

Your penalties and rewards

Naturally, everything has natural consequences. These conse-quences can usually be assigned to what you are doing and they can usually be recognized as being directly related to what they were consequences for. You need to make sure that, when your find your own motivation changing and fluctuating over time, that you realize that there are always consequences no matter what it is that you have done. Those consequences can come back to bite you if you are not careful.

However, please note that again, there is a difference between a natural consequence and a punishment. A natural consequence in the way that it is being used here is something that happened as a direct result of something else that you or someone else has done. For example, imagine that you decided that you were going to drink heavily one night before you had a major exam in college. You knew that it would be a bad idea, and yet, instead of studying, you went and got yourself plastered that night. You woke up the next morning with the world's worst hangover and yet you still had to run out the door, go into the very bright classroom and take the very intensive final exam, all while having a pounding headache, nausea, and reeking of a bar floor so badly that everyone around you had already tried to scoot away.

Is the universe punishing you when you fail your exam because you showed up hungover? Not at all—rather, the hangover was a very natural consequence—it was the direct result of your actions. In this situation, that sort of natural consequence has nothing to do with you and whether or not you were in trouble or punished by something. Rather, it had everything to do with the fact that you made a bad choice that had a very serious outcome.

Likewise, there are natural rewards when you do something right, too. If you work hard and focus at your job, you will likely get a raise. This is a natural consequence as well, albeit more of a positive one that people will naturally be more inclined to accept.

You can also sort of force the point yourself as well. You can have a reward for yourself. If you, for example, love to play video games but always have too much work that you had to bring home, a very easy reward for you is that you cannot play your game until you have completed your work. When you do this, you essentially ensure that you will not be making any bad decisions. You are eliminating the sort of desire that you may have to simply go play your game before the work is done because you know that you will be able to play—when you finish up.

If you can add these small incentives for yourself to complete what you need to do, you can actually find that it is much easier to get yourself moving and stick to what needs to be done.

Your standards

You must also have and recognize your standards if you hope to be self-disciplined. Ultimately, self-discipline is all about living a life that you can be happy with. It is about doing what you now is right for you. It is essentially your way of saying that you know that you should be behaving in a very specific way because that is what is right for you—and you need to make it happen.

Without self-discipline, you do not live up to your standards. You may simply not be holding yourself up to the standards that you should have. You may realize that ultimately, you are acting in ways that are not like what you should be doing, all because you are finding that they are not important enough to you.

If you cannot live up to those standards, you have to ask yourself something—do those standards really matter to you if you cannot be bothered to hold them up? Do they really matter enough for you to remain disciplined if you do not care to uphold them in the first place?

. . .

For this reason, you must know what your personal standards are. You need to figure out what that bare minimum sort of behavior line is for yourself so you know what you can and cannot accept.

Your drive

Finally, you must also be able to recognize what is driving you forward. This is some level of competition more often than not. That competition does not have to be against other people, though that is oftentimes an easy one to hold up. Rather, you can put yourself in a mindset that involves you attempting to outwork someone else. Or, you can make it so you compete against yourself.

If you see that you are doing something right now at a certain rate, what can you do to improve that? This is perhaps one of the most important factors to maintaining your own self-discipline. You must be willing and able to challenge yourself to ensure that you are constantly striving forward. You need this—if you cannot strive forward, how can you help yourself? How can you ensure that you are motivated and focused if you are not willing to do better than you were already doing? If you are able to achieve that level of doing better, you can usually ensure that at the very least, you are constantly trying to be at the standards that you are already at. This means that, at the very least, you are able to ensure that you are at least making forward strives.

. . .

If you cannot find that strive for yourself, you are going to suffer. You need to know what it is that is pushing you to keep moving forward so you can continue to do so. You must figure out what matters most to you so you can, in fact, ensure that you are always succeeding.

3 / WHAT CAUSES A LACK OF SELF-DISCIPLINE?

HAVE you ever woken up in the morning and realized something devastating—that you did not get anything done the night before? Maybe you had all sorts of big, important plans that you wanted to achieve. Perhaps you wanted to clean out the fridge so you could do a big meal prep that day. Maybe you were going to spend some time learning a new skill that you could use regularly. Perhaps you wanted to go out and exercise so you could get back in shape—but it didn't happen at all.

That sort of crushing feeling in the morning that people who struggle with self-discipline can become all too familiar. It can become all too frequent for them—they simply struggle to succeed and they struggle to meet standards, their own and those of others. However, it does not have to be that way. You can learn to be self-disciplined, and we will be going over that shortly. However, for this chapter, we are going to address lacking self-discipline.

. . .

Oftentimes, there are reasons that people cannot figure out how they can follow their goals or do what they have set out to do. They usually have very obvious reasons that they cannot move forward —although most of the time, they are entirely oblivious to whatever it is.

Within this chapter, we are going to address the lacking of self-discipline. We are going to consider what those common causes to struggling with self-discipline are so you can then begin to correct for the problem altogether. When you know what the problem is, you will be able to ensure that ultimately, you can better yourself. You will be able to prevent yourself from struggling further. You will be able to make the necessary changes. It will take time, but it is possible.

If you want to develop self-discipline, then, you need to stop and take a good, hard look at yourself as you read this chapter. It will be up to you to figure out precisely why this is so hard for you in the first place. Only you, and you alone, will be able to self-reflect on this to determine why you may be struggling so much, and if you can identify that, you can then begin to make necessary changes.

Aiming too Big

Sometimes, the problem with your self-discipline is not that you have no interest or you are unwilling to do something. Some-times, it is as simple as the fact that the goal that you have set out to do seems too big. You may have, for example, told yourself that you want to write a new book in two months. Now, that is a highly demanding undertaking right there—writing a book is not easy by any means. However, you tell yourself that two months seems reasonable and move on with your life.

But, two months later, and you are all of 3000 words into a 50,000 novel that you had planned. What happened?

The answer there is that you aimed too big. You set yourself up with a big goal without any real guidance or thinking about how you would get there. You essentially told yourself that you would do something, but you did not do the work to ensure that you got to that point. You did not make sure that you knew what you were doing. You did not make sure that you had a plan to get there. You just had your starting point of there was nothing written to your ending point of there was an entire novel written with nothing in between them.

When you aim too big like that, you essentially overwhelm yourself. You feel too overwhelmed by what you are doing to really get started. It seems like too much, so you continually put it off, over and over again, until the goal and the deadline have entirely passed you by. This is a huge problem—you need to learn how to better set goals for yourself so you know that you are setting ones that you know will work. Overcoming this is literally as simple as ensuring that, next time, you come up with a clear-cut plan to take you from start to finish without much of a struggle. If you can do that, you can then better ensure that, next time, you can succeed—all because you will know what to do next time.

Not Knowing How

The next point to consider is that self-discipline is not just developed—it has to be learned. You could learn it growing up from parents that wanted to help foster it. Or, it could be developed by someone who went out of their way to do better in the future. Either way, the end result is that they learn what they need to know in order to be successful when it comes to taking care of their goals and staying true to what they have set out to do. If you do not know what you will need to do, however, it might not be just out of sheer laziness—though that is always a possibility.

You could struggle with self-discipline because no one ever taught you how to be disciplined in the first place and you found that you simply fell into familiar habits that were learned from a lifetime of being around people that did not know how to behave in a self-disciplined manner. That may not be your fault, but you do have the power to change it with ease.

If you want to change this, you must make one thing happen—you must commit yourself to learning how to be self-disciplined yourself. While not knowing how may have been a valid excuse when you were younger, as an adult, it is your responsibility to make up for any gaps that you have in your knowledge that you need. This means that if you do not understand how to maintain discipline, then you must learn how to do so somehow. You cannot trust that someone else will come along and do it for you—you need to take accountability. And, the good news is that if you are reading this right now, you are on the right track. Reading this is a good sign that, at the very least, you understand that you owe it to yourself to develop those skills later on.

Self-Sabotage

Sometimes, the problem that people face is simply a matter of self-sabotage. You may find that you are not quite sure that you can do something, and so you fail it, not intentionally, but because your mind did not believe in you anyway. Let's go back to the earlier example of deciding to go and party the night before a final exam. Is it possible that you did not actually think that you could pass the exam in the first place? If you did not think that you would be able to succeed anyway, your mind could have created this sort of situation in which you had no option but to fail.

When that happened, your subconscious basically gave you an out, even if you do not realize that it is happening. Then, when you inevitably failed your exam, you would have rolled your eyes and told yourself that of course you failed—you were not prepared at all. You had not spent the time to ensure that ultimately, you would pass. You did not study properly. You did not put in the effort that was necessary to help yourself succeed. You did not ensure that at the end of the day, you took all of the study time that was given to you. Instead of any of that, you simply set yourself up to fail, knowing that if you did fail in that context, you would write it off as a problem with the alcohol and the fault of the hangover rather than making you the problem.

Fear of Failure

Maybe the reason that you were held back was because you were afraid of failing altogether. When people are afraid that they will fail, they oftentimes freeze up. They start to try to come up with some way to avoid that failure, but the failure is impossible to avoid. So, in spending all of that time constantly trying to figure out how to get out of failing in the first place, you fail.

. . .

This is perhaps one of the more ironic problems that you can have. You are afraid of failing so you struggle to get started. However, by virtue of not getting started, you failed by default. Of course, you will then use that failure to justify what happened to yourself—you will remind yourself that you failed because you are a failure and point out that the failure was entirely on you in that situation.

This is a major problem that needs to be overcome, as the procrastination that it can breed is absolutely disastrous for those that suffer from it. If you find that you suffer from failure for this reason, it is time for you to shake it off. There are ways that you can defeat that fear of failure, so long as you are willing to put in the effort that needs to happen. If you can defeat that fear of failure in the first place, you may find that you are pleasantly surprised that you could succeed all along—the success was simply buried behind too much apprehension for you to access at any point in time.

Fear of Being Wrong

Ultimately, every person has two major drives—to be right and to be liked. Of course, if you think that you are going to be wrong, you will find that you are going to struggle to remain motivated in the first place. You can see this play out much like the way that the fear of failure did—you simply freeze up and do not do anything at all because you are afraid of getting it wrong.

Oftentimes, this is linked to what is regularly referred to as paralysis by analysis. That is the phenomenon during which someone finds that they cannot make the decision on what to do next. They can decide to do one thing or the other, but the anxiety surrounding the act of being wrong essentially holds them up—

they struggle to make a decision because they cannot decide which end they want to be on.

Try thinking about it this way. Imagine that you got offered two jobs. One of them pays more but is not what you really want to do with your life. The other job is one that pays less and the hours are not as good, but it is a job that you have always dreamed of having. Which do you choose?

If you struggle with the fear of being wrong, you may find that you constantly flounder back and forth. One minute, you are telling yourself that of course you'll take your dream job. The next minute, you are thinking about the socioeconomic outcome of each job, and then two minutes later, you are thinking about whether or not you would be miserable doing the higher paying job.

The catch here is that you need to recognize that the exchange example given right there is not the same as recognizing the need to weigh pros and cons. Pros and cons should always be considered, especially when you are attempting to make such a high-stakes decision or something that is going to be life-changing. But, you must also keep in mind that if you are caught between two choices that you cannot decide between and you repeat the same questions and thoughts to yourself incessantly without ever committing one way or another, then you are going to paralyze yourself. You will lose the chances that were given to you altogether and that can destroy your ability to make a decision.

Fear of Rejection

Along those same lines, you may be afraid of being rejected by someone or something. You are so worried about how to be liked by other people that instead of doing what matters to you, you start wondering if you should simply give in to what someone else wants you to do. You decide that ultimately, you would rather be liked than do something that you enjoy, and that leads to other problems for you. You struggle to make a decision that you can live with, and you may even not make a decision at all.

Again, this fear of someone else's reaction or the fear of the consequences winds up holding you back. However, if you knew what your own personal values and desires were, and you had a sort of personal mission statement designed for yourself, you would be able to make use of that. You would be able to ensure that at the end of the day, you did make a good choice for yourself and that you did decide that what you were doing was going to be skewed one way or another.

Here is the problem with this fear of rejection as well—the more that you fear being rejected, the more you start to reject yourself. You are telling yourself that the you that you are is going to be rejected and that you need to change. You will essentially convince yourself that what you are doing is only justified by the value that other people see in you reactions. However, you do not need to do anything to make sure that others like you. It is not your responsibility to make other people like you. You cannot control them or their reactions—but you can control your own.

Lacking Motivation

Sometimes, the problem that you find is that you do not have any sort of motivation. Without motivation, you have no chance in being able to do what it was that you were hoping to do. This is quite simple—if you do not have the drive or the desire to do something that is difficult, how are you going to get yourself to move forward? You might do it to some extent—but will it be enough? You might try to ensure that ultimately, you do make a decision on how to act or what to do, but if that is not enough to actually make you act in that manner, you are not going to actually follow through.

Remember, your motivation is the desire to act. If you do not have that desire to do what you need to do for any reason at all, and you do not have some other purpose driving you, the chances of you actually doing what you are supposed to do are quite slim. Your lack of motivation will hold you back and keep you down.

However, remember this point—even if you are not motivated right this moment does not mean that you need to resign yourself to this. Find a reason that you need to care. Find a reason to drive you forward. Find a reason that will keep you acting the way that you need to in order to motivate the behaviors in the first place. If you know, for example, that you have to go to work so you can pay the bills to keep a roof over your child's head then you are going to find that, even when you do not want to get up and work, you will because you want to ensure that you can take care of your child.

Lacking Resources

Other times, the problem is not that you do not want the behavior or the motivation enough, but rather that you cannot get the necessary resources. In particular, willpower and self-discipline will both ultimately require energy. If you do not have any energy mentally due to stress, fatigue, or anything else, you need to remember that you are going to run into other problems. If you cannot make sure that you are actively ensuring that you have enough resources, such as energy, sleep, and time, then you cannot actually prioritize your goals. You need to ensure that, to succeed and to ensure that you do try to complete your goals, you will be able to prioritize them to actually get there. You need to allocate those resources where they need to go. You need to makes sure that you do spend the time working harder to make them actually get the amount of energy that they will require to ensure that you can, in fact actually succeed.

One way to help with this is to ensure that you can reduce stress. Stress, like your own self-discipline, will reduce energy. It will deplete it over time and that can be a huge problem for you. You will need to ensure that you can defeat that lack of energy and perhaps the best way to do that is to take care of yourself physically. You will want to make sure that you are eating foods that are high in all of the nutrients that you need to nourish your body. You need to make sure that you keep your blood sugar stable. You need to make sure that you not only take the time to sleep when you need it, but also that you take the time to enjoy yourself, too. You need to be able to enjoy yourself so you know that you will be able to muster up the energy that you need. When you strike a great work-life balance, you know that you will ultimately be able to protect your own energy stores and that can make remaining motivated that much easier on you in the longer run.

Having Bad Habits

Sometimes, the problem comes down to simple problems with your own habits. Maybe you have gotten used to letting other people fix problems for you. Maybe you have found that you are much happier letting other people take a defining role in what you are doing and that you are content to simply sit back without ever doing anything meaningful. If that sounds like you and you do not care enough to ensure that, at the end of the day, you do actually do what matters to you, then you are going to need to find some way to break the habits.

This has a very simple, at least in theory, fix. You need to be able to change your habits. If you can adjust your habits to be those of winners, of those that are driven, and of those that are willing to do anything that it takes to succeed, then you will be able to shed off that lack of motivation and that lack of self-discipline. However, you will need to spend the time to figure out how to make that happen and that can be a bit of a challenge for many different people.

Doubting Yourself

Another huge problem that people often have is that they doubt themselves. They simply do not believe that they are actually able to do anything that really, truly matters, and because of that self-doubt, they do not bother to act. If you doubt yourself, if you lack your own self-esteem, how can you trust yourself to be able to do anything at all? This becomes that sort of chicken and egg problem—which can you develop first? Can you really develop self-esteem while also lacking self-discipline?

Ultimately, you will need to work, little by little, to teach yourself how to trust yourself. If you can do this, you will be able to essentially remind yourself that you are trustworthy. You teach yourself that you can rely on yourself and your own actions, and that will help you begin to slowly but surely whittle away at any of that lingering self-doubt that would otherwise hold you back.

HALT

Finally, the last of the destroyers of your own self-discipline is known as HALT. When you are HALTed, you are essentially saying that you gave in to one of the following four problems:

- Hungry
- Angry
- Lonely
- Tired

Notice how the letters, when put together, spell HALT. That is very apt—when you are hungry, angry, lonely, or tired, you are going to naturally have a hard time following through with just about anything that you need to do. This goes right back to a problem with a lack of resources. However, these four have very noticeable, very obvious causes that you can essentially tap into. When you HALT, you must first figure out which feeling you are suffering from. Then, you can solve the problem. Instead of sitting back and letting all four drain on you, you can decide how to fix it.

If you are hungry, you can eat something to eliminate the problem. That may be enough to get you right back on track. If you are angry, take a few minutes to calm down and try some breathing exercises before committing to trying to better understand what had happened. If you are lonely, spend some time with someone else to make sure that you are able to meet that need to socialize— and it is a need. Lastly, if you are tired, you can try taking a break, or even a nap.

4 / THE POWER OF SELF-DISCIPLINE

ULTIMATELY, one of the most important skills that you have on your tool belt is your ability to practice self-discipline. This will keep you in line. It will ensure that you are constantly motivated. It will make sure that you are always working toward what you need and allow you to figure out how to control yourself. It is a sign that you are a strong person. You know that you can control what you are doing, how you are doing it, and why you are doing it, and you set out to do all of that at once.

Of course as well, being able to rely on your own self-discipline can come in handy. It can give you the willpower that you need to remain resolved in doing what you believe is right. It can give you that necessary mental energy and that boost to your own confidence to stand up to yourself. It can help you figure out how to navigate through the world without letting yourself be swayed constantly what other people think. You will do what you think is right, and that is something that is very important, very rare, and something that the world needs more of these days.

. . .

Within this chapter, we are going to spend some time talking all about the power that self-discipline has. It can benefit you in ways that you have never dreamed of—it can help you develop the strength to not only overcome laziness or other problems, but it can also greatly help you ensure that, at the end of the day, you are going to do what you need.

Remember that self-discipline itself will appear in many different forms, such as:

- **Perseverance:** You will not give up, no matter what has happened around you and no matter how difficult the task at hand is. You will remain disciplined and strong, and you will stick to your guns enough to ensure that, at the end of the day, you can keep yourself on track, no matter how many different roadblocks and obstacles you run into.
- **Self-control:** This gives you the power to resist any sort of temptation that heads your way because you would much rather get the long-term goals that you are working toward than to be distracted and caught up by what other people are doing or doing what will be pleasant right that minute.
- **The ability to keep trying:** You will repeatedly try to do something over and over again, even after failing because you will know that you will succeed at some point—you just have to get to that point in the first place.

As you can see, self-discipline is a very important skill to have. It will benefit you greatly. Now, let's go over several different benefits that self-discipline can bring to the table for you to take advantage of. Remember, if you can remain self-disciplined, you will be able to remember that you can, in fact, ensure that your actions will be successful. As you read over this list, consider the importance of these different actions and benefits. Consider why they matter so much and why you should ensure that you are constantly striving for them.

You Avoid Impulsive Decisions

Impulsive decisions happen often. They can be the decision to drink before a big night when you know that you need to be clear-headed. It could involve taking a big risk unnecessarily or for a reason that is not compelling enough to justify what you are risking in the first place. It could be to try something dangerous, knowing that you are doing something risky, but deciding that you should anyway.

When you make impulsive decisions, however, you are usually not the only person that suffers. Remember, everything has a ripple effect—if you fail out of college because you have not taken it seriously, that not only impacts you, but it also impacts your future spouse and any future children. It impacts your family members if you go to them to ask for financial help because you were never able to complete your degree and therefore you could not get a job that would pay enough for you to get by.

. . .

However, when you are self-disciplined, you can keep yourself on track. You can resist that temptation and remind yourself why that is a bad idea. Your own discipline will remind you why you cannot drink the night before a final—it will remind you that you should absolutely be working harder on trying to figure out how you can succeed and pass your final. It will help you focus on your schooling and resist the hedonistic pleasures of going out drinking when you know that you need to study.

You Are Reliable

When you are self-disciplined, you oftentimes will remain true to your word, no matter how hard it is and no matter what it was that you promised. You know that being true to your word is very important so you work hard to always follow through. You know better than to promise to do something just because you think that the other person would like to hear it. Instead, you focus on how you can better follow through with what you do volunteer for.

This is incredibly important. This means that anyone that you generally associate with will recognize that, at the end of the day, you are someone that can be relied on and that is a very powerful, very compelling label to have. Everyone wants to befriend the reliable one. Your relationships, both romantic and platonic will improve because you will be deserving of trust and that trust will help ensure that other people want to spend that time with you in the first place. If you can make sure that, at the end of the day, you are always reliable, you know that you are setting yourself and your relationships, all up for success.

. . .

To be reliable is difficult—there is no doubt about that. However, there is something important to keep in mind as well. Reliability is honored greatly. It is one of those traits that are always deemed valuable and in demand. If you can make sure that you avoid burning any bridges due to unreliability, you will likely find that life, and everyone around you that is in it, will be that much more enjoyable thanks to the fact that you will generally be better judged and received if you can make sure that you are always making yourself reliable.

You Avoid Procrastination

Another critically important benefit of self-discipline is the fact that you will be able to resist the temptation of procrastination. Because you will be so reliable and you will be able to drive yourself forward, you will be able to avoid that sort of procrastination that would otherwise completely devastate your ability to get your work done. You need to be able to better deal with your own motivation, and self-discipline does that for you.

Think about it this way—does anyone ever really want to do something that they know that they do not like? Not at all—in fact, most people would love to find a way to worm their way out of having to do something that they strongly dislike. However, that is something that is not always feasible. If you have any sort of responsibilities or jobs, you cannot simply procrastinate the days away and hope that you will be deemed as doing a good enough job to be kept around or doing well enough for a promotion.

By being able to defeat procrastination, no matter the cause, you are able to better protect yourself. You are able to better ensure that, at the end of the day, you can better deal with just about anything. You can prevent yourself from feeling driven to give in to those silly, hedonistic, instant ratifications that you would love because you know that it would be worse.

Consider this—you have a 5 page paper due tomorrow that you have not so much as started on yet. You know that you need to do it and you plan on doing it that afternoon. Then, your friend begs you to go to the movie theater. However, when you do go, you realize that you made a huge mistake, and now you do not get to sleep at all because you are too busy having to put together that paper early into the morning. You do not finish the paper until your alarm goes off because you spent all that time with your friend instead of working because you wanted to procrastinate.

Was that a good idea? You could have simply done the paper first and then gone out if you had time—at least then, you would have been able to sleep as soon as you were tired. However instead, you put fun first and you wound up really hurting yourself. While there were not lasting impacts other than a few days of exhaustion, you really put yourself at risk like that.

With self-discipline, however, going to the movie would have bene an instant no until you had finished up everything that you needed to do. You would have refused to go until you were done.

You Can Finish a Project

Along those same lines, when you are able to retain your self-discipline, you will know that you can always finish your projects that you start. Many people find that they lose motivation as soon as that initial excitement is gone altogether. When that excitement fades away, you realize that you were not actually very interested in the project in the first place and it becomes difficult to finish it.

However, when it comes down to being self-disciplined, you have the added benefit of being able to resist that trap. You recognize that, ultimately, you need to change up how you do anything at all. You recognize that you will need to find a way that you can prevent yourself from giving up, so you find some sort of motivation to keep yourself there and working on the project. This is important—when you can find that self-discipline, you can ensure that your motivation is intrinsic. You then are no longer going to work because you want to keep your job—you are going to work because you believe that it is right and good and you want to follow through with what needs to happen. You will be able to stick to that motivation to protect yourself and ensure that, at the end of the day, you are better equipped to finish projects because you are self-motivated as well as self-disciplined.

Your self-discipline essentially becomes a way in which you are able to keep yourself moving toward the success that you are seeking out. You are able to work hard to actually start to see it happen and this makes you more reliable. Remember, reliability and predictability are very well loved in any good professional environment.

You Will Go Out and Take Care of Yourself

When you are self-disciplined, you recognize the importance of a healthy body and because of that, you take care of yourself. This does not mean that you never do anything unhealthy that you love—you may sometimes opt to buy that candy bar or have that glass of wine, and that is okay. After all, with moderation, things will be fine.

However, when you are self-disciplined, you can resist that temptation to repeatedly skip going to the gym. You know that going to the gym is very important and you seek to make it happen. You know that you need to make sure that you can properly get everything that your body will need to stay healthy, and that includes you having to spend the time to eat healthily, exercise, and get sleep as necessary.

As a direct result, being a healthy individual and having self-discipline to make that happen are both closely related just by virtue of the way that they do connect to each other. By recognizing that, you will begin to see something important—the ones that are the most successful in their relationships, in their health, and in their careers tend to be the ones with the most or best self-discipline.

You Will Resist Temptations

Sometimes, we all get that impulse to go out and enjoy something. You may know that what it is, is something that will be harmful, but you still want to make it happen. However, this is not healthy. Choosing behaviors that you know will prevent you from succeeding is not healthy. Choosing to act in ways that are detrimental to you, your goals, and your future is not healthy. You need to be able to keep your eyes on the prize to ensure that you are able to move forward and succeed in life. If you want to, for example, get that promotion, then you cannot call out to play hooky at work just because you want to go see a baseball game that is happening during work hours.

· · ·

You must be able to remember this particular fact. You must recognize that ultimately, there is value in resisting a temptation that is going to send you far from your main goals that you have set for yourself at that point in time. You must always be paying close attention to what you value and how you can get it.

Self-discipline keeps your behaviors aligned with your goals—it teaches you to ensure that you do, in fact, focus on what matters the most to you and that helps keep you on track. You do not find that you are easily distracted from what matters the most to you and you are able to keep your eyes on the prize.

When you can remind yourself that, at the end of the day, your own attempts to try to ensure that you are enjoying the time that you have, or enjoying the current moment rather than working to get where you really want to be, will be worthwhile, you can better remember them. The entire point of your ability to remain self-disciplined is to remind yourself that, at the end of the day, you should be rejecting those immediate sorts of instant gratification, especially when they are detrimental to the bigger picture. You need to focus on the bigger picture before you focus on the little things.

Think about it this way—you are on a diet to lose weight to fit into your wedding dress. One night, you decide that you really want a chocolate cake, so you buy one on your way home. You eat one slice and decide that it is really good, so you decide that you will go get another big slice.

.   .   .

Your self-discipline, however, reminds you that the instant gratification now is not worth the setback that you will face. It sort of acts like a filter to keep yourself from doing something that will be directly detrimental to your ability to succeed. It reminds you that you have worked too hard to blow it for a cake when you are so close to your goal. It reminds you that one piece is a good treat, but it is unhealthy to eat a whole cake, and you are then able to recognize that you would rather have the wedding of your dreams in that dream wedding dress than eat an entire cake because it tasted good in the moment. You reminded yourself that the wedding was a major event that would last a lifetime and that makes it take priority over a bit of instant gratification.

You Will Wake Up on Time

When you are self-disciplined, you will know the importance of starting your day at the same time every day. This means that you will not be deciding that you reject everything that matters to you to sleep in every weekend. You will maintain your sense of normalcy and those important schedules and you will keep yourself on track. This is very, very important—when you do this, you are essentially ensuring that at the end of the day, you always keep a good, healthy schedule.

When you are oftentimes waking up at the same time every day, your body will remain healthier. Your body gets into a predictable rhythm that allows your body to continue to function optimally. When your body knows precisely what to expect and how to expect it, you know that ultimately, you need to be working hard to ensure that you do actually maintain that physical health. Self-discipline does that for you and ensures that your own healthy decisions will be made in ways that matter more than ever before.

. . .

Think about it this way, too—if you are up at the same time, come rain or shine and come Monday or Saturday, you will know that you can count on having that time. If you have personal projects that you have been working on, then, you can ensure that you have time to work on them nightly, or every morning in some instances. This is great—it means that you will be able to get more fit in because you will be able to come up with those good, functional schedules that you will need to succeed.

Your Self-Esteem Improves

When you are diligent about keeping to what you need to do at any given point and you ensure to yourself that you are able to always make what you need to happen come to fruition, you come to better trust yourself. As you trust yourself more and more, something else happens—you begin to feel like your self-esteem is better. You will feel like you are better capable of doing just about anything and you will be willing to believe that you can do it in the first place. As you begin to feel more confident in yourself, you become more likely to keep up with what matters the most to you, even if at the end of the day, what matters the most to you is not the popular decision.

When you are both self-disciplined and have a high self-esteem, you have the makings of a great leader or a change catalyst— someone who can create great changes just by virtue of being able to stay true to your values and what you believe is right, no matter how unpopular it is. You believe that your convictions and your trust in yourself will carry you through the time, so you follow through with it. You will push and push to ensure that you fight for what you think is right—and that is a good thing.

You Will Make Better Decisions

Finally, the last major benefit to living a life that is self-disciplined is that when you have that willpower, you know that you are always making the best decisions. You are able to think about a situation rationally and calmly so you can really think about what it is that you are doing. You will be able to spend all sorts of time really ensuring that you are following what you and your body need. You will be able to make decisions based on what is right rather than what is fun, and this means that you will be more successful in general.

You will be able to remind yourself that ultimately, you will be better off spending time working rather than going to the beach because you need to pay rent and you do not want to get fired. You can remind yourself that the food that you are buying is healthier and therefore better for you, even if it does not taste as good as dessert. That's okay—it is not dessert anyway and it will do its job.

You must remember that your own decision making abilities will also slowly impact everyone else around you, too. It will show you precisely how you will be able to better decide on anything according to your own values. If you can retain those values when they matter the most, you will know that you can trust yourself and that is important.

5 / THE SELF-DISCIPLINED LIFESTYLE

SELF-DISCIPLINE IS SO MUCH MORE than just a skill that you can have. It is more than a filter that will remind you that ultimately you need to make good decisions. It is so much more than either of those—it is a lifestyle. To be self-disciplined is to be someone that lives a lifestyle of self-discipline. That is not to say that you will be required to give up on general comforts or other luxuries. You do not have to reject everything to be able to live a life of self-discipline. Rather, you must make sure that you live the right lifestyle with the right habits and mindset. If you can keep the right habits and mindset, you will be able to ensure that you ultimately are able to better manage to remain self-disciplined, even in the face of temptation.

Within this chapter, we are going to look at two factors—we are going to look at the mindset that goes along with self-discipline, and then we are going to consider the several good habits that you will need to remember if you hope to be able to live a self-disciplined lifestyle.

The Self-Disciplined Mind

Firstly, you must make sure that you have the mindset of someone who is self-disciplined. That may be somewhat strange to consider at first, but it is a very important aspect of this process. To have the right mindset, you must remember four key mindsets that you will need: You must be commitment oriented, self-accepting, unafraid of failure, and self-motivated.

If you can master these four mindsets, you will be well on your way to ensuring that you are developing that proper self-discipline mindset. With those four thought processes and guiding belief systems, you know that you will be able to live with just about anything. You will be able to cope with the struggles that you run into. You will be able to focus on what matters the most. You will be able to do all of this while thinking with a clear mind that will allow you to make the kinds of good, rational decisions that self-discipline is known for.

This mindset is going to essentially be your way of building up the very lifestyle that you will be living. It will be your golden compass through doing what is right at all costs. It will help ensure that, at the end of the day, you act in ways that are compelling. You act in ways that are going to serve you well. This is very important—you will be able to act in a way that will keep you happy with yourself.

Commitment-Oriented

. . .

The first aspect of this mindset is making sure that you are always commitment oriented. You will essentially be ensuring that you always act in ways that you know are going to be true to the commitments that you have made. If you want to be self-disciplined, you must remember that, at the end of the day, you will want to also ensure that any commitment that you make is treated with the same gravity that you would give a legally binding contract.

This means that you will treat your word as binding. If you tell someone that you will do something, you will do everything in your power to make sure that it happens the way that you said it would. This is very important—keeping true to your word means that you are ensuring that you always focus on honesty and being trustworthy.

Self-Accepting

All too often, people get stuck in this idea that they have to hate themselves. They think that they are doing themselves a favor by being too harsh on themselves and they expect nothing short of perfection whenever they do anything at all. This is a problem, however—if you are trying to hold yourself to an unattainable ideal, you are constantly going to be letting yourself down. You will be constantly failing yourself at what matters the most and that is a huge problem for you. If you are constantly failing, how can you get ahead? That will weigh on you very quickly and heavily. Rather than allowing yourself to get stuck in this perfectionism problem, reject that notion. Reject the idea that you must do everything just right at all times. Let go of those feelings and move forward with fairness and compassion for yourself. Accept yourself for who you are and what you can do.

Unafraid of Failure

Reject the idea that failure is something that must be avoided or something worthy of fear. Failure is not scary—you can learn from it. Failure, when treated like a learning opportunity, can be a great way to let go of any of that fear that would otherwise hold you back. Remember, the fear of failure is a huge reason that so many people refuse to try to do anything. You are always better off giving something a genuine attempt—if you fail, at least you have learned a valuable lesson. The only time that failure is bad or should be hated is if it does not yield any lessons at all. If you have learned something from your failure, then your failure served a very important point for you.

Self-Motivated

Finally, the self-disciplined mind will let go of that idea that it must be motivated extrinsically. Rather than focusing on what needs to happen and what you will get in return for doing something, much like how people will work simply because they know that they will get paid for it, you should focus on being able to work because you want to succeed. When you can return your mindset to focus back on yourself rather than looking for reasons that the world can motivate you, you help yourself to succeed better. You are finding that drive to keep moving forward within yourself. You are rejecting that idea that you need extrinsic rewards and instead are finding the inherent value in what you do.

The Self-Disciplined Habits

When it comes down to the habits that the most successful self-disciplined people have in their own lives to help them become the successes that they are, there are many. These people often share many similarities with each other, and these habits can really help them develop the lifestyle that they lead. When you follow this lifestyle type and trend, you are able to help foster the self-disciplined lifestyle. These are not always easy. They are not always effortless. However, they will pay off greatly. These are habits that will help you learn how to recognize inherent value in what is around you. They will help you move forward and succeed in life. They will help you become able to see the world through the lens of someone who recognizes the importance of slow and steady rather than simply racing ahead.

Finding your passion

The first habit that you must remember is that you need to find your passion. If you can identify what it is that you are truly passionate about in life, you learn how you can drive yourself. This is essentially you figuring out what you intrinsic motivators are and how you can rely on them to help yourself in the future. You will essentially be learning what you can use to push yourself if you ever find yourself struggling. If you can stick to what you love, however, you will find that following through with what you have volunteered to do will come easily. This means that you should try to find a job that drives you. Find something that keeps you enjoying what you are doing. When you can do this, you know that what you are doing is going to matter to you, and it is so much easier to stick to something when it is already something important to you. We will be discussing this in depth in Chapter 7: Self-Discovery.

Managing time well

Without time management, you cannot remain self-disciplined. Remember, being self-disciplined itself is to be able to ensure that you are always doing what matters the most at any given point in time. It is being able to constantly work toward any goals that you have set and ensuring that you are constantly moving forward at a steady pace. To do this, you need to be able to manage your time. If you can set a schedule and stick to it, you know that you are able to ensure that you will be doing what you have set out to do. While sticking to a schedule will not simply guarantee that you will succeed, it can help you ensure that you have the chance to do so.

Remember, oftentimes, people afraid of failure simply do not attempt to do anything at all. You can run into that problem here as well if you cannot manage your time well. If you simply do not manage time well at all, you may never get to what actually matters the most during the day. You may simply struggle to ever actually get anything done, and that is a problem. You cannot succeed if you cannot find the time to do what you need to get done. This particular skill will be addressed in greater depth in Chapter 14: Time Regulation.

. . .

Becoming grateful

Gratitude is being able to stop and recognize what is happening around you to see how much it matters to you. When you are able to look around at what you are grateful for, you can remind yourself that the other things in life—those luxuries that could be nice to have, but that you cannot afford or attain at that point in time—are nothing more than luxuries. They are not important. When you can be happy with what you have, not only can you avoid impulse buying or impulse actions that are really only going to set you back in life, you will also be able to stop and remind yourself that any failures that happen are not actually that bad—you will be able to be grateful for the information that you learned in failing in the first place.

Essentially, gratefulness is the key to fighting off negativity, temptation, and instant gratification. We will be addressing how to develop gratitude throughout several chapters in the near future—in particular, you will see it come up in Chapter 11: Delaying Gratification and Chapter 13: Dealing with Negativity and Temptation.

Setting goals

Ultimately, when it comes down to being self-disciplined, you need to look at all sorts of factors, and one such factor is just how good you can become at setting goals. Now, we will be spending an entire chapter on this particular habit later in the book.

However, it is very important to remember that, to be successful and to be self-disciplined, you need to have these habits in place. When you set up your goals, you know precisely what you want so you can continue to work toward them and succeed. When you set your goals, you will be able to better understand the efforts that you are putting in and how you will ensure that you can make it work for you.

In Chapter 8, we will dive into more information about goals. You will learn to recognize what a good goal is and you will learn how you can set them yourself. You will be introduced to different ways to look at your goals and how you can ensure that you plan them out and form them in a way that will allow you to see precisely what needs to be done and how you can make sure that you do get it done in the first place.

Being persistent

Persistence is absolutely essential if you want to be self-disciplined. Sometimes, you will fail. Sometimes, what you are trying to do will seem impossible. However, it is possible to succeed. It is possible to be able to get what you are trying to do—all you have to do is keep moving forward. When you can remain persistent, you will do what you have to do in order to succeed. Think about it this way—when young children fail, do they give up? No! Can you imagine the world that we would live in if we all gave up the first time that we failed at something? How many of us would know how to walk? How many could talk? How many could even breathe? People make mistakes. Accidents happen. People can trip on thin air and fall down. They can accidentally inhale saliva and choke themselves. They can drop an egg or spill the food that they had on their spoon. Does any of that mean that they should quit walking or eating?

Remember, persistence is good to live by. It will involve you developing all of the necessary mental strength that you need to keep pushing forward. It will remind you that you have what it takes to succeed—you just have to reach out and take it.

Remaining organized

Organization is another very important habit to remember when it comes to becoming self-disciplined. When you are organized, you know precisely where everything is and you know exactly when you will be doing what you have to do at any given moment. You will be able to remind yourself that you need to stick to these schedules and organization so you will know where everything else is. With this comes efficiency and with efficiency comes more free time.

6 / HOW TO DEVELOP SELF-DISCIPLINE

DEVELOPING your own self-discipline does not need to be something that is concerning to you. In fact, the more that you worry about it, the more likely that you are to struggle with it just thanks to the way that anxiety tends to spiral out of control. When you are worried about whether or not you can develop self-discipline, you become that much less likely to make it happen just due to that underlying anxiety that most people often have.

Within this chapter, we are going to take a look at the six most fundamental steps that you will need to follow in order to develop your own self-discipline. When you take a look at the methods through which you can better begin to influence and regard your own self-discipline as something that you can take control of. We are going to go, step by step, recognizing the work that you will need to put into these processes to make it happen. We will look as you begin to identify what matters the most to you and how you can work toward them. We will look at the importance of role models and how you can begin to recognize the reasons that you do what you do or why you want to achieve what you want and how you can defeat the challenges that are likely to arise. We will look at how you can develop the action plan that you can use to properly develop an understanding for what you need to do and how you need to do it, and finally, we will take a look at the critical nature of accountability and how important that it is for you to manage it.

Step 1: Define Your Wants

You must start at the beginning; this is where you begin to identify what it is that you want. This is beginning to understand what it is that you hope to get at the end of this process. When it comes to developing self-discipline, you need somewhere that you can channel your energy; you need somewhere that you can aim to get this process under your own control and how you can better deal with the situations that you may be facing. Self-discipline is incredibly powerful to deal with, but it is only as powerful as it can be when it has a purpose, and that purpose will, ultimately, be looking at what it is that you wish to achieve. You must be able to point that desire that need for something as your motivator. You must be able to point out what it is that you want the most in the world around you and say that that is what you are aiming for.

When you aim for this clarity, you must be able to direct your mind. You must be able to recognize what it is that you are aiming for. You must be able to tell yourself what it is that you want to achieve more than anything else at that point in time. You must be able to identify what it is that you need to control and influence in order to develop your habits that you wish to live by as well. You must be able to state what it is that you are aiming for. It could be that you wish to achieve some new behavioral changes. It could be that you want to focus closely and intensely on something new. It could be that you are looking closely for a new achievement that you are aiming for. No matter what it is, you must clearly identify what it is that you are hoping to achieve and set your sights on it. Lock onto your target and aim. Make sure that you are pointing back at what it is that you want. Aim at it. Prepare to make sure that you have targeted precisely what it is that you are looking at, as closely as you can.

Step 2: Describe the Changes

Next, once you figure out what it is that you are looking for, it is time to begin figuring out what you must do to make it happen. It is time for brainstorming. Sit down with that goal that you have in mind and begin to focus on it—what is it that you want? Write down that goal that you have atop your piece of paper. Now, what do you need to do to make that happen? What kind of behavioral changes must you make to be able to ensure that those changes occur in a timely manner? How can you possibly begin to change up the way that you are able to work in a way that actually allows you to live that kind of life?

You will need to write down everything that you will need to know and everything that you will need to do to be able to better deal with the changes that are necessary. You must be willing and able to follow each and every one of the steps that you will be writing down here. Don't be afraid to overthink things, either; it is better for your list to be too wide-reaching, meaning that you become over prepared, than for you to be underprepared. Remember, if it turns out that some of the aspects of your list are not actually important enough for you to follow through with, then there is no harm in removing them from your list. This is fine—you can do so to allow yourself to do so.

· · ·

Consider two questions for yourself here: What will you need to do to achieve your goal—as in, which actions are going to be conducive to your success? And, what are the habits that you will need in place to achieve your goal? These behaviors and habits should be related to the core values that you are attempting to put into play here; they should always be working in tandem to ensure that, at the end of the day, you can better succeed.

Step 3: Find Role Models

The third step in this process is finding role models, or a support network for yourself. You want to make sure that the people that you keep around yourself are those that already understand these processes. They are the people that you can rely on regularly to ensure that, at the end of the day, you *can* work the way you want to. These should be primarily people that you know have already accomplished what you want as well. They are people that have already managed to do what it is that you want to do and they are the people that you need to follow to ensure that, at the end of the day, you know what you are doing.

These become the people that you go to when you are stuck. They are the ones that you seek out when you feel like you can get far greater results. Who do you know around you that has already done what you want to do? Who is there in your friends or your acquaintances that have managed to succeed with what they are doing? Who are the people around you that you think would be valuable assets to this process and to the development of the understanding of what you need? At the end of the day, the answers may come to surprise you; it may be, you discover, that you can better manage to succeed if you can involve people that you have not thought much about speaking to.

· · ·

See these people as starting points; see them as ways that you can begin to see what is going on around you. They are the ones that will provide you with the necessary background information for yourself. Even just knowing about them and their own journeys can be incredibly valuable. It can provide you with a lot of information that can very quickly transform into the methods that you can use for yourself.

Step 4: Identify Reasons and Challenges

Next, you must be able to better identify what your motivators are. You should be able to see what it is that this goal will help you with. Why is it that you want to get up each and every day and work toward that goal? Are you motivated by your own personal values or is there something else going on that is pushing you the way that you are behaving?

We all have inherent motivators that push us forward. Those motivators can help you really begin to understand and see the ways in which you are able to better cope with the world around you. They help you to better recognize the actions that you must take. They provide that energy, that forward momentum that you will need to embrace so you can succeed. If you cannot hold onto that forward momentum, you are not particularly likely to see that the way that you are behaving is going to help you at all. You must recognize that, at the end of the day, you are as limited as the drive that you have to push yourself forward. If you do not know what it is that motivates you, you are not very likely to succeed when push comes to shove.

You must also spend some time taking a closer look at the obstacles that you are likely to face. Remember, just about anything that you attempt to do in your life is going to have some sort of obstacle. The obstacle may not be particularly important or meaningful to you or the course that you are on. It may not be very big at all and at the end of the day, it will not be a big deal. However, more likely, you will find that the obstacles that you face are usually a bit more significant than you may otherwise think; it is important for you to see the ways that you can better cope with everything.

The more that you can plan out the ways that you can get stuck along the way, the better prepared that you can become. You must be able to spend that time carefully crafting the ways in which you will be able to succeed. Spend your time working carefully to understand the challenges that you foresee, and then discuss with yourself how you will prevent them from becoming overwhelming in the first place. You will be able to plan out how you can attack the challenges that you have so you can avoid running into future complications. The sooner that you are able to defeat those complications, the sooner you will be able to move forward.

Step 5: Develop the Action Plan

As you continue toward developing your own self-discipline, the next step that is of importance is your action plan. This is essentially the course that you will take to get what you are looking for. You will use this action plan so you can ensure that at the end of the day, you do know what you are doing. This is breaking down the success of your goal into step by step ways that you will be able to better deal with the plan at hand. The more of an action plan that you develop, the more likely it is that you will be able to succeed.

. . .

Now is where you will begin assigning mini deadlines to yourself. You are creating the line to which you will aim for. You will create the points that you are aiming to reach and by when you hope to achieve them. The more that you do this, the clearer it becomes that you are able to actually get that success that you are looking for. The sooner that you can succeed, the more likely that it becomes that you will be able to make it happen.

The most effective plans that you can find are those that will naturally allow you to break down your guide to steps that will break everything down to a point that it will not be overwhelming. You are aiming to get to a point in which your plan is so lined out for you and so complete, all you have to do is make sure that you take the time that you will need to follow along. It will enable you to avoid getting overwhelmed, as that feeling of being overwhelmed is what ultimately leads to procrastinating, and that procrastination can paralyze you. It can destroy that ability to make progress. When you make use of these methods for yourself, following the steps to your goal and making sure that you have a clear, articulated deadline that you have to follow, you know that you are able to ensure that, at the end of the day, you will be much more likely to succeed.

Step 6: Accountability

Finally, the last step in achieving what you are attempting to do is to ensure that you have taken accountability. When you recognizing that accountability, you know that ultimately, you are responsible. You know that it is your job to keep yourself on track and that you cannot blame someone else for any failures that you have. On top of that, however, you must also try to set up accountability with someone else as well.

. . .

This is where having that support team comes into play. When you can rely on someone else to help you stay on track whether that is a friend or a family member, you know that, at the end of the day, you have someone checking in on you. Sometimes, that added pressure of being afraid or embarrassed of failing in front of someone else is enough to get yourself moving. Sometimes, that is all that it takes to get your own work back on track and ensure that you can succeed.

Now, it is time to take a look at your values. It is time to develop the understanding of what our current mindset really entails. This step is all about discovering yourself. When you go through a period of self-discovery, you learn what it is that really matters to you. You develop that understanding of what you value, and what you may not. This is essential to figuring out what it is that you will need to emphasize and focus on when you are attempting to keep yourself motivated. The more aligned with your own values that you can keep yourself, the more likely you are to be able to succeed when it comes down to it.

Within this chapter, we are going to dive into learning to know yourself. You may think that this step is silly; you may tell yourself that it is unnecessary to take that look into yourself, and yet, it matters greatly. You must be able to spend that time considering that your own values may be something that you have not considered yet.

What are Values?

Your values are those things in life, the beliefs that you hold, and the truths that you live by. They guide everything that you do;

they keep you on track when you are doing something. They ensure that you understand the ways in which you need to change yourself. They teach you to look at the methods that you use to guide yourself. When you consider your values, you are looking at those innermost beliefs that will help you.

These will typically underlie your goals. They help you to discover what it is that you need to do and what it is that you want to do. They guide your way, ensuring that you feel fulfilled and ready to tackle anything and everything that life throws your way.

Ultimately, life works best and you feel the most fulfilled when your way of life is aligned properly with the values that you hold. For example, a very conservative person would hardly enjoy working on a highly liberal campaign, and vice versa. When you do not allow your own personal actions to align themselves to your values, you run into problems. You see issues with the way that you function. You begin to run into complications around you. You find that you cannot possibly ensure that you better deal with the world around you because you begin to become stressed. You feel unhappy and unsatisfied. You may even feel a sense of malaise as you attempt to do things that directly violate your personal values.

When it comes down to what motivates you and what you will use to keep yourself moving forward on your own in your own personal goals, you must recognize something: You must be able to see the ways in which your life and the way that you live directly influences yourself. You must begin to recognize that the cognitive dissonance that you will feel when those values do not line up can become a problem for you. While you may tell yourself that you want to do something, if it actually violates those most personal values that you hold, you will actually run the risk of simply failing altogether. You cannot succeed if you are constantly feeling unmotivated. You cannot work toward that self-discipline if all you do is feel annoyed or worried or stressed by what you are doing. You will lack that inherent drive that you will need to succeed if you do not take the time to align your beliefs and values with the goals that you set. It becomes imperative that you, and anyone else, ensures that their values and their goals are compatible, or the risk for failure is great.

The Benefits of Values

The values that you hold and that you have are there, whether you realize that they are or not. When you acknowledge those values, you can usually begin to work with the life around you with ease. You find that being able to cope with the stress of life becomes infinitely easier when you are able to stop and make sure that it is all lined up with your own belief systems. When you can acknowledge those values and you can make sure that you also plan around them and use them as the basis for any of your fundamentally important decisions that you have to make, you will find that conflict drops immensely.

For example, imagine that you want to be a stay at home parent—it has been your goal for as long as you can remember. Now, imagine that you then take a job that is highly demanding and your pay is directly correlated to the amount of time that you spend. You have your children, but now you find that you need the money, so you work. However, you are inherently going to be unhappy. You are going to feel that stress of cognitive dissonance in which your actions and your beliefs do not line up. You work long weeks, but really, all you want is to spend your time with your children. This is perhaps the easiest seen form of cognitive dissonance that you can really begin to recognize and it is incredibly frustrating for those that struggle with it. If you feel like this sort of conflict is a problem for you, you will likely become stressed.

And yet, if you can align your core values and your actions, you can find that you are able to do so much more. You feel motivated. You feel like you can better control yourself and you feel fulfilled. Instead of stressing out over the ways in which you can act and how you can deal with your own emotions. You find that your behaviors are better able to reflect what is really important to you and in doing so, you feel better than ever. You feel relaxed. You feel fulfilled. You feel like you are on the right track in life.

It is then, when you feel that inherent motivation and that inherent calmness that life becomes worth living for you. It is when you develop that inherent alignment between your beliefs and your behaviors that you find that self-discipline becomes easier than ever. You must be able to help establish this within yourself, but to do so, you must first be able to tell yourself what those values that you hold are in the first place.

Identifying Your Values

Identifying your values is quite simple—all you have to do is identify and follow a few steps. If you can work yourself through these few steps, you can usually begin to figure out where your true values lie and what you can do to help ensure that you are constantly working while aligning your beliefs to them. If you can figure out how you can better align your beliefs with yourself, you can find that you begin to feel better. You find that your motivation is inherently within yourself.

1. **Identify the point in time when you felt the most fulfilled:** To start looking for your own personal values, you must begin with looking at the times in your own life in which you were happier. You need to figure out when it was that you felt like you were on the right track. When did you feel like you were calmer than ever before? When did you go to sleep feeling good about yourself and wake up ready to take on the day, no matter what it would bring? What were you doing during that period of time? Who did you have in your life at the time? What was going on around you that may have been a direct cause for your happiness? These are all very important points to consider, but if you can do so, you will find that you can become successful in your self-discipline.

2. **Identify points of pride:** Next, it is time to think about what you have done that has left you feeling proud. What did you do? Was it in your personal or your professional life? What happened? Why were you so proud in the first place? Did other people also make you feel good?

3. **Write down the values you think that you hold:** Now, it is time for some good, simple self-reflection. You must do this by stopping and considering the ways in which you can best recognize how you need to act. You can do this step in figuring out what it is that truly matters to you. Spend some

time thinking about the traits in other people that you greatly admire and write them down. Try to put together a list of about ten and make sure that they are written down.

4. **Prioritize those values:** Now, with your list of ten most valued values, you must begin to prioritize them. Which ones are the most important to you? List out the ones that you have chosen in step 3 and write them in order from most important to least important. This is so you can get a clearer idea of what it is that you truly do value so you can then take control of it. Consider for a moment, to figure out which value you hold the highest, that you think about which of these values are those that you would prioritize above the others. Which values would you sacrifice in order to succeed with others? We all have them—we all have some values that we hold inherently close to our hearts and others that are not quite as imperative to our happiness. Figure out which values that you hold the closest to yourself and write them down.

5. **Reaffirm those important values:** Finally, for the last step, it is time to reflect upon the list that you have in front of you. Which of those values matter the most to you? It is time for you to reaffirm your values; this means that you are going to be taking the time that you need to recognize whether or not these values are important to you. It is taking the time to consider whether or not the values that you have chosen for yourself are going to really help you understand yourself. Do the values that you have assigned as your most important make you feel good? Do they make you proud? Would you be embarrassed if you talked to

other people about them? Would you fight to uphold these values, even when everyone else all around you believes that you are wrong?

It is only when you can bring together all of these steps that you will finally begin to have an idea of what your truest values are. It is then, when you finally begin to break everything down, that you will be able to see what really matters the most to you, and if you play your cards right, you should be able to ensure that you succeed.

WHEN IT COMES DOWN to it, goals are imperative to any operation in which you are attempting to make good progress. If you hope to be able to do anything at all that is remotely important to you, you will probably need to have a goal set for yourself to do it. You will need to be able to better cope in other ways. To set a goal is to create a long-term commitment to yourself and to the plans that you are making. It is to come up with a wide scale action plan that will help you get a better understanding of everything that matters to you. It is that ability to stop and consider the ways in which you are going to be able to achieve those plans that you have.

The most successful goals that you can make are those that are written out in detail—they are the goals that are able to be pushed together, to create a plan for yourself to follow. When you are able to make a successful goal for yourself, you know that you are creating one in which all of the important details are worked out. The more details that you have figured out naturally along the way of setting the goals, the more likely that you are to be able to succeed in the first place.

When it comes down to your own self-discipline, setting goals is one of the most effective ways to organize everything all into one place. When you can ensure that all of your energy is focused entirely into one aspect of yourself and one aspect of what really matters, you know that you are on track. You know that you can look at your goal and you will have all of the details laid out for yourself. You know that the details that you have been provided are everything that you will need and that is enough for you to make the necessary progress that you are trying to establish. When you can ensure that you are on track for that, you can comfortably understand the ways in which you can move forward. It gives you that nice, clear goal that you have and paints out everything that you will need to do so you do not need to worry about how to achieve everything that matters.

SMART Goals

Perhaps one of the currently favored methods of setting goals at the moment is the use of what is known as a SMART goal. The SMART goal is a goal based on one specific acronym that you can use to remind yourself of why you are doing what you are doing and how you can ensure that, at the end of the day, you do, in fact, achieve that goal that you are aiming for. When you achieve your SMART goal, you are able to ensure that you are properly managing what matters the most to you.

To set a SMART goal is to great a detailed timeline for yourself. You are going to outline everything that you could possibly need so, at any point in time, you are not blindsided. It removes those potential excuses away from you, meaning that you cannot fall back on the pretense of not having a good plan or not knowing what your goal should be.

.   .   .

Before we begin with what your SMART goal is, you must firstly recognize that a few points are inherently incompatible with becoming goals just due to the ways that they tend to work. You cannot set a goal to be in an emotional state constantly; emotions are too fleeting to be stable goals and you will only end up failing yourself more often than you can succeed when you focus on what you could be. SMART goals should not be past-oriented—you cannot get back to the person that you used to be. Finally, they should not be negative. When your goal is to avoid something, you do not give yourself any clearer image on what it is that you actually want to do. When it comes right down to it, you need to be able to stop yourself and see what it is that really matters to you and that means that your goal has to be positive.

Now, we are going to spend some time going over each and every step of the way. This goal that you will create, crafted to these standards, should give you the power to make the decisions that you are looking for that are also aligned to the values that you have. When you want to be successful with your goal setting, you must also ensure that you are successful with the ways that you conduct yourself, and it is only when you can conduct yourself well that you begin to recognize the value in what you are doing.

Specific

Firstly, your goal must be specific. Specific goals are the best ones for yourself. When you make sure that, at the end of the day, the goal that you have set for yourself is very specific, you know that you have chosen to align yourself with something that you have a clear image of in your head. The more specific your goal, the better. If you want to lose exactly 32.7 pounds in the next few months, then that is something that you can choose to set as your goal. Ultimately, the only real way that you can begin to set these goals for yourself is if you are willing and able to ensure that you can better do what it is that you ultimately need to do.

Measured

Next, you want to ensure that your goal is measured. This means that you need to be able to see the ways in which you can or cannot succeed when it comes down to your goal. You need to set some sort of standard that you can use- a metric that will guide your ability to see the progress that you are making. If you are able to stop and look at a goal based on how successful you are thanks to having a metric, you can know what your progress actually accurately looks like. Having a number that you can assign to something to tell whether or not you are being successful in taking care of the problem or with making progress on your goal is a great way that you can better understand how you are doing. Not only does this give you feedback, it can also tell you if something that you are doing will need to be stopped or tweaked at any point in time. The more that you can focus on what you are doing and how you are doing it, the more likely that you are to be successful, just because you can tell earlier on when you are not.

Achievable

Now, it is time to check whether or not your goal is actually achievable. You need to stop and ask yourself if the goal is some-thing that actually makes sense. Can you run a marathon? Maybe. Can you climb Mt. Everest? Maybe. Can you make $1,000,000 in the next three years? Maybe. This step is all about keeping your expectations relevant. After all, while goals are meant to cause you to have to work for them, there is no reason that you should be struggling to achieve them. You can help yourself here by simply paying attention to whether or not your goal is feasible. If it is, great! If not, back to the drawing board with you.

Relevant

After checking whether or not your methods are realistic, you must also recognize whether they are realistically relevant to you as well. It is important to ask yourself is the gals that you are setting actually matter to you. Are they something that you could do if you wanted? Do you want to do them in the first place? Are they meaningful to you? Do they really matter to you?

When you stop to consider whether or not something is relevant, you begin to test whether it matters. You are testing to determine if your goal that you are setting is one that you would ever reasonably or realistically pursue in the first place. If your goal is not something that matters to you at all, or something that you feel not drive or obligation to complete, then why are you assigning that to be your goal? Why would you even bother to set yourself up for that certain failure? Instead of doing so, spend the time ensuring that the goals that you have chosen for yourself are actually goals that you would attempt to pursue and that you have a vested interest in.

Timed

And lastly, your goal must also be timed. You need to have some sort of deadline in place when it comes to the goals that you are living with. You need to ensure that the goals that you are following will have very clear, defined ending points. These are relevant to ensuring that your goal *can* be failed. There needs to be a point in which you stop yourself and say that enough is enough— you have failed and you can try again some other time. If you do not have that point for yourself, you are going to struggle. You need to be able to recognize when and where that point is so you know that, at the end of the day, you can get that success that you have been aiming for. When you do so, you will find that your goal becomes so much easier to cope with.

PROCRASTINATION—WE all suffer from it at some time or another. It is that feeling of knowing that you *need* to do something, but struggling to ever find that motivation that will keep you on your feet, working toward what matters, and ensuring that, at the end of the day, you *can* defeat that feeling of stagnation within yourself. You can learn to overcome those feelings that you have; you can learn to recognize that sometimes, while you may spend your time dwelling on what needs to be done, you can also learn to hone the desire and the recognition that you need to make a change in the first place.

At the end of the day, it is important for you to remember one point: You are designed to procrastinate. The human mind is meant to function in a way in which it always prefers immediate gratification over anything else. You must be able to recognize that, sometimes, the mind will see two options—one being something along the lines of what you need to do to make sure that you are not stressed later, and the other being avoiding the stress now. Your mind will always choose to deal with the stress later on instead of in the moment; it will always naturally push off the negativity as much as it can to prevent itself from having to deal with it. When given the chance, you will naturally feel inclined to be able to do what you really wanted to do over what you really needed to do; you will naturally decide to go and have fun or go and play video games instead of taking care of you current work that needs to be done, all because your mind prefers to get that instant gratification. This is known as present bias. However, you need to be able to defeat this if you want to be successful. You need to discover the ways in which you can properly alleviate the stress and properly ensure that you do look at the cost-benefit analysis differently. Remember that, at the end of the day, you need to do what you need to do to save yourself the pain or the heartbreak or the struggle that you will otherwise face. If you can keep up with defeating that, you can usually keep yourself calmer and happier in the long-term. However, with that long-term happiness also comes some inherent sacrifices as well. You must be willing and able to make those sacrifices for yourself if you hope to ever really be successful in what really matters the most.

Defeating procrastination can be somewhat intimidating for most people. It can make you feel like, at the end of the day, you are stressed out. It can leave you feeling lost and overwhelmed. It can leave you feeling like you cannot possibly do anything. However, you can make it real. You can also draw from those benefits yourself if you know what you are doing. All you have to do is shift your focus to the right mindset.

Visualization to Defeat Procrastination

First, let's take a look at visualization. It has been shown that people are more likely to save if they have some sort of tangible proof in front of them that something is going to happen. It has been shown that people how are given a photo of themselves that has been digitally manipulated and aged up will typically save their money more readily and regularly than those that are not given that photograph. The reason for this is due to the fact that the photograph that they have makes it real. They can see that, at the end of the day, they will age. They can see that there will be a real, clear consequence if they do not save; that future them that they are looking at will suffer.

You can make use of this process yourself; you can learn to stop and consider your own future. You can stop and vividly imagine yourself with the success of having done what you needed to do so you can alleviate that stress. You can do this relatively easily. Simply imagine the problem that you need to face. See it clearly in your mind and then see yourself solving the problem. Imagine yourself doing exactly what it is that you need to do at the moment and as you do it, imagine just how much more relaxed that you will feel. Reiterate to yourself all of those important benefits of being able and ready to focus on yourself and achieve those goals that you have. As you visualize just how great these benefits are, you can begin to see the inherent value in making sure that, at the end of the day, you *do* make those changes. Make sure that you *do* understand the methods that you use. The more that you do this, the more likely you are to ensure that they work.

Commit to it

Next, consider this next method to help you defeat the procrastination that you tend to fall into. Commit to doing whatever it is that you need to do—and do so publically in some way. Tell someone that you are doing something. It does not matter who it is, so long as it is a person and it is not you. Tell your friends that you are planning on baking cookies and decorating them; when they expect those fresh-baked cookies that were decorated by you, you will feel like you have on choice but to act. You will find that acting is easier than not, and you will choose to give in rather than attempting to avoid whatever it is that you are procrastinating on.

This method allows you to create some natural accountability that you can rely on. This accountability is enough to allow you to better process your own mindset. It reminds you that you need to get up and get moving. It ensures that you understand that, at the end of the day, you can and you will make those changes that you need to see. The more that you can commit to this, the better that you will do. The better that you do, the more likely that you are to be able to succeed and defeat that procrastination that otherwise will keep you back.

Reward the First Step

Finally, the last method that we are going to approach to help you to defeat that procrastination monster is to ensure that you make the first step in the process something pleasant, or tie it to something pleasant. By making it something that you are not going to avoid, and making sure that it actually brings with it something that you want or need, you can usually sort of kick-start your mind. You can keep yourself working diligently. You can ensure that, at the end of the day, you can better work with yourself because you will be a much more willing participant if you feel like what you are doing is something that you enjoy.

For example, imagine that you really need to write that email for work but you really do not want to. Instead of continuing to dwell about it, you tell yourself that if you go ahead and write the email, you can eat a piece of chocolate while you do so. This encourages yourself to stop and really begin to enjoy the moment so you can better cope with the feelings of procrastination that would otherwise hold you back.

The catch here, however, is that you are not setting it up so you will have a reward each and every time that you make progress in the method that you are using. You must also remember that you need to be strong and that you need to resist that temptation. You are not looking to simply reward yourself each and every time that you do something for yourself or in your goal list. Rather, you are attempting to teach yourself to get up and get moving. If you reward yourself each and every time that you do something that you deep to be directly related, you are going to run into other problems as well. All that you would do if you always rewarded yourself each and every time that something happened would be to encourage yourself to need a reward to do anything at all. However, there is a simple irony in this sort of lifestyle; if you require that reward for each and every single thing that you do, you must recognize that what you are doing is bribing yourself. You are not developing that inherent self-discipline because you only do what you need to do if you can associate it with the currency for yourself that you have identified, whether it is chocolate to write that email or anything else.

BEING able to concentrate is imperative when you are trying to become self-disciplined. If you do not have the power that you will need to ensure that, at the end of the day, you can keep your focus where it is needed when it is needed, you are going to find that you really struggle in life. You will not be able to develop that self-discipline if you cannot keep your concentration where it is necessary. If you cannot spend the time to tell yourself that what you are doing is not helping you, you will find that you are going to struggle.

Staying on task is rarely simple, especially when there is always so much that you have to consider, to worry about, and to attempt to work with. Today's world is constantly connected to everything else around you. The world of today is usually entirely caught up in the moment. Even when you are taking time to be quiet and attempt to focus, it becomes incredibly simple to suddenly find yourself entirely distracted by what you are looking at. It becomes very easy for you to stop and get distracted by the next cool thing that you scroll past on your newsfeed. It is so incredibly easy to get entirely distracted by the world around you.

It is so simple for yourself to get caught off guard and be unable to focus on what really matters and on what you are supposed to be doing.

However, you need that concentration. You need to learn what you need to do so you can better focus in order to develop the necessary concentration that you will need to be able to commit to. When you can commit to your mindset, you can begin to act in the ways that you know that you need. You can improve that mental focus before it can get worse. You can teach yourself how you can better begin to process the way that you think. It will not necessarily be easy. It will take effort, as will the entire process of self-discipline. However, if you can follow these simple tricks, you fill find that your own ability to focus will slowly but surely begin to improve, little by little. More and more, you will discover that you are capable of doing anything that you need.

The Signs of Weak Concentration

When you struggle to concentrate, it will be apparent throughout all aspects of your life. Your focus is something that will stretch across everything that you do. It will determine how good or bad at something you are. It will determine whether or not you will be decent at certain jobs. It will determine how well you can cope with the world around you when you are struggling to drown out distractions around you. Remember, most of the world is always full of distractions. It is very rare that you are ever in a vacuum, away from everyone around you. You need to be willing and able to stop, calm yourself down, and remind yourself to quiet down.

When you struggle to keep your focus, you oftentimes find that your mind will wander. It will be very easy for your mind to simply wander, to go off on tangents and drift off, away from the focus that you have developed and instead focus on the areas of your life where it does not matter as much. You must be able to stop and remind yourself that you need to focus, but when you struggle to concentrate in the first place, you find that doing so is an impossibility. You feel like drowning out those distractions is too great a task for yourself. You are constantly focused on everything around you rather than the one or two things that mater the most and that can really wreak havoc, holding you back and preventing you from being able to succeed. The more it happens, the more apparent it becomes, and the more likely you are to continue to struggle over time.

If you notice that you do seem to fit the bill there, that you daydream often, that you cannot concentrate at all, and that every single little sound that you hear around you is enough to entirely derail you, you most likely have plenty of room to grow with your own self-discipline.

Eliminating Your Distractions to Boost Your Focus

One of the simplest defenses that you have against losing your focus is to make sure that you can pay attention to what really matters most in your life is to eliminate all of the distractions from your life. The more that you can remove from your surroundings, the better you can focus. Now, keep in mind that this does not meant that you need to suddenly remove everything from any room that you are in and to work in perfect and utter blankness; rather, you will bel trying to minimize what you can control while leaving behind what you cannot.

This is incredibly effective when it comes to fixing problems around you. It is incredibly powerful for you to be able to stop yourself, to remind yourself that you need to quiet down your mind, and to let yourself focus. Some of the easiest distractions that you can control include being able to turn off any electronics. You do not need to be using a television while you are working, for example, and the music that you are listening to while you write something may actually be nothing more than a distraction for you when you find yourself suddenly bopping along to the music.

You can also try to set time periods aside during which you only do the one thing that is conducive to achieving your goal. When you can do this, you are able to keep yourself more focused because you have a schedule. All you would have to do is, for example, is set the time aside that you are looking for. Make sure that, at the end of the day, you focus in that time where it matters the most.

Cut out Multitasking

So many people fall into the mistake of thinking that if you can do more at once, you can actually get more done over the long term. However, this is not true at all. When you multitask, you actually cut down the productivity of everything that you do. The attention that you have is very limited; you can only really focus on one particular thing at a time, so when you start trying to divide up your attention across several different aspects of what you are doing, you will find that you really start to struggle.

The more that you try to do at any given point in time, the less you can do overall. You are simply spreading your resources out to be thinner and thinner without paying attention to the fact that as you do so, your focus fades away as well. Rather than attempting to multitask so much, you are much better served taking that time and energy and simply dedicating it to one task at a time, over and over again. You need to be able to improve your focus by narrowing your scope and if you can do that, you can succeed.

. . .

Keep Practicing

Finally, the last way for you to really improve your own focus is to simply make use of it more often. The more that you can lock onto your focus and the more that you can make use of it, you should be more and more capable of ensuring that, at the end of the day, you will be able to better keep your mind where it belongs. Your mind and your focus, are like muscles and the more that you practice them, the more that you flex them and allow them to begin to grow, the stronger they will become. We are not talking about changing a pair of clothes here, or about cutting your hair or doing any of that; rather, you are making changes to the very way that you think and the way that your mind works. You must be willing and able to see the ways in which you change this over time and you must be willing and able to exercise those changes as well.

The more that you practice focusing, the easier that it will become. The more that you practice on focusing, the more successful you will become. You will be able to remember details better than ever. You will be able to pay attention to what really matters. You will be able to concentrate on your goals that you are attempting to achieve, and all you will have to do to make it happen is focus.

11 / DELAYING GRATIFICATION

IF SOMEONE STOPPED you and offered you $100 today, or $200 next month, which would you choose? Would you rather have that money immediately, or would you be able to wait it out to let the money grow? Would you rather take the risk of never getting that money in the future in favor of being able to have that money in your hand right that moment? When you prefer instant gratification, you will almost always default to what is better for you in the moment that you are making your decision, even if that decision is not as good in the long-term. You fall into this trap where you do not see the value in waiting or in trying to better relate to what you are doing. You stop yourself from being able to focus on the good that you could get if you were to hold off on that pleasure just a little bit longer. You feel like you need to work then and there to try to get what you were looking for. You feel like without working on what you need to do right that moment, right when it matters the most, you cannot resist that urge to have everything that you wanted and needed in the moment. The more that you work on what you are doing and the more that you begin to recognize the truth, that you do not have to let yourself be held back by the feelings that you have. You do not have to let yourself be held back by needing to have instant gratification.

Instant gratification is one of the biggest banes of self-discipline to begin with; when you give in to instant gratification, you simply do what you want, when you want it. You do not bother to see the truth of the matter. You do not bother to recognize that, at the end of the day, you must learn to resist. Think about it—very rarely is the first deal that passes by the best one. Very rarely is the first option that you have for yourself one that matters. Very rarely are you better off taking that instant gratification when there are other options for you. Think about it; would you rather put your money into a retirement account now or spend that money tomorrow? Would you rather be able to go and eat that cake today or stay on track to your goal weight?

This need to seek out pleasure can become overwhelming when you do not know how to abstain; when the option for pleasure is in front of you, you will immediately reach for it. Think of how a dog will take a piece of food that was placed in front of it just because it can and just because it is hungry in that moment. You may tell it to wait, but it would rather have that food that is there right that moment because that is a guarantee.

This is seen in people to some degree as well; children will almost always reach out for pleasure. They will typically, especially in the younger years, choose instant gratification just because the ability to understand time is so skewed in those age ranges. Pleasure is there to help us to survive; our most basic of functions are tied into these feelings. Our minds are essentially programmed to give in to this hardwiring; they are built to be able to stop, to sort of assess the situation, and then to take that pleasurable situation now rather than waiting for later.

However, you can learn to delay that gratification. You can learn to tell yourself that waiting will be better. You can remind yourself that the investment that you are eyeing is the better option. You can remind yourself that you can make those necessary changes to yourself so you can begin to thrive. If you can encourage this for yourself, you can begin to recognize something critical; you can succeed. You can learn to thrive. You can learn to grow and you can learn to keep yourself acting in exactly the way that you need.

Start Small to Delay Gratification

The first method that you can use to start training your mind to think about delayed gratification in a positive way is to start small. You do not want to simply rush into it or you are likely to fail; you are not very likely to follow through with it when you feel like the stakes are too high, so when you start with something smaller, you are able to help yourself. Instant gratification is something that you have to train your mind toward and your mind is going to inherently resist those changes that you attempt to make. Your mind does not like the fact that you are telling it that it must wait, but really, it is imperative that you do this. If you can encourage yourself to wait and relax, you can begin to recognize some very important factors; you can teach yourself that you can get more later if you do less now and that is essential if you hope to be able to proceed in your life with self-discipline.

Start by identifying something that is low-stakes for you. Perhaps it is getting that coffee that you going to buy. Maybe you were going to go out and get it, but you tell yourself that if you wait the hour and do some dishes first, you will get the larger size, or you will get that sugary treat drink that you usually resist because you know that it is not good for you. When you tell yourself that you are going to wait for these reasons, you may find that waiting a bit longer is not as big of a deal. You would much rather get that treat later than to get your coffee now.

When you are able to do this regularly, you will find that you are better able to slowly up your own tolerance to delaying your own gratification. You will slowly, but surely find that being able to embrace that delay in gratification is not that bad. You develop the ability to tell yourself that no, you will not take that instant gratification and that you will absolutely wait to get something better later on. It will get easier in time.

Maintain Consistency to Encourage Delayed Gratification

However, along with that practice, you must also make sure that you are always consistent with what you choose to do. You must ensure that, no matter what it is that you are attempting to embrace, you will always be consistent with it. As soon as you start delaying that gratification, you must remain consistent, otherwise you run the risk of slipping up and letting all of the progress that you have been making fall away. If you do not stay consistent and pay attention not what you are doing, you will find that you struggle more than ever before. You will not be able to keep up. You will struggle more than ever to hold out. This is because the more that you give in to yourself and that instant gratification, the more that you are enforcing those behaviors. The more that you do it, the less likely that you are to ensure that you are doing it properly.

Stay consistent in what you set out to do. If you are trying to lose weight, for example, remind yourself that you need to hold yourself back when you start eyeing that cake. Remind yourself gently that the end result will be worth it. Recognize that the end result, the constant striving for what you are seeking out will come together. You will find that things get easier over time. You will discover that the more you try to practice these techniques, the simpler they become.

YOUR BODY HAS VERY clear endurance. You probably feel it when you are walking up the stairs or carrying a heavy load. You can feel your body start to drain in strength. You can feel your stamina slowly but surely beginning to wear away. You can tell when your muscles begin to grow tired. You can feel as the weights that you put on them get heavier and more and more difficult to move...

But did you know that you have a mental endurance level as well? Most people fail to recognize that their minds are just the same; your mind is just as much of a muscle as your thighs or your calves. It is just as important to exercise that endurance for your mind as it is to develop the ability to understand the importance of being able to exercise your legs. You must be able to somehow develop that mental stamina if you hope to be able to better deal with the mentality that you are facing. You must be willing and able to recognize that your mind needs to be kept in tip-top shape as well. You must be able to make sure that you can build up that tolerance, and the only way to do so is with exercises.

Positive Thinking and Mental Endurance

One of the best ways that you are able to make sure that you are mentally resilient and able to mentally endure any situation is through making sure that you keep your mind rooted firmly in positivity. The more positivity that you bring to your life, the more likely that you are to be able to tolerate stress that will eventually wear down on you. Just like physical stress, such as exercise, takes its tolls on your physical body, the mental stressors that you face will pull you down as well. They will push you down lower and lower. They will make it harder than ever for you to focus on how best to fight them off. You need to build up endurance somehow, and perhaps one of the most natural places to do so is through the use of positive thinking to help yourself. When you think positively, you can remind yourself that you can fight off the stress. You can refuse to allow that stress to have that power over you. You can ensure that you are better able to fend off the threats that your stress brings with them.

To think positively, you must begin by making sure that, at the end of the day, you always try to focus on the bright side. The more that you are able to focus on the way in which you can think positively, the easier that it becomes for you to rebound when the world around you stresses you out. Remind yourself to think positively. When you hear a thought in your mind that is negative, you should focus on the ways that you can focus on the positive. Listen to the ways in which you can change yourself. Pay attention to the ways in which you are able to better cope with the stress. Hear the ways that you speak to yourself and keep the speech that you hear for yourself as positive as possible.

Contingency Plans and Mental Endurance

Another crucially important plan to remember is to ensure that the more that you do plan, the more likely you are to figure out what it is that you will need. Think about some of the ways that things could go wrong as you plan things out. If you run into a common problem that you believed that you were likely to face, you need to be able to know what to do next. When you spend some time looking at the different ways in which you can shift your focus, you can then begin to pay closer attention to working to fix the problem instead of worrying about the stress that you are under.

When you have contingency plans lined up for yourself, you already know what you are going to do when you find that you are overwhelmed by the stress around you. You already have that plan for yourself all set up and you know what you will need to do to change the ways that you should behave. When you already have those plans for yourself, you have something that you can fall back on. The more that you have things to fall back on, the more that you are able to remind yourself that, at the end of the day, you can focus. The more that you are able to remind yourself to focus around you and on what matters, the more that you are able to resist the stressors thanks to already planning to cope with them yourself.

Essentially, you skip the stress stage when you have this plan all lined up for yourself. You are able to remind yourself that the stress that you feel is not all-consuming. You are able to remind yourself that, at the end of the day, the stressors that you feel are not a big problem. You are able to see the ways in which you can change your own mindset, little by little. You are able to stop and see that, at the end of the day, you need to simply stop, breathe, and follow your contingency plans. When you can do that, all will be well.

Maintaining Physical Health and Mental Endurance

Finally, you must also consider the fact that you must maintain proper physical health as well. You must ensure that, at the end of the days, you need to keep yourself physically healthy to ensure that your mind is as healthy as it can be as well. The healthier that your body is, the better off your mind will be as well. This is crucial when you need to build endurance. You must be able to build up that physical health if you want to be able to also get that mental endurance as well.

Remember that, at the end of the day, your body and mind are both intricately connected to each other. Remember that at the end of the day, they are so closely intertwined, they are constantly impacting each other. This means that if your body is healthy, your mind will follow naturally. We know that the mind's own ability to remain clear and healthy comes from the body being healthy. Look at the ways in which the body and the mind are connected when it comes to anxiety and depression; oftentimes, you find that people are told that, when they keep their bodies healthy, they can keep their minds healthy as well. They are encouraged to begin implementing a healthier diet and healthier exercise to allow themselves to focus better than ever before. The more that you do this, the better you will feel.

13 / DEALING WITH NEGATIVITY
AND TEMPTATION

YOUR JOURNEY into developing self-discipline will see you tempted regularly. It will show you feelings of temptation sometimes. You may be working hard to lose weight, for example, but you get invited to a birthday party that has the most delicious looking cake prepared there for everyone and you cannot help but feel like you want some. You may be sitting at work one day, and there is the company potluck, filled up with endless carbs and endless fatty foods that all look and smell delicious. The more that you see this around you, the more likely that you are to begin to feel tempted.

It is very normal and very typical to feel both tempted sometimes, and feel negatively when you cannot give into that temptation in the first place. When that happens, you need to learn how to overcome it. When you learn to overcome the temptation and the negativity, you become healthier. You find that self-discipline becomes easier, simply because you know that self-discipline *is* that ability to resist the negativity and temptation. The more discipline that you have, the better you will do. There are many different ways that you can slowly but surely work harder and harder to help yourself defeat that negativity and temptation, little by little. All you have to do is realize that, at the end of the day, it must happen.

Within this chapter, we are going to look at a few of the methods that you can use to help yourself to resist that temptation when it comes trying to lead you astray. The more that you can learn to resist the temptation so it cannot defeat you or bring you down, the better you will begin to feel. Over time, you will find that your temptation is little more than a tiny nagging voice that you barely even notice any more in the back of your mind, and that is a sign that you are on the right track and headed toward success.

When temptations arise, it is easy for you to give in. Especially if you have already removed your temptations from your environment, it can be very easy for you to give in to the temptation that you have in front of you. Perhaps it is that cake at the birthday party or that cheese dip and chips at the potluck. No matter what that temptation is, however, no matter how delicious it smells and how much you really want it, it is not worth it.

Record the Start Date

One way that you can help yourself to maintain that resistance to temptation is to remind yourself of when you started to make the change. Think of how important that date is for yourself. When you set a start date to your change that you are attempting to implement, you not only give yourself a concrete option for yourself, you also allow yourself to better deal with the problems that you are dealing with.

When you focus on your start date, then, you can remind yourself that you are able to better remember when you began. This works as a running tally that you can keep in the back of your mind. Every time that temptation rears its ugly head, you can stop yourself. You can tell yourself that you have been diligently following your goals for the last several days, weeks, months, or even years at this point and that you are unwilling to give in and let that loss of focus or that temptation take that chain away from you.

When you can point out that day to yourself and point out that record that you are attempting to follow, you can give yourself peace of mind. You can allow yourself to better cope with the temptation simply by telling yourself that the short-term instant gratification is not worth it to you to let go of that chain that you have made. It is not worth it to you to lose everything when you have been working so hard.

Weigh All of the Options

Another great fix when you find yourself in the face of temptation and negativity is to stop and weigh all of the options that you currently have. What can you do about your current situation? How can you ensure that, at the end of the day, you can better cope with the situation at hand? What can you do regularly to make sure that you are more capable of defeating that negativity? What is it that really matters to you here?

Consider for a moment how many different options that you have. You have the options for many different possibilities, and you need to figure out which of the options you prefer the most. You must stop and weigh them all, one by one. Some of the decisions and choices will be better than others, and the better that you can deal with them, the more likely you are to better cope with the situation at hand. All you have to do is ensure that, at the end of the day, you pay close attention to what you are doing. Make sure that you focus on the way that you can benefit from remaining self-disciplined. Recognize the problems that you are facing in this current situation. See the ways in which you may be led astray if you are not careful. Keep this all in mind as you continue to progress; you must be able to see that, to some degree, the temptation is really just in your head and you can relieve it of its power by acknowledging that.

Keep Looking Forward

When you find that you are being dragged down by your own temptations, remind yourself that, at the end of the day, you can continue to focus ahead of yourself. The more that you focus on the future, on that idea that you are trying to achieve, the better you will do. The closer you will feel to that goal that you are trying to achieve. You will be able to make it work through the sheer force of will that you will develop to focus forward.

No matter how tempting it can be for you to stop looking forward, to stop keeping that eye on the prize in front of you, remember to keep your gaze firmly planted where it belongs. Remind yourself of how important your current situation is. Remind yourself that you do care greatly about the way that you think. Remind yourself that you need to be able to embrace your goals. You need to live by those skills that you can develop. You need to ensure that you continue to focus forward to get what you want.

When you get distracted from that straight to the point, future-oriented focus, you find that the temptation gets larger. It is easier to stop and say that those cookies will not matter in the long run if you do not actively pay attention to how it will impact your future. The next time that you feel that urge to let go and give in to the way that the world wants to keep you functioning around it, pay closer attention to what is going on around you. Remind yourself that you should be paying attention to the way that you feel. Remind yourself to pay attention to what matters the most to you. Remind yourself that, at the end of the day, you need to focus on that end goal that you have been working on. When you keep that in mind, you can keep your gaze firmly planted where it belongs. You will resist temptation. You will discover what you need to do to protect and defend yourself. You simply need to make it happen.

Perhaps one of the more difficult skills that you will need to develop to truly be self-disciplined is the ability to manage your time effectively. When you can be effective with your time management, you know that, at the end of the day, you can focus on exactly what matters. You know that you can pay attention to precisely the way that you will need to divide your day, and yet, so many of us find that time regulation is impossible. It can be hard to resist the temptations that you would face, the feeling of procrastination. The feeling of not wanting to pay close enough attention to balance out what you are going to do can keep you back. It can make you feel like you are going to be unable to really get everything done.

There is no denying it—today's lives are busier than ever. They may have become simpler in theory, but there is no denying that your current lifestyle is incredibly busy compared to that of those that did not have the modern amenities that you have. The fact that we have the internet means that we are always connected to each other. We have cars that we can use to travel widely within a short period of time. We have the electrical lights that we can use so we can better see what we are looking at at night. We are not bound by the coming and going of the sun. And yet, despite this, and despite the time that has been opened up, we are always on the go. We are always hustling and bustling around, struggling to do what we can to help ourselves figure out what it is that we can do that will really help in this situation.

To be truly self-disciplined, you must be able to regulate your time. You must be able to set up so you always have the time that you need. You must be prepared so you are always able to ensure that, at the end of the day, you are better focused on the world around you and on how everything fits together.

Create a Schedule

One of the simplest changes that you can implement into your day to not only help you with time management but also to facilitate the development of that self-discipline that you will need is through creating schedules. When you are able to remind yourself that you must sit down and follow a schedule, you are much less likely to struggle with the world around you. When you have a schedule, you have a routine. That is something that is endlessly comfortable. It is something that you can relax within. It is something that you can fall back on, knowing exactly what to predict and how to expect everything to play out.

When you have a schedule, you know that you can keep yourself on track. You know that, at the end of the day, you can better focus because you can better self-regulate. You know that your self-discipline improves dramatically thanks to the ways in which you will be able to pay attention to it. You can ensure that, at the end of the day, you are able to fall back on this schedule quickly and easily. You will see the ways in which you are better able to succeed with ease by making sure that you stick to your schedule.

Your schedule should be the same every day, no matter whether it is a weekend or not. This means that the vast majority of people are stuck to their work schedules, no matter the day of the week. This gives you that regularity that you will need to ensure that, at the end of the day, you can succeed in keeping yourself focused. You will know that you are getting everything done as well and that can be a massive help most of the time when you are worrying about whether or not you will be able to get everything done on your own.

Your schedule should not fluctuate much and should have ample time for everything that you need to do. Especially in the earlier days, you should ensure that you are always focusing on the ways that you behave. Focus on the fact that, no matter what you do or how you do it, you are able to change yourself. Pay attention to the fact that you need to spend time in certain ways and make sure that those things that you must do all get a time slot. If you can do this, you can help yourself to better manage your time regularly. Write down everything that you need to do in the day and then figure out when it fits best. You will essentially make your own sort of loose schedule in doing so and that loose schedule can greatly benefit you.

Prioritize What You Dislike

Now, this particular tip may sound counterintuitive, but it actually makes perfect sense. When you dislike something and you place it at the end of your day, you will spend all day dreading it. You will be constantly worrying about the way that you will have to do that one particular unpleasant task. It could be that you have to make a phone call but do not want to. It could be that you need to take some test that you are dreading. The more that you push off the things that you do not want to do, the more likely that you are to find that you cannot get yourself up to do ti at all. Your time management will struggle because you are resisting what is going on.

However, if you are able to instead shift your schedule around so you can focus on what matters and what really needs to get done, even if you do not like it, you can make the day go so much quicker. You are essentially going to allow yourself to let your focus remain on negativity. You are going to keep your mind stuck in that trap of negativity and as it is stuck in that negativity, it will not want to do anything at all. However, you can alleviate this; you can shift your schedule around.

When you load up the beginning of your day with all of the things that you normally dread, you can get over that hump of everything that you dislike and the rest of the day will seem much better. You will have gotten the worst of it over with and that means that you can then begin to relax. Of course, that means that you will need to also go through and do other errands and tasks as well, but they should all seem incredibly easy after you have already taken care of everything else that you dreaded!

AND FINALLY, you have made it to the last chapter in this book! Congratulations! That alone would have taken a degree of self-discipline on its own that you have shown that you possess! That is a very powerful thing and something that you should be proud of! Now, within this chapter, we are not focusing on any particular skill that is supposed to bring you closer to self-discipline. Rather, within this chapter, you are going to be getting several important tips to remember when it comes to your own self-discipline. You will be accepting the ways in which you can behave yourself to ensure that, at the end of the day, you will manage to live that life-style. These are all general tips and trick that can encompass any of the points that have been mentioned.

Recognize Your Weaknesses

These are the things that you know you will give in to no matter what. These are the areas that you are not willing to give up. It could be that you have a weakness for chocolate, or for cute puppies, or saying no to children that look at you with big puppy eyes. It could be seeing cute clothes at the store and wanting to buy them, or it could be getting the opportunity to go out with friends, even though you know that it is a bad idea. No matter what the weakness is, we all have them.

You must learn to identify yours. When you know what it is, you can then defeat it yourself. You can learn to recognize what it is so you can then stand up to it. You can prevent yourself from giving in to these feelings of stress because you will know when that temptation is looming over you. When you can see that temptation, you can tell yourself to resist it.

Eliminate Your Temptations

Along those same lines, you must also be willing and able to eliminate any temptations that you have. This means that if you know that your temptation is chocolate, you will not buy chocolate or keep it stocked in your home. You simply avoid the problem altogether by refusing to create it. You may not be able to completely eliminate temptations from your life, but you can remove most of them, allowing yourself to better focus on the world around you. The more that you are able to better deal with your temptations and the more that you learn to say no to them, the easier everything will become. Start by removing anything from your home that you know would be problem. This may be alcohol for some people. It could be a specific junk food. It could be just about anything at all. Find what it is and ban it from your house.

Start with One New Habit

Another great tip to remember is for yourself to always begin small, with just one habit. Choose a small habit that you know is not going to stress you out too much. Remember that the purpose of self-discipline is to make yourself happier. It is to help yourself to alleviate stress, not to make it worse, and that means that, at the end of the day, you must be able to change up your own habits to fit along with it. You must be able to see the ways in which your behaviors change, even if the change is small, so you can feel empowered. This creates a positive feedback loop. You succeed at your one small goal and in succeeding, you then find that you are better able to cope with everything else that follows along with it.

Focus on Smaller, Regular Meals

This next point may seem strange at first, but remember that you should eat regularly and healthily. Any time that you eat, you help to stabilize your blood sugar. When you eat regularly and focus on smaller meals, you can remind yourself that you should focus on the food that you are eating and you can then also ensure that, at the end of the day, your temperament is more even than it usually is.

Blood sugar fluctuations can be a huge problem for people. They can create great issues for people that cannot regulate themselves well and you may find that it is very difficult for you to function or resist anything at all when you are currently hungry and in need of something to eat. Rather than dwelling in that hunger, you are encouraged to eat regularly. As you do so, you will notice that everything will stabilize out. You will see the ways in which your food intake helps influence your mood in many different manners. You will see how your very temperament can change when you eat regular small meals instead of just once a day. You can find that you feel so much better and so much more empowered when you are able to eat often and your self-discipline follows with it.

Reward Yourself Sometimes

Remember that, at the end of the day, self-discipline is not a punishment. It is not here to make you feel bad. It is not here to make you feel like you are being deprived. It is a way of life in which you are able to resist your temptations in favor for getting something better later on. It is the feeling of pushing off instant gratification in favor for that better option that is there if you were just to wait a little bit. The more that you wait and the more that you become skilled at these processes, you could find that it benefits you to change up things a little bit. While it is highly recommended that you keep yourself stable and regulated and on a schedule, sometimes, you deserve the treat. Sometimes, you deserve to reward yourself somehow.

Whether you implement the reward as something that you can get after achieving a great milestone, or just as something to make a bad day a little less so, this is a very powerful method that you can use to help yourself cope with the stressors of life. Remember, a well-utilized reward can be used greatly and with much efficiency if you know what you are doing.

Forgive the Mistakes that You Will Make

Finally, consider this last tip for yourself and remember it well, as it is perhaps the most important one on this list. Remember that, at the end of the day, you must be willing and able to forgive yourself. Remember that, at the end of the day, you must recognize that change happens. You must recognize that failure happens sometimes as well, and sometimes, despite everything being set up exactly right, you can find that sometimes, those plans fail. You can find that sometimes, they fail spectacularly and far worse than you intended. This is not a problem; failures happen. You pick yourself up, you look back to the future, and you keep on trekking on. It is okay to fail sometimes; it is even expected. However, failure is not inherently bad.

. . .

When you learn to unravel those feelings, releasing that idea that all fear is bad, you can begin to recognize the truth—that being able to accept your failure with grace and tact is far more important than anything else that you could remember. The better that you do with your tact and with your own ability to handle failure, the more equipped you will be to tolerate anything.

The next time that you fall, help yourself up. Instead of getting angry, remind yourself that you can keep moving forward. Remind yourself that, at the end of the day, a stumble is not the end of the world. You can learn from that; what you should be wary for, however, is all of the bad feelings that may com out as a direct result of that failure in the first place. Forgive yourself. Let go of the frustration and keep on trying. The best thing that you can do for yourself is to simply try again.

Congratulations! You have made it to the end of *Self-Discipline,* and hopefully, as you read along, you found that you were given all sorts of imperative, crucial information that can help guide you through everything that you are looking for.

Within this book, you were taught everything that you needed to know about self-discipline. You need to recognize that, at the end of the day, self-discipline is difficult. It is not easy to learn to resist that immediate gratification. It is not easy to resist those temptations all of the time. I tis not always easy to keep yourself on track, and that is okay. It is okay that you feel like, sometimes, this process is a struggle. It is okay to feel like you are not getting it right. All that you need to do is remember that, to be self-disciplined, you will continue to try again, over and over again. You will recognize the value in being able to continue to try to succeed. You will see that, at the end of the day, you *can* succeed. You can learn to make use of these principles.

At this point, what is left of you to do is to begin to embrace these principles. It is time for you to begin to recognize that, at the end of the day, you do have this power. Recognize that, at the end of the day, you can resist that temptation that you feel. You can choose to let go of the bad feelings and simply allow yourself to exist in the world, working toward your goals. Self-discipline is a wonderful tool. It is a powerful way of life. It is something that you can rely on regularly and depend on to help you to succeed in life, so long as you are able to figure out what it is that you need to do.

As this book draws to a close, it is time to consider how you will use these tools yourself. It is time for you to begin to pull them into your life as well. It is time for you to recognize that at the end of the day, you will find that you can thrive. Do not forget the messages that this book has taught you and do not be afraid to fail. You can develop that self-discipline yourself if you know what you are doing. All you have to do is try.

Thank you so much for taking the time to finish reading through this book. Hopefully, as you read through it, you found that it was highly effective at teaching you what you would need to know and what you were looking for. Hopefully, you found that you have closed up this book with all of the information that you needed and more. Hopefully, you feel prepared to succeed in your own life. Finally, if you found this book useful in any way, please head over to Amazon to leave behind your opinions and thoughts on the material that you were provided. The opinions of the readers is always a great addition and the feedback can help so the next book will be even better than this one.

ANGER MANAGEMENT

Mindfulness Therapy Applying
Emotional Intelligence

R H O N D A   S W A N

INTRODUCTION

We all suffer from anger from time to time. It is a normal response to something that is perceived as wrong or unjust. It is a response to being threatened, and it absolutely has a time and a place. It is necessary for you to be able to feel anger every now and then in order to function properly. This is not a problem—and being angry is not ordinarily a problem, either. However, sometimes, that anger can become more. It can become devastating. It can become a major problem for you and your loved ones. It can tear families apart. It can cost you a job. It can even lead to jail time, depending on what you do in that rage that you find yourself in.

Anger can be terrifying. It can be devastating. It can be painful. People generally do not enjoy that feeling—even if you are the one with an anger problem, you could very well find that, at the end of the day, even you are unhappy with the person that you have become. You may feel like it is impossible to do what you need to do. You may feel like you cannot possibly learn to live with those around you. You may even begin to wonder if your loved ones are better off without you.

If you have ever wondered if you have anger problems, there is a good chance that you may actually have one. If you have ever had people tell you that you cannot handle your anger well, or you have found that, as soon as you get angry, you cannot control yourself, it may be in your, and everyone else's, best interest that you spend the time to take a good, long look at yourself and self-reflect.

If you know that you have anger management problems, or you suspect that you might, this book can help you. You are not a lost cause. You are not doomed to fail just by virtue of being angry. You are not unworthy of having genuine relationships or being able to find success and joy in life. However, your anger, if left entirely unmitigated and unmanaged, can lead to that. Your anger, if you never take the necessary steps to control and manage it, may very well be your downfall. However, the fact that you are reading this right now is a major step in the right direction. The fact that you are looking into anger management books shows that you do, in fact, care. It says that, at some level, you understand that you are wrong. You understand that you do need to make that change.

This book is here for you. It is here to help you learn to understand those difficult feelings that you may have. It is here to guide you through recognizing the implications of having an anger management problem in the first place. You will learn how to understand your anger, as well as the ways in which anger can manifest itself. You will learn about how to react constructively to your anger so you can prevent yourself from getting caught up in all of that negativity that threatens to overwhelm you.

You will also learn about why people oftentimes do get stuck in these sorts of problems. You will learn all about how to recognize when there is a problem and the most common causes. You will learn how to recognize when your anger becomes problematic, and how you can begin to treat an anger management problem. From there, you will take a look at how to acknowledge and manage anger in the moment, as well as how to understand your triggers. You will learn the steps that will be necessary to manage anger, and you will then see how to apply several different techniques to help you defeat your anger, looking at cognitive restructuring, emotional intelligence, and communication. Finally, you will see several anger management exercises that can be beneficial to help you really take back control of yourself.

As you finish reading this book, you will have been guided through the ins and outs of the most important information that you will need. You will see everything lined out for you so you can begin to take control of your anger. Remember, your anger does not make you do anything. While you may not be able to always stop the feeling of anger itself, you can always choose how you are willing and able to respond to it. You are always in control of what it is that you choose to do, no matter how much you feel like that may not be the case.

1 / UNDERSTANDING ANGER

WE ALL HAVE EMOTIONS. You can see it from the earliest days with infants, and you can see them in just about anyone. In fact, to lack emotions at all is usually described as being off-putting. It is described as standing out or being somewhat foreign. Emotions are a part of what makes us who we are—without them, we would not have the sort of intricate interactions that we are able to have with others. Those reactions are very important—being able to relate to someone else is a major part of what it is to be human and it is very important to make sure that you can get along with others and foster relationships.

We have all sorts of emotions. We have positive and negative emotions. However, you must release the notion that your emotions are either good or bad. Release the idea that emotions are meant to be valued differently. Even anger, an emotion that, when uncontrolled and untamed, can lead to utter destruction everywhere it goes, is very productive. Emotions are meant to be influential. They are meant to guide you to behave in different ways, and the different emotions will have very different influences over what you do.

At the end of the day, emotions are just that—emotions. They are feelings that you get. Your emotions are automatic—but the way that you respond is not. Within this chapter, we are going to spend some time going over emotions in general, and with that understanding of what emotions are, we will then spend some time taking a look at understanding anger in particular. We will take the time to look at anger, how it manifests, and why we feel it.

Remember, you are the culmination of evolution over a period of billions of years—nearly every aspect of your being is there to help you survive, and your emotions are no different. Even your anger has a very important purpose that you must consider as well so you know what it is attempting to accomplish whenever you do feel it.

Emotions: What Are They?

Emotions are tricky. They are fickle. They are annoying sometimes. They are compelling. They may even feel uncontrollable. Just about anyone knows those feelings of intense motivation to do something thanks to their emotions. They may have cried uncontrollably at getting intense news—good or bad. They may have thrown something when disappointed. They may have yelled, or even attempted to hurt someone else in a fit of passion. Emotions are designed to be motivating—they are designed to trigger sort of instinctive behaviors.

. . .

Now, you may think that if they are meant to be instinctive, you cannot possibly overcome them. You may think that you are nothing but a slave to your passions. But, this could not be further from the truth. You need to recognize that, at the end of the day, you are in control of yourself, no matter what the emotions that you have are.

Emotions themselves are quite complicated. They are believed to be the state that your body creates through the use of the nervous system that is meant to keep you alive. They are usually designed to keep you alive. You may feel happy seeing your children thriving, or you may feel angry if someone threatens them. You may feel sad at losing someone else or you may feel scared if you think that you are being threatened. These emotions are broken down into several base emotions:

- Anger
- Fear
- Surprise
- Joy
- Disgust
- Sadness

These basic emotions are there to sort of trigger different behavioral tendencies that are going to give you the best possible way that your body should survive. They are unconscious, automatic reactions to your environment. The best way to think about this is the fact that your brain always operates on two levels—it operates on a conscious and an unconscious level. Your conscious mind is the part that you are aware of. It is the part that is able to make clear decisions about what you are doing and how you are doing it. It is the part of your mind that you control. The unconscious mind is essentially there just to save resources. The unconscious mind works by ensuring that, at the end of the day, you respond as quickly and efficiently as you can. It is meant to look at your surroundings and respond automatically, meaning that you do not have to notice something, process it, think about the situation, and then decide what to do next.

While that process may be just fine for many situations, it is also a problem when you are in a life or death situation that will require an immediate response. Imagine that you are in a situation in which you have to decide what to do immediately—perhaps you are being chased by a bear, for example—how do you respond?

Sure, you could sit and debate the ins and outs of how to respond. You could debate whether or not running will work better or if you tried to climb a tree, or if maybe you should attempt to cross the river nearby. Stopping to think about all of your possible reactions in those points in time would be a major detriment—it would keep you from being able to respond to the situation in a manner that would be quick enough for you to actually change the course of what is happening.

Instead of thinking about how you feel and what you want to do, your unconscious mind overrides it all. Your unconscious will trigger the feeling that is going to be the most effective in that particular situation. You will get angry if anger is suited better to the situation. If you need to run, you will be afraid. This saves you time. It saves you effort. It triggers that instinctive reaction that your unconscious mind thinks is right.

This happens because your body will begin to change in response to the stimulus. If the cause of your emotions is seeing that bear charging at you, you will likely feel your heart begin to race. You may feel your breathing change and you will be filled with energy. That energy is triggered by adrenaline and it is there to give your body that boost it needs. As this happens, you are feeling that mental state as well. Together, these two combine to become the emotion that you are feeling. You need the physiological reaction along with the mental change, and when you have them both at the same time, you will feel compelled to respond. You will feel compelled to act in the way that your unconscious mind is pushing for.

However, you can learn to overcome that. You can fight off that instinct. You can fight back, even if every nerve in your body is screaming at you to do something. Those that are the best at managing their emotions are able to do so primarily because they are so good at taking care of themselves. They are good at being able to control what they are doing and when they are doing it, and because they have that stringent degree of control over themselves, they are able to resist what would otherwise be them responding emotionally to everything that happens around them.

This is precisely what you will need to do with your anger. Even if your body is taking that shift to fight, even if you feel the adrenaline in your veins so strongly that you feel like all you can do is respond in anger, you can resist it. You can refuse to relinquish control of your body to your unconscious mind. You can stop that instinct to lash out or fight back. You can prevent yourself from doing something that you know that you will regret.

Anger

Anger, as we have already discussed, is one of those basic emotions that you and everyone else around you has. It is just as integral to being human as, say, happiness or sadness. It is there for a very important reason—to activate your fight response. When you are threatened or you are in imminent danger, your body can respond one of three ways: You can fight off a threat, you can run away from a threat, or you can freeze up entirely. People usually go through one of these three responses, depending upon the threat, the circumstances, and how likely that it is that they could possibly fight off a threat.

In particular, anger is related to the fight response—it will help you protect yourself. It is there so, if you do feel it, you feel pumped and ready to fight off whatever was there in the first place. It is meant for defensiveness, and the more you read about anger, the more this will become true for you. You will begin to see that ultimately, you feel anger when you feel afraid or threatened. It is your response to threat that is necessary to help protect yourself.

The Signs of Anger

Before we keep moving forward, it can be very important for you to recognize the signs of anger. These signs will be your sort of key to pay attention—if you notice that you are exhibiting the signs of anger, you can remind yourself to stop, breathe, and calm down so you can protect yourself. This is very important to remember—if you can keep yourself from behaving in ways that are out of control, you can begin to tame the anger that you are feeling. That taming of anger is absolutely crucial.

Recognizing anger can be done by looking at three main factors. You must first consider the physical signs that you are angry. Then, you will want to consider the emotional signs, and finally, you will want to take a look at the behavioral cues. As you read over these lists, keep in mind that you do not have to have all of these to be angry. You can have just one or two of these signs that you are, in fact, angry—it is a very subjective state.

Physical signs of anger

The physical signs of anger are oftentimes overlooked—people may not realize that they are likely to have very specific physical tells. It can be very easy to simply get swept up in the sensations without realizing that these signs are present. However, keep a lookout for if you are actively showing any of these signs. If you do notice this in yourself, you are likely angry. If you see it in someone else, however, there is a very good chance that their body language is showing you that they are angry. These signs include:

- Jaw clenched tightly together or teeth hurting due to grinding
- Head aching or pounding
- Stomach turning or aching

- Heart rate increasing
- Sweating
- Feeling hot in the face or neck
- Shaking
- Dizziness or lightheadedness

Emotional signs of anger

The emotional side of anger is much more noticeable for most people, but unfortunately, it can be a hard one to pinpoint in the moment. Anger is incredibly overwhelming. It is very easy to get swept up in the feelings of anger and when that happens, you wind up lashing out at people without even realizing that your anger is controlling you in the first place. You need to learn how you can identify that anger early on so you know that ultimately, you will be able to stop when you realize how you are feeling. Oftentimes, the anger is actually a secondary response to something else that is going on in your life, and if you can figure out what that primary source is, you can actually begin to fix the problem instead of suffering from it. Some of the common emotional signs of anger include:

- Irritation
- Depression or sadness
- Guilt
- A feeling of wanting to escape
- Resentment
- Anxiety
- Like fighting back or lashing out

Behavioral signs of anger

There are also several behavioral signs of anger that must be considered. These are the ways in which you may act or the ways in which you may want to act. They are signs that there is something going on that is stressing you out. These signs include:

- Clenching fists, or putting one fist into the palm of your other hand
- Pacing back and forth to release nervous energy
- Touching the head or rubbing the head
- Sarcasm
- Missing humor
- Aggressive, abusive, or abrasive actions
- Yelling or raising voices

2 / TYPES OF ANGER

THOUGH ANGER itself is a universal emotion, that is to say, it is an emotion that is going to be recognizable anywhere in the world because of the fact that it knows no borders or cultural norms, the type of anger that people feel can be differentiated into many different forms. It may not be bound by borders or cultures, but at the end of the day, the type of anger that you feel is going to vary greatly from person to person, and it can even vary greatly based on the situation that you are in.

It is very important to recognize that anger can come in many very different forms. When you can recognize the differences between the types of anger that are around you, you will begin to be able to identify it with greater fidelity. You will be able to tell when someone is angry and then understand what it is that is driving that anger. The ability to classify the anger that is being felt is usually tied to five distinct factors.

Anger needs to be identified in terms of the direction of it. Is it directed inwardly or externally? That is to say. Are you directing your anger toward other people or are you directing it toward yourself? This is a very important factor to consider. Some people may become aggressive toward others while others will be harder on themselves instead.

You must also consider the reaction to the anger in the first place. Do you become retaliatory when you are angry at someone or do you withdraw and become resistant? That is to say, when you are angry, are you more likely to withdraw and give someone the silent treatment or are you going to retaliate?

Then, consider the mode of anger—how is it delivered? Do you respond with anger by being verbal or by becoming physical? Are you more likely to yell at someone or get in their face?

You should also consider the impulsivity of the anger. Are you able to control yourself? Are you able to hold back from doing something that you know is going to be harmful toward others? Can you keep yourself focused or do you find that you lose control? Are you more likely to lash out and act in ways that you will then regret shortly after? You must consider these points closely.

Finally, you will need to consider what the objective of your anger is. Are you angry because you were wronged and you want to try to restore yourself back to your previous state or are you more likely to lash out to try to teach someone a lesson or punish them?

Ultimately, there are many, many different types of anger that exist. There is no hard and fast rule that all people that are angry are one type or the other. There are no exhaustive sets of rules about the number of types that there are. However, in this chapter, we are going to go over ten different types. These are ten of the most common ways that anger can manifest, but keep in mind that there are others as well. This list is not intended to be exhaustive, nor is it likely to be exhaustive in the first place. Other books or sources may talk about different types of anger—and that is because there is no one right way to identify it.

Assertive Anger

Assertive anger will usually be the one type that is constructive. When you can make use of assertive anger, you are able to express yourself in a way that is going to get good results. You are able to essentially present yourself in a way that is meaningful and you can use your anger as a motivator. You take that anger and you use it to apply toward change in the future. You act as a sort of catalyst for the types of change that you are looking for and by doing so, you will find that ultimately, you can make a difference.

This type of anger is not afraid of confrontation—rather, those that have assertive anger know that ultimately, anger must be expressed in a way that is constructive. They know that anger can be a great way to create those necessary changes that are desired without running into the problem of simultaneously hurting someone else along the way. When it comes down to expressing anger, this is the kind of anger that you want to aim for. It is the motivated kind that you can use to fight back from any injustices. It can help you to overcome your fears. It can help you achieve just about anything, all because you are able to focus on what does and does not matter.

Behavioral Anger

Behavioral anger is different—it is entirely, or almost entirely, behavioral in nature. If you experience this sort of anger, you are usually overwhelmed by your feelings that you are having. Your anger becomes something that overwhelms you and takes over. As a direct result, you run into a new problem—you start to behave in ways that are harmful to everyone around you.

You may find that, after someone has frustrated you, you yell. If your order at the restaurant you went to was wrong, you may throw the plate on the floor and demand a new one. You may actually physically attack someone. This particular form of anger can very quickly become a huge problem if it turns into you inadvertently hurting someone. You can run into very real, very serious legal repercussions for this sort of anger.

Imagine, for example, that on your way to work, you felt like someone cut you off. They did not—they simply changed lanes in front of you. If you suddenly fly off the handle, so to speak, you may have a tendency toward behavioral anger, especially if your next response is to follow that person and honk at them, or to get ahead of them and promptly brake check them for the rest of your drive.

This anger, though highly volatile and highly destructive in many cases, can be treated relatively easily—you simply slow yourself down. If you can slow yourself down and refuse to react negatively or violently, you can defeat it.

Chronic Anger

The third type of anger that we are going to discuss here is chronic anger. As the name implies, this is long-term, general anger or resentment without anything necessarily happening. You may find that someone, for example, simply existing can be enough to frustrate you beyond belief. Just the mere existence of someone else can be enough to trigger irritation. It is important to note that this particular type of anger is typically not as extreme or explosive —however, it is most commonly identified by that constant feeling of annoyance toward other people.

Keep in mind that this sort of anger can be a big problem for people. This particular type of anger can actually begin to weigh on other people enough to negatively impact their health. If you find that you are constantly and habitually irritated at other people, you will be constantly exposing yourself to all sorts of negative emotions that you could otherwise cut out. This means that you are constantly under stress, which will then constantly weigh on your body as well. This can lead to higher levels of blood pressure and can very quickly weigh on all other aspects of your health as well.

Judgmental Anger

Judgmental anger is an idea that you are better than someone else and you assume or perceive that the other person is threatening your own beliefs. You are essentially reacting to someone else having very different viewpoints than you do. You are essentially looking at a situation and deciding that you have the better belief system. You assume that your way of looking at the situation is right and that everyone else cannot live up to that. Essentially, you believe that you are superior, oftentimes morally, to everyone else, and so you become offended when someone dares to suggest that they could have a very different viewpoint on the situation.

This anger usually comes with a sense that your own belief is better—you may try to invalidate what someone else believes, for example, or you may begin to force your own agenda or point instead. You assume that no one else could know what they are talking about and if they do have their own belief system about something that is contradictory to your own beliefs, you attempt to invalidate them.

Overwhelmed Anger

This form of anger is uncontrollable. It is typically a direct result of something happening that you feel like you cannot control. Your lack of control can spiral, feeling like you can simply not manage to protect yourself, your loved ones, or anything else. You feel like the situation is so beyond what you can control that you are frustrated. In your frustration, then, you begin to lash out in just about any way that you can.

This is a huge glaring red flag that you have decided to take on more than you can handle—usually in the sense that you cannot manage with something that is happening around you. You are attempting to cope, albeit poorly, by lashing out at others and failing to deal with the stress that you have.

Remember, anger is usually secondary, and in this case, it is secondary to being overwhelmed. However, keep in mind that even if you are overwhelmed, there are ways that you will be able to fight back. You can ensure that you protect yourself. You can ensure that you can keep yourself from becoming overwhelmed. In particular, you can reach out for help. You can ask for support from those around you. You can ask for the help that you need to help deescalate the situation rather than continuing to allow it to fester endlessly.

Passive-Aggressive Anger

When you reach the level of passive-aggressive anger, you are usually attempting to avoid the truth—you are attempting to avoid a confrontation that may reveal that ultimately, the problem that you have is your own. You do not want to be faced with the need to talk about what is happening. You do not want to be held account-able. You do not want to find out that you could potentially be responsible at all. Instead, you choose to use passive aggression in an attempt to evade that confrontation that would otherwise happen.

You may find that you deny how you feel. You may instead mock the other person or use sarcasm. This is not because you are cruel or you want to act in a way that you know will hurt someone —but rather, you are attempting to defend yourself. You are prob-ably afraid of being confronted. You are probably afraid that you are, in fact, at fault, so you try to push them away instead.

Retaliatory Anger

Retaliatory anger is perhaps the most commonly understood form of anger. If someone says they are angry, it is usually in response to this form of anger. Oftentimes, it is triggered by an instinctual response to a confrontation. This is the idea that someone or something else has threatened you, so you must lash out yourself to make it even. You feel like other people have to be punished if they do something wrong.

However, remember, two wrongs do not suddenly make a right. You cannot make the situation better just by virtue of deciding that the other person should suffer as well. You must remember that ultimately, there are better ways to cope if you feel like you have been wronged. Instead of trying to intimidate someone else, you must keep in mind that ultimately, being able to assert control of a situation is not actually necessary. You can get around having to establish and assert control by looking at other methods that you can use instead. Instead of deciding to retaliate, what would happen if you, for example, decided to instead work with assertive anger instead? What if you found some other way that you would be able to better deescalate tensions that have arisen?

Self-Abusive Anger

Some people simply respond to frustration and anger with self-abuse. Instead of attacking other people, you find that you are feeling hopeless or worthless. You feel like you have been invalidated in some way and you decide to internalize these feelings. While this is rarely actually intentional, it can still be quite problematic in many different situations. Keep in mind that if you were to act out in these ways, lashing out at others or otherwise failing to cope with your feelings, you could wind up hurting yourself seriously.

This anger can very quickly become self-harm. It can become self-sabotage. You can destroy relationships all around you, not because you genuinely do not want to value them, but rather because you would rather lash out at yourself and self-destruct than anything else.

Verbal Anger

Verbal anger is quite straightforward, all things considered. While often not taken nearly as seriously because you are not leaving any sort of physical marks on someone else, this is still a form of abuse that should not be used. You are essentially lashing out at people because you do not see a reason not to. You are lashing out at others verbally, whether through calling them names, threatening them, making fun of them, or using any other methods as well. This is a problem—if you lash out, you are hurting people. You may find that you feel bad about it after the fact, but the point still stands—you hurt someone else because you were angry and that is a problem.

This form of abuse can destroy relationships. It can lead to you losing your job. You can find that you are going to fail in general just because you are burning bridges every time that you get angry. You lash out at other people in an attempt to protect yourself, and that is a problem. You want to make sure that you avoid this—do not snap at people if you have nothing productive to say. Watch your language. Keep your negativity to yourself and learn to control that temper.

Volatile Anger

Finally, the last form of anger that we are going to discuss here is the form known as volatile anger. This form of anger is one that is unpredictable. It is a form of anger that you cannot manage at all and it seems to appear and disappear with the wind. You are very quick to overreact to even small annoyances and you then express that anger through something impulsive. You may, for example, throw something during a fit of rage, only to immediately after, go right back to being perfectly calm.

This is destructive. It can lead to everyone around you treading with caution, walking on eggshells because they are afraid that just about anything that happens around you will set you off. They are afraid that they will be the target of your anger and they decide to avoid you altogether. Your volatile anger can become violent quickly. It can become a problem for everyone in your life —and you may not seem to recognize it because you only respond very briefly in anger before you return back to your state of calmness. This particular form of anger is well known because it does come and go so much.

ULTIMATELY, though anger is one of those feelings that most people wished they could live without, it is one that needs to be considered strongly. If you are going to spend time being angry, the best thing that you can possibly do is figure out how to cope with it reasonably. Imagine, for a moment that you want to go on a vacation to Hawaii this summer. Your spouse, however, wants to take all of that money that you would spend on your vacation and dump it toward paying off debt—reasonable, but nowhere near as fun as going on a vacation, You find that you feel angry that your spouse has changed their mind and has gone from being willing to go on a vacation to deciding that it is not worth the money without giving you any sort of say. You feel like the unilateral decision is unfair and because of that, you get angry.

Now, here is the catch—your anger can be used in many, many different forms. It can be used to allow you to recognize that there is some sort of disparity that needs to be discussed. It could, for example, allow you and your partner to open up a candid discussion about the concerns that both of you have in different ways. You could point out that you are worried about mental health and wanting to take a break from the grind to ensure that you and your spouse are both well-rested and ready to take on anything that comes your way. Your spouse can then discuss their own take on the situation, which is likely entirely different than yours.

This boost in communication draws from the fact that both you and your partner are angry. It recognizes that you are both frustrated with the situation, but instead of using that anger to motivate yourself to become destructive or aggressive toward each other, you used it to open up a method of communication so you and your partner can both be on the same page.

This is very important—when you are able to use your anger for the greater good of yourself and your relationship, you know that you and your partner are well on your way to succeeding. You know that you and your partner will likely be able to better relate to each other. Rather than burning bridges, you are able to strengthen relationships and ties to other people and that is essential. If you want to live happily with people that you know or value, you need to be willing to work with them. You need to recognize that anger does not have to translate to feeling wronged —it can be used in many other different ways that have their own pros and cons.

Within this chapter, we are going to talk about constructive anger. The primary type of anger that was constructive rather than destructive was assertive anger. With assertive anger, you are able to remain balanced. You are able to ensure that you are communicating respectfully. It is the best way to figure out what everyone involved needs so you can all work toward some sort of compromise that you know is going to work for everyone involved.

There are several ways that you can work toward developing that sort of assertive anger that you can use to ensure that you are getting the best possible results. In particular, we are going to go over five different ways that you can keep your anger from becoming destructive. These five different changes to the way that you look at anger and handle the anger that you suffer from can greatly help you. When you are able to make these changes, you will find that your life becomes more enjoyable. Your relationships with others will improve. You will be happier and you will find that other people are happier as well.

Do Not Shy Away from Confrontation

The first point to remember is that ultimately, you must not be afraid of confrontation. Let's make this distinction right now—a confrontation does not need to be violent or hurtful to be effective. It does not need to leave someone else feeling worse off than ever. It does not need to make someone feel dumb or uneducated or like they are worse than the other person. Confrontation does not have to be violent or aggressive at all.

Rather, your confrontation is going to happen when you have two different opinions that clash. Bear in mind that they can clash peacefully. There is no rule out there stating that your confrontations have to be aggressive or violent. In fact, you are more than welcome to have a confrontation that involves you and the other party calmly discussing opinions and how to address a situation.

When you want to ensure that you are able to deal with your own anger, you should not be afraid to talk to others. You need to make sure that you are willing and able to sit down and discuss what is going on. This can help you have a direct heart to heart with the other party that may actually become that solution to the problem that you had. It could potentially be the way in which you are able to solve a problem just by virtue of the fact that spending time talking out how you really feel means that the other person knows now how you were feeling before, which may have been skewed along the way.

This can allow you to get in touch with how you really feel, which can also allow you to begin to understand better why you were angry in the first place. Humans are complex creatures after all—and sometimes, we are not entirely sure why certain things make us feel certain ways. However, when you can avoid running from confrontation, you can actually begin to set yourself up to identify why you feel the way that you do. You can figure out if your current actions are, for example, influenced by a past event that is coloring your vision and perspective.

Do Not Blame Others

It is incredibly easy to blame other people. Whether you were in the wrong or someone around you was in the wrong, blaming someone along the way is not going to truly help you. If all you do is blame other people, you are going to struggle. You are not going to be willing to take the blame if you feel like the blame is a problem in the first place.

However, in most situations, there is no place for blame. Most of the time, blame will not fix the problem. It will not make dealing with the problem at hand any easier. It will not help you come up with a solution any easier. For this reason, it is easier to simply skip the blame game altogether. Stop pointing fingers at other people. Stop assigning blame where it does not belong—or even where it may actually belong after all.

Instead, if you can step back from the blame and try to deal with the problem at hand, you are much more likely to find the solution to the problem. Remember, at the end of the day, the cause for the problem is not nearly as important as the solution, and unless the solution that you are attempting to implement will require you to point fingers in order to fix the problem, you are better skipping it altogether.

If you do have to point out that someone else did something egregious or something deserving of blame, then you need to do so in a way that is going to be constructive. This means that there should be no yelling. There should be no name-calling. There should be nothing other than bringing up what happened, from an objective perspective, and then, you must move on. Remember, you must remain on the subject and the instance that you are discussing right at that minute. This is not the time to air all of your grievances of the past—rather, you must only focus on the issue at hand, and only if it is actually going to fix the problem.

Thankfully, most of the time, when people are called out and the reason that they acted in that manner is called out, they will usually apologize and work together to solve the problem. No one enjoys being the one that is causing problems for everyone else—no one enjoys being the one that everyone else looks down on and because of that one particular fact, you can usually get other people to do better just by virtue of staying calm in the first place. By avoiding attempting to assign blame and avoiding causing problems with your anger, you can usually allow yourself and those around you to feel better. You can allow them to feel more confident in the ways that you are acting. You can ensure that, at the end of the day, they will listen better. You can ensure that they will work with you, all by avoiding the blame game.

Keep Your Calm

Now, you may find that you look at this step and roll your eyes. After all, if you were able to keep your calm, would you be here right now, reading a book about how to manage your anger? However, triggering calmness does not have to be difficult. When you look at this step, you are reminding yourself that at the end of the day, there is no reason to launch onto a tirade because someone did something offensive to you. You may find that, after your child broke your vase from your parents, you wanted to send him to his room. However, the way in which you approach the time out can greatly impact the way that it is recognized.

. . .

If you were to, for example, yell and blame your child for what had happened, you likely would not get very far—your child is going to shut down because you are yelling. However, if you were to, for example, calmly explain to your child that what they did was wrong and that they cannot throw their toys around indoors because accidents like breaking the vase can happen.

By remembering to stay calm in the moment, you ensure that you can have a discussion rather than a fight and that is the primary defining factor of this sort of situation.

Be Willing to Compromise

Keep in mind that compromise will always be your best friend when it comes to trying to interact with others. When you can remain someone willing to compromise, you teach other people that you are trustworthy. You remind them that you are reasonable and that you will do what it takes to ensure that everyone that you interact with on a regular basis is prepared and capable of getting together to negotiate the terms of a contract or something else without getting into an argument.

Remember, compromise is both give AND take. If you cannot follow through with both sides of this situation, if you find that you cannot properly find a way to ensure that you are making sure that everyone is happy, you are going to run into problems. If the whole plan is to compromise to make sure that everyone will work together and be satisfied, then you need to be willing to give a little to get a little.

. . .

This means that when you are arguing with someone else, you need to think about being flexible. You need to think about what you are willing to give up to ensure that, at the end of the day, you are ensuring that you are setting up for the best possible compromise. This means that you need to listen to the other party. You need to pay attention when they tell you something and be willing to accommodate wherever practical and wherever makes the most sense.

Keep it Professional

Finally, when it comes to keeping your own anger productive, the best way to remain constructive is to remember that you are going to be professional. If you are at work in particular, you need to ensure that you are polite. Even if you are confronting a family member, you must remember that you should remain respectful nonetheless and that means that you must be able to mind what you say.

It is very important, and much easier said than done, to avoid getting too emotional. Your emotions will cloud your thinking—of course, they are going to be present in this conversation because it is likely about something that you are passionate about. You may find that you have a very strong opinion that you want to assert and you will not stand for anything short of that. That happens sometimes. However, make sure that your assertions that are made are done in a way that is composed and kind. You do not want to fight aggressively, but rather, you want to make sure that you and the other person are both on the same page. You want to be sure that you are both fighting for the same end cause and that you are both diligently working together, even if you have different preferred outcomes for the situation.

4 / THE CAUSE OF ANGER MANAGEMENT PROBLEMS

ANYONE CAN GET ANGRY—WE have already established that. However, you must also consider why people get angry in the first place. This chapter is all about taking a look into some of the common causes of anger management problems in the first place. It is very important to remember that ultimately, the only person who is in control of you is yourself. You are the only one who can make the changes in your life that you want to so. You are the only one that can decide that you are ready to make a change in the first place. If you do not see a reason to want to change, then you are not likely to attempt it in the first place.

You cannot allow someone else to take the blame for you. This means that you cannot attempt to project that blame onto someone else in hopes that if you do so, you will feel better. It is not the fault of the other person, no matter what they did, that you got angry. It is no one's fault but your own. While they may have done the action that triggered your own anger, it is not their job to regulate you for them. It is not their job to placate you to prevent you from being angry in the first place. If you are angry, that is your own fault and the sooner that you can acknowledge that, the better.

Within this chapter, we are going to go over several causes that are found at the root of anger management problems. This does not mean that someone does not need work to work on the problem or attempt to be respectful to you—but you must remember that at the end of the day, you need to remember that you cannot blame other people for your own feelings. As you read through this list, you will see that the vast majority of these problems stems right back to the idea that ultimately, you are in control of yourself and how you approach any situation around you.

Attention Deficit Hyperactivity Disorder

Attention deficit hyperactivity disorder (ADHD) can be an exacerbating factor for many people and their anger. When you suffer from ADHD, you are much more likely to feel your emotions more intensely than normal. You are likely to find that your emotions will skyrocket without reason. You will find that ultimately, you will be much more likely to get angry as well.

While anger can be useful sometimes, it can also cause all sorts of problems. It can be a problem to be angry when it does not benefit you. It can be a problem to express your anger when it is not productive or useful. If it does not help you reduce your stress or solve the problem, it is more of a problem than anything else.

· · ·

Unfortunately, ADHD and aggression oftentimes go hand in hand. It becomes difficult for someone who suffers from ADHD to manage their emotional impulses and when that happens, they are very likely to fall into the habit of relying on anger, which may very well actually make the situation worse. As the situation worsens, you will find that the emotional response becomes stronger as well. It is not that you want to be hurtful—you will simply not be able to manage well without serious effort. The impulsivity of ADHD can greatly strengthen the defiance that people feel. They find that their emotions are expressed rapidly and because of that, they struggle to manage everything.

However, this does not mean that you are a lost cause or that you will not be able to succeed. Rather, with therapy and effort, you should also be able to manage the situation. You should be able to defeat the emotional impulses relatively simply.

Bipolar Disorder

Bipolar disorder is a disorder in which your emotional levels are constantly fluctuating. You may be very quick to suddenly shift from one emotion to another, or you can find that you are going to be in relatively predictable periods in which you can have episodes where your emotions are higher and then similarly predictable periods in which they are depressive.

There are ultimately several different patterns that this disorder can follow, however one thing is for sure no matter what—there is a delay and a discrepancy in being able to manage emotions> You may feel like you cannot control your emotions and that unfortunately also comes along with not being able to control your anger.

Bipolar disorder will usually cycle between depressive episodes and episodes of mania, and because anger can be found regularly in depression as well, this becomes another point of anger for these individuals. If you suffer from bipolar disorder, you may feel like your emotions are all over the place. You may feel like you cannot control your emotions. You may feel like your emotions are too far apart to be able to manage. However, you can learn to do so.

Depression

Many people wrongfully assume that if you are depressed, you cannot be angry and if you are angry, you cannot be depressed. This is due to the act that the most common symptom of depression that most people know seems almost like the opposite of angry. However, interestingly enough, anger and irritability are very common with depression.

Depression itself is the persistent, ongoing feelings of sadness or loss or a lack of interest in the world around you. Generally speaking, it usually lasts at least several weeks. It can also vary from point in time to point in time. You may be angry one day but find that you are perfectly fine the next. This has nothing to do with you and your abilities, and everything to do with the fact that ultimately, if you are depressed, your brain is not keeping itself balanced.

. . .

Depression is commonly linked to symptoms such as feeling angry and irritable, oftentimes for no reason that can be discerned. However, it can oscillate from time to time into a lack of energy or feeling hopeless. Sometimes, people usually will return back and forth between the feelings, depending upon the situation. However, do not discount depression as not being a cause of anger.

Drug or Alcohol Abuse

Alcohol is just one of many legalized drugs. However, drug use, regardless of whether it is legal or not in your state, will alter the brain. That is literally their point and why they are so highly sought after—they are meant to change the way that the mind works.

However, especially with alcohol, these drugs oftentimes lower inhibitions. They can lead to you not feeling like you need to control your anger, or simply denying that you have a problem in the first place. Rather than recognizing the problem at hand, you may be quick to sort of wave it away and move on. You may feel like you do not need to bother with the situation at hand because at the end of the day, it does not matter to you.

When you drink or consume any sort of drugs, you will eliminate your ability to think clearly and rationally. You will damage your ability to manage your own impulses. You will make controlling your emotions feel like an impossibility and that is a major problem.

. . .

Grief

Anger also happens to be one of the normal, natural stages of grief. When something happens to cause you to lose someone or something that you loved greatly, you may find that you grieve. You could have lost your partner that you lost, or you could have gotten divorced when you really did not want to. No matter how you feel, however, you must remember that your anger needs to be mitigated.

Oftentimes, the grief felt is usually related to losing a person, a place, or a thing that they once loved. To lose someone that you love, or lose something that you love can be very, very traumatic and because of that, you can need some sort of contingency plan. That contingency plan can help you protect not just yourself, but those around you as well. It not only matters to you to be able to recognize that anger is a very normal, very valid part of losing people, but also to help yourself in learning to cope with it as well. It will aid you in learning how you can address what happened. It will aid you in discovering what you can do differently and how you can make any necessary changes. These changes can vary greatly from person to person, but one thing is true—without them, you and those around you will suffer.

Intermittent Explosive Disorder

This mental health disorder is one in which you are likely to repeatedly express yourself with anger and aggression. It is most commonly noted as being widely filled up with all sorts of irritated or aggressive behaviors. It could be that you are far too impulsive for your own good—some people are. It could be that you simply give in whenever something happens around you. You could find that you are suddenly angry without any good reason and that is a problem.

This disorder can lead to all sorts of problems. You can hurt people. You can find that you are permanently on a short fuse, angry, but not set off until something bad happens.

The most common symptoms of this disorder include the throwing of temper tantrums, getting into arguments regularly, picking or getting into fights, including physically, throwing items, or even physical violence.

Usually, these people, after the fact, recognize that what they did was wrong. They understand that they have messed up and they want to try to fix the problem somehow. However, that does not mean that the next time that something comes up, they won't have similar problems.

The most defining feature of this particular problem, when it comes to understanding the people and what they can and cannot do, is recognizing that people that suffer from this disorder usually respond disproportionately to whatever is happening around them. They will always, or almost always, respond disproportionately negative, no matter how bad something really was.

Trauma
Finally, trauma can be another major source of anger for many

people. While most people are able to cope with trauma just fine if they are given enough time, other people find that they cannot cope with it at all. They may find that they suffer from a traumatic disorder, such as post-traumatic stress disorder and, directly related to the fact that they have suffered from trauma, they struggle to manage their anger.

These people may lash out unintentionally when stresses and tensions continue to rise. It is often linked to these people struggling in other ways as well. Additionally, people who suffer from trauma, or PTSD, find that they are much more likely to struggle with alcohol or other drug disorders. That increased risk of engaging in these behaviors that are already known to exacerbate the situation can be a major point of contention. They can lead to the individual lashing out even more.

Remember, anger is a response to a threat, and if you have lived through a trauma of some sort, you are going to get angry sometimes. Anger is a very normal response to terror and trauma—it is done to help you fight back whatever caused you problems in the first place. However, there is one particular problem that you must consider as well—if you are responding violently and drastically to all sorts of problems around you, you must be able to do something to prevent it from getting worse. You will need to find a way that you can cope with that stress so it does not simply weigh on everyone else, causing them problems along the way.

5 / WHEN ANGER BECOMES A PROBLEM

WHILE ANGER IS a normal part of life, and it can be normal, and even healthy, to feel anger every day, to varying degrees, it is important to note that anger should not be overwhelming. Anger should not be causing problems for you. It should not be taking over your life to the point that you cannot possibly hope to function normally any longer. It is not fair to you if you feel like you cannot control your anger, and likewise, it is not fair to other people in your life that will suffer from it, either.

When anger becomes a major problem for you and those around you, it can very quickly destroy relationships, or even land you in prison. In fits of rage that was uncontrollable, people have done horrible, heinous crimes that have led to serious injury, or even death, of other people, even if those people had been loved before.

Anger can play a major part in domestic violence in households as well. It is estimated that ¼ women and 1/7 men will suffer at the hands of an intimate partner at some point in their lives. These people will suffer from violence in a way that is unthinkable. Some may be hit. Some may be yelled at. Some may be threatened. However, at the root of it all is anger. That anger is a major problem> that anger can hurt people. It can cause problems in just about every aspect of these people's lives.

Anger can be a major problem for many people, and they may find that ultimately, they take it out on their loved ones. They may take it out on those that they feel closest to, much like how children will act out for their parents more than for others. However, this is not a good thing—it is not a sign of trust to be abused or hurt by your romantic partner. It is not a sign of affection or love to be abused.

If you have anger problems, you may have already hurt someone that you love, or you may be afraid that you will in the near future if it is allowed to continue. You may wonder if you will lose your job due to not being able to control your temper, or if you will struggle in other ways.

Ultimately, being able to identify whether your anger is a problem is the first step to being able to fix it and if you can identify it, then you can begin to work on it where necessary. Within this chapter, we are going to go over six signs that your anger has become a problem that will require you to either get help for it, or that will require you to begin working intensively on how to stop it from continuing to worsen over time. It will not be an easy journey. It is not easy to change something that has become such a deeply ingrained habit. It is not easy to make sure that at the end of the day, you are changing up what you do, but you owe it to those loved ones in your life to try. You owe it to the people that love you and depend on you to try to fix the problem and ensure that, at the end of the day, you are doing everything in your power to allow yourself to better cope with the problem.

You Cannot Control Your Anger

Perhaps the most clear-cut example of how to tell that your behavior is a problem that will need to be fixed is that your anger is simply out of control. You may feel like, no matter how hard you try, your anger is always getting the best of you. You may try to control it, only to find it very quickly escaping from your grasps and flooding into other areas in your life instead. It may also come with blaming the other party for whatever has happened—you may say that you were angry, but your anger was someone else's fault, and therefore the behaviors that you did while angry were someone else's fault as well.

However, this is not true at all. No one ever does anything to you that warrants you losing your temper on them. No one deserves to be abused and yelled at. No one deserves to be treated like they are unable to do anything right. No one deserves to have the anger of someone else thrown at them, and then be blamed for the abuse in the first place.

If you find that, when angry, you feel like you are entirely out of control, then you have a major problem. It is not normal to be unable to control yourself. It is not normal to be unable to prevent yourself from acting out in ways that are dangerous or detrimental to those around you. It is not normal to push that anger onto other people that are not responsible for the anger that you have. It is not normal for you to assume that other people have to hold the responsibility for keeping you from overreacting. Remember this—your emotions are not anyone else's responsibility. Your actions are not anyone else's responsibility. At the end of the day, you are the only one that is responsible for you how behave. You are the only one responsible for why you behave the way that you do. You are the only one that is going to be able to make the necessary changes to your life, and that begins with learning how to control your anger before your anger controls you instead.

You Are Angrier More Often Than Others

Another sign that your anger may be a problem that needs fixing is that your anger seems to happen far more frequently than that of other people. You may discover that, at the end of the day, you are far angrier than other people that you know. You may get angrier at something that is relatively harmless—and after the fact, you realize that the problem that you faced was not actually very important in the first place. You may feel like at the end of the day, you should not be getting angry so often, but you do not have that necessary control to make that a reality.

This is, to some extent directly related to the previous sign of an anger problem. When you cannot control your anger, it is only natural that, at the end of the day, you get angrier more often. You feel like you cannot fix the problem. You feel like you cannot stop yourself from becoming angry and that anger is able to overwhelm you entirely. It is able to fester, and as it does, you find that you feel angrier than ever. You feel like you cannot figure out how best to maintain that negativity. You may find that you cannot figure out how best to keep yourself calm or in control. You may find that at the end of the day, your anger just happens.

Now, you may say that the anger is related to other people. You may say that the anger is actually the fault of someone else. You may say that other people do things that make you angry and therefore you do not need to hold yourself accountable. However, all of that is just trying to come up with some sort of excuse to justify what has happened and that is not good for you. That sort of justification does not fix the problem. It does not help you begin to escape from the abusive tendencies. It does not help eliminate how often you get angry.

You Act in Ways You Regret When Angry

Sometimes, one of the easiest signs that your anger is a problem is in looking at how you respond when you are angry. You may find that ultimately, you are going to be responding negatively to anger—people usually do, unless they have mastered the art of being assertively angry rather than any other form of anger. However, when you have an anger problem and your anger is out of your control, you will frequently realize that you regret those behaviors. You will realize that at the end of the day, you struggle to keep in mind that the behaviors that you do are your own and that you must take responsibility for them.

When you act in ways that you regret, you are usually finding that you do something or another that is going to cause problems. You may find that your anger leads to you lashing out at people. You may do things that you know are going to hurt those around you.

You may decide that, at the end of the day, you do not have the fortitude to protect yourself from making bad decisions—and you feel guilty for it.

Perhaps the easiest way to see if you have an anger problem is to look at how often you feel guilty after the fact. How often is it that you find that you cannot manage your emotions well? How often is it that you wind up feeling aggressive toward someone else in your emotions, only to decide after the fact that what you did was wrong and should have been avoided? This is a major sign that you have an anger issue. It is a good sign that you can acknowledge that what you did was wrong—but it still shows that you are ultimately too impulsive at that point in time.

Your Anger is Negatively Impacting Your Relationships

When you know that your anger is making it harder to have any normal relationships with other people, you know that it is a problem. Now, this does not mean that your anger is only a problem once you get to the point of fighting with people or hurting them—rather, if you are acting in ways that put your partner or those around you on edge on a regular basis, or that hurt them in any way at all, physically, emotionally, or otherwise, your anger is a problem.

Do not wait for your anger to get to the point of raising a hand to the other person—when it comes to anger, especially in romantic relationships, you will find that anger often continues to escalate over time. It can get worse and worse over time, and that eventually leads to major problems. Just because you have not hit someone yet does not mean that you will not have the potential to hit them in the future—and this is why your anger issues should be considered earlier on before they can get to that point in the first place.

Make sure that you do not lash out at other people. Make sure that you are learning to solve the problems sooner rather than later. Make sure that you are cognizant of your behaviors and how they do impact those around you. If you can do this, you will able to ensure that at the end of the day, you can begin to correct for those anger issues and keep it from getting worse.

Your Anger Hurts Others

Sometimes, anger hurts. It can hurt yourself, especially if your anger turns into you talking down about yourself. Or, it can hurt other people as well, such as when you start to talk down to other people. You can lash out at people or say things that are hurtful. You can become louder. You can yell or threaten. You can simply stare at them with a hurtful look and your anger will be a problem for people.

If your anger is explosive, it can start to hurt people worse. It can become a problem and potentially even cause physical harm to others and that is a major sign that something is wrong. If you have ever had someone come up to you after the fact and say to you that what you did in your fit of anger was a problem and that it hurt them, that is a good sign that there need to be some very serious changes made to the way that you interact with people.

. . .

You Are Abusive

Finally, perhaps the worst of the signs that you have an anger problem is that you are abusive, especially if that abuse becomes a regular problem in your relationship or situation. If you are regularly abusing people for some reason, you likely have a problem, and there is a good chance that the problem that you have will need to be solved with the help of professionals that can help you learn why you do what you do and how you can stop it.

Ultimately, anger and abuse are very similar, but there is a difference. Calling someone a name in the throes of anger is not necessarily abusive—it is hurtful and it is wrong, but a one-off behavior where it does not happen regularly is typically attributed more toward anger than abuse. Your argument could have gotten very heated and you said something that you regret and that you did not mean.

However, when it comes to abuse, you are adding in behaviors that are toxic. They are intentionally cruel most of the time—and they are usually done to intentionally inflict pain and suffering. This is when you are considering the actions that would be present in, for example, someone who shows the anger typing of retaliatory. You may want to make them hurt because you want to punish them for what they did.

This is a huge red flag. If you are intentionally inflicting harm on someone because you want to punish them or make them hurt, you are becoming abusive. You likely will never take control or responsibility for what you are doing—you think that it is just fine to hurt. You will blame and you will attempt to punish the other person. It is not your fault—they asked for it, or at least, that is the narrative that you will tell. You will find that you are better off hurting those around you. You will find that you are better off lashing out at those around you.

Now, abuse is not just physically lashing out at someone—there are many different types of abuse that you need to be aware of at the end of the day. Any of these can be a direct result of your own anger problems. Some of the most common forms of abuse include:

- **Physical abuse:** This is physically harming the other person. It is inflicting physical pain or restricting movements. Grabbing someone's face or restricting movement is one example. It is any sort of intentional contact with the body of someone that is unwilling at that point in time. It does not even have to leave a mark—holding someone's hand firmly enough that they cannot get away or blocking them somewhere can be considered physical abuse.

- **Emotional abuse:** This is the use of any other behaviors that are not physical. It could be threats or insults. It could be constantly texting to see what the other person is doing due to your own insecurities. It could be attempts to intimidate or stalk, or isolate the other person. If you call names, yell, embarrass, threaten, or attempt to manipulate the other person, you are likely emotionally abusing them.

- **Sexual abuse:** This is any sort of act that will coerce or force someone into a sexual act that they are not consenting to. And yes—you can sexually abuse a partner or a spouse. Remember, a lack of a no is not consent—consent requires an enthusiastic yes. Any sort of sexual touch toward someone that is unwanted is a form of sexual assault. Any attempt to limit birth control or protection from sexually transmitted infections is a form of sexual abuse. Pressure and badgering into something is a form of sexual abuse— especially if it is met with anger if denied.

- **Financial abuse:** This is restricting access to money, or damaging the credit or ability to work of the other person. It could be not allowing the other person what they need, or not allowing them to see the money. It could also be causing the money to be lost or held up somewhere else, or taking it away entirely. It is the use of money to keep someone trapped and obedient. Many people do not realize that being controlling with money is a form of abuse.

If you notice that you show signs of being abusive and you can acknowledge that some of the behaviors are, in fact, abusive, you need to recognize that your relationship is toxic. If you want to salvage it, you are going to need counseling—for you alone for a long while, and then couples counseling.

6 / TREATING YOUR ANGER
MANAGEMENT PROBLEM

IF, at this point, you are heavily considering the ways in which you can better control your own anger, there are many, many options out there for you. These options that you can use for yourself are greatly important. They are incredibly powerful and ultimately, you can make use of them right in the comfort of your own home. You can learn to slow down the anger that rages within you, allowing it to quiet down just enough for you to be able to take back your control of yourself.

People encourage all sorts of ways that you can engage in anger management. They tell you to stop and breathe. They tell you to think positive thoughts. They tell you to let it go. However, none of those options are particularly useful to you. None of those methods are actually going to truly help you to defeat the anger that you may be holding onto. They are just as vague as telling you to just swim if you are currently sinking in a pool; you cannot simply tell someone to do something without giving them the resources that they will need to follow through with it.

. . .

Within this chapter, you are going to be guided through the general steps of several different forms of anger management that you can use to completely slow your own anger. These are methods that you can use to allow yourself to take back that control, little by little. As you develop that control, you can better make use of the way that you behave, allowing yourself to be more inclined to control everything that you will need to know.

Cognitive Restructuring

Cognitive restructuring is perhaps the most foundational technique that you find within cognitive behavioral therapy. When you make use of this approach, you are essentially rewiring the thoughts that you have. You are developing a method through which you are able to better manage your emotions and behaviors by ensuring that you take the time to change the thoughts that you have. It is based on the concept of cognitive meditation—the way it works is that it separates out the person from the feelings. In this concept, your feelings are not the reactions to the world around you. Rather, they are in a direct response to the way in which you think about it. Your reaction will vary greatly from person to person. It will change immensely between the way that you stop and look at the world around you and the way in which you are able to better cope with the stressors of your life. When you take on cognitive restructuring, you teach yourself that your thoughts will directly and completely alter the ways in which you respond to the world.

. . .

These methods are incredibly useful when it comes to creating a real, lasting change. Imagine for a moment that your partner points out that the way that you cooked something was a bit off, and then he or she offers advice about how you could improve on the cooking it in the future. You immediately get offended; you feel like you need to be worrying about whether or not your partner likes you. You stop and feel judged, and as you feel judged, you feel angry. You feel like it is impossible for you to be able to better deal with the feelings at hand. You begin to argue about what you feel, and in a direct response, your partner gets angry as well.

This action was caused by the fact that you felt threatened and attacked when your partner was really trying to be helpful more than anything else. This is a major problem; you become aggressive and combative, even though there is no reason for you to be aggressive and combative in the first place. You run into the issue of then lashing out in anger toward your partner as well.

With cognitive restructuring, however, you are able to better change the way that you think, allowing you to shift your attention from the negativity of the situation into an aspect of positivity. As you do this, allowing the thoughts that you have to shift away from the negativity of your life. You are able to avoid that negativity and instead focus entirely on the ways that the situation may be different. When you stop looking at the advice as a criticism and instead focus on it as a genuine way in which you can get help and advice from your partner, you stop responding to it so aggressively because you stop feeling attacked. We will be going into more detail about cognitive restructuring in Chapter 12: Anger Management and Cognitive Restructuring.

. . .

Communication

Communication is another major way in which you can begin to defeat your anger problems. When you learn to communicate clearly and effectively, you develop the ability to stop and listen. You develop methods of understanding what other people are saying, as well as the ways in which you are able to better understand how you communicate. When you learn these methods to help yourself, you learn that your words have power. You learn that the way that you approach situations, both in how you look at what other people say and how you present yourself, matters.

Communication can come in many different ways, but oftentimes, the conflicts that we get into, no matter who they are with, are due to the struggles in communication. When you do not communicate well with other people, you run into all sorts of other problems that can be a great detriment. You need to be able to best work on your emotions and how they impact you. You need to learn that it is incredibly important for you to stop and pay attention to the ways in which you present yourself. The way that you talk to yourself, and the way that you talk to others as well, becomes the best way that you can cope with the stressors of your life. If you can shift the way that you can communicate, ensuring that your body language, your words, and your tone all are what you intend for them to be, you can better deal with the negativity and the anger.

As with cognitive restructuring, we will be dedicating an entire chapter to communicate in ways that are conducive to being able to better communicate with others. We will be taking a close look at all of the ways in which you can better deal with your emotions and the words that you use when you talk to other people. The more that you worry about this and the more that you focus on the way that you can be seen when you do interact with other people becomes incredibly important.

Problem Solving

Problem-solving is the way that you will be able to look at your current situation and then know what it is that you will need to do to allow for relief in your current situation. You are figuring out the ways in which you can better deal with the world around you. You are focusing on the problems that you have that are making yourself feel worse. You stop and look at what the source of the problem could be. You stop and consider where there are ways that you can do something that you can better help yourself. You stop and wonder whether the problem that you are currently suffering from is one that you can solve, in which you are able to make the necessary changes, or one in which you are stuck or trapped with little recourse, at which point, your best possible choice is to ensure that you make good use of acceptance.

When it comes right down to it, there are things in this world that you can control and there are things in this world that you cannot control. The things that you can control are primarily just those within yourself. They are the ways that you choose to respond to the world around you. They are the ways that you behave and the ways that you think. These are all different aspects of the world that you have direct control over.

· · ·

However, so much more in the world is entirely out of your control. These areas that you cannot control can become points of contention. They can stress you out. They can change the way that you look at the world. When you feel out of control, it is entirely possible that you are left feeling anxious, concerned, frustrated, or even volatile. All of this can lead to anger as well; the more that you are exposed to these negative or different feelings within yourself, the more likely that it is that you will find that you do have these other problems. It is important to stop and think about the ways in which you can better cope with the situations at hand.

The vast majority of this book will help you with these principles. When you want to problem-solve, there are just four steps that you have to follow. These basic steps will help you begin to think in ways that are meant to be constructive. They are meant to facilitate those ways of thinking that you will be able to rely on. As you develop that ability to rely on them, and to trust that at the end of the day, you are doing what matters to you, you will find that you are much better off than ever before.

Step 1: Defining problems

The first step is to define the problem that you are currently facing. When you can stop and look at the problem that you are currently facing, you are able to begin trying to understand the truth of what is going on. When you do this, you are trying to consider the ways in which you are better able to look at the problem. What is it that is the problem here? What is it that matters to you here? You must be able to figure out exactly what the problem that you are facing is so you can then begin to correct the solution.

Step 2: Brainstorming alternative solutions

Next, when you want to solve the problem that you have identified, the natural next step is beginning to identify any alternative solutions that you may face. When you start to look at the alternatives that you face, you can begin to find potential ways to alleviate any of the stressors that you currently face. You are trying to come up with any and all possible solutions, no matter how ridiculous or silly that they may seem.

Step 3: Evaluating your solutions

Thirdly, you must stop and evaluate all of the solutions that you have. Consider the ways in which each of your methods identified in step two is actually going to be valuable. Allow yourself to figure out which of the methods is the most likely to produce the most desirable result. Figure out which ways are the most likely to help you to alleviate the situation and reduce your anger.

Step 4: Implementing solutions

Finally, you must implement that solution that you have come up with. Maybe your solution was to make sure that you change the environment. Maybe your solution was to allow yourself to spend less time with someone that is frustrating or distracting to you. Perhaps it is the case that you do not find the way that will fix the problem. Maybe the first attempt to solve the problem will not be good enough for you. If that happens, the natural solution is to make sure that you then begin to attempt a new solution. When step 4 does not give you the results that you want, you simply go right back to step 2, considering the ways that you can react and the ways that you can change your behaviors.

Relaxation Techniques

When you have an anger management problem, you likely hear on a regular basis that you need to find a way to relax and lighten up. You may find that, no matter how hard you try, you are stuck or even that the implication that you should maybe try to tone down your frustration is enough to push you deeper and deeper into your anger. When that happens, you need to be able to reclaim that control of yourself. The best way that you can do so in the moment happens to be through relaxation techniques. You will need to spend the time that you have quietly considering the ways in which you can begin to calm down. It is only when you are able to stop yourself and relax that you can then begin to better cope with the stressors of your life. It is only when you can release that tension that you have, alleviating your stress that you can then begin to take control of your behaviors as well, and that requires you to, at the very least, begin to process your feelings and find that soothing method that you need.

When we get to chapter 15, we will be focusing on all sorts of exercises that would be defined as this sort of method that you could use to begin to alleviate your tension and begin to relax. As you identify the ways in which you can focus on yourself and the behaviors that you have or the behaviors that you would like to alleviate, you can begin to relax. You can begin to remove that stress from yourself.

EVERYONE FEELS angry from time to time. We all have those feelings that we are stressed out, or that we are overwhelmed by what we are doing, and we all lash out at other people at points in time. This happens from time to time and it is important to note that the rare outburst is not, on its own, a sign of an anger management problem. However, repeated instances or patterns may be.

If you are suffering at the hands of your anger, you may feel like there is no real way for you to better deal with the stress at hand. You may feel like you are trapped. You can feel that pressure within yourself, bottled up deeply ad being shaken, little by little. Think of the pressure that builds up within a bottle of soda as you shake it. The pressure builds more and more as you constantly attempt to keep yourself under control. The more that the anger and frustration get jolted around and the more stressed out that you begin to feel, the worse the situation becomes.

. . .

Your anger, if not properly alleviated, can continue to build up to dangerous levels. Over time, it can build and grow, until eventually, you snap. That is where the problem lies; when you are able to better cope with the anger and frustration that you feel, you can find that, at the end of t e day, you cannot manage as well as you should be able to. However, you can begin to alleviate that pressure, little by little, through the use of gently beginning to alleviate the stressors that you face. In acknowledging your anger, you can begin to alleviate some of that pressure and in alleviating that pressure, you should be able to defeat the problems that your anger brings to you.

Recognize Its Validity

To recognize and acknowledge your anger, you must first start by stopping and reminding yourself that anger itself is not a problem. You must remind yourself that, at the end of the day, to be angry is not to be a failure. It is not to be someone that is struggling. It is not to be deemed someone incapable of success. Rather, anger is believed to be a method through which you will be able to better cope.

Your anger is not a part of you. Your anger is not who you are. It does not define you, nor does it control you. Your anger is just that: An emotion. The anger that you feel is something that you must be able to remember; you must be able to recognize that it is real and that it is there within you. Rather than attempting to bottle it up and hide it away, you must be able to quickly and carefully calm yourself down. You must remember that, at the end of the day, you need to be able to better cope with the stressors that you face. You need to be able to see how the ways that you may normally attempt to deal with your emotions, such as through the use of fighting off the threat or attempting to avoid the anger altogether is not actually going to help you.

Anger needs to be acknowledged. The more that you try to ignore it, the louder it will become. The more that you ignore it, the worse that it will become and the harder it will be to resist that tendency to lash out at the people around you. In attempting to ignore everything around you, you cannot simply make the ager disappear. You do not solve the problem by ignoring it; if you were to ignore it, all that would happen is that it would bubble up, worse and worse, until it blows up and you find that your entire situation fails.

Remember, to acknowledge your anger is not to accept that everything that you do is exactly as it should be. To acknowledge that anger within yourself is not to allow yourself to be held back by it. It is not to keep you down or prevent you from changing. It is not an acceptance of the negative behaviors that you feel. Rather, your acknowledgment of that anger is little more than stating that you see it there. You can tell yourself that you can see it there and that you can understand why it is there. Your ability to stop and gently acknowledge that anger as a valid feeling, as it is exactly what you are feeling in that moment, and that is enough.

Remember that, at the end of the day, you do not have to be justified in your feelings for them to be valid. Any emotions that you currently feel are automatically valid. The way that you can identify your way of feeling is enough to make the emotions that you feel as valid as they could be, and that is enough here. It is enough for you to tell yourself that your emotions are what they are and that you should recognize them.

Recognize the Reason

Once that you have acknowledged the validity of the feelings that you are experiencing right that moment, you need to move on toward recognizing the why. Here, you are going to be looking at why it is that you have these feelings. Here, you are going to be considering the ways in which you can better cope with your emotions so you can then begin to understand the ways that you will be able to tackle them. You will be able to tell the ways in which you can better deal with the emotions at hand. You will be able to recognize all the ways that you will be able to better deal with those feelings that you have when you can see why you are feeling the way you do in the first place.

Keep in mind that being able to understand the reason that you behave the way that you do is not the same as justifying it. There is a difference between being able to stop and look at a situation, pointing out to yourself that you feel the way that you currently feel thanks to the interaction that you just had with someone else and blaming someone else for the feelings that you have just had. When you can stop and recognize the difference between the two, and understand that there is a difference between the way that you feel as the cause of those feelings versus making someone else the one responsible for your anger, you can begin to make more progress.

·   ·   ·

Remember, it is not the interaction that you had with someone else that is the problem. Remember that you cannot blame someone else for your own anger. Remember that at the end of the day, the only one responsible for the anger that you have is yourself. Your thoughts that you have are very important when it comes down to dealing with the anger that you feel. You must be able to find the thoughts that you have that are the problem; it is not a matter of identifying the thought that is making the situation problematic in the first place.

When you focus on thoughts in these ways, you can usually allow yourself to begin to process the truth of the matter. With careful introspection and reflection, you can begin to uncover the reasons that you are angry in the first place. To identify the cause of the anger—the real cause and not the one that you have attempted to pass off by blaming someone else—is a great way that you can better understand yourself. By recognizing what the truest cause of your anger is, you can then begin to recognize something important; you can recognize that your anger has a very real source and by learning what that very real source is, you can remove the power that the source has over you in the first place.

Avoid Downplaying Anger

Finally, when it comes to actively acknowledging and embracing your anger, you must avoid the trap of downplaying your anger. When you downplay your anger, you try to assert that it is not actually a problem. When you are able to pinpoint your anger and begin to recognize where it actually falls, you know that you can better deal with the anger and the frustration that you face. You will face it head-on instead of looking at the way that you can attempt to disregard it.

Consider for a moment what you do when you downplay your anger. You tell yourself that it is not valid. You tell yourself that it does not matter. You remind yourself that the anger that you are feeling is not something that should be felt at all. You are minimizing. You are telling yourself that the way that you feel is illegitimate and that is not fair to you. That is not a way of approaching yourself and your situation in a method that is going to be conducive to the successes that you will need to have for yourself.

To recognize your anger as valid, you must make sure that, at the end of the day, you are willing and able to see the ways in which your anger is there. You must be honest with yourself and the severity of the anger that you are engaged in. You must be willing and able to see the ways in which your mind is overrun with the anger that you feel. You must be willing and able to see the ways that your anger impacts you and that means that you cannot attempt to downplay it. You cannot attempt to minimize it. You must see it for exactly what it is.

When you have acknowledged your anger, the next natural step is to ensure that you are able to begin to manage your anger in the moment. Within this chapter, we are going to take a look at several techniques that you can use that will aid you in discovering your own calmness. These are techniques that are designed to help you discover what it is that works for you. These are techniques that you can use when you feel like your anger and frustration is getting the best of you. When you feel like nothing is going right, or when your anger is at the end of your rope, it is important for you to stop and look at the ways in which you can better cope with the stress and anger. The better that you get at handling your anger, the easier it gets to manage it.

Take a Pause

Perhaps one of the greatest things that you can do when you feel that rage build up within yourself is to stop, to acknowledge that you are angry, and to pause. Different people have different ways that they do this. Some stop and take a deep breath. Some people have a phrase that they repeat to themselves. Some people simply freeze in the moment to give them a second to process everything that is going on around them. No matter the method that you chose to make use of, remember that at the end of the day, you can make this work. Take some time to calm yourself down. Remind yourself that, at the end of the day, what you really need to do is give yourself that moment.

Sometimes, this break gives you that split second that makes the difference between an overreaction and a more productive manner of handling the issue at hand. When you can stop yourself and pay closer attention to what it is that you are doing, as well as pausing when you know that you need to give yourself a quick break, you can remind yourself that you can, in fact, keep control of yourself.

When You Don't Have Anything Nice to Say, Don't Say Anything at All

Another way to manage your anger goes right back to kinder-garten, and if you think about it, it makes perfect sense. If you cannot say anything kind in the moment, you should not be saying anything at all simply due to the fact that when you do say some-thing unkind in the moment, you are going to find yourself making the situation worse. You should never be using your words to hurt other people and the very idea that it is acceptable to do so is a major problem for many people; you must be willing and able to recognize that, at the end of the day, you must be able to relax. You must be able to remind yourself that you cannot simply say anything that comes into mind.

. . .

When you feel yourself getting ready to say something abrasive or aggressive, you have a problem. You need to be able to change the way that you respond in some other manner. It could be that you spend the time to remind yourself to quietly reflect upon what you are doing around you. It could be that you are taking the time to remind yourself that you need to stop and focus on the way that you can approach the situation with kindness and compassion.

Before you speak, it is highly recommended that you take a moment to stop. Take the time that you need to quietly focus. Listen to the words that you have on the tip of your tongue for a moment. Are they kind? Are they acceptable to say to someone else? Would you mind having those words said to you? If not, then you should probably abstain from saying them at all.

Take a Mental Break

Another way that you can focus your efforts on solving the problem is by making sure that you are better able to cope. Usually speaking, the best way to make that happen is through ensuring that at the end of the day, any time that you are feeling on edge or tense and it makes sense for you, you need to be able to step back and take a break. You need to be able to remember that you get time for yourself as well. You need to be able to ensure that you can better cope with the stressors and sometimes, the best way to be able to cope with the stress that you feel at hand is to take time away from it all.

This is both preemptive and used to cope in the moment. You should be better able to regulate yourself. You should be able to better deal with your daily stress if you are able to relax from time to time. Mental health breaks are some of the best ways that you can better deal with the world. They can help you recognize that at the end of the day, you need to better spend time doing what you love so you are mentally well-rested enough to focus on what really matters in your life.

As you take mental health breaks, you help yourself to eliminate that stress that would otherwise overwhelm you because you reduce the stress hormones of your life. When you do this, you can help yourself. You can ensure that, at the end of the day, you can cope when you get stressed out. When you can cope with the stress, you can resist the anger that would otherwise overwhelm you.

Mantras

Another method that you can use to better manage your stress and anger is through the use of mantras. A mantra is a specific thought or phrase that you have for yourself. It is a word or phrase that you are able to repeat to yourself over and over again to allow yourself to begin to unwind. It allows you to develop the ability to better cope with the stressors that you are handling. It makes sure that you are capable of reminding yourself that you need to stay in control. It ensures that you are able to release the tension that you have and the anger that you are feeling. The mantras that you repeat are ways to control your thoughts. They direct your mental energy to somewhere that you know that you can trust and rely on. They allow you to see the ways in which you can better regulate yourself and in regulating yourself better than ever before, you find that you are more capable of controlling yourself. You discover that, at the end of the day, you can mitigate the stressors in your life.

Your mantra can be anything for you. They redirect your attention elsewhere. They encourage your mind to think clearer and they ensure that your focus is kept exactly where you want it. When you deal with anger, you need to be able to accept that you are feeling what you are feeling, and sometimes, those mantras can really help you. There many different ones that work for various people. For some, it is something as simple as, "Let it go." Or "Inner peace." Other people may get a bit more ambitious about it and begin to add in other aspects as well. Some people may, for example, take time to craft the perfect mantra for them. They may take a look at the ways in which they are going to be able to best defeat whatever the feelings that they have are.

"I have peace within me that this anger will not challenge."

"I am in perfect control of my reactions."

"I am strong enough to resist the stress that I feel."

"I will let go of this anger."

Release Physical Tension

Another way that you can really help your mind release the anger that you are feeling is through making sure that you slowly but surely release the physical tension within yourself. When you are to release the tension that you are holding within yourself, you are usually able to do so in many different ways. You can, for example, work with yourself to make sure that you do release all of that tension that you are feeling at any point in time. It is important for you to feel like you can, at the end of the day, really relax, little by little.

To release physical tension, there is a very simple trick that you can remember. The next time that you need to get yourself to relax, stop and take a deep breath. Feel the tension in one of your body parts. It could be that you feel it in your legs or your shoulders or your jaws, or anywhere else. Take a deep breath and let yourself tense up that area even more than it was before. Hold onto that tension tightly for a few moments, and then suddenly release it entirely. Let it all and feel the way in which your body part feels when you release it. By forcing the point, you can help yourself develop the ability to manually loosen up your muscles, little by little.

Deep Breathing

One of the greatest ways that you can take control of your anger is through developing the ability to breathe. When you breathe, you are sort of powering the way that your entire body works. You are taking control of the way that your body regulates itself. It allows your body to slow itself down, or speed itself up. To change your breathing is just one of the many ways in which you are able to better deal with the world. Your breath is one of the first parts of your body that changes in direct response to any sort of stress that it feels. When you are stressed out about something, your body make an attempt to deal with it. It increases your heart rate, which then in turn speeds up your breathing. This is normal and natural—it happens because you are better prepared to run and to react to stressors that have been deemed a threat when your body's heart is racing and you are breathing heavily to give yourself more oxygen.

Of course, the opposite holds true as well; when you breathe deeply, you can start to slow down your body as well. You can help your body begin to unwind and let go of the stress that it clings to all by ensuring that you breathe deeply. When you breathe deeply, you trigger what is known as a vasovagal response. This means that your body is responding by lowering your heart rate and it is also ensuring that your breathing slows down as well. That is the power of your deep breathing.

The best breathing patterns that you can use will make sure that your breathing is slowed down, regulated out, and relaxed. It requires you to make sure that you remember to keep yourself calmer. It reminds you to slowly and carefully breathe deeply and as you do so, you will feel your body unwind.

Then next time that you are attempting to calm yourself down or get your anger out of your system, try taking a deep, slow breath. Inhale deeply and slowly from your nose for at least five seconds. As you breathe, really focus on the sensations that pass through your body. Then, slowly and surely breathe out of your mouth with the same count of five. That is all you have to do. You simply repeat the breathing exercise and continue to use it, over and over again until you feel calm.

9 / UNDERSTANDING YOUR
TRIGGERS

ANGER RARELY HAPPENS IN A VACUUM; when you are angry, usually, something has triggered it. Typically, these triggers are thoughts that you have in your mind and they almost always are rooted in some sort of negative thinking pattern that needs to be defeated. Until you can defeat that negative thought pattern, whatever the source of your anger is will continue to plague you, over and over again. You must be able to separate yourself out from these emotional triggers so you can then defeat your anger.

By learning what your triggers are, you can then begin to see the ways in which you are likely to react. You will be able to see how, when you act in a certain way, you will be more likely to behave in others. You will see that shift between how you behave, what you do, and why you do it that will guide you. When you learn to recognize what your triggers are, you can begin to catch the patterns in your behavior before they can be triggered. When you can figure out the way that you will behave before it happens, you can then take the steps necessary to ensure that you can prevent it.

. . .

We are going to be addressing these triggers within this chapter. You will be guided through the ways in which you can better understand your own behaviors. You will see what there is that you can do to help yourself to succeed. At the end of the day, you need to be able to keep control of yourself, and in learning your triggers, you can then begin to defeat them.

What Are Triggers?

Before we begin, let's take a look at what triggers are. They are the actions or behaviors that happen around you that are likely to make you angry. They will set you off. They will make the situation that you are in worse and worse. As you are triggered by something into anger, your anger then begins to cause problems. You suddenly fly off into a rage and most people are left not knowing what they did to cause it or how they can fix it. However, one thing is certain: When you know what your triggers are, you are better able to help yourself. You are better able to ensure that you can, at the end of the day, prevent your anger from worsening.

Keep in mind that triggers are quite different from person to person. They vary greatly from individual to individual and because of that, they can be incredibly unpredictable. Some people may be very quick to anger over the way that they are treated. Others may respond poorly to the words that are used with them. Others still may find that they struggle the most with other aspects, such as the idea of being wrong, of being vulnerable, or of anything else.

. . .

Why Triggers Matter

When you are triggered, your brain is shifting right back into your primitive activation. Instead of being able to stop yourself from continuing to struggle, you will find that you are stuck. However, if you can see that a trigger is coming, you can stop it. You can preemptively prevent it from becoming an issue. When you can anticipate that you are likely to be angered by something, you know that you can stop yourself. You can begin to predict your response, and in being able to predict that anger that you have. In being able to predict the anger, you can talk yourself out of it. Think of how, when you stand on a boat and you can see a wave coming that will rock it, you can sort of brace yourself. You can keep yourself from struggling and falling over because you can correct for it. Very similarly, you can do that with your anger as well. You can teach yourself how best to deal with the frustrations at hand, which means that you will then be able to better keep yourself from losing that emotional footing, which would be a lack of emotional control.

When you make sure that you control yourself and your mind, as well as your body, you can begin to tame that anger. You can ensure that the response that you have is one that is considered acceptable. You choose a response that you can use to protect yourself; it is one that you can use to ensure that, at the end of the day, you *are* able to cope with the stress. You can choose a response that you know *will* protect you. You will develop that self-control to maintain your own composure, allowing you to protect yourself and respond in ways that are practical.

Common Anger Triggers

People everywhere can have very different anger triggers, and there are some people whose triggers you would see as entirely absurd, or even as something that seems not to make any sense. No matter what the trigger is that you are considering, remember this; the person that is triggered is validated in feeling the way that they do. Just the fact that they have those emotions in the first place means that they are valid and you cannot just shift them off as anything else.

Some of the most common triggers, however, include:

- Feeling wronged or like the situation is inherently unfair
- Feeling disrespected or like someone is mocking you
- Feeling threatened or like someone has invaded your personal space
- Being subjected to abusive name-calling or other language
- Being blamed for something or shamed for something
- Being threatened overtly, physically or otherwise
- Being insulted
- Being lied to or mislead
- Fighting within a relationship
- Being regularly disappointed due to carelessness or something else that is a problem
- Being out of control in that particular situation or feeling like you want or need a control that you do not have

Identifying Your Triggers

Identifying your own triggers is a relatively simple process. All you have to do to identify your own triggers is to remind yourself that you must sit back and consider the ways in which you respond to the world. It requires a degree of self-awareness and focus that will help guide you. When you are trying to find that cause of your own anger, it is very important that you stop and you focus on the fact that it could be anything—but at the root of it all, it is likely on you. It is how you perceive the situation that becomes your trigger. It is the way that you respond that becomes the problem here. It is what you chose to do and how you choose to do it that really matters at the end of the day.

To identify your own trigger, you must stop and consider the last time that you felt angry. What triggered it? What led to it? How can you control it? What can you do this time that will protect yourself or ensure that, at the end of the day, you are not left vulnerable? There are all sorts of ways that you can make sure that you are able to protect yourself; it is simply a matter of figuring out which is the right one for you.

The next time that you are angry, when you realize it after the fact, ask yourself what happened. What was going on? Who upset you? Why were you upset? How can you protect yourself from being that upset again in the future? What are the thoughts that were going through your mind? If you can consider these, you will likely find that the trigger itself has to do with the list that was provided.

Now, at this point, you may be feeling pretty confident in where you are. You can recognize what it is that is bothering you and you can see how you can change the approach that you must take to ensure that, at the end of the day, you do succeed. You can approach the fact that ultimately, you are in control of yourself. However, without making sure that you admit some very important truths, you are not going to be able to manage that anger.

This chapter is all about recognizing those five steps that will bring you anger management. When you can follow these five steps, you will be able to identify that you are angry and then begin to take control of it, little by little. When you are able to make use of these methods, you will find that you are better able to respond to the world around you. You may find that, for example, what you really need to do is make sure that you are better responding to the world around you. You may find that what you need to do is stop and take control. You may find that there are all sorts of problems weighing over you; you simply need to stop and figure out which ones are relevant here and which ones you can defeat. When you can defeat your anger through these five steps, you know that, at the end of the day, you will succeed. You know that, at the end of the day, you can do better. You know that you will be able to maintain your composure, no matter what happens because you will understand what you are doing.

Admitting Your Anger

The first step to managing your anger is to admit that it is there. You may find that what works best for you is that you admit it to yourself. You may tell yourself, within your mind or out loud, that you know that you are angry. You may find that you work better by telling someone else that you are angry instead. Sometimes the sheer relief that you get for labeling your anger and then telling someone else how you are feeling is enough to help yourself to succeed in containing those feelings. Sometimes, that is enough for you to manage to control yourself and the emotions that you are carrying.

When you are able to admit that you are angry, you do two things: You not only own that anger yourself, allowing yourself to better deal with the stressors at hand. You may find that you are better off figuring out what it is that you need to do that will actually begin to help yourself. In labeling those emotions, in recognizing the power that they have and the gravity of the situation, you can oftentimes find that you can actually completely and entirely take yourself away from the situation.

Believing You Can Control Your Anger

Then, you must also be willing and able to believe that you can control your anger. This is critical- if you do not trust that you can control your anger, then you run the risk of that anger controlling you. The more that you believe that you cannot control that anger, the less likely you are to be able to actually make it happen. It may be that, for example, as you continue to try to provide that anger control for yourself, that you are actually self-sabotaging—instead of believing that you can solve that problem, you focus instead on the fact that you *cannot* solve the problem.

If you do not think that you can control the anger that you have, there is a great chance that you will simply not be able to. At every step along the way, you will likely find that you resist yourself. You do not listen to what your body and mind have to say. You refuse to acknowledge the differences or the ways in which you can protect yourself. You tell yourself that you are not strong enough to control your anger, and because you believe that, you will simply fail to ever gain that control.

At the end of the day, your own beliefs will rule everything. At the end of the day, you must be willing and able to state that you can, in fact, control your anger. You can only do this, however, if you believe it. If you do not believe that you can, why not? What is it that is holding you back? What makes you so thoroughly doubt that you can ever contain your anger? Why would you never be able to defend yourself or help correct the feelings that you are having? There has to be some reason that is guiding you; there is always a reason that you are either unwilling or unable to better deal with everything that you are doing. Find the underlying hesitation that you have and begin to correct it.

. . .

Repeat this to yourself:

"I can control my anger."

"I am in complete control of myself and how I respond to the world."

"I can ensure that I am controlling my own emotions so they do not overwhelm me."

Calming Down

The third step in the process is triggering that calming down. This is the point in which you see your anger; you feel it surrounding you and you must be able to fight it off. Calming down typically involves exercises such as deep breathing, guided meditations, or other methods that you can use to help yourself calmly and quietly return back to your own mind without disturbances or distractions. When you are able to quietly return back to your mind, you can remind yourself of something—you can remind yourself that, at the end of the day, you can better take care of yourself.

If for you, crying is what you need to do, then do it. If you are better off with deep breathing exercises as you count to ten, or any other methods, that is fine as well. The calming methods that you choose to use are ultimately the ones that will work best for you. You must be willing and able to make use of these methods if you hope to really succeed with what is going on. You must be willing and able to accept any methods that you need to help yourself calm down, short of hurting yourself or others. So long as you are not inflicting any sort of harm with what you are doing, you can use it as a coping method.

Problem Solving

The fourth step of problem-solving is one that, at this point, you would be at least somewhat familiar with. At this point, you are taking a look at the ways in which you are better able to keep your own problems under control. You can usually do this through the methods that you use to protect yourself. When you ensure that, at the end of the day, you have those problem-solving skills in your back pocket, you know that you can begin to alleviate the problem.

It is very important to note that this stage does not occur until after the fact. This step occurs after you have begun to calm yourself down and after you have figured out how best to stop the anxiety or anger that caused the problem in the first place. When you enter this stage with a calm mind, you have the potential for great, quiet, productive meditations that can really help ensure that, at the end of the day, you do what you need to do.

This step should never be foregone; you should make sure that, upon reaching that state of calmness, you stop and figure out what went wrong. Why were you angry in the first place? How can you solve those problems in the future? What can you do to prevent these problems from getting worse and worse? Is it possible for you to better cope with the situations at hand? Is it possible for you to better deal with the fact that, at the end of the day, you better solve problems?

Articulate Yourself

Finally, that last step in the anger management program is to ensure that you articulate yourself clearly and effectively. You must be able to point out exactly what it is that you need when you need it. When you can do that, you can figure out the best way to get your own point across. Oftentimes, there is some degree of miscommunication that occurs when anger has been triggered. It is quite typical that the anger is actually related to many other aspects instead. It is very common for people to feel like they were not heard, but in reality, the real problem was actually that there was a lack of articulation in the first place.

Being able to articulate your elf is to be able to clearly tell other people what you need, assertively and respectfully. When you can articulate what is going on with you or with your own mind, you can usually allow yourself to better deal with the emotions that are plaguing you. When you can articulate yourself, other people will listen, and as they continue to listen to you, you find yourself feeling more validated. You find yourself feeling much more like you can succeed. You find yourself feeling like, at the end of the day, you can get what you need, no matter what it is, because you know how to ask for it in ways that other people understand and relate to.

11 / ANGER MANAGEMENT AND SELF-REGULATION

EMOTIONAL SELF-REGULATION IS one of those life skills that every functional adult needs. In order to be a functional individual, you must also be able to self-regulate yourself. You must be able to see how you are feeling, understand the ways in which your behaviors may be harmful or destructive, and then allow yourself to step away from them. When you can do this on a regular basis, you can usually begin to defeat the process. You can begin to figure out how you will be able to alter your own reactions to the world around you because you need to. You will be able to change the way in which you interact, knowing that at the very least, you will be able to control the way that you feel. You will be able to see when your emotions may begin to run a little high, and when that does happen, you can remind yourself that, at the end of the day, you need to slow down. You can remind yourself that you must slow down and calm down to better cope with the situation at hand.

Self-regulation is something that you begin learning in childhood. You learn it early on, when you start aging out of tantrums.

Think about it: A two-year-old that gets told that he cannot have a cookie will probably cry, yell, and scream while flailing on the ground in a tantrum. However, a three or four-year-old might pout, but they will be much less likely to have such an emotional reaction. This is because the children that are older have that degree of self-control. They have that sense of self-awareness and self-regulation that they need to know that they may feel bad, but they cannot simply respond in any way that they want to. They know that, even though they are feeling badly, they can better cope with the situation at hand. They know that if they are struggling, they can better deal with everything that they have to deal with, all because of the way in which it is functioning for them.

When you have the self-regulation skills that you need to thrive within yourself, you know how you can control yourself. You learn to keep your temper in check. It is essentially everything that you need to develop within this book, all summed up into one little phrase. However, self-regulation itself is not difficult or hard to manage. It is not something that is going to be difficult to use. It is as simple as being able to stop and pause before you do something. It is as simple as ensuring that, at the end of the day, you pause before you act so you know that you are better able to cope with the situation at hand. When you are able to make use of these processes, when you know that what you are doing is something that will work for you, you will find that the control becomes easier. You will find that it quickly, like any skill that you work on, becomes something that you can manage easily and readily.

Self-regulation does not need to be something that is difficult. It is not something that has to hold you back or become an impossibility. It does not have to stress you out unnecessarily. All you have to do is acknowledge this point: Every person, no matter the situation that they are in, can control something. Every person, no matter the situation, can control themselves. You will always have the opportunity to control who you are, what you are doing, and how you choose to respond in any situation. Being able to honor that is incredibly important; it is very important to recognize that, no matter what happens around you, you have several choices and the choices that you make will matter greatly.

When it comes right down to it, when you are in a situation, you can break down what is available for you to do into one of three actions. You can approach the situation closer—you can choose to continue to interact with the situation and ensure that you are better making sure that you do follow what you need. You can avoid the situation entirely, withdrawing from the situation. You can do this by trying to retreat somehow, either physically leaving the situation or emotionally removing yourself. Finally, you can make use of an attack—this may not be a method that is highly recommended, but it is an option when it comes to how you respond. When you make use of an attack over the other forms of action, you get angry. You lash out. You try to hurt people.

With self-regulation, you learn how you can choose your actions yourself. You learn how you can sway the way in which you align yourself. You know that you are going to be taking the time that you need to ensure that you are aligned one way or another, and if not, you are going to be able to stop yourself from continuing to struggle. At the end of the day, you must make sure that you take the right step toward the right action plan. You must make sure that you choose the actions that are going to be facilitative to the results that you want.

To develop your own self-regulation, you begin to choose the methods that you need. You begin to see the ways that your body responds. You realize that the way that you move can begin to tell you what is about to happen. You learn to stop and pay attention to those little cues that you have; those subtle signs that you are going to lean one way or another with the way in which you respond and the more that you get caught up in this, the more likely that it is that you will continue to struggle.

One of the greatest methods that you can use to control yourself is the use of mindfulness. Mindfulness is the act of taking a quiet analysis of how you are doing in that particular moment. You assess your body's current state, latching onto the feelings that you have, the ways that you behave, and what you hope to see happen. As you do this, you teach yourself something important—that you can control the way in which you control yourself.

To engage in mindfulness, you need to stop yourself and quietly pay attention to your body. You need to quietly go over the feelings that you have, from your head to your toes and everywhere in between. As you do so, you catch onto those small feelings that you needed to identify. You realize that the way in which you behave greatly influences how well you can better deal with the world around you.

To develop your own mindfulness to use as a self-regulatory tool, try taking a few moments of quiet breathing. Starting at your head, work your way down your body, little by little. What are you feeling? How are you holding yourself? Is anything standing out? What does your current body language tell you? Is it possible that your body language is implying that you are angry? If so, you may genuinely be angry and that is okay.

Learn to read the signs of your body that it gives out. If the body language given out by your body right now says that you are angry, you may genuinely be angry. If it says that you are calm or relaxed, that is fine too; the most important takeaway point here is that your own ability to better cope with the situation at hand is powerful. Your own ability to deal with the stressors at hand is great. Your ability to calm yourself down, using these cues as your sort of way to check whether or not you are feeling okay is powerful. All you have to do is ensure that, at the end of the day, you are following along with what you need to do.

12 / ANGER MANAGEMENT AND
COGNITIVE RESTRUCTURING

YOUR BRAIN IS a vast expanse of wiring. It is little more than a vast map of endless connections that all come together. They all send electrical impulses throughout the entirety of the brain, processing the thoughts within it and becoming aware of the ways in which it works. The process of the mind is a particularly complex one from the standpoint of science; it is there to allow for endless control over the body. It allows you to think. It allows you to feel. However, your mind is absolutely a creature of habit. The creature of habit within you is one that will constantly work as hard as it can to provide itself with whatever it is that it thinks you need. It will do this through sheer repetition. It will do this by drawing on background information and creating judgments for itself. It will figure out how best to figure out what it is that it should be doing and it will make it happen.

Unfortunately, this is a very easy concept to take advantage of. It is very easy for this to be exploited, and because it functions with these habits within itself, it is better able to regulate itself. It falls into habits that re sometimes problematic, such as one in which your default response to being questioned about something becomes an emotional trigger for you. Instead of seeing the validity in asking you what you thought or if you were sure about something, you take it as a threat and that can trigger you into anger.

Cognitive restructuring teaches you to go in, change up the wiring, and get out without disturbing anything if at all possible. It is there to convince your mind that there are other ways to behave. It changes the ways that you feel by altering the thoughts that you have about the world around you.

When you make use of cognitive restructuring, you are looking for ways in which you can change the thoughts within your mind to become something that is more manageable. You are looking for solutions within yourself that will help you to figure out the best ways in which you can interact. You are looking for methods that you can use to aid yourself.

Cognitive restructuring ultimately works for several reasons, but they all boil down to one: You break free from your negative thought patterns and that freedom is what gives you power.

When you take a look at cognitive restructuring, you will see that there are several benefits that make it work. It allows you to get organized mentally-- you feel like you know what you are doing better because you have a sort of working tally of what is going on in your mind. You have to slow down because you are busily focusing on the information that you can get about yourself. You are looking to see if the emotional levels that you are feeling make sense given the current situation or if you seem to be overreacting.

Cognitive restructuring can be broken down into six steps that you need to follow to help you begin to rewrite that narrative in your brain. If you can follow these six steps, you will find that you are able to better cope with the situation at hand. You will be able to change the underlying thoughts that guide everything that you need to do.

Step 1: Pause

The first step is to pause. As soon as you feel the feeling of negativity that you need to change, which is likely anger in this particular situation, you must stop yourself. Pause and look at the situation around you. What is going on? How can you change what is happening? What can you do to better cope with the situation at hand? If you can stop and inhibit the response that you have—that negativity must be identified and studied. What can you learn from it? How can you make it work for you? How can you ensure that, when you do feel negatively, you do not make a mistake with your behaviors?

The best way to get yourself to pause is to identify an emotion, particularly a strong one, and have that be your sort of cue—that emotion would remind you that you need to change the way in which you interact at that point in time. If you can ensure that you change your reaction accordingly, you should be able to fix the problem over time.

. . .

Step 2: Identify the Trigger

As soon as you have paused, you must stop and look for the trigger. What is it that is causing you to feel as bad as you do? Typically, you have been triggered by something and you need to identify what that trigger is so you know what you need to do to succeed in quelling your anger later on. Remind yourself to stop and look at your environment in the moment. What is going on around you? Who is with you at this point in time? What is going on? When did the feelings of upset begin? Where did everything happen around you?

Put all of this together and analyze the situation until you can figure out what is going on. Where is the stressor that is impacting you? Can you defeat it?

Step 3: Notice the Automatic Thought

The next step is to identify what the automatic thought is that is underlying that trigger. They are typically spontaneous thoughts that we use as default judgments of the world around us. They are typically built up over time with you looking at the ways in which you have experienced the world. Essentially, your mind will build up this sort of stereotype to embrace what is going on. It will look at the situation and declare that the situation is strange or unusual. These are little more than snap judgments that your body has made and you can learn to defeat them. These judgments are made to help protect you. Your automatic thoughts are typically reactionary.

. . .

For example, imagine that you are sitting at your desk, late at night while you are reading a book or having fun by yourself. You hear your phone vibrate and you see that it is your boss, texting you late at night. Your immediate automatic thought is that you are in trouble because your boss never stops to text you, and when they do bother to text you, it is never this late.

Other automatic thoughts can be more detrimental as well. Sometimes, they are thoughts that wonder whether or not you can do anything right. Sometimes, the thoughts that you have are to question yourself and your surroundings. They may question the way that you interact and the way in which you are able to fix the problem.

The sooner that you begin to identify those underlying thoughts, the ones that arise entirely unbidden within your mind, the sooner you can begin to defeat the negativity that is holding you back.

Step 4: Identify Your Reaction

The next step to remember is that you must begin to identify what the reaction to that trigger was. How did you respond practically speaking? What did you do with your behaviors? How did you change the way that you responded? What can you do with yourself to ensure that you do properly cope with everything?

You need to look at the way that you are feeling so you can then begin to create alternative ways of looking at the situation entirely. If you are currently angry that someone questioned you, for example, your automatic thought would likely have been something along the lines of wondering why everyone around you thinks that you are so stupid. You then take that thought that gets stuck in your head and you work to try to eliminate it. You try to remove it from your thought processes, but you can only do so if you can identify the original thought and the feelings.

Step 5: Create Alternative Thoughts

When you understand what your default reaction is when you are upset or frustrated, you can then begin to shift the way that you think into something more productive. You can ensure that, at the end of the day, you do think a bit easier and more positively just through the alternative thoughts that you create. Perhaps, instead of feeling like everyone thinks that you are stupid, you could say that they are questioning you and making sure that you double-checked, not because they think that you are dumb, but rather because they want to be able to be sure that everything that you are doing in the moment is correct and done properly.

The idea here is that your alternative thoughts should be there to sort of mitigate the damage so to speak. The thoughts are there so you can better control the way in which you can interact with the world around you. When you are better able to see the ways in which you can interact with the world, you can begin to tackle just about anything. You create a new thought that you will remind yourself of. Every time that you find that you have that feeling of anger or that feeling of struggling, you can then begin to remind yourself of that new thought.

. . .

If you were to do this, you could remind yourself that there is no reason for you to have that negative thought. There is no reason that you should let that negativity grind you down and hold you back. Rather, you should be working to ensure that, at the very least, you can focus on the way that you are thinking now.

Take that negative thought and the cue that negativity to something that you can control. In particular, you should turn it into something more positive that you know will actually benefit you. Instead of thinking that the people around you are causing problems for you, remind yourself that you are lucky that you have friends that care enough to bring you this positivity in the first place. Remind yourself that, at the end of the day, you are incredibly lucky to have someone that cares enough to ask about you, what you are doing, and make sure that the way that you are currently behaving actually works.

For any one negative thought that you have, you should have at least two or three ways that you can counter it. These are the messages that you can tell yourself; they are the ways in which you can retrain your brain to think, little by little. You should be able to ensure that your thinking can be corrected no matter what. Any time that you find those negative thoughts are in your mind, it is time to drown them out with the positive ones.

Step 6: Reassess

Finally, after reiterating those positive thoughts in the moment, and after reminding yourself in the moment that you should be thinking positively, it is time to reassess the situation.

How can the way that you have shifted your thoughts help you change your mindset? How do you feel now after reiterating that positive mindset? How has it helped you to figure out what you are doing, how you should be doing it, and why it matters? Make sure that you have the time and energy to spend going over the way in which these corrected thoughts helps you. If you find that you feel better than ever through the use of these thoughts, then great! It is working for you! If not, however, you need to consider what is going on and why the problem is there in the first place.

If your own corrected thoughts do little to alleviate the problems that you have in the moment, there is a chance that there is more to the story. There is a chance that you are not yet addressing the right positive thought. There is the possibility that you have not yet gotten to the root of the problem and that means that you have to keep digging deeper. Keep looking for the source of the problem so you can then begin to correct it entirely to ensure that, at the end of the day, you are doing better for yourself.

13 / ANGER MANAGEMENT AND EMOTIONAL INTELLIGENCE

EMOTIONAL INTELLIGENCE and anger management go hand in hand. Emotional intelligence is the ability in which you are able to understand and alter your own emotions while also understanding the way in which your own emotions influence other people around you as well. It is essentially the ability to understand people—it is your people skill competency, and if you are not particularly good at managing your anger, you likely also struggle in emotional intelligence which is also an incredibly important skill to remember as well.

When it comes down to success in life, professional, personal, or otherwise, the most important skill that you can have is emotional intelligence, which happens to encompass anger management. What emotional intelligence does for you, however, is that it provides you with the fundamental information that you would need to know and understand to be able to properly handle the ways in which you interact with the people around you. When you make use of these methods, you note that, at the end of the day, your ability to interact with other people improves dramatically.

Emotional intelligence is made up primarily of four key points that you must remember:

- **Self-awareness:** This is your ability to understand your own emotional state at any point in time. You are able to sit down and understand where something leaves you and how you feel at any point in time. You are able to stop and listen to your own mind and understand what is happening within it. This encompasses your ability to understand when you are angry and why you are angry so you can better understand what is going on with yourself.

- **Self-regulation:** This is the skill that we have already been introduced to—it is the ability to be able to regulate your own emotions at any point in time to control yourself. This would encompass anger management skills.

- **Social awareness:** This is your ability to understand what is going on with other people. It is being able to look at how what you do with your own actions and behaviors and recognizing that your own actions and behaviors directly impact other people as well and that you must be willing and able to recognize that point. When you cannot recognize that your own emotions impact other people negatively, you run into other problems as well.

- **Relationship management:** This is your ability to influence other people; it is the ability to be charismatic and trustworthy on your own without feeling like you have to do anything at all. It allows yourself to be able to recognize the way in which you are able to interact with other people in order to get them to do things for you.

All four of these come together to become an emotionally intelligent individual that is capable of success. When you become emotionally intelligent yourself, you teach yourself everything that you will need to do and become in order to allow yourself to move forward. If you want to be able to see the ways in which you can succeed with your relationships, you need to have the emotional wherewithal to do so, and emotional intelligence can help you.

When you have developed your own emotional intelligence, you become capable of so much more than you were before. You become capable of succeeding when you interact with other people. You learn how you can communicate to get others to do just about anything that you possibly want them to do. You can get people to give you just about anything that you want, all because you are willing and able to learn how to interact. You can become persuasive. You can become well-liked. Above all, you become emotionally regulated.

Emotional intelligence teaches you to have a balanced view. It teaches you to stop and step back when it comes to how your emotions are making you feel. It requires you to stop what you are doing and think about the way in which you are going to interact with the people in your household or in your social circles. It makes you contemplate whether or not the ways that you are attempting to behave are actually appropriate or beneficial. You learn to control your anger. You learn to hone your emotions, remembering what you need to do to be able to completely control the emotions that you are under. When you can do this, you can succeed with ease.

If you think that you could benefit from emotional intelligence, the good news is that most of the techniques that we have talked about within this book already will naturally aid in it. The vast majority of what you have been learning about throughout all of this time is actually closely related to the art of emotional intelligence. However, it may be worthwhile for you to stop and take the time to read a book or two about emotional intelligence as well to help develop better understandings of what is going on, how you can stop and think about the world around you and what it is that you need to know.

Consider talking to people that you would deem to be emotionally intelligent yourself. See if you can find a good friend or family member that you know is great at keeping their own emotions together. Talk to them. What can they do for you? What can they do to keep you engaged in what is going on and ensuring that, at the end of the day, you will be able to better process everything that is going on? You can learn considerably from what other people around you have to say and if you can learn to recognize that, you can truly learn everything that you need to know. You can develop the mindset that you need to become emotionally intelligent, ensuring that you are driven intrinsically rather than extrinsically. You can become someone that is great at respecting other people and their inherent value as people rather than attempting to step on everyone else. You can learn to tame your anger and ensure that your emotions do not get the best of you. All you have to do is take the time to build up your own emotional intelligence.

COMMUNICATION IS fundamental in any relationship. Whether you communicate with a loved one on a regular basis, a strange at the grocery store, or even your pet dog, communication happens everywhere. However, despite the fact that communication is something that we all use on a daily basis, it can be very easy to miscommunicate. It is all too common that people get into arguments or they find that tensions are rising because no one can communicate within the group. The lack of communication can really only make the problem worse as well as tensions continue to rise, little by little, making the situation worse.

Of course, that leads to the perfect breeding grounds for stress, arguments, and anger. Anger is our response when we feel misunderstood, meaning that struggling to communicate effectively can actually just make the situation worse if you are not careful. You need to be able to stop yourself, to recognize the ways in which you need to communicate with those around you, and then, really commit yourself to doing so. If you can make that happen, you will be able to communicate better and in communicating better, you can alleviate the anxiety and anger that go along with those miscommunications that you may have in the first place. Within this chapter, we are going to go over some of the most important ways that you must remember to communicate, especially when you are angry. These methods will allow yourself to keep a positive focus. They will enable you to better deal with the way that you feel in the middle of a conflict and can really help yourself to calm down and articulate yourself in a way that you can be heard.

"I" Phrases to Avoid Blame

When it comes down to talking about something where tensions are already on the rise, one of the easiest ways that you can shut down all communication is incredibly simple—you just have to say, "You," and mean it in a blaming manner. If you were to say, "Well, *you* didn't take the dog out this morning!" as a point of contention in complaining about cleaning up the accident in front of the door, you are immediately putting the other person on the defensive. As they go onto the defensive, you immediately see a spike in the tension. You need to be able to avoid that entirely by trying to avoid blame in the first place.

Rather than trying to talk about the other person, or blaming them for anything, including your own feelings, make sure that you phrase your points with "I" and "I feel..." When you do that, you are able to ensure that you can better communicate. You do not shut down the other person. You do not make them feel attacked and as a result, you do not risk making the situation worse.

. . .

This can be difficult, especially when you are already angry at that point in time, but remember, adding fuel to the fire is not going to help anyone or fix anything. You are better off trying to stay civil and trying to fix the problem.

Calm Tones

Next, make sure that you remember to keep your voice down, especially when you are angry. Make sure that you take a deep breath if you feel yourself getting heated and focus on carefully keeping your voice down. We all want to yell sometimes, especially when we are mad. We all want to fight back and defend ourselves when we do not agree with what the other person is saying. We all want to have this way in which we can force our own point, and sometimes, we defer to yelling as the manner to make this happen. Some people yell in hopes of it meaning that they will be heard better.

However, if you are in an argument with someone and one of you starts yelling, one of two things will happen: The person being yelled at will shut down entirely, meaning that any meaningful communication that you were aiming for is gone, or that person is going to start yelling back as well. Either way, you are not communicating effectively and you will not be able to get to the root of your problems like this. You need to be able to figure out how you can actually have a normal conversation, even if you do not actually want to have that conversation in the first place. You need to ensure that there is actually communication happening rather than attempts at talking to each other where no one hears a thing.

. . .

Watch the Body Language

A lot of people seem to forget that the vast majority of the communication that we do as people is through nonverbal means. We communicate heavily with the ways that we move our bodies. The way that we shift from foot to foot, or the way that we cross our arms can say a thousand things that we are actually avoiding talking about, and yet so often, people forget to listen to it.

Of course, that means that people also forget about it when it comes to their communication with other people as well. You need to remember that, at the end of the day, the best way to communicate with people is to ensure that you have open body language. This means that you should not be coming across as threatening, even if you are angry. Arms should not be crossed.

Instead, try thinking about ways to open up your body language. Make gentle eye contact—this means that you break it every now and then. Make sure that you are ensuring that, as you speak to those around you, you appear to be open by making sure that you do not put anything in front of yourself. This naturally shifts the interaction into one that is far more open than the ones before it.

Stick to the Topic at Hand

When you are already airing your grievance about something, it can be very tempting to begin trying to load more into the argument as well. You tell your partner that they forgot to take the dog, but then you are suddenly arguing about other aspects as well. You complain that they left their cup on the counter, and that their socks are currently strewn across the floor. You mention that on top of that, you have other problems as well; you point out how there is a major problem with just about everything that you are talking about and suddenly, your attempt to come to some sort of agreement has become a contest of who can blame the other person for more annoying things at one time. When this happens, you run into problems—you see that there is a lot going on there that is inherently problematic.

Instead, pay attention only to the topic that is relevant at that moment. If it does not matter right that moment to what you are saying exactly then, then leave it out of the conversation. This keeps you from setting the other person off into what would probably just become an endless standoff in which you both blamed each other incessantly for everything that you believed was going wrong with the other person.

Pick Your Battles

Finally, the last point for you to remember is that you must pick your battles. This means that, at the end of the day, you cannot simply dive in head-first to each and every problem that you have with the current situation. You must be mindful of the ways in which you feel about the people that you are interacting with. You must be mindful to remember that, sometimes, it is simply not worth the effort to put up that fight. Sometimes, it truly does not matter enough to bring up those problems because, at the end of the day, you will not be doing anything about them anyway. Rather than dig up a problem that you do not particularly care about in the first place, you decide to let it go. This is essential when it comes to communication when you are trying to manage your anger, and when you can let go of those battles that you once would have vehemently stood behind, you know that you have achieved what you set out to do. You know that, at the end of the day, your desire to learn how to manage your anger must have been effective after all.

FINALLY, in this last chapter, we are going to go over several anger management exercises that you can use and rely on to ensure that at the end of the day, you are able to manage your expectations and your emotions readily and easily. These are simple exercises that you should take with you to help yourself. Make sure that you practice all of these methods beforehand. By taking that time ahead of time, before you actually need these exercises, you experiment with them. This allows you to better understand what is going on with you and how you can allow it to help you. You are essentially looking at it as practice; when you are already familiar with the situation, you will then be able to better cope with the situation as well.

Visualization

The first method that you can use to help yourself begin to reset your anger is through the use of visualization. This is essentially your ability to take control of the situation around you and making sure that you are able to better visualize everything. It is your ability to ensure that, at the end of the day, you can stop and relax by retreating, at least temporarily, into your mind. You are essentially going to be pulling yourself away; you are trying to figure out the best way in which you can alleviate the stress that you are in by starting to imagine that you are somewhere very calming in your mind.

This is what people mean when they say that they are going to their happy place—they are retreating deeper into their own minds so they can then begin to cope with what is going on. You must be willing and able to retreat into your own mind if it becomes necessary, but on the bright side, it makes anger go away and can actually have some great health benefits if you make use of it on the regular.

You will begin by closing your eyes. Then, you bring yourself somewhere that you have always wanted to go. It could be somewhere that is beautiful. It could be somewhere that you went for an anniversary or where you met your spouse. It could be a memory that you revisit. No matter what it is, it should be something that brings you that sensation of calmness that you will need to keep yourself feeling calm and in control. If you can make that happen, you know that you are better able to control yourself. You will retreat to this place in your mind and allow it to let you better see the future that you were hoping for. When you can keep this position in your mind, you will recognize that you see a wondrous image in front of you that you can genuinely enjoy and that can help you to eliminate the negativity.

· · ·

Walk it Off

Another way that you can try to help yourself calm down in the moment is to get up and walk away—and keep walking. In fact, any sort of exercise in the moment is a great form of stress relief. From walking to jogging to anything else that you can think of, these methods are great for you to ensure that you can begin to unwind and enjoy the comfort of your own body and mind. You can erase that negativity. You can help yourself eliminate the pain that you have suffered. You can ensure that, at the end of the day, you are better able to calm yourself down, all by tapping into your body's natural mechanisms.

Walking, yoga, running, swimming, sports, weights, hiking, and just about anything else that will get your blood pumping will readily help you greatly to discover the movements that you need and the body that you should appreciate. If you can achieve this, you can ensure that, at the end of the day, you *do* begin to defeat your anger.

Use Humor

Humor is a fantastic way that you can help yourself to eliminate tension. This is because, if you play your cards right, you can trigger yourself to laugh. When you and the other person that you are fighting with or that you are angry with are already feeling tense, this ability to rely on someone else to laugh and enjoy the situation is great at bringing you both back together. Humor is a great way to essentially restart the body. You are essentially going to restart the way in which you are going to be able to interact with the people in your life. You are looking for the methods that you can use to bring yourself a smile.

. . .

When you smile or laugh, you trigger your body to engage in positive functions. You are shifting your mind away from the negativity of your anger and into a positive, happier state. With your body laughing or smiling thanks to the humor, your mind should also begin to release the tension that you were feeling as well. In doing so, you can allow yourself to slowly alleviate that anger, releasing it and getting back to a normal, positive state of mind.

Use Your Senses

Another method that you can use to help your anger is to engage with your senses. Stop letting the negativity in the world hold you back. Let go of those feelings of stress. Remind yourself that you can pull yourself out of your mind by beginning to engage with the senses as well. Essentially, what you will do is shift away from feeling like you need to dwell entirely in your thoughts and force yourself to engage the world around you. Sometimes, that can be enough to sort of reboot your mind, breaking away from that negative feedback that anger usually provides.

This method of helping yourself to calm down is largely entirely up to the individual. It is entirely up to you how you will do this. You may decide that you want to drink your favorite tea—preferably decaffeinated to avoid the added arousal that you can get from caffeine that may only exacerbate the situation. You may find that you choose to get a massage instead, allowing yourself to calm down and relax. You may choose the method of ensuring that, at the end of the day, you better cope with the situation through the use of your senses.

. . .

Maybe you focus entirely on one of your senses for a moment. Feel the ground underneath your feet and try to describe it as much as you can. Focus on the way something around you looks, and really absorb each and every detail that it has to offer. Perhaps you listen to the sound of the clock in the room ticking as you wait for the tension to begin to melt away, or you do some combination of them all. No matter which senses that you choose to engage with, however, one thing is true; you will be able to engage in ways that will slow down that anger and frustration if you stop and make an effort to do so.

Count

Finally, one last method to take a look at is counting. This is the most efficient if you also paired it with, for example, breathing deeply as you go along. When you do this, you can allow yourself to better relax. You ensure that you are focusing on the ways that you can calm your body by making use of a quiet meditative state, so to speak. When you count, you are shifting your body from engaging in that negative emotional manner and forcing it right back into using its rational side. When you do this, you once again sort of reboot your mind, allowing you to then recognize that, at the end of the day, what is happening is actually not as big of a deal after all.

Typically, this method works best if you count down from ten. With each number that you count, you breathe in slowly and you exhale slowly before moving to the next. You force yourself to not only slow down your body when you do this, but also to slow your mind. You alleviate that tension and anger and allow yourself to calm yourself down, taming that anger that you were feeling. Use this one in the moment, when you feel like you are about to snap. It can really help you to become calmer and more capable of coping with the stressors that you have.

CONCLUSION

Congratulations! You have made it to the end of *Anger Management*. Hopefully, as you have read through this book, you have discovered all sorts of information that is beneficial to you. Hopefully, you have learned to uncover the darkness that your anger can shed over your life as you have read through this book. It is with the utmost hope that, as you did read over everything within this book, you did find that there was valuable advice within it. Hopefully, as you read over everything as it was provided, you found new insight about the process of controlling and managing your own anger. Anger is something that we all must face at some point in time, but not everyone ever develops that ability to be fully cognizant of how to manage it. At this point, you should now understand what you can do to begin to control that anger for yourself. You should be able to recognize that, at the end of the day, your ability to control the situation is just as limited as you believe that it is.

Within these pages, you were introduced to all sorts of different methods that you could use to better control yourself. You were guided through the ways in which you were able to better process the ways that you can control your own anger. You were taught how you could begin to understand the ways that your anger is something that you are capable of controlling. You have discovered the ways that you can begin to change your life, little by little, looking at your own current situations better and better.

We all know that anger is a problem to some degree. We all know that anger can be a huge problem for people and that it can be a major part of the way in which people struggle. We all know that anger is hurtful and detrimental to healthy relationships. All you have to do is ensure that, at the end of the day, you control it. That is always easier said than done; significantly so, in fact. However, if you can begin to take the steps that were provided to you within this book, you will find that you can succeed. You will see that success and your own ability to develop what you need is within grasp. All you have to do is work hard to claim it.

If what you seek is the ability to control your anger, you must remember to validate your anger. Recognize that your anger is there and it is real and that is enough to recognize the validity of it. You must accept that you feel angry and begin to look for the true source of that anger in the first place. What is there that is going on around you that frustrates you? What is it that you do not like about your anger and about how it impacts everyone around you? How can you make the changes that you need to see in your own life to better protect yourself?

You must remember to recognize the cause of your anger and how you can take that anger that you are feeling in order to redirect it. If you can redirect it toward where it belongs, toward becoming constructive with it, you can allow your anger to work for you. Remember, however, that there is a fine line between your own anger being too much and it being assertive. You must remember what an anger problem looks like.

Remember the ways in which you can manage your anger, and

the methods that are likely to work for you. Focus on each and every one as you get through this process. Remind yourself of how you can work to treat your anger. Remind yourself to acknowledge your anger. Remind yourself of those general ways that you can better yourself and manage your anger. Do not forget how you can find your triggers, and do not forget all of the exercises that you have been guided through that are designed to help you discover what you need to do, how you need to do it, and why it needs to happen in these ways.

Remind yourself of everything that you can do at the end of the day that will help you develop the ability that you need to control yourself and the world around you. If you can remember the ways in which you should treat yourself to help yourself succeed, you will be that much more likely to make it happen along the way. You must work hard. Fighting anger is not easy. It is not simple. It will take time and energy. It will take ample effort to push you further and further toward that success that you seek but at the end of the day, it will be worth it to give you that power. It will be worth it to give you that contentment.

Thank you for taking the time to make it to the end of this book. Thank you for spending the time that you have, looking through everything that has been provided for you. Hopefully, as you wrap this book up, you see that you can actually begin to control yourself. Remind yourself of everything that you can do to help yourself. See the ways in which you can better control your anger and your frustration. Discover the methods that you can use to ensure that, at the end of the day, you *can* succeed. You can do this. You can control your anger. You can learn to see what it is that you need and what you want. You can learn what it is that matters for you. You can discover the ways in which you need to behave for yourself and if you master them, you will own your own anger.

Finally, if you have found that this book has benefitted you at all—if this book has been a guiding factor that you could rely on, please feel free to head over to Amazon to leave a review behind. The reviews of the readers are always taken into consideration for next time!

DIALECTICAL
B E H A V I O R
THERAPY

DBT Guide to Managing Your Emotional Regulation,
Distress, Anxiety, Depression, with Mindfulness

Rhonda Swan

Despite the bad reputation that therapy gets, it is not something to be ashamed of. Needing a little bit of extra help to ensure that your mind is healthy is no different than needing some extra help for the body to be healthy. Think about it—no one in their right mind would ever criticize someone else for spending time trying to fix their body. Cancer treatments are not frowned upon—instead, those suffering from cancer and going through treatment are commonly called warriors or brave or strong—all because they are fighting back to bring their bodies back to healthy. They are fighting for their lives, oftentimes poisoning themselves in hopes of killing the cancer so they can survive. People do not just look at cancer patients and tell them that they need to try harder to think positively. They are not told that they can just will the cancer away. They are not told that needing to see the doctor—the medical professional that has spent years upon years trying to learn how to heal the body—makes them weak. On the contrary— they are celebrated for it.

Seeking mental health support should be looked at no differently. Whether to make sure that your thought processes are healthy or to ensure that your body is functioning properly, taking care of your health—all of it—is admirable. Whether you need treatment for your mind or your body, it is all one you. It is all a part of you, and you need both parts to be healthy. You deserve to be healthy.

Of course, it is not always that simple. Some people suffer from trauma. Some people suffer from abuse. Others are born with a difference in brain chemistry. Others still eventually develop unhealthy coping mechanisms through life experience. When something does go wrong, however, you are not stuck without any options. You are not trapped with no recourse to help you better cope with what has happened. You do not have to simply live with your suffering or struggle in silence. You can get help. You can learn how to become healthy.

This book will introduce you to one type of therapy that you can use to begin to correct you own mental health problems. You will be able to make sure that, at the end of the day, you will be able to cope with problems and stressors that come up in life. You can learn how ot manage those mental health problems that you may carry with yourself for a lifetime—but in learning to cope with them and learning to live with them, you can learn how to begin to thrive.

Dialectical behavioral therapy is a type of therapy that has been developed as a sort of subsidiary to cognitive behavioral therapy. Just like cognitive behavioral therapy, dialectical behavioral therapy (DBT) will make use of all sorts of principles that are meant to address the problem from their roots—your thoughts.

This particular therapy pushes for changes to thinking to allow you to then create positive changes to behaviors as well. It has been used for many different self-destructive behaviors, from suicidal tendencies to other sorts of disruptive choices. It will provide you with the skills that you will need and the arsenal that you will require to change those unhealthy behaviors. You are able to break that loop, allowing you to change from those negative, harmful tendencies that you may not even realize you do. You may be self-sabotaging without realizing it. You may be the cause of all of your problems without recognizing that, at the end of the day, you could take control. You can learn to cope.

This form of therapy is unique in many ways—it draws from cognitive behavioral therapy, but will bring together two distinct principles that are fundamentally opposite—you will be bringing together both acceptance and change together to allow for better coping. You will be able to work through your problems that you have. You will be able to find those harmful behaviors and make the meaningful changes that you need to see. You can get results, and you can change your life. You are not a lost cause—if you want to change, then you can.

Within this book, you will be guided through everything that you need to know to get started with dialectical behavioral therapy. You will learn what it is, how it works, and why it matters. You will learn about the components that go into making this therapy successful, as well as what can be treated with this form of therapy. Finally, you will be guided through the key steps to DBT, the ways that this sort of therapy can be mimicked at home, and the four key steps that go into using this form of therapy. You will be guided through the process of how to change your mind and be guided through the proper exercises to make it happen.

This book is not some easy cure. It is not a book that you can simply read and suddenly be better. It will not solve your problems and it cannot promise you that you will get better if you read from start to finish. The reality is, there is no easy way to cure mental health disorders. There is no easy way to fundamentally alter core beliefs that underlie everything that you do. The process is not easy at all—but no process that promises to be life-altering is easy.

If you can make use of these principles, you can learn to better cope with the world around you. Remember, you reap what you sow, and if you put in the effort, you should begin to see results. Remember that it will be difficult, but you can do this. You can come out on top because you are a fighter and you are a survivor. You can take control of your own mental health issues and become the person that you were meant to be.

DIALECTICAL BEHAVIORAL THERAPY is very powerful. We all have thoughts and feelings that underlie what we are doing. These are our core beliefs—they are beliefs about ourselves or the world around us, and they are strongly influential on how the mind responds to the world around you. Though you may feel like you are in complete control of yourself and your behaviors, this is not quite the case. You *do* get to control many of them. You can learn to change your thoughts and your behaviors to ensure that you are functioning healthily.

Within this chapter, we are going to dive right in to the process of doing so. You are going to learn what DBT is, how it works, and how effective it is at being able to change unhealthy behaviors. With this therapy, you can learn to overcome just about any negative or unhealthy behavior. You can learn to defeat those problems that would otherwise plague you or make things difficult for you.

What is Dialectical Behavioral Therapy?

Ultimately, dialectical behavioral therapy is its own sort of cognitive behavioral therapy. It is focused on taking a look at negative behaviors and then how to change those negative patterns of behavior to something positive. This is possible for one simple reason—your thoughts, your feelings, and your behaviors are all intricately linked to each other.

Your thoughts, especially the unconscious ones can influence your behaviors. If you, for example, think that you are a failure, you are going to act in ways that follow that assumption. You may not try to do something with your fullest potential because you feel like it does not matter anyway. You may feel like it does not matter—you do not need to try as hard as you could or attempt something to the best of your ability simply because you doubt that you would be able to succeed in the first place.

This is self-defeating—this sort of thought processing can be hugely detrimental to you. You cannot possibly hope to succeed if you get stuck in this mindset that you can never succeed in the first place. Those self-limiting or self-deprecating thoughts and feelings can actually become incredibly detrimental to you. They can prevent you from doing what, ultimately, you need to do. They can make you act in ways that are harmful. They can make you fail to acknowledge that, at the end of the day, you could change what you are doing. You could prevent yourself from failing if you chose to make sure that your thought processes were positive or productive.

When you use dialectical behavioral therapy, then, you are looking to defeat those strongly negative thought processes to defeat those strongly negative behaviors. This is precisely why DBT is used so regularly to manage self-destructive behaviors. It is meant to help people cope with their thoughts and feelings so they stop trying to cope in ways that are harmful.

Note that this therapy is not there to stop your mental health disorders—rather, it is there to help you cope with any that you may have. It is meant to help you learn how to better manage your negative feelings. It is meant to help you accept that, sometimes, there are things that you cannot change, but you can change how you respond to them. This idea of acceptance with change is the driving factor behind DBT that make it so incredibly effective in the first place.

Dialectical Behavioral Therapy and Cognitive Behavioral Therapy

DBT is really just a branch from cognitive behavioral therapy (CBT), and CBT itself is driven by this idea of thoughts, feelings and behaviors being intricately linked together. It takes a look at thoughts, or the cognitive, and how they impact actions, or the behavioral aspects of your life. You will see this feature heavily in this book. Your thoughts about something will ultimately greatly color how you respond to it. This is precisely why so many people will have different responses to just about anything that they address in their lives.

If you think, for example, that a giant dog that is running toward you is cute, you probably will not be very afraid of it. However, if you have this thought underlying everything that dogs are terrifying, such as a thought that may have been driven by some degree of trauma, you will probably panic if you see that same dog, which may be perfectly friendly, suddenly charging toward you. This is because your thoughts about something influence your feelings about it. Your feelings about something will then influence your behavior. While one person may readily accept a big, fluffy dog charging at them for pets and cuddles, someone else may not. The thoughts that people have can greatly change the way that your behaviors are colored.

Like CBT, DBT also takes that same goal-oriented approach to psychotherapy. It is designed to work to change patterns of thinking and patterns of behavior—it just so happens to be that most of the time, these two are intricately linked together. These two oftentimes entirely overlap with each other—just as your thoughts can influence your behaviors, your behaviors offer valuable feedback to your thoughts as well. Imagine this: You have this underlying thought that ultimately, you are incapable of acting responsibly. You feel like you are never going to be able to make the right or the responsible choice. This directly influences your behaviors—if you know that you always fail anyway, you do not see the point in resisting or the point in going through all of that necessary effort to prevent it from repeating itself. You do not see the inherent value in protecting yourself. You do not see the point in trying to fight what you take to be true, so rather than attempting to do better, you simply fall into old habits entirely. You fail because you always fail. Of course, when you do fail, however, you will only manage to reinforce that thought process. You will essentially justify to yourself that it always happens like that. You tell yourself that of course you failed—you always fail. This then makes that thought process that much more deeply ingrained in your head and that much harder to resist in the future. Rather than being able to fight it off, you are stuck. You cannot figure out how to prevent it.

This is precisely why this form of therapy seeks to eliminate that loop. It sets out to ensure that, at the end of the day, you do not just give in. It is there so you do not repeatedly do something that is going to be a problem for you. Instead of continuing to think that you are a complete and utter failure that will never manage to get anything right, you can interrupt that process. You can learn to disrupt that entire thought process, and since thoughts, behaviors, and feelings are all intricately linked together, you will be able to change them all if you can alter just one.

DBT attempts to do this as well—however, it does so in a very specific way. DBT is essentially a specific method through which you can make this happen. It is a very specific treatment plan with its own sets of tools and methods to ensure that the negative thoughts that you have are altered. It is meant to disaffirm those thoughts—it is trying to prove yourself wrong, so to speak, so you know that, at the end of the day, the thoughts that you were having are actually able to be better managed in other ways instead.

Dialectics—the Unique Aspect of Dialectical Behavioral Therapy

At the heart of DBT is the philosophical concept of dialectics. This is the most important concept that you will need to understand for this process—this concept is how the entirety of DBT is able to function as effectively as it does. It is a concept that is meant to exhibit precisely how your mind works. It is meant to show that many of the concepts that you live with, or the emotions or behavioral tendencies that you have cannot exist without the opposite. Think of it this way—you cannot have hot without having cold as well—it is only in having both hot and cold that you are able to have any temperatures at all. This sort of divide is crucial to remember in this therapy.

Imagine trying to explain colors to someone that was born blind and therefore has no concept of what it means to be colorful. What would it mean to explain to them that the sun rises and falls, changing the darkness or light in their area if they are blind and cannot see it anyway? How can you know what it means to be happy if you have no concept of the difference between happiness and sadness, or you cannot feel in the first place?

For people that have never experienced these concepts, they cannot know. You cannot know warmth if you do not know both hot and cold. You cannot know light without also knowing darkness. This is inherently the way that the human mind works. For everything there is an opposite, and without that opposite, neither would exist.

Dialectics like these are precisely how DBT is able to operate. It introduces to the people the idea that they cannot fully understand what it is that they want if they cannot appreciate that there is an opposite as well. These sorts of opposites are said to be bipolar—they exist on a spectrum between two extremes that must be managed. Despite the fact that dialectics inherently divide something into opposites, they become the most unifying concept in this entire therapy. They are there to help you begin to recognize that you must be able to appreciate all ends of something.

. . .

This works because in order to understand concepts, you must understand the opposites—however you must recognize that opposites are not entirely incompatible. They are simply different—think about it this way: When you are learning about the stock market, you are probably going to find that the best time to invest is when no one else wants to—the other people are so afraid to invest that they do not want to. However, this drives down the price, making it paradoxically the best time to invest in the first place.

You can see this in ways that are related to behaviors and mental health as well. If you are highly anxious about being a bother to other people, for example, and you decide that everyone around you would be better off if you were to attempt or commit suicide, you are inherently causing them to suffer. It may have been unintentional, but in thinking that they would be better off without you and therefore removing yourself from the equation, you inadvertently wind up making things harder on those that loved you to begin with. You tried to fix the problem for your loved ones, and by doing so, you actually just burdened them more.

This manifestation can lead to overcorrection or problems in making the situation worse. They are closely related to each other —you are afraid that your presence is a problem for people, but making your presence nonexistent is also one as well. As you can see, then, opposites can actually exacerbate a situation. You can absolutely overcorrect if you are not careful, and that is important to understand.

. . .

However, in DBT, you will be looking at one particular dialectic: The dialectic between acceptance and change. Acceptance itself is inherently related to believing that something cannot be changed. It is leaving something as is without attempting to alter it. To accept something is to recognize that it is valid or correct. In the consideration of DBT, you will be taking the definition as recognizing that it is valid. However, you must also look at changing something as well—you are recognizing that you have the power to change.

This dialectic is where you begin to see the real magic of DBT—you will be both accepting and changing yourself. You will be balancing the two, attempting to find that middle ground in which you are able to properly accept who you are. You are accepting yourself while simultaneously changing the ways that you think—usually those changes are to the ways in which you interact with yourself. They are meant to help you change the thought processes that you rely on when you are considering who you are and how you treat yourself. It is both accepting that you are worthy and changing how you treat yourself at the same time. In the instance with this therapy, it is so effective because acceptance and change become one in the same, so to speak. You change your views to accept yourself.

This may seem problematic or contradictory—you may ask how you can possibly change yourself to make you accept yourself. After all, to accept yourself is to say that you do not need to change —but if your current mindset is that of not accepting yourself, then pushing to accept yourself seems to be a contradiction on many levels. To some degree, this is true—but this is where the magic of

DBT comes into play. It is effective to act in this way, and in changing the way that you think about yourself or your situation, you can then learn to accept yourself for who you are, rather than attempting to change who you are.

The Effectiveness of Dialectical Behavioral Therapy

DBT has proven itself to be incredibly effective for people suffering from borderline personality disorder, which we will be addressing in more depth later. It has also, however, been found to be effective in many other conditions as well. It works by disrupting and altering dangerous, self-sabotaging, or self-destructive behaviors to begin to alleviate the problems that are there to begin with.

Studies have been done to attempt to identify just how effective DBT is at treating problems in the first place. In particular, there was a study done to test the effectiveness of this sort of therapy. It took a look at the brain activity before and after going through a 7-month long treatment plan that pushed DBT. Studies have shown that those suffering from borderline personality disorder (BPD) typically presented with lower levels of activity in the prefrontal cortex than those without BPD. This is significant—that is the area in the brain that allows for control over emotions and behaviors.

This study took a look at the brain scans for brain activity of 29 patients with a BPD diagnosis and active self-harming behaviors. Through a computerized activity while being scanned, the base brain activity levels were able to be recorded. These people were then studied again after a 7 month treatment session. They were asked to once again complete the same computerized task while also being monitored once more.

As a result, the people not only reported that they were not self-harming as much, they were also associated with higher levels of activity in the prefrontal cortex. This therapy not only helped in reducing self-harm, it also helped with managing to teach people how to avoid taking impulsive actions. It showed that people's literal brain activity was altered after therapy and that is incredibly important to remember. This therapy literally rewired the ways that these people's brains worked. The therapy not only helped to stop the self-harming, it also helped them to become less impulsive in general.

These results are promising—the use of DBT can actually rewire the brain. It can remove that level of impulsivity that may come with the other symptoms of your mental health struggles. It can help you learn to become better at coping with problems. It can ensure that, at the end of the day, you do better. It can teach you to avoid self-harming as much as possible. It can provide you with the power and the skills that you will need to be able to better manage yourself. It can help you achieve real, meaningful change once and for all.

Behaviors are the responses that we have to the external world, as well as to our own internal stimuli. Everything that you do is a result of your behaviors. Your behaviors can vary greatly based on thoughts, feelings, preconceptions of a situation, people that you are around, your mood, and just about everything else. Behavior is incredibly fluid. It can change from person to person or from day to day in many other situations. However, behaviors exist on a spectrum. Many behaviors are considered normal. Others are considered abnormal or uncommon. This is important to under-stand. Some are considered acceptable and no one will judge you for them. They are considered healthy. Others are considered unacceptable and are arguably behaviors that will need to be changed. Look at laws that we have—acting within the constraints of the law is usually considered acceptable. It is acceptable to drive down the road at speed limit. However, it would not be acceptable to drive down your neighbors' front lawns, parallel to the road, at the speed limit.

. . .

Within this chapter, we are going to take a closer look at behaviors in general—specifically those that may become problematic. We are going to identify what behaviors are and how you can begin to recognize the difference between conscious and unconscious behaviors. Finally, we will take a look at being able to change human behaviors in general. These are all very important points to remember as we continue throughout the rest of the chapters in this book. As you seek to understand behaviors, you are coming to understand the primary targets of the therapy process. You need to be able to target these processes and practices to ensure that, ultimately, you can make the changes that you need.

What Are Behaviors?

When you hear the word, "behavior," you may think of attitudes—sometimes, people will say, "I don't like your behavior right now," in reference to attitudes. However, there is more to it than that. Behavior is highly general—it is meant to apply to all actions by an animal or a person. There are ultimately several aspects to this sort of behavior that can all come together. Behavior is not just what you can observe about someone or something else. It includes many different aspects. These aspects include:

- **Externally visible activities:** These are actions that animals or people may do. This would be anything that is inherently observable. For example, you may consider the act of talking to other people a behavior. It is—you are choosing to go up and do something, and that action is all observable. Other people can see you going to someone else and talking.
- **Changes to an external condition:** Changes to the external condition can also be considered a form of behavior. This includes changes to body language, for

example. You can change your stance intentionally or inadvertently, but this is a behavior nonetheless. If you choose to stand somewhere with your arms crossed, you are exhibiting a behavior that can be observed by others.

- **Changes to an internal condition:** Changes to internal condition, though unobservable for most people, must also be considered. These would be changes of the mood, changes of thoughts, or other changes to an internal state that other people cannot readily observe. You may not be able to hear what someone else is thinking, but that does not mean that thinking would not be classified as a behavior. If you were, for example, to constantly think that you are a failure, that is a behavior—the simple act of thinking that you are a failure is the behavior being discussed. Of course, this will then go and influence future behavioral choices as well.

- **A response to a sense:** Some behaviors are in a direct response to a sensory stimulus. It could be that, for example, you see something coming toward you and you choose to respond. Let's reconsider that example earlier of being chased by a dog. You may respond to this happily if you know that it is friendly, or you may become scared if you are unfamiliar. This is a different sort of behavior—it is reactive, but it is a type of behavior nonetheless.

- **A response to a thought or idea:** Sometimes, the behaviors that you have are direct responses to your thoughts or ideas. You may decide to write a book, for example—you write the book because you had a thought or an idea for it. Sometimes, you may decide to cook something as a response to being inspired by your own thoughts.

As you can see, behaviors vary greatly. Some are self-motivated. Others are reactionary. However, they are all still behaviors. They are all still ways of acting and behaving that are directly influenced by the world around you, or the world within yourself as well. Essentially, behavior is a response of an organism to either an internal or an external stimulus.

Conscious and Unconscious Behaviors

Typically, you can divide your behaviors up into conscious and unconscious behaviors. The best way to sort of iterate this difference is to take a look at the difference between someone nervously changing their body language without thinking about it —they may cross their arms or shift from foot to foot. They are responding to the stimuli around them—something about their own internal state or the state of those around them is threatening or disconcerting enough that it creates a change in behavior. Now, contrast that with intentionally walking to exercise. That is taking a conscious behavior.

Ultimately, much of what we do *is* unconscious—we simply do not think about it. Think of it this way—how much of driving is automatic versus conscious? You probably do not pay attention to every little aspect of your driving. You probably do not pay attention to the way that you move your wrist to be able to turn on the blinker. You may not pay attention to the way that you shift from the gas pedal to the brake when it comes down to ensuring that you are going the same speed or trying to stop moving to avoid hitting a car or running a red light.

. . .

SO much of what we do throughout our day is automatic. It has to be—think about how exhausting it would be if you had to stop and consider, for example, every aspect of what you do. How draining would it be if you had to remember to breathe or remember to beat your heart every second? Having to remember these aspects of your body's functioning would be tedious at best, but outright fatal at worst. It is very important that some of the responses that your body has are automatic.

Consider for a moment instinctive behaviors or habitual behaviors. We can return back to the idea of driving a car. Driving, at first, may be quite tedious because you have to focus on everything that you are doing at any given moment. You have to ensure that you are focusing on the pressure you put on the pedal. You need to take time to ensure that you are keeping your car in your own lane and how to correct for any sorts of movement or changes in the road. This is important—you need to focus on everything because it is new. You do not yet know what you are doing.

However, the more you do something, the easier it becomes. The more habitual it becomes and the more likely it is that the behavior will be reinforced. You can turn the behavior into a habit, and as it does become habituated. As you develop a habit like this, you do not have to think about it any longer. You do not have to spend time trying to force the behavior—it just happens without thinking about it.

This is a good thing—when you have behaviors or tendencies that happen often, you do not have to waste valuable resources from your mind focusing on them. You are able to instead of focusing on how to do something, focus on other aspects as well. Think about how much struggle you would have with typing if, for example, you had to stop and think about how to press each and every letter rather than it becoming automatic? That could carry on to other aspects of your life as well and that would put an extra drain on your conscious mind.

However, this sort of automatization of your behaviors by your unconscious mind is not infallible. In fact, it comes with all sorts of other problems that must also be considered. Your efficiency comes at the cost of nuance. You stop considering the options or thinking about the behaviors—you just act. This can be a major problem for people if the behavior is a negative one. You can create tendencies and habits that can either be destructive to other people or be destructive toward yourself and that is a major problem. There is no benefit toward behaviors that are going to hurt you or other people, and yet, they can become an unconscious habit if you are not careful.

Imagine, for example, that you are the type of person that, every time that you get stressed out, you reach for a bottle of beer. The first few times, you may have consciously decided to drink. After that, however, it could get easier and easier to reach for the bottle every time that you are stressed out or struggling in some way. This is a huge problem—your coping mechanism is essentially being overtaken by this negative habit.

. . .

However, if you can replace those unconscious behaviors with positive ones instead, you can do yourself a huge favor. What if, instead of stressing out about what you were doing and reaching for a bottle, you changed your tendency to drink with one to work out instead? You could get to the point that, without thinking about it, you would simply head over to work out every time that you got frustrated. If you can make this shift in behavior, you can greatly improve the behaviors that you are exhibiting. You can majorly change up the ways that you respond to the world. You can change how you are likely to deal with a situation. You can make sure that, at the end of the day, your unconscious and automatic responses to the world are those that are productive or beneficial, and in doing so, you can greatly improve your own outcomes and mindsets.

Changing Behaviors

Consciously changing behaviors, whether those behaviors are conscious or unconscious, can be a bit tedious. It does not happen overnight—in fact, it can sometimes take weeks or even months to properly change a behavior that you have developed into a habit. This is not an easy feat—but when you are trying to correct negative behaviors, it can be one that is worth undertaking. You need to ensure that you are constantly driven by healthy behaviors. You need to know how to ensure that you are making positive changes to your life. You may be able to do so for a few days, but to make a long-term change can be much more difficult.

Changing behaviors is difficult. It requires several processes—six, in fact—that will support the necessary changes that you are hoping to see. If you can go through these stages, you can alter a behavior. As you will see, the act of changing your behaviors intentionally is a very deliberate one. It is also one that will very closely overlap with the changing of your mindset as well. Remember, the thoughts and behaviors that you have are intricately linked and you will need to remember this as you progress.

For now, however, let's go over the stages of changing your behaviors:

Stage 1: Prior to contemplation

This is the stage that you are at in the beginning. It is that state in which you have not considered a change or you have not done so seriously. You may not realize that you have a problem in the first place. You may have been told by someone else that you should change, but you feel threatened by the suggestion that something that you are doing is wrong. You are usually quite fond of your current habits, or at the very least, you do not feel like you are being strongly negatively impacted by them at that point in time. After all, if you were not at the very least comfortable in your current habits, you would likely not maintain them. This is the state of resistance—the state of not yet remembering or recognizing that you need to change.

Stage 2: Contemplation

At this point, you begin to recognize that you do, in fact, have a problematic behavior that needs to change. You may feel like the behaviors that you have been leading with may actually be a problem. It is time to consider whether or not you do want to change your behaviors at this point. This stage is marked as the change from an idea or an assumption to a deep, personal belief that you will need to change in some way. Consider the difference between, "Stress management is a good skill to have," and "I need to manage my stress in a healthier manner." They are both, more or less, stating the same concept, however, in one, you are generalizing, and with the latter, you are recognizing that you personally need to do something to change as well.

Stage 3: Motivation

At this point, you need to find the motivation to make the change that your body needs. This point is marked by you recognizing that something is wrong with the way that you are currently act and you are able to discover what it is that you will be able to motivate yourself. Consider for a moment that someone is a moderate or heavy drinker. They get told that if they do not cut out the alcohol, they will die. It may not be the fact that their doctor has warned them that continued drinking will result in them becoming quite unhealthy that becomes the motivator here. Rather, they may look at how their drinking is taking up the money that they would like to save up for their grandchildren to go off to college. The motivator for each and every person is going to vary, and it may not be the obvious one. You must be able to find that motivation if you want to make real, longer-lasting changes to your behavior.

Stage 4: Determination

. . .

Next, you must begin the mental preparation. You may need to make very real mindset changes, or you may need to change your physical behaviors at this point. This usually involves some sort of catalyst that will launch you toward the change in behavior that you want to see. You may, for example, decide that you will dump out the rest of the alcohol that you have on hand at that moment in time. You may decide that you are going to only carry enough cash for the groceries that you are going to buy at the store so you cannot buy a bottle of alcohol as well. You may declare that you will not drink at all, barring certain special occasions. No matter what, however, one thing is important to remember: This should be what propels you forward.

Stage 5: Action

This is the starting point to your change. When you take action, you force the point. You do not drink. You choose to go to the gym if that was what you are trying to change. You may decide that you will not be spending time eating sweets anymore, or you may declare that you are going to give up some other bad habit. This is where you finally start to see those desired changes in your behaviors once and for all, and those changes are very important to see manifested.

Stage 6: Maintenance

Finally, the last step of this process is maintenance. This is you continuing to take action. You continue to refuse to buy alcohol.

You continue to go to the gym. You continue to make good choices. You may decide that you are not going to be spending money unnecessarily, and stage 6 is all about continuing to maintain it. This is the hardest part of changing your behavior—if you cannot maintain the changes that you want to see, then you have failed, and this is why so many people fail in the long run. They fail because when it comes down to it, they cannot permanently make those changes. As they get further and further out from the changes that were made, they may decide that they will no longer make sure that they are constantly maintaining the changes. They may see the constant effort and management as no longer important—they may buy that bottle of alcohol because it is a special occasion and they want a bottle of wine to go with it. However, that slip-up is quite likely to happen more and more often if you have let go of that change. These occasional slip ups can slowly but surely eventually manifest into real, problematic situations that suddenly undo everything that you have worked on.

No matter what the changes you choose to make throughout this book are, whether they are aimed to help you better reject negative thoughts, correct self-harming behaviors, or anything else, you must remember that maintenance is the hardest part of all. You need to remember that maintenance, constantly ensuring that you do continue to manage to fend off the temptation to slip back into old habits, will be the most important part, and you must remember that these changes that you are making will require life-long commitment. It is all too easy to regress or slip back into old habits if you are not careful. It is very easy to suddenly give in to everything that you are trying to avoid if you are not able to fend off those changes. It is very simple to undo all of that change without meaning to—and all you have to do to have that slip back into problematic behaviors that you had before is to stop trying to maintain your change. Relapse is far too easy to run into. However, keep in mind that even if you do relapse, you have already kicked the problem once. You already changed the behavioral tendencies and you can do it again.

3 / EMOTIONS, REACTIONS, AND BEHAVIORS

ULTIMATELY, before we continue, we must take a look at the difference between emotions, reactions, and behaviors. So far, we have been entirely focused on how to connect thoughts and behaviors. However, there is one more important aspect to consider as well—emotions. Your emotion is like the intermediary between the thoughts that you have and the behaviors that you exhibit. They are the communication between the unconscious mind and the behaviors that you have. They are reactionary—they occur in response to something else, whether that is in response to thoughts or events.

Within this chapter, we are going to take a look at what emotions are. After all, if you are suffering from a mental health issue, the emotional component is perhaps going to be the one that you notice the most. It is the part that is more likely to weigh heavily on you thanks to the fact that your emotions are so powerful. Those emotions are unavoidable—they happen whether you want them to or not. However, that does not mean that you have to act upon them. You are under no obligation to react to your emotions. You are under no obligation to respond to the way that you are feeling, and in fact, you would be well advised to avoid allowing emotions to run your life in the first place. We are going to look at how those emotional states then directly influence your behaviors as well. Understanding this cycle that exists between the thoughts, feelings, and behaviors that you exhibit at any point in time is very important for you. You cannot defeat the cycle if you do not recognize that it is there in the first place.

What Are Emotions?

Emotions are influential. They are there to influence how you feel in hopes of then influencing how you act. They are there for a very good reason—to motivate you toward action. They will either encourage you to repeat behaviors, such as feeling good or happy when you eat a good, healthy meal, or they will encourage you to avoid a behavior in the future, such as feeling sad after getting into a fight with your spouse. These emotions, in being able to alter your mental state, are incredibly motivating. They are incredibly skilled at making you act in different ways—and for good reason. The emotions that you feel are meant to keep you alive.

Before we get to that, however, let's go over what an emotion is in the first place. It is believed that humans all experience emotions. In fact, there are six in particular that are commonly deemed to be universal, with all others being combinations or branches off of one of these main six. These six emotions are like the basis for everything else and they, and their body language and expressions, can be seen anywhere in the world. Even the most remote tribes in the world with very little outside contact will be able to read this body language. These six emotions believed to be entirely universal are:

- Happiness
- Sadness
- Disgust
- Fear
- Surprise
- Anger

Each of these are rooted in very important motivation of your behaviors. They are all there to keep you functioning in certain ways. They are there to drive you toward survival and interacting with others. As a social species, your emotions are very clearly spelled out in your body language. Emotions are used for communication. They are used to better relate to others. They are used to push people to act in ways that are good for more than one person, especially when you add empathy to the mix.

Essentially, if you wanted to break down what an emotion is, it is a mental state that is characterized by being natural, instinctive, and motivating. It is intuitive and automatic—you do not think about how you should feel when you feel something. The feeling itself sort of just happens. They can happen for reasons that make sense, such as being sad after losing someone important to you. Or, they can be a bit more irrational or not make much sense, such as being upset about a bit of milk spilling when you have no shortage of milk in the fridge and no shortage of money to go out and replace it with.

The problem with emotions, however, is that they are irrational. They are unpredictable. Something that may have been entirely acceptable to you one day may anger you the next, depending on other factors. Just about everything can directly alter the way that you are feeling. You can be more upset that particular day because of the way that the wind blew your hair into your face, or because you burnt your breakfast. You may simply wake up feeling worse for wear one day, with no clear reason why. This is a problem because your emotions are meant to motivate you. If your emotions are irrational and will be altered by anything from the way that the wind blew to the way that someone looked at you, how can you possibly think that relying on them would be a good idea?

The Purpose of Emotions

Nevertheless, emotions have very important jobs: They are meant to motivate and they are meant to discourage. They are meant to reinforce a behavior or they are meant to influence you into acting in a certain way. Though these sound more or less the same, they are different in their own ways. Some are meant to be reinforcing in the sense that you will base future actions on past results. Others are meant to push you to behave in that moment.

When your emotion is meant to reinforce something, it is meant to make you feel like you should repeat a behavior that led up to the moment, or you should feel like you should avoid that behavior in the future. This is why emotions are so powerful in the first place —they are there to drive you. They are meant to make you think that it is, in fact, a good idea for you to continue interacting with this person, or why you should choose not to have that interaction. This is why so many emotions are uncomfortable. While happiness is going to encourage you to repeat behaviors, you should also look at emotions such as sadness and fear—they, and many of their subsidiaries, such as guilt, are there to make you feel bad. They are there to make you correct something or change how you behave next time to avoid running into that same problem again in the future. This is very important for you and it is evolution's way of keeping humanity alive. Remember, evolution rarely develops something that will be counterintuitive to survival—it is always working to encourage and reinforce fitness. Your emotions are all very important for this reason.

On the other hand, your emotions have another important job—they are there to encourage behaviors in the moment. Think about it—in a period of anger, what do you want to do? If you are frustrated with someone, how do you want to respond? Most people respond to anger in particular by entering a fight response. This is the biological purpose of anger in the first place—it is a response to a threat that is meant to encourage you to fight it off to protect yourself. Let's look at those six universal emotions again and take a look at their purposes:

- **Happiness:** This encourages you to repeat those behaviors again in the future because they gave you a good result or they made you feel good when you completed them. This is meant to ensure that you continue to do so. Happiness is like the universal reinforcement—it is meant to feel good so you naturally feel inclined to pursue it.
- **Sadness:** This encourages you to avoid repeating behaviors because you were hurt by loss. Sadness usually comes when you have lost something, whether because you made a mistake or because someone else did.
- **Anger:** This encourages you to fight back to protect yourself because you feel like you are under a threat. It

390 / RHONDA SWAN

is usually considered secondary to fear and comes from the fight or flight response. Anger is the manifestation of the fight response.

- **Fear;** This encourages you to avoid something because you perceived it as a threat that you will need to escape from. You may feel like running away to protect yourself from the threat. Sometimes, this will shift over to anger to encourage a fight to protect yourself.

- **Disgust:** This is meant to discourage you from approaching something that was so intensely revolting that it will probably make you ill. This is that feeling of something being rotten and you deciding not to eat it.

- **Surprise:** This is meant to encourage you to pay closer attention to see what is happening because something does not line up with your current expectations. The physiology of the body changes to allow for more focus and attention on the surroundings.

The Cause of Emotions

Ultimately, there is no complete, perfect consensus on the proper combination that triggers emotions. We do know that they are typically reactionary and they are typically created by certain electrical impulses and releases of hormones within the body that lend themselves to the emotions that are felt. However, what is not quite understood is the way in which it all works. There are many different theories on what causes it, however. Within this section, we are going to take a look at three different explanations. If you ever took a basic psychology class in high school or college, these three will probably look quite familiar to you. The three that will be discussed here are the James-Lange theory, the Cannon-Bard theory, and the Schacter-Singer theory. Each have their own reasons to find them compelling, but at the end of the day, it is hard to pinpoint down exactly how the process of emoting occurs in the first place.

James-Lange Theory

The James-Lange theory posits that the emotion that you feel begins as a physical response to the world around you. It starts off with something happen. In this instance, let's go back to the example of a dog running at you. You see the dog running at you. In response, you feel a physiological change. You suddenly feel your heart begin to race as your body prepares to respond. You may become tense. You may brace yourself. You are able to see that this dog is running for you and you are unsure why it is. The emotion comes after the fact—you may realize that you are scared because you can feel the changes to your body. Your mind then creates the sensation of fear in response to the physiological changes to your body based on the stimulus that you were exposed to.

Cannon-Bard Theory

Next, let's consider the Cannon-Bard theory. This theory, rather than seeing the entire process as linear the way that you did in the James-Lange theory, looks at it slightly differently. You see the stimulus—in this instance, the dog running toward you—and you then have two reactions simultaneously. You begin to feel the physical response of your heart pounding and your body becoming tense as the dog barrels toward you. Then, you also feel the emotion at the same time. This theory states that it is a two-part simultaneous reaction rather than them being sequential. You are having a concurrent response instead.

Schacter-Singer Theory

Finally, the Schacter-Singer theory is a little bit different. Rather than the reaction being the result of the stimulus, in this case, you must look at it slightly differently. You will see the dog running toward you and have your physical response to the stimulus. You feel that level of arousal—in this case, the pounding heart and feeling tense. However, that is joined with it by cognition—you have some sort of preconceived notion of the event. Something about the event must tell your body what to infer and therefore what to assume is about to happen. If you are afraid of dogs, you may have the thought of being afraid of dogs pop into your mind. Together, the physical response and the preconceived notion come together to create the sensation of the emotion that you felt. In this instance, you feel the fear that came along with it.

Emotions and Behaviors

Of the three theories that you have just been introduced to, the Schacter-Singer model is going to best-explain the process that you use in DBT, and in CBT in general. This particular theory looks at the nuances. It looks at the fact that your thoughts that you have are able to alter the emotions that you will feel. After all, how many of the emotions that you have all include very similar responses? Think about it—a pounding heart can be felt in excitement, in anger, in fear, and in just about any other excitatory emotions. This makes sense—the increase in heart rate is there to encourage you to act. It is there to make sure that you do respond to whatever is happening around you. It is there so, if your response is to something that will require a reaction quickly, you are prepared. The pounding heart is not specific to fear. However, you can pair that pounding heart with the idea that dogs are frightening, or the idea that dogs will attack and alter the response.

However, what if you changed that thought—instead of looking at a dog and thinking, "Dogs attack me!" you changed that thought to something that is not as negative toward dogs? What if you had a thought process that was more along the lines of, "Dogs are cute, but I'd rather keep my distance," or something else that was relatively neutral or indifferent? You likely would not respond in fear. It may instead be annoyance. If you were to change that thought to something positive, however, you may get even better responses— rather than being afraid of that dog running toward you, you may suddenly feel happy. You may feel glad that you see a dog running to play with you.

The only real difference there is that you are looking at the situation in a different light. Your change in thought to the physical reaction to the stimulus is enough to change the emotion that you feel. This means that you are able to take control of your emotions, albeit indirectly, by making sure that the thought processes that you have are designed to be more constructive or more positive. Essentially, you will have thoughts at the beginning of your cycle— the thoughts will influence those behavior-influencing emotions. Between the three, changing thoughts is oftentimes the easiest of all, which is why you will often see an emphasis on cognitive restructuring—the restructuring of the thoughts that are had at any point in time.

Of course, the emotions that you feel will then directly drive your behaviors. We have already looked at the behaviors that the emotions that you experience are meant to encourage or facilitate. They are important to consider and remember. They are there to help guide you and your reactions to what is happening around you.

ULTIMATELY, DBT is highly effective for many chronic and severe mental health issues. It can help eliminate self-destructive habits or help alleviate negative thoughts that are holding someone back. It is able to do this primarily through the way it works. This particular form of treatment is comprehensive, meaning that it is attempting to treat all aspects of life rather than just the symptoms. It is meant to help people that have struggled when they were treated by other therapies that may have been aimed at alleviating the problem in the first place. It is meant to focus on being able to solve the problems that can be solved and accepting and coping with the ones that cannot. This works by operating within its own dialectical methods, with the primary dialectic being the one between change and acceptance.

This therapy system is highly effective in treating those people that would otherwise struggle, and when you consider the purpose of this therapy being to change what you can and accept what you cannot change, this makes sense. Other therapies may be designed to help you alleviate a trauma or to make it no longer traumatic—this therapy, however, instead provides you with the tools that you would need to help yourself cope with the trauma in the first place. By providing you with all of the tools that you will need, you are able to develop important techniques that you will need to create real, meaningful change and begin to improve your own wellbeing.

In particular, you will use methods from several components to help yourself begin to improve. These different components all serve very important purposes to helping you become well. These components are essentially the livelihood of this particular methodology and without them, it would not be nearly as effective as it is. These components are capability enhancement, generalization, motivational enhancement, and structuring of the environment. These are joined with the tools and methods that are commonly given as a sort of support as well for those that are engaging in this particular form of therapy.

These will usually occur in several forms. People will traditionally go through their individual therapy with their therapist to get that one-on-one guidance that they will need. They will also be guided through skills groups in which they are able to practice the skills that this particular therapy advises for without the struggles that are otherwise seen. It will offer up phone coaching if necessary, and finally includes a consultation team. Ultimately, the fact that there are so many elements to this therapy is one of the main reasons that it is so incredibly effective and it is so capable of creating real, lasting change for people. With these elements and all of the different people present and active, you not only get to work with others, you also get the support from others as well and sometimes, that added support of everyone, from your therapist to your group leader, to even the people that you are attending your classes with, will make all the difference in the world. We will take a closer look at this all later, but for now, we are going to focus on those key components of this therapy that make this particular therapy as effective as it is.

Capability Enhancement

The first aspect of DBT is the capability enhancement. The first stage is all about providing the individual with the skills that they will need to help themselves later on. The entire idea behind this is best summarized by the saying that you can help a man for a day by giving him a fish, but you can help him for a lifetime if you teach him to catch his own. This therapy will teach you to catch your own metaphorical fish for a lifetime rather than attempting to give you that first fish. Both of these are valid methods of helping someone else, but they have very different implications. You can help someone short-term with a specific problem, or you can help someone long-term by giving them the tools to help themselves. This particular therapy wants to incentivize the improvements to oneself rather than to helping them just solve one problem, knowing that more will come down the line.

Let's face it—life is difficult. Coping with life can be a huge problem for some people. Being able to deal with people and their reactions can be incredibly difficult. However, you can also recognize that ultimately, you will be able to do so much better if you have the tools that you will need to help yourself. This therapy is not meant to be long-term—it should be relatively short-term and offer you everything that you will need to take care of yourself.

The tools that you will be taught will primarily vary from person to person, but one thing holds true—they will fall into one of four categories, each of which will be emphasized in later chapters in this book. These skillsets include emotional regulation, mindfulness, interpersonal effectiveness, and distress tolerance. You will essentially be given tools that will help you regulate out your reactions to your emotions to prevent you from behaving impulsively. You will be taught mindfulness, a method that you can use to stop yourself and consider what the emotions that you are feeling at that moment are in the first place rather than simply getting caught up in the moment. You will be taught how you can interact with other people in a more meaningful, healthy manner. Finally, you will be taught how you can better cope with the stressors that you have in your everyday life.

All of these tools will help you prepare for just about any situation. They will give you those tools that you will likely use for a lifetime. You will be able to prevent yourself from struggling. You will be able to prevent yourself from hurting others or yourself. You will learn how you can fend off that desire to be impulsive as well—all because you will have the tools to help.

Generalization

The next set of techniques that you use in DBT include those that will help you generalize. This is essentially teaching you how you can apply those same skills that you have already begun to learn to other areas in your life as well. You are essentially learning how you can take those important skills that you learned to solve your one specific problem that you were hoping to change and then apply them elsewhere. You do this so you can prevent yourself from struggling long-term with other problems as well.

Essentially, you are learning to project those learned skills and coping mechanisms to all areas in your life. You are taught to apply your solutions to work-related problems to other relationships as well. Think about it this way—you may find that you really struggle with a conflict with one person. You and your therapist can work together to come up with the necessary tools to solve that one conflict. However, after that conflict is solved, you are then taught the tools that you will need to apply those same tools and skills elsewhere in your life as well. You are taught to take those conflict-solving skills with your coworker, for example, and bring them home to your spouse as well.

The goal with this is to give you tools that are nonspecific—they should be effective for you no matter what the situation. They should be able to help you in any situation to learn how best to fix your problems and how best to help you. When you can use your skills in all aspects of your life, you are able to prevent yourself from struggling in other situations that may arise. You are extrapolating from what you have learned. You are becoming creative and skilled at problem solving in general.

Motivational Enhancement

Next, DBT uses what is known as motivational enhancement. This is coming up with individualized treatment plans that are meant to help you specifically. It is adding a layer of customizability to the entire process. It is allowing you to begin to recognize that your quality of life will be impacted if you do not spend the time to learn how these tools will work for you, and it involves you discovering just how these tools do work for you.

With this concept, you will be tracking the changes that are made. You will usually be guided through tracking sheets that you will have to fill out over time to help you figure out precisely how it is that these techniques are working for you. Think of these are your feedback providers—they will tell you whether what you are doing is working well, therefore motivating you to continue with those actions, or they will prove to be unbeneficial to you in general, therefore showing that you may need to change what you are doing.

Without this element, you are going to struggle. You will not have the necessary feedback that is there to help you figure out what is working and what should be changed. Your therapist will be working hard with you, especially if you are tracking your changes and writing down how it is working for you. In having these points recorded for you, you will begin to understand how certain responses and behaviors can be highly beneficial to you while others really struggle to benefit you. You learn what works and what does not—and ultimately, that is crucial.

Structuring of the Environment

Finally, when you consider the structure of the environment that is given to you, you begin to see that the therapy itself is designed in a positive manner. The goal of this therapy is to make sure that your positive behaviors are developed. However, we can develop very situational habits. You may learn to pick up the habits and behavioral changes that you need to see in your therapist's office, but that is a very controlled setting. Those skills are oftentimes much harder to use in real time when they matter the most.

For this reason, DBT tries to structure the therapeutic process to ensure that you are able to better manage the situation. It is designed to help you make sure that you are getting treatment in a wide array of situations, from at home to in public to in groups of people, as well as alone. This is usually done because DBT will have you attend several different sessions. DBT oftentimes involves a degree of one-on-one therapy along with others as well. You are given multiple treatment programs within one particular office or agency that are meant to help really reinforce the skills that you are learning. You are meant to be learning that, at the end of the day, you should be able to use these skills no matter the setting that you are in. You will want to, for example, be able to come up with good problem solving in a one-on-one setting, but also in a group.

You will usually interact with your therapist, or you will be asked to practice your skills, in many different settings. You will be encouraged to do this so you can get a better degree of reinforcement at the end of the day. You will be meant to ensure that, at the end of the day, you are better optimizing your behaviors. The more practice that you get and the wider that practice spreads, the more likely you are to be able to cope and use your tools when you will need them the most.

The Bottom Line

At the end of the day, all of this comes together for you. It all comes together to help you in a way that is meaningful, that is beneficial, and that is going to emphasize the development of the skills that you will need to reinforce. This therapy may be off-putting to some—especially when you realize that you will have no choice but to interact with other people as well—but it is powerful. It is very good at ensuring that, at the end of the day, you can succeed. It will help you if you give it the chance.

In using this therapy, you will be practicing your own skills regularly. You will be expected to spend time completing homework. You will be encouraged and pushed to ensure that you are working with other people. You will need to better your relationships with others. All of this has to happen—it is necessary to help you succeed with the changes that you want.

5 / THE COMPONENTS OF DIALECTICAL BEHAVIOR THERAPY

WITH THAT PREVIOUS information in mind, then, there are several components of DBT that you should also consider. This is a complex therapy, and in some ways, it is a bit unorthodox—after all, most therapies are not designed to have you spend so much time in so many different settings. DBT will encourage you to become involved with four different settings—the therapy itself, the group skills training, the phone coaching, and your own personal group therapy consultation team. These are like the most fundamental building blocks of the therapy itself and are precisely why it is so effective. Beyond that, however, there are also other tools that you will need to keep in mind. These tools are the ones that allow the therapy to be practiced regularly. They are the tools that will work to help you reinforce what you are doing and that will be the driving force behind the change.

When you consider DBT, then, you are considering wide range of resources, tools, and techniques that will all come together to help you. They will help you in making meaningful changes to your own life. They will encourage you to be able to better cope with the world around you. They will help you begin to break free of those negative habits that have been hurting you, and in doing so, you will be able to succeed.

Therapy

As with just about any other form of therapy, you will be sitting down, one on one, with an individual therapist. This is meant to help you get that one-on-one focus that you need. It will help you create a tailored, individualized plan that will allow you to understand what it is that you will need to do. You will learn all about what it is that you will need. You will get feedback on what you have been doing. You will learn which tools you should focus on.

Typically, this happens regularly—it should be roughly 60 minutes per week spent together in this one-on-one setting with the hopes of being able to address any individual or unique challenges that are happening. This is important—while you will also be spending time in skills groups, you still need that sort of personal connection. You will still need that sort of personal application to make this therapy useful and beneficial to you. Think of this as the way in which you will be able to bring everything back to yourself. It involve your therapist relating the problems that you are suffering from back to yourself. Your therapist will be able to point out how what you are doing may be problematic, and may be able to make suggestions on how to fix the problem in the first place.

Group Skills Training

While the individual therapy is a very crucial part of this process, you actually should be spending more time during the week in your skills training setup. These are essentially classes that are designed to teach the tools and skills that you will need in a group setting. This will involve a group leader that will act as a teacher, along with several other students in the class as well. The leader is able to teach skills, lead the class, and assign homework that will need to be completed to remain in compliance with the program. You will be surrounded by other people that may or may not have similar problems, but are there to get the same toolset that they will be able to apply to themselves in their own individual therapy classes.

These classes are a bit lengthy—usually, they met weekly for best effectiveness. During each weekly class, you can expect to be instructed and asked to work in group settings. You may be encouraged to roleplay or act out settings with other people. You may be asked to lead discussions with other people. You may be encouraged to ensure that you are able to process what is happening better by taking tests that they can then score to see if you do, in fact, understand.

Generally, these classes meet weekly for roughly 2.5 hours. Usually, to get through the entire class, you are able to do so in about 24 weeks. If you want to learn the entire range of DBT skills, you would be in a class that is longer or denser. On the other hand, there are also plenty of programs that offer just subsets of the skills that you will need to know. These can be quicker options for you if only one or two of them may be relevant to your life or your problem.

. . .

Despite the structure that goes along with your class schedule, it is important to note that this is endlessly flexible, and your individual therapist will likely be tailoring it to you with their own homework.

Phone Coaching

DBT is unique in the sense that it allows for in-the-moment coaching. If you ever felt overwhelmed in a situation, for example, you would be able to call in to your therapist, or to another therapist in your particular office, and begin to talk to them. This is great if you find that you are in a rut sometime and cannot figure out how to get through it, but you still have several days until your next scheduled appointment.

Essentially, this aspect elevates your therapist to accessible nearly all the time, though they may have their own personal stipulations on when you can call for help if it is needed. However, this is a unique feature that can be great for people that find that they need a bit more guidance than they would get through a weekly session or some other situation in which they are not getting that constant degree of availability from their tutor or therapist.

Therapist Consultation Team

Finally, DBT makes use of a sort of consultation team that you, personally, do not have access to, but is oftentimes heavily involved in the process of your care and treatment plans. The consultation team is comprised of your own individual therapist, several other therapists, and the group leaders that you are likely interacting with regularly. Especially if you have a disorder that is difficult, a situation that is relatively unique, or anything else that would make you harder to manage, this can be the perfect way to get more eyes on you and helping you. You will be able to essentially ensure that other people are working together. It involves the therapists that are involved in your care coming together and discussing the case or figuring out how best to proceed.

Though you will not be meeting with this group, it is important to recognize that this means that you could have an entire group of people looking at your case. This is an entire group of people that is dedicated to ensuring that you get the help and care that you will need to allow you to better cope with the situation that you are in that has pushed you to seek therapy in the first place.

Homework

The therapy that you will do will involve homework. You will be told that you need to do the work outside of the classroom as well, and this makes perfect sense if you think about it—you need to be able to ensure that, at the end of the day, you can recognize the ways in which this therapy can work. You are going to be tasked with all sorts of different tasks and activities that you will need to do.

While this may not be enforceable most of the time, you can run the risk of being dropped as a client if you simply do not manage to complete the homework on a regular basis. You need to ensure that you are always working hard to help yourself as well—after all, you cannot make the change that you want to see in your life if you are not motivated and actively working toward it. One such way to maintain that effort and motivation is through this homework.

Homework can take several different forms. It could involve you being asked to go out of your way to do something that you are uncomfortable with. It could involve you learning to do something new. It could involve emphasizing mindfulness or attempting to help you meditate. Your homework is essentially you applying the work that you have been doing elsewhere in your life as well. It is pushing you to make sure that you are actively working to take care of what needs to be done. It is ensuring that you are always actively taking care of what you need to do. It emphasizes really solidifying and reinforcing the work that you have been doing and it is crucial if you want to make sure that you will be successful.

Usually, you will find that this particular technique is going to make use of a mixture of worksheets, journaling, and also actively attempting to change what you are doing. It may ask you to apologize to someone that you have wronged, or to attempt to patch up a relationship. It may provide you with a technique to try out the next time that you are stressed out. It may involve other situations that you have not yet attempted to navigate yet. However, it is very important that you complete it to get the fullest effect that this therapy has to offer you.

Diary Cards

Diary cards are another very important aspect of this particular form of therapy. You can very readily find a template for one online that you can print out to make use of yourself, or if you are seeing your own therapist, they may provide you with your own. These cards are meant to be your way to hold yourself accountable. They are meant to help you track what you were feeling, how you were feeling, how you were able to act, when and why you acted the way that you did, and how what you did in response. You will be asked to rate your behaviors and mindsets in a way that is easily glanced over to get a good idea of how you are feeling and how you are able to make these techniques really work for you when it comes right down to it.

. . .

Generally, these cards will have two sides to them—one side will list several different skills that you are expected to be using. It will be your job to, once a day, rate the skills that you have been using. You will need to record how often you make use of these skills and whether or not they are effective for you.

The other side of these cards is usually meant to sort of summarize any of the behaviors that you have deemed problematic in the first place. It will be designed to record your urges that you are trying to defeat. Usually, these are the most problematic of your behaviors. It could be that you are trying to prevent yourself form self-harming—and that would be written down as an urge. Other examples could be the abuse of drugs or alcohol, or hurting someone else. You will want to record how often on those days that you felt the urges, as well as how many times that it happened. You will also be asked to specify what happened and why. This is important—it will allow you to track the behaviors and the patterns, as well as why you may do what you do.

This side will also ask if you managed to use the skills that you were taught in your therapy sessions. If you did, then great—you write down the skills that you used and whether or not they worked for you. If you did not use the skills, you will know that they are there, unused, and you will recognize that you will need to use them in the future.

. . .

This should be recorded during the week and brought to your therapist to discuss. If you are not using a therapist, it is still of the utmost importance that you record these thoughts as they occur so you will be able to recognize your behaviors. They are there so you will be able to reference them at a glance. You will be able to tell whether or not your skills that you have been working with as much as you can are actually working.

Behavioral Tracking with Journaling

One final component that you are likely to encounter regularly is being asked to reflect on what has happened. You will need to be able to consider whether or not what you have done is actually going to be effective for you in the first place. You need to understand what the underlying problem is if you hope to solve it, and the best way to do so is if you can track it, your triggers, and other behaviors through journaling.

This is essentially a slightly more personal version of the diary card, which is meant ot reduce everything down to something that can be glanced at in a few minutes by a therapist that is on a limited amount of time. However, you will also find that you are greatly benefited by being able to track your behaviors regularly.

When you are journaling, you are going to want to record several different aspects to help you begin to learn what you struggle with. You will need to record down what happened during your day. If you found that there was a major problem for you one day, what was it? Did you get into a fight with someone? Why?

. . .

You will also want to record how you were feeling before it happened. This is imperative as well as it can give you a clue as to what sets you off. If you were hungry, you may note that down. If you were stressed or overwhelmed, you may include that as well. What matters here is recognizing what the problem is and how you can fix it if necessary later on.

You will also want to record any reflections upon what has happened. How do you feel about it? Was it a problem for you? Why or why not? It was most likely a problem for you if you are writing it down—what does that problem entail?

The more that you can journal about what goes wrong in your life, the more likely you are to be able to come up with good solutions. Remember, nothing in life was fixed by figuring out how you should have responded in the past or how you could have changed how you reacted. Rather, you get the most benefit when you decide how you will be have next time to prevent the same situation from reoccurring.

DBT IS INCREDIBLY FLEXIBLE, all things considered. It can treat all sorts of issues, ranging from borderline personality disorder, which was the initial reason that it was created, to many other issues that exist as well. There has been a lot of luck helping people with a wide range of disorders or tendencies that needed help learning how they could regulate their emotions, discover how they could better tolerate their stress that they are suffering from, and how they can begin to better tolerate negative emotions of all kinds.

The skills that are taught in DBT, despite being tailored to help those that have borderline personality disorder, are not actually specific. When you make it a point to work through how best to discover the ways in which you can learn how to change your mind, you can begin to start seeing great progress. You can begin to learn how to better focus on how to tolerate stressors in the moment and how you can then begin to interact better as a direct result.

. . .

Within this chapter, we are going to take some time to consider each and every one of the different types of people that are likely to see great benefits. These are people that vary greatly in the complexity and the differences in how their particular disorders tend to present. Some of them may suffer from mood disorders. Others may be addicted to drugs. Others still may have eating disorder. However, DBT is there for all of them. The skills that you can learn with DBT are great. They are powerful. They are compelling. They can help all sorts of people in many different ways. Now, before we continue, let's understand a bit more about the people that DBT helps the most.

Borderline Personality Disorder

Borderline personality disorder (BPD) is typically identifiable by the struggles that they have regarding their ability to be able to manage the emotions that they have. For these people, emotions are typically quiet intense. They fluctuate greatly from extreme to not so extreme at rapid paces. They constantly shift around between their emotions and that can lead to all sorts of other problems. They struggle with keeping themselves regulated, and when they have been set off into an emotion, it is very difficult for them to be able to return back to that stable baseline. They instead fluctuate around widely.

This is a problem for people with BPD. They struggle underneath their attempts to better manage their emotions. They are impulsive by nature thanks to a lot of the problems with their emotional regulation and they oftentimes get caught up with dangerous or destructive actions that can become major problems if not treated quickly.

. . .

BPD is believed to impact roughly just under 1.5% of the adult population within the US, and of those, ¾ are women. However, this may not be entirely accurate, and current research has shown that men may also suffer from this disorder at a roughly equal rate, though they are oftentimes misdiagnosed as suffering from depression or post-traumatic stress disorder instead.

Those that suffer from BPD typically are diagnosed as suffering with symptoms such as:

- Perceiving being abandoned by loved ones and desperately attempting to avoid it, even if there was no threat of being abandoned in the first place
- Struggling with personal relationships that are typically constantly spiraling between love and hate
- Struggling to create a healthy or normal self-image—instead, they see themselves as damaged or flawed, which can lead to all sorts of other problems as well.
- Impulsivity in many different aspects with little regard for the consequences
- Self-destructive or self-harming behaviors, including suicidal ideation, threat, and attempts
- Moods that seem to fluctuate to extremes
- Regularly feeling empty or bored
- Regular intense and uncontrolled anger that is a great source of embarrassment or guilt
- Dissociating from the body

It is not yet known why people develop this disorder but it is believed that it is likely due to some combination of genetics and environmental function.

Suicidal Behaviors

Some people more than others tend to suffer with the idea of wanting to commit suicide. It is not specific to any particular disorder, nor is suicidal ideation itself a mental illness on its own. Rather, these are symptoms of a mental illness that needs treating. People who find that they wish to commit suicide regularly need serious help to ensure that they do not pay the ultimate price— their life.

There are many warning signs for those that are potentially suicidal, ranging greatly and falling into the categories of most other disorders that you will see within this chapter, including:

- They suffer from sadness that seems to persist longer than normal, along with suffering from mood swings that can vary wildly
- They oftentimes feel entirely hopeless about what the future holds. They do not quite believe that they can recover from the problems that they are suffering from and they do not see any sort of hope for the future
- They suffer from sleep disturbances, either sleeping too much or not getting sleep at all
- They may suddenly, after they have been suffering and behaving erratically for a long while, suddenly present as calm. This is a major warning sign that should be considered.
- They pull away from those that they love, trying to avoid having to interact with other people.
- They suddenly appear to be slower or quicker than

normal; their personality may change greatly from what it normally was.

- They engage in dangerous behaviors and seem to be impulsive; this is commonly assumed to be a sign that they do not care about their own life any longer
- They have recently gone through some sort of major trauma or loss
- They may begin clearing out their belongings and giving up their items, or otherwise getting their affairs in order

Suicide can typically be reduced if you can identify that it is coming. If someone that you know or love appears to show signs of suicidal behaviors, reach out to t hem. Encourage them. Let them know that you are there for them and that you want them to know that they are valued

Mood Disorders

Mood disorders are a classifications of mental health disorders that can range greatly. They are the varying types of both depression and bipolar disorders, all grouped together into one. When you take a look at these different disorders, they can vary greatly. However, the most common ones are major depression and dysthymia, both of which are forms of depression.

Major depression is that which lasts for longer than two weeks and is a persistent, heavy, and constant feeling of hopelessness and sadness. The people that suffer from this typically do not see much value in anything that they do. They do not want to engage in the behaviors that they once loved. They do not want to work on themselves. They do not want to do anything at all and that is a problem for them.

. . .

Those that suffer from dysthymia, on the other hand, are suffering from chronic, but low-grade depression. They usually have much longer lasting symptoms, but they are rarely anywhere as severe as that of someone suffering from major depression. These people are the ones who are still going out with their friends and family and seem to function pretty well, but they are still chronically feeling low about themselves and about the world around them.

Other common mood disorders include:

- **Bipolar disorder:** This is depression that can become manic, fluctuating between extremes from time to time. These people suffer from their moods being largely varied and fluctuated.
- **Seasonal Affective Disorder:** This is a manifestation of depression that is rarely as long-term as you would usually see. It usually makes an appearance when the weather is cooler and the days are shorter, especially when you are near one of the poles of the earth.

These mood disorders can be difficult to cope with, but at the same time, they can be treated relatively regularly if the individual suffering from them is willing and able to go through the effort of doing so.

ADHD

ADHD (attention deficit hyperactivity disorder) is a medical condition in which the brain has some differences to it that lead to varied brain activity. This leads to changes in the way that the individual functions. You will see changes in their behaviors, in their ability to sit, their self-control, and more. You will see that these people are likely to become quite impulsive. They may find that it is difficult to pay attention or that they cannot really cope with the way that things are provided. Typically, it will prevent with one of the following three presentations:

- **Inattentive:** People classified as inattentive struggle to pay attention. Oftentimes, their attention span fluctuates greatly and they struggle to keep it where it belongs. They struggle to keep up with what they need to do and they oftentimes completely forget what they are doing at various points in time.
- **Hyperactive:** People who are hyperactive are typically going to struggle to sit down and stay down. They cannot keep themselves quiet and they cannot manage to keep up with their own self-control. They are likely to constantly be fidgeting or moving around.
- **Impulsive:** These people struggle to stop and think before acting. They typically act first and think later. When that happens, they can cause all sorts of problems for other people.

Post-Traumatic Stress Disorder

Post-traumatic stress disorder (PTSD) is a form of anxiety that develops after a trauma. When someone has suffered through a trauma of some sort, they can typically bounce back. They are typically able to begin recovering and healing from that traumatic event relatively simply. However, sometimes, they do not do that at all. Sometimes, their minds simply do not recover from the trauma in the same way that the other people do. Sometimes, they simply cannot keep up with the methods that they are thrown. Sometimes, they struggle to keep their reality separate from their mind.

These people oftentimes suffer greatly through being forced back into memories of the trauma; they commonly find that they are thrown right back to the way that they were feeling before. They feel trapped. They cannot cope with themselves. They struggle to keep moving forward or to be able to change their focus so they can avoid harm.

Each and every one of these different disorders are just several of the examples of what can be readily treated by DBT. They all come with very different struggles. Some cannot control their emotions. Some cannot manage behaviors. Some cannot keep control of their thoughts, and they will all benefit from the way in which they can learn to better cope with the stressors that they are exposed to. They can all learn a lot from this process and how they can better begin to deal with their emotions.

7 / THE STEPS TO DIALECTICAL BEHAVIOR THERAPY

At this point, it is time to dive right into the processes that we are considering. From here on out, the book is going to be focused on the information that you will need to begin embracing the ability to use DBT by yourself at home. You will be seeing the steps to which you will need to focus your attention within this chapter. Over time, as you continue to embrace these methods, welcoming the ways in which you can better deal with the problems that you have on hand, you will be able to better cope with the problems that you have developed over the course of your life.

This chapter is going to guide you through the four stages of treatment that become the center of focus. Most therapist work toward each step, one by one, starting with the worst problems and slowly making their way down to the problems that are not nearly as severe. By doing so, slowly but surely shifting from the worst behaviors down to creating the life that you want to live, you ensure that you have the quality of life that you will need to protect yourself. This is the perfect self-preservation pattern; when you work hard to stop the most dangerous behaviors first, you can ensure that, at the end of the day, you are better able to see the ways in which you want to enjoy your life.

We will go through these steps, one by one and figure out what it is that the goals will be. As you quietly read along, you will want to keep in mind that each of these will matter to you as well. You will need to be willing and able to quietly apply each of these patterns to your own life as well. When you can do that, you know that you are better able to ensure that everything is happening according to plan. You will be able to begin foreseeing what this process will look like for you, and that visualization and planning will help you immensely.

Stage 1: Treating the Most Self-Destructive Behaviors

Stage 1 is all about discovering what the worst situation is. It is trying to stop anything that is incredibly self-destructive. As you recall, some of the people that DBT treats are suicidal; that desire for suicide would be at the top of this list. When you use DBT, you will be treating your worst, most destructive tendencies before anything else. Some people may be hurting themselves. Others may be using drugs or they may be engaging in risky behaviors that, if they do not stop, have the very real potential to kill them.

The riskiest behaviors are usually there because the patients either do not value their lives at this point in time or they simply do not care about what is going on around them. The people that are more likely to be more self-destructive will also probably, unfortunately, be the most resistant to this process as well. When this happens, you are going to see all sorts of other problems begin to manifest as well. When these problems all arise all at once, you will recognize that something needs to be done. Perhaps you wish that you could die. Perhaps you are currently drinking an entire bottle of vodka each day, or you are engaging in other risky behaviors. No matter what it is, you need to look at the ways that you will be able to better deal with these problems.

This stage has one goal: It is trying to achieve control. At the beginning of this stage, the patients that are suffering and trying to get their treatment typically describe themselves as out of control —they cannot stop themselves from spiraling and they cannot prevent it from getting worse. They continue to struggle greatly during this time period and they desire to get that control back. By the end of stage 1, they should have that control.

Stage 2: Addressing Quality of Life Skills

At state 2, the individual is no longer in crisis, and that is a major step forward. However, usually, there are other problems that will need to be considered as well. When you take a look at the way in which these people in stage 2 live, they are finally afloat, but, they are not out of the water yet. They are still in danger. They are able to keep their behaviors under control, but just barely—they are still suffering underneath everything. They still struggle to find that quality of life that they are going to need.

Usually, these people have suffered due to trauma or being invalidated. Sometimes, they did the invalidating. Other times, they were the ones being invalidated by other people. No matter the situation, however, they often found that they were stuck. They could not get out of that rut. They could not figure out how best to deal with the stressors that were facing them, and as a result, they suffered. They are no longer emotionally volatile, but at this point, they are also not enjoying life either. They have faded into a position of quiet desperation, in which they are quietly suffering rather than finding the joy that they need.

The entire goal of this stage is to learn how to fix that quality of life. It is to figure out how the individual is able to begin breaking away from that desperation and learning how they can then begin to deal with the problems that they are facing. They are looking for the ways that they can leave behind that lack of emotionality to discover what it is that they truly need in life. They are being taken from that feeling of quiet distance and desperation from everything and into one that involves healing and discovering that quality of life that is missing.

Stage 3: Focusing on Relationship Quality and Self-Esteem

The third stage focuses on creating a life to live instead of one to suffer within. At this point, the individual should have broken out of that state of being desperate for normalcy and into being able to feel again. This is the point in time where the individual is learning to do everything that he or she will need to better deal with their problems. They are developing the skills that will be there that will help them for an ordinary life.

The entire point of stage 3 is to get to that stage of normalcy. It is to recognize that there are certain key aspects that come along with a normal life, and to reach those stages of normalcy and to develop that happiness, you must be able to get yourself out of that position. You must ensure that you are better able to process the situation at hand. You must be able to better able to follow certain life skills. You will need to learn to live. You will need to learn to have goals in life, both short and long-term. You will need to develop that self-esteem that you will need in life. You need the skills that you will need to begin to develop the relationships for your life.

Essentially, this stage is creating those life skill that will bring the greatest sense of normalcy to them. They are the skills that are needed in many different contexts they are the skills that will be enough for them to better understand what needs to be done and how to do it. When you are able to get out of stage 3, you know that you have the skills that you will be able to live a life that is ordinary – both in its happiness and its unhappiness, as they are both part of a normal existence and experience.

Stage 4: Promoting Joy

The fourth stage is not always necessary, but for those who do need it, it can be greatly beneficial to remember. This stage is all about being able to develop that further, deeper meaning in life. For some people, that ordinary sense of happiness is not enough; other people want to take it further. They want to discover what it means for them to better develop their life goals. They want to feel more connected. They are looking for the ways that they are able to better achieve what it is that they are ultimately looking for. These people want to go a step further—they are looking for purpose and connection, and they feel like, until they get it, they will be unsatisfied. They will feel incomplete until they discover this point. They need this to better themselves and to figure out what it is ultimately that they want and need.

. . .

To complete stage 4 is to be moving toward a life that is set up so you will be able to better cope with the life that you live. It is the necessary skills that you will need to better ensure that you are prepared. It is trying to figure out what it is that matters the most to you so you can embrace it.

8 / DIALECTICAL BEHAVIOR THERAPY AT HOME

DBT will, ultimately, be more effective if you were to spend the time to go through it with a proper therapist. It is always simply always going to be more effective to have a professional guiding you through the steps, one by one. When you use DBT at home on your own, however, you are not getting that guidance. Instead, you are focusing entirely on what you can provide yourself. You are ensuring that you can better manage the situation on your own. You are looking at the ways in which you are able to help yourself.

Ultimately, you are already on the right track if you want to be efficient on your own. The biggest hurdle for yourself to pass was being able to find a book with the material that you will need, and you have that right here. It is very important to recognize the ways that you are better able to help yourself and to be prepared. What you will ultimately need to ensure is that you can focus on what it is that you need to do. You must make sure that you are dedicated. You must be diligent in being able to pay attention to what it is that you need to do the most. When you can focus on that, paying attention to what it is that you can do, you will be able to make progress on your own.

The skills that DBT teaches heavily are mindfulness, emotional regulation, distress tolerance, and interpersonal effectiveness. Each of these are crucial skills to develop. They allow you to understand that fine balance between what you can and cannot change. The more of these skills that you develop yourself and the better that you get at managing them, the better you will get in how you approach the world around you. You will be able to stop and pay attention to the way in which your training will be able to help you.

Ultimately, even if you are not in one of the groups of people that were discussed earlier within this book, it is still highly possible that you are able to make use of these processes. There is no rule that says that you must be a certain person or you must have a certain problem if you hope to make use of these processes. In fact, it is not required at all. All you need to do is have a problem that you need to face and have the strength to tell yourself that you need to fix it. If you can do that, you will be able to get moving.

Remember That These Skills are a Lifestyle

Before we move on to the real work, it is time for you to consider that these skills are for a lifetime. These skills are for someone who want to see their effects and ultimately, their effects will be the most apparent if you are able to make use of them regularly. You need to remember that at the end of the day, you will get what you put into this process. If you want to get more out of these skills, then you have to put more into them.

. . .

These skills work as a lifestyle more than as a quick fix therapy. You are not being given the magic answer that will solve your problem. You are not being guided to one single answer. You are being given skills that you can apply—and you *should* apply them regularly. You need to be able to recognize that you can apply these skills. You need to remind yourself that you will be able to better control yourself the longer that you are able to make use of these principles and the sooner that you are able to apply them to yourself. You will be applying them, ideally, anywhere that they are relevant.

Practice Regularly

Similarly speaking, you must make sure that you are able to practice these methods regularly. Spend some time stopping and reminding yourself what you need to do. Take the time to sit down and review over your skills. Take the time to quietly reflect on yourself and the way that you are dealing with the problems at hand. Remind yourself that, at the end of the day, you can get better—so long as you continue to practice with these methods as much as you can.

DBT will give you what you put in. If you want to practice regularly and ensure that, at the end of the day, you are regularly working with your skills and learning how best to cope with them, then great! You will get a lot out of this book. If you are looking for an answer that will fix your problem, such as a perfect "A-ha!" moment, you are not going to find that. There are no perfect epiphany moments where everything beautifully falls right into place like in the movies—you need to work. You need to put in the work hard if you want to make use of these. You need to make sure that you are able to better use these processes to ensure that, at the end of the day, you can better cope with any of the problems that you will find yourself facing. If you put in the time that you will need, you will find that these tools are actually greatly helpful. They can actually carry you far if you are willing to make them work for you.

Use These Skills in Other Contexts

Similarly, remember that nothing exists in a vacuum. While these skills are largely present to give yourself that boost in quality of living, you need to remember that at the end of the day, they can be used elsewhere as well. What if you took that mindfulness or that resilience and you took it with you to work so you could better focus there? What if you made use of your skills when it came to solving a conflict with your partner? The more that you make use of these abilities in these manners, the closer that you can become to understanding what it is that you are going to get in the future. You will be constantly reinforcing your skills. The people around you may not be entirely sure what you are doing when you start using them, but that is okay—if they help you, then they are doing their job, and the more that you can make use of these skills, the better you will be.

Do Not Give Up

Remember that this process will not always be easy. It is not always simple to go in and retrain your mind. In fact, it rarely ever is. It is difficult to go in and rewrite what is effectively years and years of your own programming. This can be a problem for people, especially if they are more firmly aligned with the idea that when the going gets tough, it is time to give up.

If you really want to get those results that you are looking for, you need to make use of your own ability to stay resilient. If you give up, you have already failed—you must be able to remind yourself that you can tolerate the stress that you are under and that you can begin to make better use of these therapies as they are for you. The better that you become at coping with this, the better you will do.

When you start to feel doubtful that this is right for you, remind yourself that you can do better. Remind yourself that you can be better. Remind yourself that you *deserve* better and that you will do anything in your power to make it happen. The closer that you can get to that point, that moment in which you know that you are going to succeed, the better, and the more fulfilled that you will feel. You can do this for yourself—you just have to reach for it.

Do Not Be Afraid to Reach Out for Help

And finally, if you are practicing DBT at home, do not feel like you have to stay that way. You have endless resources available to you. There are many people online that can help you. There are therapists trained in DBT all over the country. You can find people that have already been through DBT and know what the process is. You can find people that are practicing DBT and those who coach it. You can find support groups and you can find others.

There is no rule that you must isolate yourself, and in fact, in this instance, isolation is the exact opposite of what you are looking for. You want to ensure that, at the end of the day, you do develop those skills. You want to ensure that you are able to better cope with the stressors in your life.

If you find that this is too much for you, do not be afraid to reach out to friends and loved ones. This process can be stressful for people. It can become too much sometimes, and sometimes people can find that, no matter how hard they try, they cannot deal with the processes around them. If you feel like this process is causing you more distress than it is helping, then you may be best served underneath the guidance of someone who knows what they are doing and that will be able to give you exactly what it is that you need.

THE FIRST OF the four cores of DBT that we are going to look at is mindfulness. Mindfulness itself is the act of being present. It is simply being there in the moment. It is being able to ensure that you are able to stop and simply observe the world around you, completely free and devoid of judgment. It is being able to look around and recognize what is going on. It is being able to stop and hear the way in which your mind is working without making yourself feel bad or ashamed for your thoughts. It is simply being in that moment.

Ultimately, most people go about their lives perpetually distracted. They may try to focus but find that they are constantly inundated with distractions. It could be your own thoughts that distract you, or it could be the radio blaring in the car. It could be the chattering of your children, or the whining of your dog, or a million other things. It is incredibly difficult to be able to stop and be mindful without really thinking about anything at all. Achieving that is difficult when you do not know what you are doing, and yet, it is an integral part of this process. Without the mindfulness, you cannot ensure that you are better able to cope with the world around you. Without mindfulness, you cannot be able to stop and see the way in which you interact with the world. Without mindfulness, you cannot remind yourself of what you need to do at any point in time.

Within this chapter, we are going to dive into mindfulness as a topic. We are going to look at the ways in which you can become mindful in your own life. We are going to consider the methods with which you can be sure that you better deal with the world around you. We are going to go over the ways that mindfulness and DBT fit together. Finally, we will go over some of the exercises in mindfulness that you can use for yourself.

Practicing Mindfulness

To practice mindfulness is very simple in theory. All you have to do is stop and focus your mind on current state. You do not have to do anything at all while you do this; you simply observe the state of your mind, or of whatever else it is that you have ultimately chosen to focus on. At the end of the day, mindfulness does not need to be difficult. It does not need to be some impossibility that you cannot manage. Mindfulness is a simple skill that will involve you stopping, taking a step back, and then enjoying the moment.

When you practice mindfulness, you are going to stop and listen to yourself. You are listening to your mind and your thoughts. You are reminding yourself that, at the end of the day, your thoughts are just that—they are thoughts. They are not you. They do not define you. They do not determine your worth. You are not what the thoughts say. If your thoughts are currently angry, that does not mean that you are an angry person. If your thought is that you are dumb or stupid or unable to otherwise deal with yourself, you must be willing and able to recognize that that is nothing other than a thought. Your thoughts only have as much power as you are willing to give them and that is entirely dependent upon you.

When you can make use of mindfulness, you will be distancing yourself from those thoughts and the emotions that you feel. You are learning to develop a position of quiet observance rather than of being caught up in what is happening around you. You are learning what it means to be in your current state without worrying about anything else at that particular point in time.

Mindfulness and DBT

When it comes down to it, DBT is meant to treat emotional dysfunction. It is to figure out the way that you can defeat that dysregulation in order to be able to begin to move forward. Imagine for a moment that you have a job that you enjoy. That job could be doing anything at all. Whatever it is, you genuinely enjoy about 95% of the work that you do. You enjoy the people. You enjoy the clientele. However, you realize that, for that last 5% of the time, you are busy regularly doing something that you hate. When it is your time to go and take care of whatever that hated thing is, you find that you get stuck. You sit there and wallow. You tell yourself that you hate the job. You tell yourself that you should quit. You spend so much time during that 5% period dwelling on how awful it is, slowing yourself down, that you then begin to find that you are stuck there, longer than you expected that you would be. You have essentially trapped yourself there—you have no choice but to keep on going, but that very fact leaves you frustrated and unwilling to continue working. You drag your feet more and more. You find that you begin to resent the job, and the longer that you have to do that 5% of work every day, the more that you become frustrated. The more that you get frustrated, the more that you feel like you want to quit. You tell yourself that quitting would be the best possible solution here. You tell yourself that if you were to quit, you would be better off because you would not be miserable any longer.

However, stop for a moment—you are miserable, but why? What is it that the problem is here? Is it really that you have to do that 5% of work that you dislike when you love the other 95% of your job? Is it really worth it to get that worked up over what is the equivalent of just about 25 minutes of your day? If you are loving the other 7.5 hours of your work day, why would you throw that away over one 25 minute session a day?

Notice what the problem is here—the problem is that your own inability to regulate is keeping you back. You see that at the end of the day, the fact that you are stuck, and the fact that you have to keep on going are problems. You see that it is not a problem with the job, but rather that you are having a difficult time accepting being unhappy with a very small aspect of your job. This is not abnormal—we all have areas in our lives that frustrate us. We all have to do things that we do not like sometimes, and yet, at the end of the day, it is important to remember that you can defeat that. You can overcome it. You can learn to cope with those negative emotions.

Mindfulness helps you with that. Mindfulness in this sense is meant to guide you through accepting what is happening. It is guiding you to accept what you cannot change and accept what you dislike. It may not be your favorite thing to hear, but at the end of the day, you must recognize that you have no choice here. You must recognize that, at the end of the day, the best thing that you can do is learn to cope with the world around you.

In this instance, mindfulness helps in three ways:

- **It facilitates acceptance:** You discover that at the end of the day, you can accept what you are stuck with. You can learn how you can become better willing to cope with what you dislike or what you cannot control.
- **It facilitates level-headed decision making:** Your mindfulness can also aid in ensuring that you make good decisions. When you struggle to watch your emotions, you can discover that, at the end of the day, you will make impulsive decisions that do not actually help you. You will realize that you are able to better cope with these emotions so you can then make decisions that actually make sense for you.
- **It removes the struggle with your emotions:** When you take a step back from everything that is happening around you, you realize that, at the end of the day, you can cope with just about anything. You can create that distance that you need to help yourself with your most difficult emotions and that can help you greatly. In finding that distance, you can better deal with the ways in which you can cope.

Mindfulness can be difficult to use at first, but the more that you can bring it into your life, the better that you will become. We are going to take a look at the methods that you can use here that will help you begin to implement mindfulness into your own life so you can begin to succeed with it. The more that you work with your own mindfulness, the easier it will become over time.

Mindfulness Exercise 1: Short Observations

This first exercise is to sort of dip your feet into the process. For this particular exercise, you will need just one item. It can be any item that you would like—it could be a photograph or it could be a pen, or a rock, or literally anything else. The only restriction that you have is that it should not be an electronic device and it should not be a book or another media source.

Sit down somewhere that you will not be interrupted with your item. Take it with you and pull it out. Look at the object that you are holding and set a timer. You must spend the next 5 minutes doing nothing but observing your item. This may seem strange at first, but take that time to slowly but surely go over all of the details that you can of the item. Look at the way that it is shaped. Go over the texture. What color is it? Does the color change? How does it feel in your hand? Spend the entire five minutes going over these details with yourself so you can better understand what it is to be mindful.

These minutes are spent quietly focusing on an object; you are learning to quietly direct yourself into juts one item so you can then begin to understand it. This is the inherent mindfulness that you are attempting to achieve. You are essentially teaching your-self that you must be able to stop and look at an object and only that object in its entirety for a period of time.

. . .

After your timer is up, you need to quietly reflect on it. What did it mean for you to focus your attention entirely on something? How did it impact you? What does that mean for you in the future? Will you try to use it again sometime? How did it make you feel? Why? Why not?

Mindfulness Exercise 2: Mindful Eating

Another simple introduction to mindfulness is mindful eating. When you use mindful eating, you are focusing your attention on just one thing for that one point in time. You are rejecting anything other than the simple act of eating in that one moment. To eat mindfully, you are going to slowly and gently go through the process of eating with nothing on your mind. This means that you should not be thinking about anything at all. Your mind should solely be focused on what you are eating. What does it taste like? How do you like it? What is the texture?

Spend three minutes quietly and mindfully eating something today. Let yourself quietly focus on just the food. During this, there should be nothing else on your mind. There should be nothing else in existence but that food that you are consuming. If you can do that, you will find that you are able to better focus than you thought.

Mindfulness Exercise 3: The Body Scan

This next exercise is known as the body scan. This is to help you begin to stop and pay attention to exactly what you feeling right that moment. You are ensuring that you know exactly what the state of your body is right that moment. As you go through this, you are going to quietly pay attention to the way that you feel.

. . .

Take a deep breath and start at the top of your head. Slowly, as if imagining that you were drying yourself off, little by little, study each and every part of yourself. You are looking for anything and everything here. Look for the feelings and sensations within the body parts as you slowly make your way down. Where is the tension in your body? Which parts of your body are entirely relaxed? As you continue to go through this process, you should find that, at the end of the day, it is not actually that bad to go through everything in this manner. You will work your way down until you get to your toes. What did you notice? How did it make you feel?

10 / DISTRESS TOLERANCE

THE NEXT CORE concept for DBT is distress tolerance. This is the method through which you are able to tolerate the stress within yourself. It is essentially emotional self-regulation—it is your ability to remain in control and ready to function even when you are stressed out. It can be difficult at times to regulate your emotions—that is just a fact. We all face rough emotions sometimes, but the key here is that you must be able to develop that degree of stress tolerance to know that you are better able to cope if you need to.

Within this chapter, like the last one, we will be addressing the relevance of distress tolerance and what it is to the entire principle of DBT. We will be taking a closer look at what it is and how it works so, at the end of the day, it does become possible to change. We are looking at what it means to be able to become emotionally resilient so you can begin to tolerate the ways in which you are surrounded in the world.

. . .

When you are able to go through developing distress tolerance, you are able to begin developing that ability to be resilient, no matter what is going on around you. You can learn to cope with the stress that you will face. When you learn to be emotionally resilient, you are able to cope with just about anything that you face. You are able to change the way in which you see the world around you in the sense that you learn to accept it and in becoming accepting of it, you learn how you can better deal with everything else.

Essentially, distress tolerance boils down to this idea of radical acceptance. It is trying to ensure that, at the end of the day, you are able to accept what you are doing and what you are surrounded with. If you can accept that, you know that you can begin to change the way that you react. You know that you will be able to tolerate the stress.

The idea here is that ultimately, pain is a part of life. We can never entirely and utterly escape the pain of reality. We cannot avoid the negativity in our lives on our own—negativity and pain will always be there, and so it is better to teach the acceptance of them. The idea, then, is that instead of you feeling like you must avoid the source of your pain, you begin to approach it instead. There is no point in shying away from what stresses you out simply because, at the end of the day, no matter what it is, it will always be there somehow. Think of it this way—if you are afraid of rejection, what will you do?

. . .

You could choose to avoid all people in hopes of avoiding rejection. Sure, you would not be rejected, but the end result is the same—you are still alone. Or, you could choose to embrace it. You could embrace the possibility that you may be rejected at some point and then move forward in like. If that pain is inevitable anyway, why should you attempt to avoid it? Instead, you can control the way that you feel. You can accept the reality of the world around you and in doing so, you can then also make sure that you control your own feelings. At the very least, when you attempt to accept to the possibility of failure and you try your hardest to be able to better deal with yourself, you will be able to better deal with the world around you. You will not be afraid of that failure that could potentially threaten you. You will not be afraid of being stuck somewhere. You will not be afraid of being rejected, or whatever else your fears are. When you learn to recognize the legitimacy of that fear that you have, and recognize that, at the end of the day, you need to work to be able to tolerate and respect it. There is ultimately nothing wrong with being afraid—so long as that fear does not hold you back and so long as that fear does not hurt anyone.

When you practice distress tolerance, you learn to recognize the ways in which your life changes. You recognize the way that you will have to suffer sometimes, but also, that you will be able to succeed in the future. Think about it—you take the risk of being rejected, but when you are not rejected, the reward is worth it. It is all about teaching you to understand that sometimes, the reward is worth the risk and when you do find that you are risking something, you must be prepared to fail—and if you do fail, you must be prepared as well to tolerate it.

Distress Tolerance and DBT

In DBT in particular, this is an incredibly important factor.

This is necessary if you want to be able to help yourself to be able to develop that understanding of your needs. If you want to be able to understand the ways in which you can better deal with the problems that you are facing, you will better begin to deal with the entirety of the situation. You essentially learn you are able to cope when you are suffering, either physically or emotionally. It grants you the ability that you can use to endure the pains of just about any situation, learning to recognize that will occur so there is no point in running.

With radical acceptance, you are recognizing that you cannot change anything that is happening around you at that moment. It means that you are willing to experience what you are surrounded by right in that moment. You are going to be willing to focus inward for the duration of this; you are able to be in the situation rather than attempting to find some sort of escape. When you can embrace that radical acceptance, you are able to trust that you can take care of yourself. You are able to push yourself back to where you need to be. You are able to bring yourself into the moment and focus on being able to tolerate what is happening. The more that you can learn to tolerate what is happening, the better you will be able to cope with life and all of the surprises and challenges that it has a tendency to throw at people. The more that you practice these policies, the easier it becomes for you to begin to accept the world around you.

It is crucial that you remember that acceptance does not mean that you like what is happening. It does not mean that you agree with it, nor does it mean that you are okay with it continuing to happen indefinitely. Rather, radical acceptance in this situation is simply acknowledging what is happening around you at that one point in time for that one point in time and not fighting it right that moment.

Distress Tolerance Exercise 1: Visualization

The first method that we are going to discuss that can be used for distress tolerance is visualization. When you make use of visualization, you are learning the ways that you can better tolerate the world around you by retreating within yourself. You are essentially giving yourself the ability to stop what you are doing, return back to your own mind, and then allow yourself to better focus on the image that you have created. This allows you to step back from the pain that you may be feeling.

You can paint any picture that you want when you are visualizing away the pain. All that matters is that what you are doing is helping yourself to be able to better deal with the problem so you can, at the end of the day, get through the problem that you are in. When you make use of visualization, you are better able to remind yourself of what really matters. You are able to help yourself to retreat just long enough to make the situation bearable.

To visualize, all you have to do is stop and distance yourself away from what is going on. Remember your mindfulness practice and quietly focus inwardly. Within your mind, you can now create yourself a beautiful picture that you can be on. You can create paintings in your mind of a beach with beautiful white sands or you could be in the middle of a rainforest that has birds singing all around you. No matter what the image is, all that matters here is that you must paint it within your mind. Make sure that you make the image as clear as possible for yourself. Really imagine every last detail that you can. As you do this, allow yourself to calm down. Allow your body to settle down and relax as you work your way through everything. The more that you do this, the easier that it will become. The easier that it becomes, the better you can do for yourself. All you have to do is focus and wait it out.

As you continue to imagine the image that you paint yourself, make sure that you continue to keep your breathing as steady as you can and focus as much as you can on what it is that you have to do and how you have to do it. When you can do this, you know that, at the end of the day, you can better deal with any problems that may be thrown your way.

Distress Tolerance Exercise 2: Breathing

The next method of distress tolerance is one that sounds like it would be common sense—breathing. However, so many people find that they accidentally forget to breathe, especially in times during which they are stressed out, angry, or otherwise upset. When those emotions run high, it is incredibly difficult to remind yourself that you must slow down and breathe deeply to ensure that you can, in fact, keep your calm and ensure that, at the end of the day, you do manage to distance yourself from the stressors that you are facing.

In particular, we are looking at deep breathing in this exercise—you must be able to breath deeply to allow yourself to better recognize what you must do. When you breathe deeply, you are able to help encourage your body to slow down. Deep breaths trigger the *vagus nerve*—that part of your body that regulates out your heart rate, blood pressure, and just about every other function that your body has. Your vagus nerve is involved highly in stress regulation, and when you breathe deeply, you trigger that nerve to activate. You allow yourself to better deal with the emotions because you can return to that state of quiet calmness after you have done so. This is crucial when it comes down to it. You must know some way in which you can better distance yourself so you are able to better succeed at the end of the day, and the way to do so is through breathing.

To begin, you must lay down somewhere. This will not be a requirement in the future, but to make sure that you know what you are doing and that you are breathing in a way that is effective and is going to help you, you should start on your back for now. Place one hand on your chest and the other hand on your stomach. Then, take in a deep breath. Hold it in for a moment. Which hand was it that moved? If the hand on your stomach is the one that moved the most, then you know that you are breathing correctly. If it did not, then shift your energy so you breathe and move the hand on your stomach.

From then on, in any position, all you have to do is make use of deep breaths. Take a big, deep breath when you are ready to start the exercise. Hold it in for a few seconds, and let it go. You want to repeat this process. Ideally, you would do a five second inhale and a five second exhale after a brief pause, but you may need to work up to this. If you can make it work, then do so. If not, simply shorten the breaths to what is comfortable for you.

Distress Tolerance Exercise 3: Grounding

Finally, the last exercise that we are going to consider here is the use of grounding. When you make use of grounding, you are looking at a way in which you can remind yourself to stop, to calm down, and to begin to focus inwardly. This is commonly used in anxiety and panic attacks, but it works here, too—when you need to be able to calm yourself down, you can make use of grounding the next time that you need.

Essentially, to ground yourself, all you have to do is engage with your own senses. You are simply trying to identify the way in which you can properly interact with your senses to ensure that you are calming yourself down. You do this because you force your mind to shift out of that feeling of emotionality to shifting instead to one of rationality. You essentially force your mind to shift its gears to allow for you to take back that control and then begin to make use of it the way that you need.

To begin this process, take a deep breath for yourself. Then, you are going to work all the way down your senses. You will start with what you can see all around you. Look around. What is there? Identify at least five things that you can see right this moment. As you do, name them off. You see a chair. You see a table. You see a dog. You see a couch. You see a toy that a kid left on the ground. Or, you would fill that in with whatever is relevant for you.

Then, shift over to what you can hear. You should be able to list out four things all around you that you can hear surrounding you. What is there? Can you hear the fan running? Do you hear a vent? Birds chirping outside? A busy road? List it all out for yourself, one at a time.

. . .

Now, shift down a little bit further. It is time to identify what you can feel with your body. What is it? Do you feel carpet under your feet? Can you feel a breeze from a fan? What about the tickle of your hair on your back? Figure out the three things for yourself and then move on.

It is time now to do two things that you can smell around you. Perhaps you can smell the scent of the food cooking in the kitchen, or the lingering smell of your shampoo. Identify that for yourself and then move on.

Finally, you must choose the way that you are feeling right that moment. Identify the biggest emotion that you are currently feeling so you can be aware of it. Name the emotion. Now, stay in your quiet mental space that you are in.

To summarize, when you want to use grounding methods, you are looking at:

- 5 things that you can see
- 4 things that you can hear
- 3 things that you can touch
- 2 things that you can smell
- 1 thing that you are feeling

We all have emotions. These emotions can be varied greatly from person to person, but at the same time, they are all going to be different. Remember that your emotions are there so you able to better regulate yourself. They are there to help you to change the way that you act and the way in which you feel. They are motivators. They are there to either encourage your behaviors or discourage your behaviors. They are either good or bad. They are positive or negative. When you can recognize this, you can then begin to understand the roles that emotional regulation plays. They vary greatly. You may find that your emotions oftentimes feel like overkill for the situation that you are in. Sometimes, it makes no sense for you to be interacting the way that you are. You need to understand that sometimes, you will need to change your emotions.

Think of your emotions as your mind's attempt to guide itself. Your mind is trying to guide your body to change the way that your body responds. Your mind will encourage you to shift from behavior to behavior to try to figure out what is going to work the best for you. Think about it—when you are afraid, you want to run. You may lie to someone because you are afraid of the consequences of telling the truth. You try to cover it up by lying, and this can actually be a huge problem to you in your relationship. While fear may be greatly useful in many situations while you are out in the wild, such as being able to keep you alert when you are trying to avoid being found while walking somewhere. Your fear in one situation may be necessary or even good for you to have, while in other situations, it is a huge problem for you.

No matter what the emotion is, it has its own time and place. It is important for you to be able to recognize that sometimes, your emotions are spot on, but sometimes, you must also be able to stop and tell yourself that you need to change them. You must be able to criticize your own emotional triggers to prevent yourself from being led astray sometimes. This is done primarily through the process of emotional regulation.

Emotional regulation itself is the act in which you are able to pay attention to your emotions so you can understand them. To be able to regulate means that you are able to understand that you have influence. You can develop that ability to change the way that you process the world around you and your emotions that you have. When you are able to remind yourself to stop and consider those emotions in the moment, you are able to ensure that you protect yourself as well.

Emotional regulation comes along with three key points. It involves being able to stop actions that are triggered by emotions. This means that when you feel that you are about to do something that is going to be a problem, you are able to stop yourself. You are able to ensure that you can prevent yourself from doing something that you will regret and by refusing to do something that you will regret or that will be harmful for you, you can do better for yourself.

It also brings with it the ability to start actions related to emotions. When you are able to start those actions, you are then able to ensure that you can better figure out what you can do to change the way that you are behaving. Essentially, you can step in and tell yourself that you will or will not do something based on emotions.

Finally, you are able to change the behaviors that are associated with your emotions as well. This is the best process that you can make use of—it allows you to stop what you are doing when you do it so you know that it will not be problem in the future. You are essentially figuring out what you can do to help yourself to ensure that you only make good emotional responses.

To be able to regulate your emotions is to be able to modify your behaviors. You are able to use it as a sort of filter for yourself. You use it so you are better able to change the way that you can respond to anything around you so you know that you ultimately make the right decisions for yourself. Of course, this is not easy, but when you can do it right, you are better able to stop yourself and figure out the ways that you are able to better motivate yourself. You are able to change the ways that you will behave so you can better regulate yourself out. When you play your cards right, this allows you to figure out what it is that is truly important. It allows you to figure out how to control yourself and your emotions so you can ensure that, at the end of the day, you do not get caught up in being impulsive.

When you are impulsive, you run into all sorts of other problems that you will have to deal with. You can create problems for yourself simply by being impulsive or by giving in to those negative emotions. However, when you can regulate yourself well, you can ensure that you make good judgments. You ensure that at the end of the day, you are better able to regulate yourself, judge yourself properly, and figure out which behaviors that you can use.

This becomes a crucial ability to have, especially in DBT.

When you are able to keep your focus on how you can change your emotions so you are able to address the mental health issues that you are going to be facing. Oftentimes, DBT treats problems that are related to struggling with emotional regulation, and because of that, it becomes imperative that you are able to better regulate. To be able to regulate means that you are able to better control. To learn to regulate means to gain those skills that you need. To be able to regulate means that you can control yourself.

Emotions are tough for us all, but if you have the skills of emotional regulation, you can learn to express those emotions that you have in constructive manners that you know will be better for everyone involved. DBT focuses heavily on these processes. It focuses highly on learning to identify the emotions that you will need to use in order to change the way that you are behaving. When you are able to do this, you know that you are better able to cope with the stressors of your life and that is powerful. The better that you do with those emotions, the more likely you are to be able to cope in the long run.

Emotional Regulation Exercise #1: Cognitive Reappraisal

This first skill is all about being able to change the way that you think. It is the ability to look at a situation and essentially change the way that you look at it entirely. You are essentially able to ensure that you change up the way that you look at everything so you can better deal with the problem. Imagine, for example, that when your friend does not text you back right away, you get caught up in wondering what you did wrong because they must hate you if they did not answer the text. Rather than feeling like that, however, which is incredibly unfair to put on someone else anyway, you change the way that you think. Instead of focusing on that manner, you are able to shift it around. You change it so you focus on the fact that your friend must be busy instead.

When you want to use cognitive reappraisal, you will need to ensure that you are focusing on being able to challenge any of those thoughts that are highly emotional. When you are able to remember to challenge those thoughts as they occur, you are able to sort of alleviate the problem. You teach yourself to reject those ways of acting. You encourage yourself to resist the problem. You tell yourself that you are not willing or able to deal with that negativity and that you want it to be positive instead.

By taking back that control and refusing to allow those negative feelings control you, you are better able to cope. You are better able to deal with the emotions because you have turned down the problematic ones. You challenge them every time that they arise and over time, they stop.

For example, imagine that you are still convinced that your friend hates you after they explained that they were driving and could not respond. Instead of being able to deal with the possibility that someone else is actually being honest with you and is not free every moment, you tell yourself that you must be the problem.

However, if you were to correct that though, you would remind yourself that, at the end of the day, you must be able to accept that sometimes, other people are busy. It has nothing to do with whether or not they like you and everything to do with the way that they are trying to remain safe.

Emotional Regulation Exercise #2: Positive Thinking

Another method to help with your own emotional regulation is through the use of positive thinking. When you think positively, you are essentially able to show yourself that you are not willing to tolerate that negativity. Negative thoughts have the tendency to bring us down and because of that, you must be able to erase them entirely. You must be able to reject that negativity in favor for the positive thoughts that you have in your mind.

For example, imagine that as you are walking one day, you drop something. You immediately tell yourself that there is a problem with yourself. You blame yourself for being so clumsy and say that it is your own fault that you are so problematic in the first place.

However, if you can think positively, you can prevent yourself from falling for those negative thought traps. You stop yourself when you hear that kind of negativity and you remind yourself to show yourself some compassion. You remind yourself that it is okay to make mistakes sometimes and that it does not mean that you are a failure or a problem or anything else. Rather, you must be sure that you are better able to deal with the stress and the negativity. You must remind yourself that you are not actually broken or a problem. It is okay to be clumsy and it makes you quirky and you. You shift away from that negativity to something that shows that you are gently and kindly accepting yourself rather than attempting to push yourself away and make the problem worse.

Emotional Regulation Exercise #3: Gratitude Challenge

Finally, the last exercise that we will see for emotional regulation is the gratitude challenge. This challenge is there to remind you that, at the end of the day, you must be able to be grateful for what you have. You must remind yourself that, at the end of the day, you are able to thank the world for giving you what you have. The more that you are able to focus on the ways that the world has provided for you and the way that things have gone right, the more positive that your own thinking becomes. This happens over and over again. The more gratitude that you put out into the world around you, the more positivity flows into the world around you and you know that. You latch onto that.

For this challenge, you are officially challenged to spend the next two weeks figuring out three things every single day that you are grateful for. They should all be different objects and you cannot simply say that you are grateful for your food every day. Try thinking outside of the box a bit more than that—look at other ways that you can think about gratitude. Implement it everywhere that you can.

The more gratitude that you invite into your life the better your life will become. The more positivity that you can bring, the more likely it is that the positivity that you find will help you immensely. So, every night, before you go to bed. Sit down and think about the day. Consider how it went. Was it a good day or a bad day? What did you like? What did you dislike? What went well? What went wrong? What are you grateful for at the end of it all?

It is only when you can truly embrace gratitude, bringing it into your life, that you can begin to regulate your emotions. You must be able to implement them regularly if you hope to better get your own emotions under control. What better way to control your emotions than to implement a gratitude challenge? If you could feel any emotion at all, why not make it gratitude? Why not make it something beautifully positive that will help you feel joy and thankful for everything?

FINALLY, the last skill that people need to have is interpersonal effectiveness. When you can develop he interpersonal effectiveness that you need, you know that you can begin to interact with other people. At this point, you have the skills to tolerate the distress that you are in. You know how to handle emotional states. You can cope in many different situations, but, so far, you have not yet gotten that focus on what you will need to do for relationships with other people. To have a relationship with other people is to make yourself vulnerable, and if that vulnerability scares you, then you will need to pay close attention to the ways in which it leaves you feeling.

Now, you may be thinking that people skills are not that important —why would you need them? However, the fact of the matter is, that throughout your life, you will run into many different people. Some of them, you will interact with, others, you will pass up entirely. Either way, however, it is important to recognize one important feature: You need to be able to get along with the people that you do meet. When you are able to focus on being able to get along with people, you know that at the end of the day, you can do better. You know that you can interact in ways that are meaningful and when you can do that, you know that you are better able to manage those important relationships that you have.

When it comes down to interpersonal effectiveness, you are looking at your skill to do four things:

- You should be able to attend to the relationships that you have
- You should be able to juggle the constant war between the most important priorities and the demands that others put onto you.
- You should be able to balance the things that you want with the things that you should be doing
- You develop a sense of the mastery that you are looking for.

Each of these four skills are crucial to develop. The more that you are able to develop, the better you can do. When you get through this development, you are able to begin to relate better to other people. You are able to better cope with those that are around you. You are better able to manage the relationshps that you have because you are better able to manage the skills that you need to do so.

When you have the ability to interact with someone else, you are going to be doing so based on goal. What is it that you want to do with that relationship? What is it that you want to do with that particular interaction? How do you want it to play out? What can you do about that? How can you ensure that you make it happen?

There are ultimately three ways that you can do so. There are three distinctive interactions that can play out for you when it comes right down to it. You can have a goal to ensure that you get what you want. This is the first one—sometimes, you are only really interacting with someone else because you view it as the only way to get to that end that you are looking for. It becomes the only method through which you are better able to deal with the problem at hand or to get what you want. These are typically selfish interactions—these are designed to ensure that you are taking from other people without really attempting to give in return. The next goal to interactions with other people is to maintain or facilitate a relationship. This could be a conversation that has just one purpose—to make sure that you get to enjoy it with the other person. This is where many of the interactions with friends and families comes in. Finally, the last potential goal is to preserve your own self-image or self-respect. This is essential for you—you do not want to be seen as something that you are not. You do not want to feel like you are seen as less than. You do not want to feel like, at the end of the day, you are seen as a problem in the relationships around you.

All of these different attempts to interact with people are very important in their own ways. However, at the end of the day, the most important priority of you during this period of time is the relationships maintenance. You need to be able to see the ways in which you can better deal with the emotions that of yourself and those around you.

. . .

However, the interpersonal skills come into play with the other two as well. When you work toward your objective, you must be able to communicate clearly. You must be able to tell someone else what it is that you want and how you want to make it happen. You must be able to better interact with the other person and ensure that, at the end of the day, you can better begin to be understood. When it comes to your self-preservation interest, you use those same skills to ensure that you keep your image that you want shows up.

Interpersonal Effectiveness and DBT

This particular skillset is incredibly powerful and is essential if you want to be able to maintain your relationships with other people. It is only when you are better able to put yourself in this position in which you are able to interact with other people that you can begin to see the ways in which your own skills matter.

In DBT, you are going to be communicating constantly. You are constantly going to be working on how to better communicate with other people because, at the end of the day, you want and need to be able to communicate with other people. Communication is essential in just about any setting. Whether you are at school, in a relationship with someone else, being able to interact in other ways, or anything else, you must be able to interact and communicate effectively.

Think about it—if you cannot communicate effectively, what will happen? You may find that you are frustrated because you cannot get your point across. You may feel like you are frustrated because the other person seems to be entirely missing your point, over and over again. You feel like you cannot fix the problem because you are stuck in this rut where no one seems to understand what you are saying or why you are saying that.

Of course, then, the failure on your part to communicate would then have a direct impact on the way in which you feel about yourself. Your wellbeing is dependent upon both your self-esteem and your self-confidence, which are both developed through the use of your own relationships. You cannot have high self-esteem or high self-confidence if you feel like you cannot communicate effectively. You will struggle. You will find that you cannot simply succeed at anything that you try because you cannot communicate.

In particular, when it is time for you to begin to practice communication, it is important to recognize that there are two key points that are going to be pushed here. You must firstly be able to ask for the things that you currently want, and you must be able to say no when someone asks something of you. When you can do these two basic tasks, you know that, at the end of the day, you are more in control. You know that you are able to better cope with the situation at hand and that is important.

Now, at this point, we are going to take a look at three different ways that you are going to be able to stop and think. You need to see the ways that you can better deal with yourself and how to remember the ways that you can better cope with the feelings that you have at any point in time. You will have three acronyms here to remember; they will help you remember the steps that you must go through when it comes to ensuring that you can keep up with the relationships that you have.

Interpersonal   Effectiveness   Exercise   #1: DEAR MAN

This first acronym is a bit of a long one. However, it is great for helping you to develop objective effectiveness—it will help you begin to understand how you can communicate with those people around you to help yourself to figure out how to get your point across clearly and articulately.

- **Describe:** The first thing that you must do is ensure that you are able to describe what you want. This means that you must be able to come up with very specific words—you want to be as clear and concise as possible. The clearer that you are, the easier it becomes to understand what you are doing and what you are seeking. If you can master being clear, you can ensure that the people around you are more than happy to give you what you want.

- **Express:** Next comes express—this means that you are expressing yourself. You are clearly showing to those around you how you are going to feel at that point in time. You are telling them and showing them how you are feeling without expecting anyone to simply understand what you want without you saying a word. At the end of the day, they are not mind readers and as nice as it would be if they were, they simply are not. You need to cope with that and deal with it. Tell other people what you are thinking rather than hoping that they will simply catch on by themselves.

- **Assert:** Next, you need to remember assert. This means that you must ensure that you are straightforward when you speak. Tell everyone what you want and assert yourself. Remember, this does not mean forceful—it means firm. There is a fine line there and you need to ensure that you do not accidentally completely and utterly overblow it.

- **Reinforce:** This is essential. This means that, when someone does help you, you offer up your own reinforcement for it. You reward those people that have helped you. Especially if what you want is something that is positive, it becomes crucial for you to be able to show other people how appreciative you are when you see that they have done something for you. You essentially want to make everyone else feel like they are happier that they helped you. You want them to feel rewarded and fulfilled for helping you.

- **Mindful:** You must remember what the initial purpose of your interaction was in the first place. You do not want to allow yourself to become distracted— those distractions can be a huge problem for you. You must ensure that you stay with your eyes on the prize. Do not get distracted by arguments or anything else.

- **Appear:** This is to remind you to remain confident in your interacting with the people around you. When you better interact with the people around you with the right kind of confidence that you will need, people will be more likely to oblige you with what you want. This means that you must remember that your body language should be kept confident. Do not forget eye contact and posture.

- **Negotiate:** Finally, you must be willing to negotiate if you need to. This is important—when you are interacting with other people, you must be willing and able to interact better. You must be willing and able to give up what you wanted sometimes. You must be willing to see that sometimes, you have no choice but to negotiate to better get what everyone needs.

Interpersonal Effectiveness Exercise #2 GIVE

The next acronym is to help yourself to focus on your relationship effectiveness. This is going to ensure that, at the end of the day, you are successful in the interactions that you have with people. The acronym here is GIVE.

- **Gentle:** This is simple—you must remain gentle in your demeanor when you are trying to foster relationships. You should not attack other people when you talk. Make sure that you are not threatening at all during your interaction as well. You must be willing to avoid passing judgment on people and you must also be willing to be told no every once and a while.

- **Interested:** Next, you must consider how you can show everyone around that you are feeling interested with the interaction. You are ensuring that you are able to show them that you are happy to hear them. You do this by making sure that you show the other person the interest that they deserve. Listen without attempting to cut them off and pay close attention to the way in which you interact.

- **Validate:** Next comes validation. At this point, you are making sure that you acknowledge the way that the other party feels. You make sure that you recognize the way in which you interact with the other party. You ensure that you are able to listen closely and tell the other person that you hear them. You must make sure that you are outwardly validating when you are—you show them that you are listening to them and recognizing their feelings.

- **Easy:** The last letter here stands for easy. This is to remind you to keep your attitude and demeanor easy. Essentially, you do not want to accidentally scare anyone off. You do not want to make them feel like you are a threat or that you are not interested. Smile often. Have fun. Enjoy the time with the other person.

Interpersonal Effectiveness Exercise #3 FAST

Finally, the last acronym that we will consider here is FAST. FAST will help you make sure that you are able to remember how to remain effective in demanding your self-respect. This ensures that you are able to keep consistent in your own current beliefs.

- **Fair:** You must make sure that you are fair to everyone that is involved in every situation. This means that you must be fair not only to those around you, but also to yourself.

- **Apologize:** Next, consider that apologies have a time and a place and you must make sure that, at the end of the day, you do not apologize when it is unwarranted.

This will reduce your confidence. Make sure that you only apologize when necessary, and remember that you do not have to when you have asked for something, expressed your own opinion, or disagreed with someone.

- **Stick to Values:** Remember that you must be willing to stand up for your values. Do not give up on what you hold close in your heart just because someone else does not like them. Make sure that you always stand up for what you believe to be true and you should always be entirely firm on your own values. There is never a reason for you to give up on them.

- **Truthful:** Finally, the last point to remember is that you must be truthful at all costs. Do not lie to people. Also avoid other deceptive methods such as trying to exaggerate or attempting to manipulate other people.

And with that, you have made it to the end of *Dialectical Behavioral Therapy*. Hopefully, as you have finished up reading this book, you have great ideas for how these principles can guide you as you continue on your way through life. Remember, ultimately, you must be accepting and willing to change at the same time. You must be willing to see that sometimes, you must accept the change that is coming. You must see that sometimes, you must simply accept what is happening around you, and that other times, you actually can make changes. When you remember this, you learn that you do have the power that you are looking for. You learn that you do have that ability to make the changes that you are trying to find around you. You recognize that you can begin to ensure that your processes that you make use of and the tools that you use, can help you succeed.

This therapy can be difficult for some people. It can be challenging. It can be painful in some ways. You will be asked to dig up some of the deepest wounds that you have. You will need to be able to walk yourself through how you can begin to reclaim your life without emotions ruling over it. You will be learning what you can and cannot expect and the ways in which you can better begin to cope with the world. When you practice DBT, you learn that you can control yourself. You learn that you have the power to change the way that you think and feel, and in doing so, you can help to stabilize your behaviors. No matter where you have been or how long you have struggled, when you remember what DBT consists of, you can succeed.

Remember how mindfulness can help you accept what is happening. It can help you begin to recognize how you feel in the moment. It can help you see the sensations that you have for your-self and recognize how they feel for you. It can help you to accept the world for what it is and to see the truth as you do so. It is important to be able to be mindful when you are attempting to heal yourself, as that mindfulness teaches you to be able to better cope with anything.

Remember how distress tolerance teaches you the ways in which you are able to begin distancing yourself from pain that you feel. Remember that you can use these methods, from visualization to changing the way that you are breathing, to even working to ground yourself in other activities, and these will aid you in helping to distance yourself further. You can use these as sort of mental distractions that can help you to tolerate what is happening around you and it is in that acceptance in what is happening that allows you to continue to employ these tools.

Remember that emotional regulation teaches you everything that you need to know and how you can begin to control yourself in order to ensure that you can react properly. Remember that this is one of the ways that you actually can control the world around you; you can control your own input into the world. While you may not be able to dictate what comes back after the fact, you can still recognize that, at the end of the day, you have done something positive for yourself in being able to control what you can.

Finally, remember that interpersonal effectiveness is crucial when it is time for you to begin to interact with the world around you. It is how you control the way in which you interact with your friends, and how you interact with the people that you are surrounded with. When you are able to interact with the world in a way that is positive and actually constructive, you are able to better these relationships that you have so you can then begin to see the ways that you do need to improve yourself. The more that you are able to take control of your own behaviors, the more capable you become of navigating the world around you.

When you make use of the fact that, at the end of the day, you have the power to both accept and change at the same time, you can really begin to make use of the ways in which DBT asks that you behave. When you use DBT, you must accept the world. You must accept the stressors that you face and accept the pain that you are likely to encounter. When this happens you are able to recognize that sometimes, you must do nothing more than accept the world around you. However, you can also change as well—you can change your reactions to the people and things in your environment. It is only when you can master both of these skills—acceptance and change at the same time—that you can really begin to see the improvements that you have set out to find.

From here, all that is left for you to do is make sure that, at the end of the day, you must make sure that you also make use of these methods. Make sure that they become regulars in your repertoire. Make sure that you pull out these tools and these concepts any time that they become relevant so you can then begin to see the ways in which you need to act.

If you can begin to implement these processes regularly no matter what is happening around you, you can then begin to make the changes that you want to see. You can then understand the ways in which you can help yourself to grow. As you continue to grow, you will be able to better improve yourself. As you continue to improve yourself, you can begin to see possibilities that you may not have seen before. All you have to do is be willing to move toward them.

Thank you for taking the time to read through this book. Hopefully, you have found that with reading this, you gained some new methods that you can use to help to manage your own stress. Hopefully, as you make use of these new methods, you will start to see those results that you need so you can better cope with the world around you. Finally, if you have found that this book was useful to you in any way, please consider heading over to Amazon right now to leave behind a review. Your opinions, thoughts, and experiences in reading this book are always greatly appreciated and greatly welcomed!

HABIT

Building Self-Discipline, Persistence, Goal
Setting, Gratitude, Forgiveness & Meditation

Rhonda Swan

If you have picked up this book, you likely are someone who is sick and tired of being trapped within the same bad habits that you can't get out of. You probably want more for yourself than just constant procrastination and continuously doing things that won't add any value to your life. If this feels like you, I can help. I can teach you everything you need to know about from habits starting from how they are formed and which ones you should be incorporating into your life.

The trick to building habits is that it is hard work in the beginning. However, once the task that you want to turn into a habit actually become habits, you'll notice that it doesn't require as much energy as it used to complete it. This is the magic of building habits as learning how to do this means automating certain behaviors and tasks that are healthy for you without shedding a second thought. This is what I'm going to teach you to do throughout this book.

There are many things that are required for you to do before you can properly build new and good habits. For one, you need to practice self-discipline as that will be used in the first stages of habit reinforcement. Secondly, we need to learn how to break bad habits that are constantly holding us back like procrastination. That is the most common and worst bad habit that you can have. I will teach you ways to prevent and overcome your procrastination habit, so you have the capacity to learn new and healthy habits. I will also teach you about the challenges that you need to expect when you are actually trying to break out of bad habits. It's hard to do but definitely possible. By understanding the challenges beforehand, we can make a plan to help you overcome it as best as possible. Lastly, I will teach you how to use Cognitive Behavioral Therapy to build better habits. This is a new type of therapy that can be used to treat various disorders and can even be used to treat things like procrastination or to build new habits. There are many theories and practices that I will be teaching you to use.

So, in this book, you can expect to not only learn about new strategies and what types of habits you should build – but you will also have the opportunity to understand the science and theory behind it all. This is crucial in the learning process as understanding the *why* is just as important as learning the *how*. Without further ado, let's begin!

1 / BUILDING NEW HABITS

THE FIRST THING I will teach you about in this book is what it will require from you to make habits. The answer to this is simple; it's self-discipline. In order to exert self-discipline, you also need to have willpower. A common belief in people is that they think they can change their lives for the better if they simply could just have more willpower. If people had more willpower, everyone would be able to save responsibly for retirement, exercise regularly, stop procrastinating, avoid alcohol and drugs and achieve all kinds of their noble goals. This is true to an extent; however, you will learn later in this chapter that once an action becomes a habit, you no longer need to exert willpower anymore. Let's take a look at what willpower is and how this will play into building new habits.

What Is Willpower?

In various scientific articles related to studies on willpower, it was reported that the biggest obstacle when it comes to people achieving change was the lack of willpower. Although many people often place blame upon the scarcity of their willpower for their unhealthy choices, they are still grasping on to the hope of being able to achieve it one day. Most people in this study also reported that they think willpower is something that can be taught and learned. They are absolutely correct. Some research recently has discovered many ways of how willpower can be strengthened with training and practice. On the contrary, some participants in the survey expressed that they think they would have more willpower if they had more free time to spare. However, the concept of willpower isn't something that increases automatically if a person has more time in their day. So that leads me to the next question, how can people resist when they are faced with temptation? Over the last several years, many discoveries were made about how willpower works by scientists all over the world. We will dive a little deeper into what our current understanding of willpower is.

Weak willpower isn't the only reason for a person to fail at achieving their goals. Psychologists in the field of willpower have built three crucial components when it comes to achieving goals. They said that you first need to set a clear goal and then establish the motivation for change. They said the second component was to monitor your behavior in regards to that goal. Willpower itself is the third and final component. If your goal is similar to the following; stop smoking, get fit, study more, or stop wasting time on the internet, willpower is an important concept to understand if you are looking to achieve any of those goals.

The bottom line of willpower is the ability to achieve long term goals by resisting temporary temptations and urges. Here are several reasons why this is beneficial. Over the course of a regular school year, psychologists performed a study that examined the self-control in a class of eighth grade students. The researchers in this study did an initial assessment of the self-discipline within the students by getting the students, their parents and teachers to fill out a questionnaire. They took it one step further and gave these students the task of deciding whether they want to receive $1 right away or $2 if they waited a week. At the end of the study, the results pointed to the fact that the students that had better test scores, better school attendance, better grades, and had a higher chance of being admitted to competitive high school programs all ranked high on the self-discipline assessment. These researchers found that self-discipline played a bigger role than IQ when it came to predicting academic success. Other studies have found similar evidence. In a different study, researchers asked a group of undergraduate university students to fill out self-discipline questionnaires that will be used to assess their self-control. These researchers developed a scale that helped score the student's in relation to the strength of their willpower. They found that the students that had higher self-esteem, better relationship skills, higher GPA, and had less alcohol or drug abuse all had the highest self-control scores from the questionnaire.

Another study found that the benefits of willpower tend to be relevant well past university years. This self-control study was conducted in a group of 1000 people who had been tracked since birth to the age of 32. This is a long term study in New Zealand, where they wanted to learn more about the effects of self-control well into adulthood. They found that the people who had high self-control during their childhood grew up into adults that had better mental and physical health. They also had less substance abuse problems, criminal convictions, better financial security, and better money-saving habits. These patterns were proven even after the researchers had adjusted external influences such as socioeconomic factors, general intelligence, and these people's home lives. These findings prove why willpower is extremely important in almost all areas of a person's life.

Now that you have learned the importance of willpower and the role it plays in multiple stages of a person's life, let's define it a little further. There are many other names used for willpower that is used interchangeably; this includes; drive, determination, self-control, resolve, and self-discipline. Some psychologists will characterize willpower in even more specific ways. Some define willpower to be:

- The capacity to overcome unwanted impulses, feelings, or thoughts.
- The ability to resist temporary urges, temptation and delay instant gratification in order to achieve goals that are more long-term
- The effortful and conscious regulation of oneself.
- The ability to engage a "cool" cognitive system of behavior rather than a "hot" emotional system
- A limited resource that has the capability to be depleted

Delaying Instant Gratification Is Key to Fostering New Habits

Over 40 years ago, a famous psychologist studied self-control within children using a simple and effective test. You may have seen this study used before in modern-day experiments. His experiment is called the "marshmallow test." This test has become extremely famous over the years as it laid the groundwork and then paved the way for modern studies of self-control.

This psychologist and his colleagues began the test by showing a plate of marshmallows to a child at the preschool age. Then, the psychologist let the child know that he had to go outside for a few moments and that he would let the child make a very simple decision. If the child could wait until the psychologist came back into the room, she could have two marshmallows. If the child could not or doesn't want to wait, then she can ring the bell which then the psychologist would come back to the room right away but then she would only get to have one marshmallow.

Willpower can be defined as simple as the ability for a person to delay instant gratification. Children who have high self-control are able to give up the immediate gratification of eating a marshmallow so that they can be able to eat two of them at a later time. People who have quit smoking sacrifice the satisfaction of one cigarette in hopes of having better health and lower the risk of cancer in the future. Shoppers fight the urge to spend money at a mall so they can save their money for their future retirement. You probably get the point here.

This marshmallow experiment actually helped the researchers develop a framework that explains people's ability to resist or delay instant gratification. He proposed a system that he calls "hot and cool" in order to explain whether willpower will succeed or fail. The 'cool' system is naturally a cognitive one. It means that it is a thinking system that uses knowledge about feelings, sensations, goals, and actions that remind oneself, for example, why the marshmallow shouldn't be eaten. The cool system is very reflective, while the hot system is more emotional and impulsive. The hot system is responsible for quick and reflex-based responses to specific triggers, for example, eating the single marshmallow without thinking about the long term ramifications. To put this in layman's terms, if this framework were a cartoon, the hot system would be the devil and the cool system would be the angel on your shoulder.

When somebody's willpower fails, their hot system essentially overrides their cool system, which leads them to make impulsive actions. However, some people are more or less affected by the hot system triggers. That susceptibility to emotional responses plays a big role in influencing a person's behavior throughout life. The same researcher discovered that when he revisited his experiment with the children that had now grown up into adolescents, he found that the teenagers who were able to wait longer to have two marshmallows when they were children were more likely to have higher SAT grades and their parents were more likely to rate them of having better ability to handle stress, plan, respond to reason and exhibit self-control in frustrating situations and could concentrate better without being easily distracted.

Funnily enough, the marshmallow study didn't end there. A few other researchers tracked down almost 60 people who are now middle aged, who had previously been a part of the marshmallow experiment as young children. These psychologists proceeded to test the participants' willpower strength using a task that's been proven to prove self-control within adults. Surprisingly, the participants' various willpower strengths had been very consistent over the last 40 years. Overall, they found that the children who were not successful in resisting the first marshmallow did poorly on the self-control tasks as an adult and that their hot stimuli seem to be consistent throughout their lifetime. They also began to study brain activity in some of the participants by using magnetic resonance technology. When these participants were presented with tempting stimuli, those who had low willpower exhibited brain patterns that were very different from the brain patterns of those that had strong willpower. They discovered that the prefrontal cortex (this is the region of the brain that controls choice making functions) was more active in the participants who had stronger willpower and the ventral striatum (an area of the brain that is focused on processing rewards and desires) showed increased activity in the participants who had weaker willpower.

Can A Person Run Out of Willpower?

The hot-cold framework does a great job of explaining people's ability to delay gratification but there is another theory that is called 'willpower depletion' that has emerged in recent years to explain what happens to people after they have resisted multiple temptations. Everyone exerts willpower every day in one form or another. People resist to surf the web or go on social media instead of finishing their work report. They may choose a salad when they are craving a slice of pizza. They may hold their tongue rather than make a snide remark. Recent growing research indicates that resisting temptations repeatedly takes a mental toll on a person. Some people describe willpower as a muscle that can get tired if overused.

．．．

The earliest discoveries of this concept came from a study that was conducted in Germany. The researcher brought participants into a room that smelled like fresh-baked cookies. The participants sat down at the table that held a bowl of radishes and a plate of those freshly baked cookies. The researchers asked some of the participants to taste those cookies while the others were asked to try the radishes. After this, the participants were assigned to complete a difficult geometric puzzle in 30 minutes. The researchers found that the participants who had to eat the radishes (therefore resisting the urge to eat the cookies) took 8 minutes to give up on the puzzle while the participants who got to eat the cookies tried to complete the puzzle for 19 minutes. The evidence here seems as if the people who used their willpower to resist eating the cookies drained their resources for future situations.

In the late 90s, this research was published, and since then, numerous other studies have begun looking into willpower depletion or otherwise known as ego depletion. One study, for example, the participants were asked to hold back and suppress any feelings they had while they watched an emotional film. These participants then participated in a physical stamina test but gave up sooner than the participants who watched the movie and reacted normally without any suppression.

Depleting willpower is very common in today's society. You have probably tried to make yourself be diplomatic when you are dealing with an aggravating customer or forced to fake happiness when your in-laws come to stay with you for an extended period of time. You must have realized that certain social interacts demand the use of willpower. There is also existing research that has proven that people interacting with others and maintaining relationships often is a high depleter of willpower.

Willpower depletion is not solely just a simple case of feeling tired. During another study by the same researcher, she had the participants in her study go through a whole day of sleep deprivation and then asked them to watch a movie but to suppress their emotions and reactions during it. She then proceeded to test the strength of the participant's self-control and found that those participants who didn't get sleep were not much more likely to be depleted of willpower compared to those who got a full night's sleep.

So if willpower isn't related to physical fatigue, then what exactly is it? Research studies recently have discovered a few different mechanisms that are possibly responsible for willpower depletion, some that were at the biological level. The researchers found that the people whos willpower became depleted after completing self-control tasks showed lowered activity in the region of their brain that controlled cognition. When willpower is being tested, a person's brain may begin to function differently.

Some other evidence indicates that people who have depleted willpower might be on low on fuel quite literally. Since the brain is an organ that requires high-energy that is powered by glucose, certain professionals suggested that the cells in the brain that are responsible for maintaining a person's self-control uses up glucose quicker than it is being replenished. They performed a study with dogs where the dogs that were obedient and were asked to resist temptation showed lower blood glucose levels compared to the dogs that did not need to use self-control.

They found similar patterns in humans during scientific studies. The people who needed to use willpower in tasks were tested to have lower glucose levels compared to the participants that weren't asked to utilize their willpower. Moreover, replenishing glucose levels tend to help reboot a depleted willpower source in individuals that were depleted while drinking a sugar-free drink did not.

However, there is still evidence that suggests that the depletion of willpower can be maintained by a person's attitudes and beliefs. Different research and other colleagues found out that the people who felt the need to use their willpower (usually in order to please other people) were found to be more easily depleted compared to the people who are driven by their own desires and goals. These researchers, therefore, suggested that the people who are in better touch with themselves may be better off in life compared to the people who are often people-pleasing.

Some other researchers also studied how the effects of mood could affect a person's willpower. A study that took place in 2010 discovered that the group of people who believed that willpower is a resource that is limited were more likely to have willpower depletion. However, the group of people that did not believe that willpower can be depleted didn't show any symptoms or signs of willpower exhaustion after using their self-control. During the next stage of the same study, the psychologists manipulated the participants subconscious beliefs by getting them to unknowingly fill out a biased questionnaire. The group that was manipulated to believe that willpower is for a fact a limited resource exhibited symptoms of willpower depletion/exhaustion while the group that believed that willpower was not depletable didn't show any signs of declining self-control.

So at the end of all this evidence and discussion, do you think willpower is a limited resource? Many ideas point to evidence that supports both spectrums of this answer. They argued that willpower depletion in the early stages could be buggered by factors such as belief and mood. However, more research is definitely required for us to explore how moods, attitudes, and beliefs might be affecting a person's ability to resist temptation.

Understanding the Relationship Between Willpower and Healthy Habits

A person makes decisions every day in order to resist urges and gratification so that they can seek a more healthy and happy long term life. This could be in the form of refusing another portion of fries, forcing yourself to go work out, denying a second round of alcoholic drinks, or overcoming the temptation to skip early morning meetings. Willpower within everyone is being tested on a constant basis.

Lack of willpower is often known as the main obstacle to people's ability to maintain a healthy weight and physique. A lot of research actually supports this idea. A study found that children that had better self-control had less likelihood of becoming overweight when they grew up into their adolescence years due to their ability to delay gratification and control their urges.

. . .

However, just like we talked about earlier, resisting those urges may diminish a person's willpower to resist the next temptation. A researcher proved this in a study where they offered students that were currently dieting some ice cream after watching a sad movie. Some of the participants were asked to watch the movie like any other normal day while the other group was asked to not show any reactions or emotions, which is a task that requires self-control. The psychologists discovered that the participants who had to use their self-control to withhold their emotions and reactions indulged in more ice cream compared to the participants who were allowed to watch the movie normally and react as they'd like.

A lot of people often place most of the blame on their bad moods for causing their 'emotional eating.' However, that study found that the participants' emotional states were not the cause of the amount of ice cream that they consumed. In layman's terms, the depletion of willpower had more significance than a person's mood when it comes to determining how much ice cream the participants ate.

We have to keep in mind that the reason behind why someone is on a diet will also play a role in willpower depletion. As we had just discussed, researchers found that people's attitudes and inner beliefs may create a buffer for them in terms of the effects of willpower depletion. In a further example that this based on this theory, the researchers asked participants to resist the temptation of eating cookies that were placed in front of them. He then tested the participant's strength of self-control by getting them to squeeze an exercise handgrip until they couldn't anymore He discovered through this exercise that the people who refused to eat the cookies for their own reasons (such as finding enjoyment in resisting treats) showed better control in this physical test compared to the ones who refused the cookies for reasons that were external (wanting to impress the experimenter).

At this point, it is obvious that willpower is a required component when it comes to eating healthy. If a person is living in a surrounding where there were plenty of unhealthy but delicious food options, the action of resisting temptation is more likely to deplete willpower and even making it difficult for highly motivated healthy eaters. Since the behaviors of overeating are very complex, the role of willpower is argumentative when it comes to discussions for obesity treatments.

Some of the experts in the field of willpower believe that using self-control and personal choices causes people to be stigmatized which makes them unlikely to be motivated to lose weight. Many dieticians advise against using willpower as a tool and argue that dieters should be focusing on lowering the effect that their environment will have on their eating habits and behavior. Ultimately, when it comes to the world we live in today, resisting the temptation to eat unhealthily can be a hard challenge. We are constantly exposed to ads for delicious high-calorie foods. Cheap and fast processed foods are available at our fingertips 24/7 and are less expensive compared to healthier options. A person's willpower and the environment that they live in plays a big role in people's choices when it relates to food. Having a better understanding of both of these elements will help individuals and dieticians that are battling obesity.

. . .

Not only does willpower play a role in eating healthy, but it also plays a role in the use, and possible abuse of alcohol, tobacco, and drugs. Children who have developed self-control may avoid substance abuse in their adulthood and teenagehood. Researchers in this field studied the self-control of adolescents as they moved from sixth grade to eleventh grade. They discovered that the kids who had problems with self-control in sixth grade, such as not speaking in turn during class, had more likelihood of using tobacco, marijuana, and alcohol as high schoolers.

This may not come as surprising, but willpower also plays a signifi-cant role in curbing alcohol abuse and usage. In another study, a researcher discovered that people who drank socially very often that used their willpower during the lab proceeded to go out and consume more alcohol compared to the other participants who didn't use their willpower stockpile. In a different study, the researcher found that the social drinkers who had used a lot of their self-control that day were more likely to infringe on the drinking limits that they created for themselves. This finding shows evidence that exerting self-control excessively in one situa-tion can cripple a person's ability to fight off other temptations in different parts of their life.

We are talking a lot about willpower because understanding the role that it plays is very important for developing effective treat-ments and plan to battle serious issues like addictions to help guide people in making healthier choices for themselves. Willpower research offers people lots of suggestions on how to stick with healthy behaviors.

. . .

Let's take a look at an example of how willpower affects a person's decision making skills related to willpower. Professors from the University of Minnesota did a study that focused on impulse buying and willpower depletion. They showed the participants a silent movie with a series of words that appeared on the bottom of the screen. A group of those participants was asked to not pay attention to those words which were a task that required the use of self-control. After the movie, the participants were asked to look through a catalog with products like cars and watches and they wrote down the money amount that they were willing to pay for every single item. The participants that used self-control during the movie were willing to spend more money, about $30,000, while the participants who didn't deplete their willpower were willing to spend approximately $23,000.

In the next experiment, the researchers tested the spending behavior of the participants by showing them the opportunity to buy lower-cost objects like cups and decorative stickers. The group that had done self-control in the previous experiment expressed that they felt a higher temptation to buy those items. In fact, They purchased more items and spent more money compared to the participants who hadn't done the self-control exercise.

The task of making decisions financially can be much harder for people that are impoverished. researchers conducted various studies in India to explore the relationship between poverty and will power strength. in one study, this researcher visited two different Villages one that was poor and one that was richer. The researcher offered people an opportunity to buy a luxury brand name soap at an extremely discounted price tag. This item was a great deal in terms of cost but it still showed that people who live in poverty had difficulty making financial decisions as such.

The participants in the study were told to squeeze a handgrip made for exercise, which is a popular test of strength regarding self-control, before and after the soap was offered to be purchased. The researcher found that the participants who had more money exercised the handgrip for the same amount of time prior and post to the opportunity to buy that soap. However, they found that poor participants squeezed the handgrip for a smaller amount of time after making a purchasing decision. Their willpower was depleted, and the researcher had concluded that it was likely run down by the difficulty of making that financial decision.

This research may sound depressing but there is a silver lining. If impoverished people have a higher chance of using up their willpower, then it could possibly mean that lowering the amount of hard decisions that they have to make every day to help prevent the depletion of willpower will give them the ability to make future decisions. A different researcher studied this effect amongst thanking customers in Southeast Asia. They offered customers the opportunity to open a savings account but it comes with a catch. These customers would only be able to withdraw their funds after reaching a targeted saving goal or target date that they have decided for themselves. A year later, the participants that signed up for these accounts saved 82% more than the participants who had not opened the special savings account. When the decision to save money or spend money is taken away, it helps customers avoid failing at self-control.

· · ·

All of this evidence collaborated shows that the people who are in the lower end of the socioeconomic spectrum are more likely to deplete their self-control resources. It's not that people who don't have money have less willpower than rich people; rather, the people that are living in poverty have to make more willpower draining decisions. This means that every decision they make, whether it is as simple as buying soap, will require self-control which, therefore, dips into their limited resources of willpower.

Self-Control Improvement

A ton of research has been developed recently in order to explain the numerous elements of willpower. Many professionals that study this area of self-control to this with one goal on their mind. They are about these types of questions: If willpower is a limited resource, what can we do to conserve it? How can we strengthen willpower?

One effective tactic for maintaining willpower is simply to avoid temptation. In the marshmallow study, children were given a choice of being allowed to eat one marshmallow right away or having to wait an undefined period of time to have the opportunity to eat two marshmallows. They found that the kids who started at the marshmallows during the whole time were found to be less likely to resist the treat compared to the kids who shut their eyes and refused to look, looked away, or created a distraction for themselves. The technique of out of sight, out of mind, works with adults as well. In a recent study, researchers found that office workers who kept unhealthy snacks such as candy in their desk drawer consumed it less compared to when they would put the candy on top of their desks at eye level.

. . .

A technique called "implementation intention" is another helpful tactic that helps improve willpower. These intentions are usually in the form of "if-then" statements that aid people in planning for situations that are likely to disrupt their goals. For instance, a person that is monitoring their consumption of alcohol may tell themselves before entering a drinking part that is anybody offers them an alcoholic drink, then they will request a plain soda with lime. Research has found that amongst adults and adolescents, implementing solutions will increase self-control, even if people already had their willpower depleted by other tasks. People that have a plan ahead of time allows them to easily make decisions in the moment without needing to draw upon their bank of willpower resources.

This research suggests that people have a bank of willpower that is limited raises a few troubling questions. Are people destined to fail if they are being faced with too many temptations? The answer is not necessarily. Many psychologists have the belief that a person's willpower cannot be ever used up completely. Instead, people often have stored some back up willpower that is being saved for future demands. Those reserves are only available for the right type of motivation, allowing them to accomplish things even when their willpower has seemingly run out.

In order to demonstrate this idea, a researcher further found out that individuals who had their willpower used up 'completely' continued to be able to accomplish self-control tasks when they were being told that they would be compensated well for their actions or if their actions would bring benefit to other people. He concluded that having high motivation can overcome weaken self-control.

Will power can also be controlled in the first place to be less vulnerable to being completely depleted. Psychologists often use an analogy to describe will power as being similar to a muscle that will tire out after a lot of exercise. However, there is another element to this analogy. Although muscles will tire due to exercise during the short-term, they become stronger when regularly exercised over the long term. Just like physical exercise, self-control can become stronger when a person exercises willpower.

According to one of the earlier experiments that supports the idea above, the researchers asked participants in the study to follow a two-week guide to improve their moods, track their food intake, or improve their physical posture. Compared to the group that didn't need to exercise self-control, the participants who had to use their willpower by performing willpower heavy exercises were not as vulnerable to the depletion of self-control in a follow-up study. In another set of research, this researcher found that smokers who exercised willpower for two weeks by avoiding sweet foods or regularly squeezing an exercise handgrip, found more success when it comes to not smoking than other participants who performed two weeks of tasks that didn't require any self-control.

Other researchers have also discovered that using your willpower muscles can help a person increase the strength of their self-control over a period of time. Some researchers in Australia did a study where they assigned participants to a physical exercise program that lasted two months; this is a willpower-required routine. In the conclusion of this program, the participants that finished it scored better when measuring self-control compared to the other participants who were not assigned the exercise program. The participants that did the program were also reported to have been smoking less, eating healthier food, drinking less alcohol, improving their study habits, and monitoring their spending habits more carefully. Regular exercise of a person's willpower using physical exercise seem to have led to an increase of will power in components of their daily lives.

The research findings regarding how glucose levels are tied to willpower depletion suggest a conceivable solution. A person that is maintains their blood sugar by eating regularly and often may help their brain replenish their storage of willpower. Those who are dieting aim to preserve their willpower while calorie reduction may be more effective by eating frequent and small meals compared to skipping out on entire meals like lunch or dinner.

All this evidence founded from studies of the depletion of willpower proposes that people making resolutions for the new year is the worst approach possible. If a person is running low on willpower in one specific area, it often reduces their willpower in all of the other areas. Focusing on one goal at a time makes more sense. In other words, don't try to get into a healthy diet right away, quit smoking, and start a new workout plan all at the same time. A much better technique is to complete goals one by one. Once you have one single good habit nailed, people no longer need to use their supply of willpower to maintain that behavior. Habits that are healthy will eventually become a part of a person's daily routine and would not need to use the energy of decision-making at all.

There are still many questions regarding the nature of willpower that needs to be answered by future research. However, it seems like if somebody has clear goals, good self-monitoring, and does a little bit of practice, they can train their self-control to be strong when faced with temptation.

THERE ARE many reasons as to why one would require self-discipline. The first one being self-discipline will be what drives you to achieve your goals, and the second reason is that you will require self-discipline in order to build new habits and to change your life. Although the thought of exercising self-discipline may sound exhausting to you, there are various benefits that come along with it. Understanding the benefits of self-discipline will help motivate you to practice it more often. In this chapter, I will be explaining five extremely important benefits that come with practicing self-discipline and I will be going over some causes of low self-discipline.

1. Self-discipline will help increase your chances of success.

When a goal can be achieved with great ease, some would argue whether or not it should even be considered a goal. Goals require a person to stretch and grow; to improve skills, attitudes, and to improve one's knowledge. When an individual meets those requirements, they improve the quality of their life along with improving their capability to take on larger and harder challenges. Ultimately, goals should be challenging. Everyone will face barriers and obstacles in which they would need to overcome. This is the action that is needed in order to create personal growth. In order to overcome these obstacles and barriers to achieve your goals. It will require a lot of self-discipline and self-belief. A person's ability to persevere and overcome obstacles when faced with difficulty is often times the difference between failure and success.

1. Self-discipline fosters character and inner strength.

According to a famous psychology book, there was an important statement that the author wrote. He stated that everyone is the person that they wish to be. All that is stopping you from behaving in the manner that you want to behave is your emotional mind. Let's think about that for a second. Although you may be a very kind and caring person, if you have a tendency to lose your temper easily, other people may see you as a hothead or an angry person. In this example, you don't necessarily need to change who you are as a person. Instead, you need to change the way you behave. Once you change the way you behave, other people will then see you for the person that you truly are. For example, you already are that kind and caring person but your short temper is preventing you from showing that personality to the world. Self-discipline is a tool that can help you to stop acting on your impulses and instead act based on your true character.

1. Self-discipline helps you resist instant gratification.

As we discussed in chapter one, our modern-day lives are filled to the brim with temptations that can throw people off track and prevent them from achieving their goals. Often, these temptations are temporary, and by exercising willpower, most people can overcome the urge. In our modern workplace, temptations tend to take the form of distractions like checking your phone, a conversation at the water cooler, or scrolling through social media. Those examples are just the tip of the iceberg when it comes to our modern-day potential distractions. When you are able to recognize what your temptations are, you can place a strategy in order to prevent caving to it. This requires less self-discipline compared to ignoring the temptation with brute mental force. For example, if your coworker locks her phone in the drawer of her desk and refuses to check her phone during the workday. She may make this strategy easier for her by telling all of her friends that she does this so that her friends do not expect an immediate response.

As we already learned, temptations also exist in the form of addictions and bad habits. When self-disciplined is coupled with effective strategies, it is a very valuable tool that can be used to overcome most urges in life.

1. Self-discipline improves your self-esteem and confidence.

People with more self-discipline tend to be calmer, assured, and more confident. They know who they are as a person and what they believe in. They will always do what they believe to be the right thing. As we mentioned throughout this book, although the task that needs to be done may not be something that they want to do at that very moment in time, the strength of self-discipline demands them to be true to their values and beliefs. One of the major benefits of this behavior of a self-disciplined person is that they can always be confident that they have done their best. If a person knows that they tried their very best and couldn't have done any better, they will be able to hold their heads up high, knowing that any insults or criticism are meaningless. However, this person would also be prepared to listen to any constructive criticism but negative feedback does not affect them much at all. To maximize the benefits of self-discipline, a person must have goals that are effective in motivating and inspiring them.

1. Self-discipline helps improve relationships.

Take a minute to think about some of the things that you value in a relationship. This could be a friendship, a romantic relationship, or a familial relationship. You may value important things like integrity, dependability, loyalty, and honesty. All of these traits require a person to have a strong character. It requires someone who is able to be true and act true to their values and beliefs, even when it would be easier to fall into temptation. As we already discussed, those with self-discipline are more likely to develop a stronger character. They have a lot of practice in doing the things that they know need to be done, even though they would probably rather be doing something else. Generally, they are a person that most people can count on. They are more effective when it comes to gaining respect and building trust amongst their peers.

Do You Have Low Self-Discipline?

If you think you have low self-discipline, now is the time for you to assess your own willpower and self-control. If you think you are someone with high self-discipline, then learning new habits shouldn't be hard for you as you already have the fundamentals down. Let's discuss some of the causes as to why some people have low self-discipline. Having low self-discipline, not unlike having high self-discipline, affects people's performance in multiple aspects of their life. This includes the performance at work, school, relationships, sports, and financial well-being.

By identifying the common causes of low self-discipline, you can better identify which areas in your life may be holding you back from building better habits. Pay attention to these causes, and try to see if any of these resonate with you. If they do, you know exactly where your low self-discipline may be coming from and you can start there for any improvements.

Lack of self-discipline shows up in all the different things that people do in their lives. Some people make sure that they do the big things in life but end up neglecting the little things. They do this to impress other people who don't know them very well. However, they tend to annoy and disappoint those that are close to them because it shows that they don't care enough about the people that they should be showing respect to. When people choose to not perform certain chores or duties, don't do what they say they would, don't show up for appointments, or don't make themselves presentable for every day, they are showing low self-discipline. So you may be wondering, why don't we take more responsibility for these everyday obligations? Below are two reasons why:

1. Lack of commitment

The first reason why people don't take more responsibility for everyday obligations is because of the lack of commitment. A person's commitment, enthusiasm, and interest to a task determines the degree to which they can be distracted. When their commitment is very high, very few things have the power to distract them, but if they are doing something that is meaningless to them, their attention is easily distracted. This proves a strong link between self-discipline and commitment. People who have the inability to ignore, control, or bypass thoughts means that they have low self-discipline.

By learning the reasons behind why a person does not take more responsibility for every day obligations, we are ready to learn the eight causes of poor self-discipline.

1. Negative attitude

The second reason why people don't take more responsibility for everyday obligations is that they don't believe in its importance. Why is this? Why do some people take the time to be considerate, clean, trustworthy, and honest While others believe that those things are important? The answer is their attitude towards themselves, other people, and life itself. The former believe that people, including themselves, and other forms of life, are worth investing their energy, time, resources, and interest into. They are able to see the importance of Life while the latter have less regard for life and for themselves. All of the simply relates to love. When people have a love for life, they tend to respect all components of it. They take the time to appreciate and experience life as if it's a pleasure. Self-discipline comes from the willingness to take care of ourselves, other people, and other types of life. The lack of discipline shows less willingness to respect themselves or other things.

Common Causes of Low Self-Discipline

Now that we have a better understanding of why some people don't build good habits for themselves, let's take a look at the common causes of low self-discipline:

1. Lack of self-respect and self-esteem

A person who is lacking self-respect often doesn't put a lot of effort or importance in achieving personal excellence. They often don't really care what others think about them or whether or not they are helping out other people in their lives. You might be wondering what self-respect has to do with self-discipline. The answer is that it takes self-discipline in order to produce excellent results, to achieve goals, and to help people who require it. When a person doesn't think about their own self-improvement, they tend to focus on other things that bring them pleasure such as instant gratification. They don't necessarily practice self-discipline because they are comfortable in indulging the instant gratification that life throws at them. If a person lacks respect for themselves, they are more likely to indulge in unhealthy conveniences like fast food or shopping impulses that we discussed in chapter one. If a person does have self-respect for themselves, they understand that this instant gratification may bring them joy and pleasure at the moment, but does very little in helping them achieve healthy long-term goals.

1. Lack of awareness

The primary cause of low self-discipline is a lack of awareness. This component is important specifically to our imagination and thinking. People are unaware of the thoughts that take our attention are actually negative and can damage a person's well-being. These thoughts are fed into the conscious mind by the negative mind power to ensure that people have minimal time to spend just simply just being mindful. If people are aware of the things that are happening within their own minds, they would know that self-discipline is needed to refocus our attention away from the flow of negative thoughts.

1. Laziness

There are many temporary reasons as to why a person is not exhibiting self-discipline to do the things that need to be done. This could be sickness, tiredness, apathy, or something that is more appealing that is immediately available. If you find that these excuses are occurring often when you were trying to complete the task needed to reach a goal, you need to dig deep and find the real reason why you are choosing options that aren't the ones that will help you achieve your goal. Laziness is often the culprit in a lot of cases. The reasons for laziness usually runs very deep into an individual's psyche. If a person believes that there is a goal that is worthwhile, they will be motivated to keep working and applying themselves and making the decisions that make sense when it comes to achieving their goal. However, if they don't have any motivation to achieve their goal, it likely means that their goal isn't important enough, or the person has a natural tendency to be lazy and uninterested.

1. Lack of ambition

Ambition is very effective in creating self-discipline by giving us a reason to work towards our goals, although we might rather be doing something else. However, it has a negative effect on our self-discipline if our ambition is in an honorable, ethical, or fulfilling one. It is obvious that people who lack the ambition to achieve goals in life will have a harder time building strong self-discipline because they don't have a reason to do it. This is why we discussed in chapter one that one of the main steps in developing strong self-discipline is coming up with clear and attainable goals. By coming up with a goal that is realistic, an individual can then create a plan of action that they can then hold themselves accountable to. They also need to continue finding the motivation and ambition to keep them striving towards their goals.

1. Having goals of low-importance

People that have goals that aren't that important tend to lack the ambition to achieve them and, therefore, will not be able to practice their self-discipline. If people set goals that looked good on the outside but didn't actually believe that they were necessary, or didn't see them as goals that are important enough to accomplish in the first place, then they may find it very difficult exercise self-discipline in order to put in the work to achieve them. One of the main motivating factors of self-discipline is having a goal that a person is able to stand by or is important to them. By having an important goal, or something that is meaningful to them, they will be able to find the self-discipline needed in order to complete the tasks required in order to achieve their goal.

Do you resonate with any of these causes of low self-discipline? If so, don't worry. I will teach you many strategies and ways that you can build up self-discipline to promote healthier habits in your life. In the next chapter, we will learn about how habits are formed and which good habits you should be building.

3 / BUILDING HEALTHIER HABITS

IF YOU ARE READING this book, you likely want to build healthier habits to improve your life. An important part of learning to build new habits is understanding what habits actually are and how they are formed. If you've ever read any psychology books in the past, you would know that a lot of what a person does every day is very habit-driven. You might even know from your own experience, that some people don't like to stray away from their habits and routines. This means that if a person develops the right habits, they would be able to have stronger self-discipline without feeling like they are draining their willpower. People tend to lose self-discipline when they feel like their willpower has been drained and they can no longer resist the temptations in their lives.

So where do habits come from, and how are they developed? Why is it that when many people try to change their habits by breaking the bad ones or building good ones that they only stick with it for a certain amount of time before they give up and go back to their old ways? The biggest problem here, especially with habits that people have had for many years or even decades, are the neural pathways that have been imprinted into people's brains. This happens on a biological level. These neural pathways are responsible for linking up the neural networks in a person's brain to perform a specific function like preparing a cup of coffee in a certain way, walking up the stairs, or smoking a cigarette.

These neural Pathways help a person automate behavior that is constantly used in an effort to reduce the energy needed for the conscious processing power in a person's brain. By doing this, it allows a person's mind to focus on other things rather than the habitual tasks that they have done a thousand times. This function actually stems from our early days as humans and his part of our DNA; it allows humans to have a more efficient mind that can be used for other things rather than mundane things.

In this case, it's normally the mundane behaviors that are often repeated which hold people back from building good habits in most cases. People tend to have more bad habits that are adding negative value to their lives rather than good habits that help them achieve their goals further. Since the cause of this is the neural pathways that get ingrained deeper and deeper over time, it makes it harder for people to break their bad habits or even form good ones when all of the bad ones are constantly getting in the way. However, if you can try to ingrain the next following habits we will be discussing into your life, you will find that strengthening your self-discipline may become easier. Again, these things don't happen overnight. Remember that habits take lots of time to form and even to break. If you start small and take baby steps, and build, you will stop thinking about how much longer you can discipline yourself since you will have ingrained those habits into your brain which then automatically promotes the self-discipline that you seek.

Healthy Habits That You Should Be Building

Now that you understand the science behind how habits are built let's take a look at some healthy habits that you should be building. By building healthier habits in your life, you will increase your chances of gaining more success and achieving your goals and dreams that you have.

1. Persistency

No amount of self-discipline would ever be complete without the presence of persistence. Persistence is a type of habit that helps us to not give up even when we are faced with failure. Persistence is what helps us get back up on our feet to keep trying even when we do fail. Persistence plays such a huge role in self-discipline that without it, achieving self-discipline is probably impossible.

You might be wondering why that is. This is because achieving our goals is not an easy thing to do. It is really hard. Getting discouraged is easy and something that happens to everyone along their journey. In addition, giving up takes far less energy and effort compared to continuing to push through even if it's something that causes a lot of pain in the process before it can give us any pleasure.

. . .

However, this hardship that is required to achieve any goals is simply something that you have to persevere through because that's just what it takes. We all have to realize that even the most successful people in the world have failed numerous times over and over again. Failure is simply a part of life, and rather than avoiding it and not pursuing your goals at all in fear of failure, we should learn to persevere and push through even during the hardest of times. Without fail, we wouldn't be able to achieve the big goals that we have set for ourselves.

There are many ways that a person can go about instilling perseverance as a habit, but the best and most effective weight is to come up with the reasons why you want to do the things in life that you aim for. If the reasons behind your goals are strong enough, they can motivate you so you can get through anything.

1. Organization

Have you ever noticed that when your home is messy, it makes it very hard to be comfortable and therefore leads you to be unfocused and distracted? Naturally, humans don't like living in a dirty and messy environment. In order for a person to achieve their goals and accomplish self-discipline, they need to be organized. Organization also needs to become a habit that is fully incorporated in a person's personal life and professional life. This includes the physical act of organizing the things you have in your home and the mental act of organizing the things on your mind.

By living an organized life, you are living a disciplined life. If you are someone who is constantly scattered and disorganized, start small with your organization skills. Just pick one small space each day for yourself to organize. This can be just one single drawer in your kitchen, the things lying around on your desk, or just straighten out the things on your coffee table. The next day, pick something else to organize like your bathroom drawers or the clothes in your closet. The more time you spend living in a clean and organized environment, the less you would want your home to become cluttered and messy again. You will start to begin to notice when clutter builds up and by having a habit of organization, you will immediately organize things as you use them so you don't have to spend time organizing it later on.

By decluttering your home or your working environment, you will have plenty of different areas where you can sit down and work on your own goals. Has your home ever been so cluttered that when you do have the motivation to start working on something, you simply just don't have the space to do it? In order to avoid this, keep your home clean and organized at all times so that when you have a rush of motivation, you can find a workspace that is clean and ready for you to work.

Like a lot of other habits, the habit of organization can be learned and built over time. It does require your attention and effort, but it is something that will pay off tremendously in the long run. When you are living in a physical space that is organized and clean, your mind will automatically become more stress-free, relaxed, and give you the ability to focus. In turn, by becoming more organized, you are increasing your ability to be more self-disciplined. Begin to incorporate this good habit of putting things back where it belongs when you're finished using it rather than leaving it out. Little things like this we do on a daily basis have the largest impact on the quality of life. Pay attention to the small things and you'll begin to see big benefits.

1. Regular exercise

Exercise is one of the most important habits to build within all people. It acts as a cornerstone habit to help a person's life be filled with positive habits and be rid of the bad ones. A person that is truly able to discipline themselves has to instill the habit of exercise into their everyday routine. As you all may already know, there are endless benefits when it comes to exercise. This is something that is talked about not only by psychologists but medical experts as well. Even though exercise is such an important component of a person's life, not everyone actually makes it a priority. Why is this?

In our busy modern-day lives, everyone is caught up with trying to get all the things that they need to get done and are often busy running around completing errands and fail to simply tackle exercise head-on. Often, people have a bad mindset when it comes to exercise and think that they won't be able to build it as a habit because they simply have "too many other things to do." This is where most people are wrong. There are ways to incorporate exercise even if their day is jam-packed from beginning to end.

When people think of exercise, they may automatically think of a minimum one hour intense weight-lifting session at the gym, a one-hour long expensive spin class, or a one-hour yoga class. If that's what they are thinking about then yes, it is true that the people that have busy lives may not be able to incorporate the time to get to their exercise class, the time it takes to complete the exercise class, and then get to wherever they need to go after that. However, exercise doesn't necessarily have to be a formalized session that takes a long time. It can simply be getting some sit-ups, push-ups, or some jumping jacks in the morning before you head to work. It can also be you choosing to walk to work instead of taking the bus, or it could be a brief walk around your neighborhood park after dinner.

By instilling exercise as a keystone habit of your life, it can help you become more disciplined and can also improve your life in numerous ways. First of all, exercise is extremely effective in reducing stress levels and pain because it causes the brain to release feel-good endorphins and neurotransmitters like serotonin and dopamine. Secondly, exercise helps increase the oxygenation and blood flow of body cells which is responsible for helping boost the immune system and fighting off diseases. Lastly, exercise increases a person's ability to focus on the task at hand due to the increased activity in the brain which allows us to live a more disciplined life.

· · ·

So start building the habit of exercise in your life by simply just going for a 10-minute walk or just doing some sit-ups and push-ups right after you wake up. Just a few minutes is fine. Try to do this for one week and then increase the amount of time you spend on that session for the next week. Keep up with this pattern and soon enough, you will have a healthy amount of time every day that you set aside to get your exercise in, and this is when it will become a full-blown habit.

1. Healthier sleeping schedules

Since the theory behind willpower is that it gets its energy from the brain, which gets its energy from glucose levels and rest, then it's safe to assume that sleep is directly connected to how the brain is able to acquire energy. When a person doesn't get enough sleep, their brain spends most of its energy focused on just keeping your basic body functions up and going. This does not leave much energy for a person to spend on exerting their willpower, prac-ticing self-discipline, or even simply just remembering their self-discipline. Getting the proper and healthy amount of sleep is a vital requirement for accomplishing anything. When a person doesn't get enough sleep, it affects their ability to focus, their judg-ment, their mood, their overall health, and their diet.

When people suffer chronic sleep deprivation such as insomnia, things go from bad to worse. Many research studies have found evidence that people who don't get the proper amount of sleep on a regular basis have a greater risk of catching specific diseases.

Lack of sleep also has a significant and negative impact on a person's immune system. This can cause a person to frequently catch colds or cases of flu that cause them to not have the ability to go to school, work, or get anything effective done.

For an adult, it is important to get at least six hours of sleep every night. A healthy amount of sleep should range between eight to ten hours every night but the minimum amount is 6 hours. Avoid eating or drinking anything that contains caffeine at least 5 hours before your bedtime so that it doesn't affect your natural sleep cycle. Make a note to also stay away from ingesting too many toxins during the day such as cigarettes, alcohol, drugs, or prescription medicine if it can be avoided.

In conclusion, the benefits of getting enough sleep are extraordinary. Aside from the fact that it can help you stay focused and be more disciplined, it also helps you curb inflammation and pain, lower stress, improves your memory, jumpstart your creativity, sharpens your attention, improves your grades, limits your chances for accidents and helps you avoid depression.

1. Healthier eating habits

Raw fruits and foods actually offer the biggest boost of energy for humans because they require less energy for the body to process and provides more energy for the body to use after that. This process is called an enhanced Thermic Effect of Food (TEF) or otherwise known as Dietary Induced Thermogenesis (DIT).

Like we learned in the previous chapter, our brains use up a large amount of glucose in order to keep it functioning. Therefore, the amount of energy that a person has is very responsible and how focussed they feel. When a person is focussed, they can achieve their goals using less willpower than if they weren't focused. When a person is feeling too comatose from the unhealthy food that they have eaten, staying focused is something that is very hard to achieve. They often spend too much of their time feeling too sluggish and tired to work on achieving their goals.

You commonly hear that breakfast is the most important meal of the day. However, it's important not only to eat a healthy breakfast but to eat multiple healthy meals throughout the day. In order to do this, you have to actively plan what you're going to eat during these meals in order to break some of your bad habits. For example, if you are planning to eat five healthy smaller-sized meals per day, but you haven't prepared any of those meals, you are more likely to feel hungry and indulge in unhealthy conveniences like fast food. If you are someone that eats fast food or processed foods often, your body won't be able to create enough energy to help you approach your goals with focus or help you have the willpower in order to start working at them.

Since the food that a person eats can change the neural chemical makeup of their brain, it also heavily influences a person's mind and body connection. Take a look at the things that you eat during your day. Try to find the meals where you often indulge in unhealthy food or junk food. Plan in advance so you can substitute those meals with raw, organic, and healthy foods. By buying this type of healthy food in advance and preparing it for the times that you become hungry, you will be less likely to visit your nearest McDonalds.

1. Setting active goals

Active goal setting is very different from passive goal-setting. Passive goal setting means you are setting goals in your mind, and they are passive because they lack many details are planning. Passive goal-setting means that a person hasn't properly defined the actual goal which makes it hard for them to keep track of their progress and knowing what needs to be done in order to achieve that goal. Active goal setting is the complete opposite of passive goal-setting. Active goal setting means writing out these goals and making sure that they have an important meeting. These goals have to be measurable and very specific. To successfully have an active goal, a person has to make a plan towards achieving it. this is why people set long-term goals, but also engage in smaller goals on a daily basis in order to work towards achieving the bigger goal.

By using active goal-setting, it ingrains the discipline in us because you are forced to give it direction. By breaking down your big goals into smaller daily goals, it helps people avoid distractions by only looking at the things that they need to get done in the present day.

This way, a person isn't left constantly thinking about one large intimidating goal but not knowing how to approach it.

Active goal setting works by taking the first step in setting your long-term goals. If you are someone that has long-term goals like; wanting to own your first home, wanting to pay off your student debt by the next three years, or wanting to take 6 months off to travel Europe. If you are someone that has long-term goals, then you need to actively participate in daily, weekly, and monthly goal setting and planning. You have to play an active role in tracking your progress towards your goals and making changes in places where you feel like aren't working for you.

So take out a pen and a piece of paper, and start writing down what long-term goals you have. Once you have some long-term goals written down, break it down into monthly, weekly, and daily goals. Start slowly by accomplishing your daily goals and when you reach the end of the month, assess to see if you have achieved your monthly goal through accomplishing your daily goals. If you haven't, look back on your daily goals and see if there's anything you can change so that you could achieve next month's goal.

1. Practicing gratitude

Gratitude is an important action in human life that helps not only people with self-discipline but is often used to help people that are facing self-esteem and self-confidence issues. A huge problem in our modern world today is that we are constantly presented with millions of materialistic things that cause us to always be wanting something more or something else. This causes people to spend too much time thinking about all the things that they want, and not enough time thinking about the things that they already have. Building a habit of gratitude helps people move away from constantly wanting the things that they don't have and move forward towards appreciating the things that they do have. When people do this, they can begin to make remarkable changes in their lives.

The effects of practicing and showcasing gratitude are extremely crucial. It does everything from improving mental health, emotional well-being, a person's spirituality, gratitude is capable of so many things. Practicing gratitude is an exercise that is constantly used in therapy to help the client move away from thinking about things that aren't in the present and focus on being mindful. Most importantly, gratitude helps people move away towards a state of abundance and away from a state of lack. When people live in a state of lack, it makes it impossible for them to focus on achieving their goals and being self-disciplined. They spend too much of their mental energy and capacity worrying about the things that they don't have or living in a fearful way, to the point that they forget about the things that they do have.

The state of lack can also show up in someone as physical symptoms. This state produces a lot of stress because the brain automatically releases cortisol and epinephrine, which are the stress hormones from our brains. These hormones impact numerous systems within the human body. When someone is stressed, their immune systems, digestive systems, and reproductive systems are all affected. We must spend a few minutes every day writing down all the things that we are grateful for. Even if you feel like you don't have anything to be grateful for, try hard to find something. It doesn't have to be anything large like winning the lottery or finding $20 on the ground. It could be something very simple like the nice weather, the nice conversation that you had with your barista, or even just seeing a cute dog on your way home.

1. Forgiveness

If you are someone living a fast-paced life, how often do you find yourself feeling angry, frustrated, or annoyed? Due to the insane amount of convenience we are offered in our daily lives, simple annoyances that happen in a person's day can cause a spiral of negative emotions. For example, if you are in a hurry to get to work and you happen to be running late that day, the coffee shop that you normally stop at to get your morning coffee is taking forever to make your order. When you finally get your coffee, you realize that they had made your order wrong but now you have no time to get it fixed. That one simple human error has spent you into a spiral of anger and annoyance, and you struggle to let go of it and you find that it is still negatively impacting your whole day. This causes you to have spent most of your energy upset about the coffee shop that wronged you and you don't have enough mental capacity to focus on other things like practicing your self-discipline. When people spend most of their days feeling the emotions of anger, regret, or guilt, they actually are creating more problems than they are with solutions. The emotions of anger and hate consume much more energy in a person's body compared to positive emotions like forgiveness and love. Forgiveness is something that can be learned. When people learn to forgive, only then will they be able to let go of certain things.

Without learning the habit of forgiveness, people would simply not be able to achieve self-discipline. When a person is too worried about how someone or something has wronged them, it makes it impossible for them to focus on achieving their goals or on their personal discipline. If someone has hurt you in the past, learn to forgive them. It doesn't mean that you have to forget about what they did to you altogether. Simply just forgive and let go of that negative energy and give it back to the universe rather than keeping it within your body. When we perform the act of forgiveness, we are actually letting go of the negative energy that inhibits our ability to practice self-discipline. If you want to master self-discipline, you have to get rid of sources that are sucking away at your mental energy. Holding on to negative emotions like anger is a sure way for your energy to be drained. While forgiveness might not seem like a discipline habit when you first look at it, it is an extremely crucial one to build in the process.

Try to think about the people or situations that you are currently angry with. It could be someone that you think has wronged you recently, or simply just an annoying situation that has happened to you. Instead of just thinking about how it made you feel, try to put yourself in their shoes. What would be the things that you would do if you were in their situation? Make it light-hearted and try to find some humor in it. Rather than thinking about it as a situation that shouldn't have happened, try to find a lesson learned in those situations. I know that it is very hard to forgive certain people, especially if they have really hurt you or wronged you in life. However, it isn't until people are able to let go of those feelings of animosity and hurt before things in their life really began to improve. People are often so busy stressing and worrying that they don't spend enough time thinking about how they are going to change their future.

1. Practicing meditation

Just like gratitude, meditation is a commonly used technique to help people practice mindfulness in cases where they are suffering from an anxiety disorder or depression disorder. Meditation is something that can be used to help put people's minds at ease. Provide people with a spiritual centeredness that can be used as an avenue of growth. When people meditate, they take their awareness away from things of the past and the future and focus it on the things of the present. When this happens, they are able to connect themselves to the universe, which also helps them with increasing gratitude.

In the later chapters of this book, we will learn the specific ways of how meditation can help a person improve their self-discipline. Meditation actually plays a big role in a person's ability to use their willpower. Its function is to clear the mind of any thoughts and simply focus all attention on the present. From a self-discipline perspective, meditation helps set the right tone for a person's day. In addition, it helps people improve their physical, emotional, and mental health all at once, allowing them to gain some of the biggest benefits for the least amount of time invested.

There are many types of meditation, some of which focuses on mindfulness and some of which focus on love and gratitude. There truly are too many different types of meditation for humankind to keep track of, but the most popular and beneficial type that is used amongst many therapies and within self-discipline is mindfulness meditation. Contrary to common belief, meditation doesn't have to take a long time. It can be done in 10 to 15 minutes. However, the hardest part of meditation is actually bringing yourself to do it. A person has to be able to keep their mind still and train it to stop wandering all the time. The trick behind mindfulness meditation is not to stop wandering thoughts altogether, but simply to acknowledge these thoughts, and reroute yourself back to the present. There are many types of breathing techniques that can be accompanied with meditation to help with achieving mindfulness. We will be diving deeper into these techniques in the meditation chapter.

Some people believe that meditation is about aligning the physical human body with its spiritual body. However, for the purpose of this book, we will stay away from spirituality and focus more on the practical benefit that being mindful can bring.

4 / BUILDING STRONG SELF-DISCIPLINE TO ENFORCE BETTER HABITS

THROUGHOUT THIS BOOK, I have emphasized the need to have self-discipline to enforce better habits. The trick to this is you don't need to constantly use self-discipline in order to stick to your habits. Once your habit actually becomes a habit and the right neural pathways are created in your brain, you actually require much less self-discipline and willpower. The beginning stages of building a habit, however, does require a lot of self-discipline so this is what I am going to teach you

Step-By-Step Guide to Build Stronger Self-Discipline

Everyone faces difficult decisions when they are presented with temptations that are hard to resist. A person that is looking to eat healthier may struggle with their self-discipline when they are offered a hot fudge sundae. A person who is looking to gain some muscle mass may face a temptation of wanting to sleep in rather than going to the gym. People that have stronger self-control often spend less time thinking about whether or not to indulge in temptations that are bad for their health. Luckily, self-discipline is something that can be taught. I will be walking you through a guide of step-by-step instructions on how you can improve your self-discipline.

1. *Understand what your own weaknesses are.*

Everyone has their own set of weaknesses. They could range from a certain type of food like chocolate, or it can be social media like Instagram, or even the latest addictive video game. Regardless of what it is, it has a similar effect on everyone. The first step to mastering your self-discipline is to acknowledge your shortcomings, no matter what they might be. People often try to pretend that their weaknesses don't exist in order to portray themselves as a strong person. This is extremely ineffective when it comes to self-discipline. The purpose of acknowledging your weaknesses is not to make yourself feel bad. Instead, it helps you recognize what they are and will help you plan in advance to overcome them. Acknowledge your flaws; it is impossible to overcome them until you do this.

1. *Remove likely temptations around you.*

Once you have acknowledged your weaknesses, you can now move on to step two, which is to remove your temptations. Just like we mentioned in step one, everyone has their own set of weaknesses and it can range from small things like an unhealthy snack all the way to something that hinders your productivity like playing a video game for hours on end. By understanding what your weaknesses are, you can make accommodations for yourself that will help remove some of those temptations.

For example, if somebody is looking to lose weight and get fit at the gym, but they know that their weakness is that they always eat chocolate after dinner every night. Their temptation removal, in this case, would be to not buy any more chocolate that they keep around in their home. By not having chocolate in the home, they would be unable to fall into the temptation of eating it, which will hinder their progress of getting fit. However, this does not mean that they will never be able to eat chocolate again. This only means that they can indulge in their favorite snacks when they have achieved a certain portion of their goal. Rewarding oneself is important to self-discipline as well.

1. *Make CLEAR goals for yourself and build a plan around it.*

In order to continue strengthening your self-discipline, a person must have a clear vision of what goals they are trying to accomplish. They must also have an understanding of what success means to them. If a person doesn't know where they're planning to go or what accomplishing their goals even and Tails, it is easy for them to lose their way or to get sidetracked.

. . .

Make sure the goals that you are setting have a clear and concise purpose. For example, don't use goals like "I want to be rich by the next five years." This goal is too broad for it to have a strong meaning. Instead, you should make a goal that is quantifiable like "I am planning on saving $20,000 by the end of this year". Then, when you have a quantifiable goal, you are able to make a plan that makes sense for yourself. In this example, a person can plan to save $2,000 each month for the rest of this year in order to hit their goal of saving $20,000 by the end of it. They can break down these goals even further, and figure out where in their budget they can save money or how they can make more money to accomplish that goal.

1. *Practice building your self-discipline whenever possible.*

Self-discipline is not something that people are born with; it is mostly a learned behavior. Self-discipline is just like any other skills that people may be looking to grow; it requires repetition and lots of daily practice. Similar to going to the gym, the more you work out your muscles, the bigger and stronger they will become. Changes do not happen overnight, instead to strengthen your muscles and to grow them; it will take at least several weeks for a person to be able to see their progress. The effort and focus that training self-discipline requires can be extremely tiring.

The more time you practice self-discipline, it can become more and more difficult to keep utilizing your willpower. Sometimes when a person is faced with a big temptation or decision, they may feel that overcoming that large temptation makes it harder for them to overcome other tasks that also require self-discipline. The only way to move past this is to have a good mindset. By having a good mindset, it creates a buffer for how quickly your willpower becomes drained. In addition, like the muscle example we used, by exerting your willpower more often, you will have a higher tolerance and therefore be able to exert it more than if you were just starting out.

1. *Start with creating simple habits first.*

To strengthen self-discipline, you need to work on instilling a new habit, which can feel very intimidating at first, especially if you are focusing on the entire goal all at once. To avoid this daunting feeling, keep it very simple. Break your bigger goal into smaller doable ones. Instead of trying to accomplish one huge goal all at once or to change all of your habits all at once, focus on doing just one thing consistently and exercise your self-discipline with that one small thing.

For example, if you are somebody that is looking to get into better shape, start by exercising for 10 to 15 minutes per day. Instead of trying to go to the gym for 2 hours every day, which can be very daunting, start with a smaller goal in mind first. By taking baby steps, you can get your mind used to that habit and slowly increase the amount of time that you spend at the gym. eventually, once you feel like that goal has become a habit, you can then begin to focus on other small goals and keep building up words from there.

1. *Eat a healthy diet, and eat often.*

We learned in the earlier chapters that glucose levels play a big role in a person's brainpower which controls a person's willpower. The sensation of being hungry can cause people to feel angry, annoyed, and irritated. This feeling is real, and everyone has felt it before and often has a huge impact on a person's willpower. Research has found evidence that having low blood sugar weakens a person's ability to make good decisions.

When a person is hungry, their ability to concentrate suffers a lot, and their brain doesn't function as optimally. Therefore, a person's self-control is likely to be weakened when their body is in this state. To prevent this, make sure to be eating small meals constantly to prevent yourself from feeling that annoying hungry feeling that causes people to have a lapse in judgment. Since exercising willpower takes up a lot of energy from a person's brain, make sure to keep fuelling it with enough glucose so that the brain is able to keep functioning at an optimal level.

1. *Get a new perspective on 'willpower.'*

We learned in the earlier chapters that a person's point of view or their beliefs can create a buffer of how long it takes to have their willpower drained completely. Although most researchers believe that there is a limit to how much we can tap into our willpower, they also found that the people who believe that there wasn't a limit had a bigger will power stockpile. If a person believes that they have a limited amount of willpower, they probably will not be able to surpass those limits. However, if a person does not place a strict limit on themselves, they are less likely to use up their willpower stockpile before meeting their goals.

A person's internal perception about their own willpower and self-control plays a huge role in determining how much willpower they have. If a person can remove these obstacles by believing that they have a large stockpile of willpower, and believing in themselves, then they are less likely to drain out there will power compared to someone who believes that they don't have much of it. So try changing your own perception of how you see your willpower. Try to think of it as a source that can run out, but because of your beliefs, you have a larger amount of it. This is a much better mindset to be in compared to thinking that willpower will run out so therefore you should be stingy with it.

1. *Make yourself a backup plan, and ALWAYS have one ready.*

Many psychologists use a famous technique that helps with boosting willpower called "implementation intention." This technique is where you give yourself a plan when you are faced with a potentially difficult situation. We used this example earlier; if a person is trying to reduce the amount of alcohol that they drink and they know that they are going to a party where they will be asked if they want to drink alcohol, instead of always asking for a beer like they normally do, they will instead ask for a plain soda with lime.

By making a plan before going to a situation that you know where you will be confronted with big temptations, you will have an action plan in place where you can automatically use rather than having to come up with an excuse on the spot and risking failure. When a person goes into those situations with a plan, it helps give them the mindset and the self-control that is necessary to overcome obstacles. They will be able to save energy by not having to make sudden decisions or make sudden plans based on their emotional state. This will make them less likely to cave in to temptations and more likely to exercise their self-discipline.

1. *Treat yourself.*

Just like anything else in life, it is necessary to give yourself a break and to give yourself a reward. Give yourself something to look forward to by planning an appropriate reward when you accomplish your goals. This is not much different from when you were a little kid, and you got a treat from your parents for showing good behavior. When a person has something to look forward to it gives them the extra motivation that they need to succeed.

Anticipation is a powerful thing. It gives people something to focus on so that they are not only thinking of all the things that they need to change. When you have achieved one of your goals, you can find yourself a new goal and a new reward in order to keep motivating yourself to move forward. However, the reward should not be something unhealthy. For example, in the previous example of the person that is trying to lower their alcohol intake, their reward for not drinking as often should not be that they will go binge drinking next Friday. Their awards should be something healthy that won't make them lose progress on all the work that they've done.

1. *Forgive yourself for any mistakes and keep moving forward.*

Even if a person has all the best intentions and the most well-made plans, sometimes they will fall short when practicing self-discipline. Avoiding failure altogether is impossible and we should not build a mindset around that. Everyone will have their ups and downs, their successes and their failures. The key to overcoming the failures that you will face is to simply to keep moving forward. If you stumble on your journey of self-discipline, instead of giving up altogether, acknowledge what caused it, learn from it, and then move on. Don't let yourself get caught up in frustration, anger, or guilt because these emotions are the ones that will de-motivate you and get in the way of your future progress. Learn from the mistakes you have made and be comfortable with forgiving yourself. Once you have done that, you can get your head back in the game and start where you left off.

ONE OF THE worst and most detrimental bad habits that many people have is procrastination. Typically, this bad habit is the one that holds people back from building better habits or achieving their goals. Although overcoming procrastination and breaking that habit isn't an easy task, it is one that must be done. You have to break through this habit to make room for all other healthy habits that you want to implement for yourself.

The Root of All Bad Habits Is Procrastination

In this chapter, I will focus on helping you overcome the main bad habit that is typically the source of all other bad habits. I will teach you about what procrastination actually is, why it happens, and how you can overcome it. When you begin to get an understanding of how procrastination actually works, it helps you overcome it much easier. Let's start by learning about the science behind procrastination.

What Is Procrastination and How Does It Work?

Through an abundance of psychology research, psychologists have discovered a phenomenon called "time inconsistency," which helps explain why procrastination affects humans so largely by pulling us away from needed tasks despite our good intentions. The term time inconsistency refers to the habit of the human mind to value immediate gratification or rewards more highly compared to long-term and future rewards. The best way to further understand this is to imagine that you have two alter egos. The first is your present self, and the second is your future self. When a person sets goals for themselves, such as getting fit by working out more or learning a new language, they are actually making plans for their future self. They are envisioning what they want their life to be like in the future. Evidence has shown researchers that when a person thinks about their future self, it is not difficult for their brain to see the value of doing actions that will lead to long-term benefits. The future self is the one that values long-term rewards.

On the contrary, while the future self can only set goals, the present self is the one that is responsible for taking action. There will come a time where this individual will need to make a decision, but they aren't making a choice for the future self at this point. In the present moment, their brain is focused entirely on the present self. Research shows that the present self prefers immediate rewards over long-term ones. This means that the present self and future self don't often get along. While the future self wants to be healthy and have a sic pack, the present self wants some chili cheese fries. Everyone knows that eating unhealthy will prevent health problems in the future when you're at an old age, but those things are so far away, so why worry about them now right? This is the thought process that many people have when they are faced with a choice of immediate gratification or achieving long-term goals.

. . .

Very similarly, most young people know that saving money for their retirement during their 20s and 30s is extremely valuable, but the benefit of this is many decades away. It is much easier for a person's present-self to see value in buying themselves a new iPhone rather than putting away $1000 for their 75 year old self! This concept of "time inconsistency" may be the reason why people often go to bed feeling motivated and inspired to reach their goals and change their life but they find themselves completely falling back into bad habits when they wake up. This is due to the fact that the human brain values long-term benefits when they are thinking about the future, but it prefers immediate gratification when it comes to the present moment. Let's dive into a little bit more of the science behind this.

For the sake of example here, let's pretend for a little while that you are a giraffe living in the plains of the African savanna. Your neck is 6 feet long, and occasionally you will see a group of human tourists driving in a car with a safari tour taking pictures of you. However, it's not just your long neck that separates you from the humans. It could be that the biggest difference between you and your other giraffe friends and the humans taking pictures is that almost every single decision that you make brings an immediate benefit to your life. For example, when you see a storm coming, you will find shelter under a tree or if you are hungry, you walk over to the nearest tree and begin to eat, or when you spot a predator hunting you, you begin to run away.

Everyday, most of the choices that you make as a giraffe such as where to sleep when to avoid a predator or what to eat, makes a direct and immediate impact on your life. You are entirely focused on the present and the furthest you would think about in the near future. You are living in an 'Immediate-Return Environment,' this is what scientists call this environment due to the fact that your actions deliver very immediate and clear outcomes.

Now let's change things up and pretend that you are one of the human tourists that are traveling in Africa on the safari. Different from giraffes, humans live in a 'Delayed Return Environment.' Most of the choices made in this type of environment will not benefit you right away. For example, if you save your money now, you'll have enough for retirement in forty years or if you work hard at your job today, you will get paid in two weeks. Rewards are designed to be delayed until some point in the future in many aspects of modern day society.

While the giraffe is worried about problems that are immediate, such as avoiding predators, seeking shelters, and finding food, humans worry the most about the problems of the future. For instance, while the humans are on the safari, they may be thinking, "This trip and safari has been tremendous fun! It would be so awesome if I could work as a safari tour guide and be able to see the giraffes every day. Speaking of work, is it time for me to change my career? Am I really working the kind of job that I enjoy? Should I start looking for new jobs?" Unfortunately for us, humans that are living in a Delayed Return Environment tend to lead to a lot of anxiety and stress. This is because the human brain wasn't designed to solve problems of a Delayed Return Environment. In fact, this is why there has been a rise in depression and anxiety over the last decade. Where people of the past focused more on their immediate problem like harvesting their crops for food or boiling water so it's safe to drink, people nowadays focus on problems that are in the future since most of our basic needs are already taken care of.

Why Do People Procrastinate?

With your new understanding that most of us live in a Delayed Return Environment, let's learn a little about why people procrastinate. Most people are more than capable of achieving great things in their life, but many fail to do so. Procrastination is probably one of the biggest obstacles that hinder a person from being able to achieve greater things. Everyone has procrastinated before and anyone is capable of it. Many times, people don't even know that they are procrastinating. However, there are also those moments where people know that they are procrastinating but fail to do anything to stop the process. So why do people procrastinate anyways although they are self-aware? There are numerous reasons why people begin procrastinating; I've created a list of the most common ones for you to go over. Take a look and try to identify the reason behind your procrastination.

- You are resistant

You might have experienced this phenomenon before, where there are times that it would be easier for you to just complete a task than procrastinate but yet you still chose to procrastinate! The main reason for this is rebellion. There is a class of procrastinators called the 'rebellious procrastinators.' They are very common. These people deliberately delay tasks, defy standards, falter expectations, and impedes protocol. This type of procrastination can be done by anyone especially if they feel like they have been mistreated.

The reasons that cause people to procrastinate are different for every individual. The exact reason why for each individual may not be obvious but the obvious reasons may be caused by something that is underlying. On the contrary, the reasons that we had just discussed are seen as the most common ones. Trying to avoid this type of behavior is not an easy task as it often involves a person to identify their bad habits and actively try to break them down and create new ones. Whether you are the procrastinator or you are suffering at the hands of one, the important part here is to take action immediately. You have to take action in order to correct your situation. Keep in mind that procrastination is a serious issue that if left unresolved for a long time, can cause some serious and long lasting problems in your life.

- You lack interest

Everyone has their own special set of interests. Just because your friend is passionate about a particular topic or job, it does not mean that everyone else is interested in the same thing. People have the tendency to put off doing jobs that they do not find interesting because it is more difficult to find motivation. There are multiple ways that people can deal with jobs that they have no interest in depending on if you are the person that is actually doing the job or if they are the person that is simply assigning the task. Let's take a look at the perspective of a person that is physically doing the job; they could try the following things:

- Check to see if this task actually has to be done
- Ask yourself if there is someone else who is much better suited to completing this task. If possible, you may be able to swap it or delegate it (e.g., if someone else likes that job better, you can trade with them for theirs that you might like better)
- If your tolerance for frustration is low, try to break down this job into smaller pieces and complete them one at a time
- If your tolerance for frustration is higher, you can schedule a block of time where you take away all distractions and just do this task until it is done

From the perspective of the person who is assigning the job/task, you will likely find more success if you assign this specific task to someone who you know will be passionate about it. By choosing someone who has an interest in that task, the job will be completed in a much faster fashion and at a higher standard as well.

- You have a skill deficiency

In order for a person to achieve their goals, it requires them to learn and to have personal growth. People will have to develop new skills and knowledge related to their set goals. This is a huge part of their journey. However, people often fail to see this fact. They see their lack of skill or knowledge as an obstacle that is permanent and cannot be overcome. This mindset causes people to give up on their goals before they have even done anything to start it. Rather than giving up, people need to be able to assess the skills and knowledge that are required to achieve their goal and then compare it to their own skills and knowledge that they possess. The difference between the two is nothing more than just an opportunity to learn and train. Instead of just giving up, people need to create a plan that will help them develop and learn the skills needed in order to bridge that gap. So is it procrastination if you are pushing the date of your goal achievement back? Absolutely not. This is just effective planning. By understanding that you require more time to reach your goal means that you are identifying the right steps, you need to take to reach your goal.

- You have a fear of failure

There are a lot of people who have the belief that failure is devastating. They often see failure as a final result that is set in stone and cannot be rectified or changed. Failure to them is a permanent stain on their reputation, which means that every time that they fail, their ego takes a huge hit. This lack of confidence causes them to avoid taking action on tasks where they are not 100% absolutely confident in its success. Keep in mind that in the era that we live in today, many tasks that people face will be new to them and it is entirely impossible to be able to be 100% confident in every single chance of success. Due to this, procrastination is something that happens frequently and in an endless spiral.

. . .

On the contrary, there are the people out there who see failure as a stepping stone towards success and a learning opportunity. They have the understanding and belief that mistakes are unavoidable and they will be made. Their attitude consists mostly of realistic optimism which enables them to believe that they will be able to successfully achieve their goal/task even if it's something that requires more than one try. As you might be able to tell, these types of people have a much lower tendency to procrastinate. Instead, they often approach new challenges with excitement and preparedness to deal with obstacles.

Since learning and growth are important parts of a successful life, it is unrealistic to believe that you can succeed without experiencing any obstacles or failures in your journey. If you are constantly worrying and are scared at the idea of failure, try to identify extra steps or measures that you can take in order to lower the chances of failure and increase the chances of success. Factor in time that you can take to review and assess your own actions and try to learn something from every experience. You will soon start to change your mindset into one where you see every challenge as an opportunity for learning and growth.

- You lack motivation

People often have the wrong mindset where they think that they need to feel fully motivated before they start working on a task/job. This mindset is unrealistic. People's motivation often does not arrive until they have started that task and is beginning to see progress. When people see progress, they start to see the fruits to their labor, and they become even more motivated to keep working until they have completed their task. You might be wondering what about the motivation that is needed in order to start working altogether? The answer to this is that a person needs to have a good understanding of the 'why' and the vision of that particular job. Before you even begin working on it, you should know what the benefits are going to be. You would be surprised at how many people waste a lot of time doing work that actually does not need to be completed. Moreover, people should be using prioritization in order to get the most urgent and important work out of the way first. By understanding the benefits of completing a task or job, you will fully be able to estimate its importance. In terms of smaller tasks/jobs, simply understanding what the benefits are of completing that task should be enough for motivation. For larger tasks and jobs, it is important that you have a way to measure your progress so you can further gain motivation and confidence from your work.

- You have a fear of success

Many professionals of the self-help industry have talked or theorized about the fact that people's biggest fear wasn't necessarily failure, but our biggest fear is actually the fear of success. Many people view success as stress and pressure. When they think about achieving greater and more things, they often think about the negative aspects that come with it. For example, they believe that when a person achieves more, people will begin to demand and expect more from you. They often doubt their ability to deal with the increased expectations so they decide to procrastinate to sabotage their own chances of success.

The reality here is that there is no reason that a person should fear success. As a person begins to succeed by overcoming challenges of all difficulties, they begin to become more knowledgeable and have developed new skills. Their resilience will begin to increase. If a person is able to learn the necessary skills of personal organization, it really doesn't matter what type of task or work that they are doing, they will be able to find a way through. Long story short, every task is simply just a task that needs to be completed. When you are able to break down every large task into a number of smaller tasks, there should be nothing that would be able to overwhelm you.

How Do I Overcome Procrastination?

By reading the most common reasons why a person procrastinates, you may have felt like you resonated with one or some of those reasons. Don't feel bad because this is a bad habit that 90% of people have. The difference between you and them is that you are not making an effort to change it. I can help you with this by walking you through a step-by-step guide to help you overcome it. Use this guide over the course of the next 2 – 3 weeks and you will begin to see a change in your approach to completing tasks.

1. Break down big tasks into smaller and more manageable ones.

one main reason that people put off doing the work that they need to do is because they subconsciously find that their work is too overwhelming for them. Start by just breaking down whatever that task is into littler parts and then focus on one at a time. If you find yourself still wanting to procrastinate after you've already broken it down, then break it down even more. You will eventually get to a point where the task that you need to do is so easy that you would feel very badly about yourself if you didn't just do it.

Let's use a simple example of filing your taxes. Imagine that you are feeling overwhelmed as you don't even know where to begin filing your taxes. You have a bad habit of avoiding tasks related to money as it scares you. You are also afraid that you may owe money to the government that you might not have. Here is how I would break down the large and broad task of 'filing taxes':

1. Research the best way to file taxes for beginners
2. Explore my options (either downloading software for DIY or going to a tax filing company)
3. Pick which option suits you best
4. Gather the documents that are suggested based on which option you chose in step #2
5. Follow the instructions given to you by the tax software or the tax professional

Now, your one large task of 'filing taxes' became much more manageable. Instead of thinking about filing taxes as one large unit, you are now starting with a simple google search of the best way to file taxes for beginners. From there, now you can make an educated decision on which method is easiest for you to proceed with. By taking things one step at a time, you feel less overwhelmed and are more likely to do the task rather than putting it off.

1. Change your working environment to improve your productivity.

This may be obvious to some but different types of environments produce different impacts on a person's productivity. Take a look at your workspace, does looking at it make you want to go back to bed? Or does it look inviting enough to make you want to jump right into work? If it's the former, you may want to consider changing up your workspace to make it more inviting. For instance, I used to have stronger feelings of procrastination when my desk was cluttered. It did not look inviting and in fact, it added stress as now I needed to clear up my workspace before doing a task that I didn't even really want to do in the first place. By keeping your workspace clean, tidy, and inviting, you can skip the step of having to tidy up before getting your hands dirty with work.

1. Build a plan surrounding tasks you want to accomplish, including all details and deadlines.

When a person just has one singular deadline for a large task, it's basically an invitation to procrastinate. This is because people get under the impression that they have time and continue to keep pushing things back until the deadline is looming over them. In step one, we discussed breaking down your task into smaller ones. In this step, we will actually make our own deadlines for each small task. The purpose of this is so you have a general idea when you have to finish each task. If you don't finish one step by the deadline that you have set, you are jeopardizing every step that's planned after that. This helps create some urgency.

1. Remove any temptations you have that can cause you to procrastinate.

If you are someone who is a constant procrastination offender, it may be because you make it very easy for yourself to be distracted. Be self aware – what are the things that you typically find yourself doing when you're supposed to be doing something else? Is it browsing the internet? Scrolling your phone? Identify what exactly it is that is tempting you to procrastinate and try to prevent yourself from being tempted in the first place. If you are easily distracted by your phone, turn it off for an hour, put it in a drawer, and begin to work. Some people may extreme and go as far as disabling all their social media accounts so they can prevent themselves from endless browsing. It doesn't have to be extremely drastic but take preventative measures, so it's not too easy for you to procrastinate.

1. Spend more time with people who inspire and motivate you.

Choosing who you spend your time with heavily influences your behaviors. If you are spending time with people who also procrastinate and don't see anything wrong with it, then you are likely to think that that is okay. Instead, try to surround yourself with people that are motivated and have achieved many goals before. You will soon be able to gain some of their motivation and spirit as well.

1. Find someone to hold you accountable/to get things done with you.

When you have a large set of tasks that you need to get done, having a buddy will make the process way more fun. Your buddy should ideally be someone that also has their own large set of tasks/goals that they want to complete. The two of you will hold each other accountable for the tasks that need to be done. It is not required that both of you need to have the same goals but if they are, even better! Many people that have goals of getting more fit will likely find themselves a workout buddy that will help hold them accountable for going to the gym, or even planning workout sessions together.

1. Share your goals with people around you.

This serves a similar function as the step before but on a much larger scale. Tell your friends, family, and colleagues about the goals that you have in mind. This works better if you tell them details like your deadlines or the plan that you've made for yourself. Now the next time you see these people they will likely ask you what your status is on your goals, therefore, creating motivation for you. Also, people tend to not want to 'fail' in front of others, so if you know that you are seeing those people soon, you are more likely to make sure that you have made some progress so you can update them on it.

1. Reach out and network with someone who has achieved similar goals that you want to achieve.

If your goal is one that you think other people have accomplished before, try to find out who these people are. Seek them out and connect with them in order to ask them about their experience. You can learn about what obstacles and failures that they faced along the way, and they'd be able to provide you with some tips that may have made their journey a little bit easier. Moreover, seeing living proof that your goals are ones that are achievable may help you take action even sooner.

1. Reevaluate and re-clarify your goals on a frequent basis.

If you are someone that has been procrastinating for a long time now, it might be due to the misalignment of what you're currently doing and what you want. People often outgrow their goals when they begin to learn more about themselves. However, they don't always adjust their goals based on those changes. Try to take a weekend to yourself and regroup. Ask yourself, 'what exactly do I want to achieve? Are the things that I am doing now aligning with that? If not, what can I do to change it?' Adjusting your goals to something that lines up with who you are presently is crucial in terms of creating motivation and value for yourself.

1. Don't overcomplicate.

This relates back to a point we talked about earlier in this book. There is never a 'perfect time' to do a task that you need to do. You may be identifying all the reasons why the present moment is 'not the best time,' but that is the wrong mindset to have. Even if you only had 10 minutes, you can surely get SOMETHING done that is related to your goal. Abandon this thought of waiting for 'the perfect time' because there will never be one. After you break down your goals into smaller ones, start doing them whenever you have 10 minutes free. It's as simple as that.

1. Will yourself to just DO it.

At the end of it all, everything comes down to simply just taking action. Motivation comes from starting something and not before, just simply taking the first step to doing something will create the motivation you need to keep you going. A person can do all the planning and strategizing they need but if they don't actually take the first step, nothing will happen.

Dismissing Your Procrastination Excuses

In this final subchapter, I will be teaching you to dismiss your procrastination excuses. Typically, when a person begins to procrastinate, they usually are not aware that they are procrastinating. Instead, they will come up with a series of excuses for why they aren't able to do a certain task at this time. To help you better overcome your procrastination, you need to learn to identify the common excuses you make. Once you are able to identify them, you will know that you are trying to procrastinate and you can will yourself not to.

Popular Excuses People Make to Procrastinate

Let's start learning about the most common and popular excuses. When you are reading through this, be sure to relate it back to yourself. Ask yourself if these excuses are prominent in your life, and if they occur a lot. If you notice one excuse in particular that you heavily resonate with, that excuse is likely the one that's been holding you back from building better habits and achieving more goals.

1. "I'm too stressed, tired, angry, sad, ...etc."

This excuse is probably the most used, common, and tempting one of them all. If a person finds themselves in a negative mood, all they want to do is to stop working and do something that will make them feel better. This could be just sitting at home relaxing or going out for a beer. This results in the person rationalizing with themselves that their work would be done faster and with more productivity if they try to attempt it when they are feeling better. There are two important aspects to note here. First of all, it is impossible to tell what kind of mood someone will be in the future. For all we know, this person could be in the same exact mood tomorrow and fall into the same excuse, like some sort of unproductive loop. Secondly, this is not a common thought but working through a hard task can actually enhance someone's mood. The feeling of achievement and satisfaction that comes with finishing a task, no matter how pleasant or unpleasant, often lifts people out of a bad mood. Especially if they can get a reward after that they feel like they deserved.

1. "This task isn't important enough to do right now; I have more important things to do."

This excuse comes in multiple forms. The first form of it is that you believe that this task should not even be your responsibility in the first place. For instance, your manager could have given you a task that generally isn't your responsibility. In this scenario, you may be procrastinating because you resent the fact that you got extra work. If there is an opening for you to negotiate with your boss about this task, then, by all means, go for it. However, if you know that there is no getting out of it, you might as well start sooner rather than later. Secondly, a task that you deem not important enough may be something that is of a preventative or routine measure. These tasks tend to take a backseat in comparison to more urgent tasks but they are also often swept under the rug when a person thinks they are insignificant. If you find yourself thinking that certain tasks just 'aren't important enough,' remind yourself that routine upkeep tasks prevent large problems in the future. If we use dental cleaning as an example, it's a lot cheaper to just get your routine check up and cleaning every year rather than putting it off and having to do costly dental work when something does happen to you.

1. "This task is too important, it requires all of my attention, and I can't do that right now."

The most common victims to fall into this excuse are your nervous professionals. For instance, let's pretend that there is a huge project that's been neglected for a while, but there are a ton of your daily tasks that you still need to complete. If you truly believe that your project is the most important thing right now, you may decide to do it at a time where you aren't distracted by other trivial tasks. It does sort of make sense on one hand when it comes to a person doing their best work when they have minimal distractions. However, there will never be a time where there are no distractions. People will always have interference and just like what we learned earlier, there is no 'perfect' time to do something. Rather than saying now is not the best time to work on it, break it down into smaller tasks and just do one of them amidst your other tasks.

1. "Once I finish doing A, THEN, I'll start working on B."

When a person has two competing tasks or goals, inevitably, one will take a backseat. It is important to have more than one priority, but dividing your attention entirely is not the ideal way to confront this. For instance, let's say that you are working on two projects that have the same deadline at the end of the week. By the end of your first day working, you've already made a huge impact on project A but you don't want to start project B because you don't want to shift gears. In order to not make the excuse to put off project B, start doing some preliminary tasks that project B requires in the background. You can take short 5 minute breaks from project A just to make a plan for project B. This way, when you complete project A, you already have a whole plan mapped out for project B and you can get your feet wet right away without losing momentum.

1. "This task is too hard to do at the moment; I will do it later."

We talked about the concept of having a large task a lot throughout this book. People that set themselves up for large tasks without making a plan often fall victim to this excuse. When a person looks at a huge set of tasks, all they can see is how big and overwhelming that one entity is. When all you're thinking about is how big that workload is, it's almost natural that you would want to avoid it for as long as possible. Rather than looking at your one large task as a monstrous unit, break it down into smaller chunks. We already talked about this but by breaking down your task into smaller ones and focusing on those smaller ones individually, you are giving yourself an in that feels much less intimidating.

1. "I don't have the time to do this right now; I'll do it when I have more time."

The people who rely on this excuse the most are busy professionals. They never feel like they are using an excuse because it is true that they are actually always busy. If someone is constantly on the go and completing tasks but still never getting to the end of their to-do list, it may feel natural to think that you don't have time for whatever task you promised yourself you would do. However, there is a huge flaw in this type of mindset. There will always be time to work on something; you just have to make room for it. We talked about how you can do a lot in 10 minutes of time. Simply just set aside 10 minutes of time in the morning or right before bed. That is really all you need. You'll then start to make gradual progress without the need to interfere with your daily schedule.

1. "I'll do this tomorrow."

This excuse usually appears during a person's childhood. However, a large number of adults use this excuse on a daily basis.

There is an old saying that goes, "never put off till tomorrow what you can do today." Unfortunately, this saying does not stand up well in the face of temptation of instant gratification. Instead of resisting temptation, try to think of it in a way where you're doing yourself a favor. Promise yourself some type of reward (e.g., getting your favorite take out or drawing yourself a nice bath) if you do that required task today instead of 'tomorrow.'

So there you have it – these are the most commonly used excuses for people who procrastinate. Now that you know what the most common excuses are, which ones do you feel like you use most often? When you know which excuses you use most frequently, you can begin to test them to see if these excuses have any truth in them. Now, let's move on to learning how to test your excuses. I have made a simple chart that you can follow to help yourself identify procrastination when you begin to make excuses. Test your most frequently used excuses by asking yourself these questions.

YOUR EXCUSE: QUESTIONS TO ASK YOURSELF IN ORDER TO TEST SAID EXCUSE

"I'll do this tomorrow."

- What is my schedule like tomorrow?
- Do I actually have more time tomorrow?
- What are the reasons why I can't do this task right now? (If you don't have any reasons, just get started!)

"I don't have the time to do this right now; I'll do it when I have more time."

- How much time do I have? (If you have at least 10 minutes, you have time)
- What smaller tasks can I do in a short amount of time?

"This task is too hard to do at the moment; I will do it later."

- Why is it 'too hard'? Is it because the tasks itself are too large? (If so, break down the task into smaller ones)
- Will this task be too hard tomorrow? (If yes, then it's not a matter of time, it's a matter of breaking your tasks down properly)
- What will make this task easier to do right now?

"Once I finish doing A, THEN, I'll start working on B."

- Is there nothing I can do between finishing A and starting B that will make my tasks easier?
- Can I at least start a plan for task B?
- What is the likelihood that I will be able to simply dive into B after I'm done A? (If it's a low likelihood, start some of task B before you are finished task A)

"This task is too important, it requires all of my attention, and I can't do that right now."

- Is there going to ever be a time where my attention is 100% undivided? (If no, this time is as good as any)

"This task isn't important enough to do right now; I have more important things to do."

- What else is more important right now?
- Why do I think this is not important enough?
- If I neglect this now, will it catch up to me later? (If yes, then just do it right now)

"I'm too stressed, tired, angry, sad, ...etc."

- Am I going to be less tired (or any other negative emotion) tomorrow?
- How will I know for a fact that I will be feeling better tomorrow?
- Can anyone know how they are going to be feeling in the future?

6 / CHALLENGES YOU WILL FACE
WHEN BREAKING BAD HABITS

As you may already know, you will be faced with numerous challenges on your journey of breaking bad habits and building better ones. In this chapter, I will focus on teaching you what some of these habits may be. By understanding these challenges, you are better equipped to deal with them when they come your way. The main challenge that we will focus on in this chapter is your inner-critic, as that is the one that typically prevents people from doing the things that they truly want to do. We already have a good idea of the role that unhelpful thinking styles play in a procrastinator. We will also learn a little about bad habits that people develop over the years and how people can practice self-discipline in order to overcome bad habits and learn good ones.

Managing Your Inner-Critic

A person's inner-critic plays a huge role when it comes to things like mental health, self-esteem, and in our case, procrastination. We notice that our inner-critics usually live in a world that is black and white, a world with very little room for grey areas. Inner-critics share words with you, such as, "You should just give up." Or "What makes you think you'll succeed?" Instead of creating an open space that allows for mistakes, growth, and development, our inner critics causes us to question our worth which makes it difficult for us to have the right mindset to complete needed tasks.

For some people, their inner-critic is reflective of a voice from their past. It could be their mother, father, the boss that fired you. For others, it could simply be your own voice talking down at you. Often times, anybody who makes an offhand comment to you may cause you to take it so deeply that those words become a part of your identity.

This is why mindfulness is very important when we are looking to overcome procrastination by training our inner-critic. Mindfulness helps people see their own negative thoughts that are said to themselves in a repetitive cycle of self-detriment. When we continue to judge ourselves harshly, we may think that we are making progress in terms of improving our flaws when, in reality, we are only reinforcing the feelings of unworthiness.

In our world today, it is a cultural norm to believe that self-criticism will bring motivation to achieving goals and avoiding procrastination. This type of self-criticism functions under the false belief that when a person realizes that their actions or performance isn't good enough, they'll want to change. Our inner-critic is also guilty for giving us a sense of control, but not in the right places. We also use our own judgmental thoughts as a way of coping with emotions like shame, fear, and the unknown. Over time, these comments made by yourself or other people manifest inside of you and eventually become your own unique "inner-critic." To put it in its simplest form, your inner-critic is the persistent negative self-talk that keeps us stuck.

. . .

Unfortunately, the type of communication that our inner-critic uses with us are very anxiety-provoking and shaming, which actually creates something that is the complete opposite of motivation. It triggers us to stay safe, reduce anxiety, and to avoid. Avoidance with the goal of reducing anxiety is not the same as having motivation to change. In fact, avoidance is usually made up of things like procrastination, addictive behaviors, or self-distracting behaviors (constantly checking your phone, excessively browsing the web). If the messages that our inner-critic is telling us are often shameful, such as "why are you so lazy?" or "what's wrong with you?" we often become paralyzed. When people feel shame, they feel that there is something that is so flawed within them that they don't feel worthy of connections with other people. Shame is the emotion that disconnects us from other people and teaches us to feel alone. As humans, it is within our nature to crave a certain level of human connection. When we often feel feelings of shame caused by our inner-critic, these feelings make us want to withdraw from the world and further trigger avoidance behaviors like procrastination as a way to soothe or comfort ourselves. Ultimately, shame and self-criticism work hand in hand to prevent us from doing the things that we need to do in order to reach our goals or simply just to take care of ourselves.

Awareness is the first step that needs to be taken in order to recognize your inner-critic and to reshape it into something that is less critical and more supportive. Try to pay attention the next time you are feeling distracted, numb, or anxious. Try to identify who's voice is the voice of your inner critic. Try to find the situation where your inner-critic awakens. Allow yourself to dig deep and identify the most vulnerable feelings during situations where your inner-critic is awake. These feelings or these situations are likely what your inner-critic is trying to protect you from feeling. However, by protecting you, they are holding you back from meeting your full potential.

Let's take a look at this example:

Julia went shopping over the weekend. She hasn't gone in a while and is unsure about her sizes at this one store, and she tried on a few items. She thought to herself, "These pants are too tight, they don't fit, I feel so fat, ugly, and unattractive. I am such a failure."

What is Julia afraid of exactly? Her thought process is this: "I've gained weight, which means that I failed. It also means that I'm old and I am scared of aging and gaining even more weight."

What are Julia's vulnerabilities in this case?

Julia responds why "I feel that I don't have any control and that I am afraid. My body is functioning differently than it used to, and I'm having a harder time maintaining a healthy weight and muscle tone. I feel like this is hopeless. I feel overwhelmed and scared."

What does Julia really need to do in this situation?

. . .

Julia says, "I can deal with this change. By acknowledging my vulnerability, it causes me to make more effort to take better care of my physical health. When I feel worthless, I am unproductive. Shaming myself is not motivating."

A person's inner critic may say negative things to you but its true intention is to prevent you from harm by demotivating you from doing things that may result in failure in order to prevent you from feeling negative emotions. For example, Julia's inner critic may be telling her that she's a failure and overweight in order to prevent her from taking better care of her body. From doing this, Julia will be demotivated by working out at the gym or eating healthier. If she doesn't do this, she will not fail. This is what the inner-critic is trying to do. By demotivating the person to a point where they'd rather not try is the safest protection of them all, if you don't try, you can't exactly fail.

Breaking Out of Your Bad Habits

Humans are creatures of their own habit. You may know from your own experience that you don't like straying away from your existing habits and routines. It feels uncomfortable. Humans tend to find comfort in old habits and routines. Unfortunately, a lot of the times our habits are not positive ones. Most people tend to have bad habits such as indulging in the conveniences of junk food, drinking alcohol every night or skipping the gym for an extra hour of sleep. If you have a couple of bad habits yourself, you may know very well that the urge to act out these habits are very strong. However, there is a silver lining to this. If bad habits can be so strong and tempting, it means that good habits can be like that too. It all comes down to a matter of incorporating those good habits in your life and ingraining it so deeply that it feels wrong or uncomfortable to not act out those habits.

. . .

So where exactly do our habits come from and how are they developed? Why is it that when people try to change their habits by breaking out of bad ones and building good ones that they can only stick with it for a short amount of time before they give up and revert to their old ways? The biggest problem here is that the bad habits we have are likely the habits that we've had for many years and maybe even decades. Our habits are made up of neural pathways that have been imprinted into our brains. This is something that happens on a biological level. These neural pathways are responsible for linking up the neural networks in a person's brain to perform specific functions like pouring a cup of coffee in a certain way, smoking a cigarette, or walking up the stairs.

These neural pathways help a person automate certain behaviors that are constantly used in order to reduce the energy needed for the conscious processing power in a person's brain. By automating certain actions, it allows this person's mind to focus on other things rather than the mundane tasks that they have done a thousand times. This function actually stems from our very early human days and is actually a part of our DNA. This function allows us to have a more efficient mind that can be used for many things and not just entirely focused on simply daily tasks.

It is often the mundane behaviors that are repeated which then holds people back from being able to build good habits. Most of the time people tend to have more bad habits that add negative value to their lives rather than good habits that help them reach their goals further. Since neural pathways get ingrained deeper and deeper over time, it makes it difficult for people to break out of their bad habits or form good ones when they are constantly acting out on bad habits.

Unhealthy Thinking Patterns

You will have an opportunity to learn more about unhealthy thinking patterns later on in this book. Unhealthy thinking patterns is one of the biggest challenges that people face when they are looking to overcome procrastination. The difficulty comes from first being able to be aware of your own thoughts and then paying attention to what types of patterns your thoughts occur in. When a person is able to recognize when those thinking styles are happening, that's when they can begin to interrupt them, challenge them, and change them.

For instance, let's say you need to hand in a report to your boss by the next weekend. You know for a fact that it will take you several hours and that you have a jam packed week coming up. You're sitting at home, and your thoughts begin to mindlessly wander. You begin to think that this report is too hard (although you haven't started yet) and that you are going to fail. You begin to feel stressed and anxious and then you say to yourself, "I'm too stressed right now to do this report. I'll start on it tomorrow." We learned in the previous chapter that there are multiple things wrong here. Firstly, since you were being mindless when thinking about the report, you looked at the report as one giant hard task. That is the first mistake. The second mistake here is letting that one giant report cause emotions of stress and anxiety which led you to "feel too stressed" to start the report right now. The third mistake is saying to yourself, "I'll start on it tomorrow," as you fully know that the rest of your week will be very busy.

· · ·

Therapy like Cognitive Behavioral Therapy becomes useful here because if you were being mindful of your current thoughts, rather than exhibiting the jumping to conclusions unhelpful thinking style, you would be able to catch yourself thinking that the report is too difficult before even tried. If you were able to stop yourself there and take a few steps back and instead think, "I believe this report is a big project so in order to make it easier for myself, I have to break it down into smaller and more manageable pieces." By doing this, you likely will not end up feeling those emotions of anxiety and stress which then led to procrastination. Do you see how simply just being aware of your thoughts and challenging yourself can change the outcome of a situation entirely?

When a person learns to be able to tolerate the discomfort of challenging their own thoughts, they can overcome bad habits and things that they never thought they were going to be able to. It may sound easy, but it requires a lot of practice for a person to be able to start paying attention to thoughts that they have ignored for years. So the next time you feel like you're about to procrastinate doing something, just pay attention to the emotions you're feeling. Work backwards. Ask yourself, 'why am I feeling these emotions right now?" "what triggered these emotions" "if ABC trigged these emotions, what can I do to make it more manageable?"

7 / CHALLENGES YOU WILL FACE WHEN DEVELOPING HEALTHY HABITS

AFTER DISCUSSING some challenges that come with overcoming bad habits, let's talk about some challenges that you will face when you are practicing self-discipline to build healthy habits. We already know that hardship and failure are a part of the process of life and the process of building self-discipline. By understanding what these challenges might be in advance, it gives you an idea of what to prepare for when you are faced with an obstacle. Like we mentioned earlier in this book, having a plan prepared when you are in the face of a challenge or temptation can help you react in a way that is good rather than in a way that negatively affects your progress.

One problem that people normally face when they are trying to strengthen their self-discipline to build new habits is falling into a self-defeating loop. It looks like this: Fail to engage in desired behavior > negative/physical/psychological consequences > low mood, shame and self-criticism > low motivation to engage in healthy behaviors. In this chapter, I will be addressing a few challenges that are most commonly experienced when a person is looking to practice their self-discipline.

1. You are constantly fighting against your 'natural tendencies.'

Often times, people feel like their natural state should be to sit on their couch, with a plethora of snacks, and watching their favorite TV show. During those days, the idea of going to the gym or even just eating a healthy meal seems to be totally absurd. It is interesting that people nowadays have been conditioned by the expectations of society to think that their natural state is lazy. We live in a world where if you are not constantly on-the-go or working your butt off at work, then you are not working hard enough. The result of these feelings is that people tend to get trapped thinking that practicing self-discipline is the constant battle of fighting against a person's natural state. Their mindset is one that is a psychological battle of laziness versus self discipline. Having this type of mindset makes it difficult to practice self-discipline.

One of the reasons that I suspect behind this mindset is the fact that people tend to mistake the need for rest to be lazy. Lots of mental or physical exertion creates fatigue in the human body. Rest is a recovery process so that the person can not only get stronger but also be able to repeat and exceed that mental and physical exertion. If your mindset regarding self-discipline is one that is constant and uninterrupted work, then you deny your body's natural need for recovery and rest. This need for recovery will show itself as a type of sabotage of your self-discipline efforts and you will automatically label it as being lazy. Be careful when this happens, as this label is very incorrect.

Rather than mistaking any urges of rest as a sign of being lazy, think about whether or not you have exerted yourself already. If so, it is all right to stop what you're doing and take a quick break to recharge. Getting into the mindset that you are lazy, or that resting is for lazy people, then you will always feel negative about yourself every time your body shows you a natural symptom when it is asking you to rest.

1. People normally don't care about your attempts at building healthier habits/self-discipline.

When a person makes a decision to actively and purposefully restructure their life and behavior, the universe doesn't just magically make things easier for them. On the contrary, it will likely throw many challenges at you. It may rain the day that you decide to go out for a run, or your coworker might buy you a whole box of chocolates just to be nice on the day that you decide to eat healthy.

Since the world isn't built on fairness or justice or reward, it is silly to think that the universe will consciously support the changes that you are trying to make in your life. There are people who claim that the universe is presenting opportunities to them when they have decided to change their life. This is inaccurate because if a person is looking to change their life, they likely have taken on new activities. By being exposed to new people and new information, this is what creates new opportunities that have nothing to do with the universe trying to help you. So don't spend time thinking about whether or not your self-discipline plan is something that the universe will help you with. Spend your time instead preparing for all the obstacles that will get in your way of achieving your goals. If you do run into obstacles, which you will, don't think that they were placed there deliberately to throw you off but they were already there in the first place.

1. It is difficult to break down emotional behavior pathways that are well-worn.

One of the most well-known concepts in Psychology is that the emotions that people feel are very powerful influences on their behavior. These emotions and feelings are developed over the course of human evolution in order to help us with survival. Negative emotions that people often feel like fear and anxiety lets them know that danger is nearby. Feelings of happiness or excitedness tell us it's okay to approach the situation. The feeling of anger lets us know that it may be an opportunity where we would need to fight. Sadness lets us know when we need to seek comfort from our loved ones.

However, as people, we have learned that emotions and feelings aren't always the best guide to how we behave. People may get anxious in situations that don't actually have any real danger or they may get angry in situations where fighting isn't an appropriate reaction. Over the course of our lives, we've learned to pick up different habits of ways to react when it comes to responding and managing our emotions. For example, if someone had a rough day after work, their habitual behavior would be to drink a couple glasses of wine. They do this because this action has worked for them in the past, but they may not realize that they need to change it when they may have outgrown his habit. Some people may try to numb their feelings of sadness or stress by scrolling on their phones in order to prevent themselves from thinking about other things.

Oftentimes these types of emotional habits derived from the roots of somebody's childhood, where they first learned how to deal with their emotions. Without knowing, people may learn that numbing their emotions is the best strategy for not dealing with the negative ones, or they may try to distract themselves with unhealthy things like alcohol or food. These strategies become reinforced when a person repeatedly uses them and has received success in the past from it. By the time children become adults, they have built some emotion to behavior pathways that are not very well-established and hard to break. This is why people have so much trouble when it comes to strengthening their self-discipline because habits that have formed over the decades require lots of time and willpower to break down and be rebuilt.

In the process of establishing new habits, it also means that people will have to confront their well-worn habit. For example, if a person's goal was to eat healthily and get in shape, they may have to face their habit of comforting themselves with food and abandon it altogether. Although it may not seem like this is an emotional event, people subconsciously grow very attached to their coping mechanisms. By giving that up altogether, people often feel like they are stripped of their safety net. This means that strengthening and practicing self-discipline is very hard and emotional work. The emotions and feelings that people have managed through using their own coping mechanisms now become very apparent to them because the coping mechanism has been removed. This typically doesn't make people very happy and they often have trouble dealing with their emotions without the safety net that they would always fall back on.

By understanding this important concept, you can prepare yourself for the difficulties that you will face when you are practicing your self-discipline. Some of the practices and work that you put in will be very emotionally challenging. You may be able to initiate changes in your life using some simple and concrete goals that you've made for yourself but you may quickly learn that if there is emotional baggage, you would have to face them head-on along your journey.

1. Self-discipline and healthy habits do not make you a popular person.

When people first begin practicing self-discipline and are excited to make him good changes in their lives, they often hope that their efforts will inspire other people to get into good habits as well. They think that by changing into a better person, and achieving the goals that they've always wanted to achieve for themselves, that they will gain respect from other people. This thought process is normal because why wouldn't you want to share with your loved ones that you are changing your life for the better?

However, in reality, most people will just think that the person who is trying to change is annoying because they go from being easy-going about what they eat to having major food restrictions if they are trying to change their diet. They will begin saying no to certain activities that get in the way of them achieving their goals. They will begin to prioritize other important things regarding the goals that they are going after rather than spending time with people that may not be exactly beneficial to them. Being self-disciplined is not something that is going to make a person more likable.

In order to be a socially desirable person, you have to be willing to spend a lot of your time with other people doing things that are often unhealthy like eating out and drinking socially. Let's say that this person manages to strike a really good balance between achieving their goals and still remaining socially desirable. Any success that they achieve isn't necessarily going to inspire others. This is because of two reasons. The first reason is that people won't really care because most of the time they have their own problems to deal with. The second reason is that watching someone else have success when it comes to achieving goals while they're struggling with their own goals is not always inspirational; they may even see it as annoying. People may even consciously or unconsciously attempt to throw you off track because they can't bear to look at their own lives due to jealousy or other emotions.

Just to clarify, other people may not be trying to throw you off track maliciously. I don't think that people would intentionally want you to fail. However, I do think that your attempts at practicing self-discipline to take control of your own life is not something that gets you admiration and respect from other people. Relationships are very complex interactions and sometimes doing I'm healthier things in life gets you more respect and admiration rather than living a healthy life. The message I'm trying to get across here is that self-discipline should be something that you pursue for yourself and for your own intrinsic reasons. You should not be doing it to seek congratulation or respect from others because you will likely get the opposite.

1. You may not have any motivation or inspiration at all.

Some people may have multiple goals that they are looking to achieve. For example, it could be a mix of getting more exercise, eating healthier, pursuing a musical instrument, and being successful in their career. However, it may be that not all of those things can create inspiration or motivation. Out of those goals, there may only be one item that produces the most inspiration and motivation for a person.

Somewhere along the way of self-discipline, a lot of people realize that motivation and inspiration actually precede action. With this belief comes the expectation that the presence of inspiration and motivation will tell people what they need to do with their lives. They think that wherever there is motivation and inspiration, that is the direction that they should be heading. Although this is a lovely notion, it is not one that lines up with reality. Take someone's university degree as an example. I can almost guarantee that there were many days where a person doesn't feel inspired or motivated to do their schoolwork, but it doesn't change the reality that having a university degree is a very beneficial addition to your life. If a person were to be using motivation and inspiration as a guide, that degree likely wouldn't be finished.

A person's choices of where they focus their self-discipline need to be carefully selected and initiated using the most logical thinking that they can muster. People may try to eat healthily or work out frequently in order to have a healthy body but that does not mean that they are inspired to do it. Keep in mind that I am not saying that inspiration and motivation are worthless feelings. What I am trying to get across here is that the presence of these two feelings can be an unreliable source for somebody to make decisions regarding their life. For some people, inspiration and motivation don't show up until they have already put in quite a bit of work towards their goals. For example, somebody who is looking to get more muscular might not actually feel motivated to work out until they got into a regular habit of lifting weights at the gym.

1. You may not be practicing the right techniques properly.

If you have tried to achieve a goal using various different types of angles, but you are constantly failing repeatedly at a certain area of self-discipline, you might have to face the possibility that you have selected something that you simply might not ever be able to engage in on a regular basis. Self-discipline is not only about picking a goal or an activity and doing it despite all costs. Self-discipline is about picking the important activities and goals and doing them against all obstacles. It may be a possibility that you have simply picked a goal or activity that isn't all that important to you. It is all right to admit that and move forward. The good thing about this is that if it turns out the goal our activity was important to you, after all, it will pop up in your life again thematically and you would be able to take it up again.

1. Your willpower/self-discipline can be fatigued.

As we have learned in the earlier chapters of this book, it is extremely tiring and exhausting to be consciously fighting temptation and selecting healthy activities and choosing the productive activities over the unproductive ones. It is tiring because it constantly drains on your willpower resources. It takes lots of energy and effort to turn away from the wrong choices and pick the ones that are right for your goals. It takes lots of resistance to choose healthy food over unhealthy food that may be quicker and much more convenient. It takes a lot of effort to drag yourself out of bed on a rainy morning to get to the gym to work out rather than sleeping an extra hour.

The only way to really battle this problem is to practice your required tasks until they become a habit. You want those daily tasks that you need to do to reach a level of automation that you no longer actively think about it, and it no longer consumes your willpower resources. Some people may think that all they need is a few weeks or even just a few months to build a new habit. This mindset is absolutely wrong. The reason why our bad habits are so hard to break is because they have been built up through multiple years. Good habits will take the exact same amount of time. If you have been repeatedly binge-eating whenever you feel upset for the last 10 years of your life, except that it will take multiple years before you can break out of that habit and into a healthy eating habit. However, once you do get into that stage, you no longer have to consciously make decisions about that have it anymore and they will function on its own.

The good thing is that eventually, with repeated practice and some failures and obstacles along the way, new and better behaviors will become a habit. When this happens, it will consume far less mental resources than it did before. For instance, you probably don't feel stressed out or tired by the idea that you have to brush your teeth at least twice a day. However, if someone asked you to simply workout for 10 minutes a day, which is the same amount of time that brushing your teeth takes, you may find this much harder to do because it isn't already a habit. Like I mentioned before, it just takes a significant amount of time before a new behavior becomes a learned behavior.

Here are some ways that you can address the fatigue that self-discipline may bring:

- There are days where you should incorporate into your schedule where you can relax and don't have to worry about the things that you have to do in order to reach your goals like dieting or exercising. You can call these 'cheat days' or 'treat days.'
- You can incorporate something called the 80% rule. This means that you are accepting that you won't be a perfect 100% all the time with your tasks or goals, and getting 80% on your goals is acceptable.
- Make sure that you were getting enough rest and sleep. We learned that this is your body's and mind's time to recover from the fatigue that we have put it through on a daily basis.

IN THE LAST chapter of this book, we will be discussing an extremely important strategy and technique to help you build better habits and break bad ones – Cognitive Behavioral Therapy. We touched on this briefly earlier in the book, but I want to make sure that we spend enough time learning about this as it can really help you change the way you think and to build better habits. I will teach you about what CBT is, how it works, and how you can use CBT to become more mindful of your existing unhealthy thoughts and bad habits. I will also teach you about how you can use certain techniques of CBT to change these unhealthy thoughts and habits into better ones.

What Is Cognitive Behavioral Therapy?

Cognitive Behavioral Therapy is used to treat mental disorders, primarily anxiety and depression. Due to its long history and development, CBT is a practical and time-saving form of psychotherapy. CBT focuses on your here-and-now problems that come up in daily life. It is used to help people make sense of their surroundings and events that happen around them. CBT is very structured, time-saving, and problem-focused. These advantages are the reason why CBT is one of the most popular techniques when used to deal with mental disorders in our fast-paced modern lives. However, CBT can also be used to treat less serious problems such as self-esteem, building better habits, and overcoming hardship.

In the present day, CBT works by helping clients recognize, question, and change the thoughts that relate to the emotional and behavioral reactions that cause them difficulty. By using CBT to monitor and record thoughts during undesirable situations, people begin to learn that the way they think is a contributor to their emotional problems. Modern-day Cognitive Behavioral Therapy helps reduce emotional problems by teaching individuals to; identify any distortions in their thinking process, see their own thoughts as ideas rather than facts and take a step back from their own thoughts to look at situations from another perspective.

CBT suggests that a lot of the emotions that we are feeling is completely due to what we are thinking about. In other words, our emotions are entirely based on how we perceive and interpret our environment or a situation. Sometimes these ideas and thoughts become distorted or biased. For example, an individual may interpret an ambiguous text message as personal rejection when they may not have any evidence to support that. Other individuals may begin to set unrealistic expectations for themselves regarding being accepted by others. These thoughts contribute to illogical, biased, or distorted thinking processes, which then affect our emotions. In CBT, clients will learn to distinguish the difference between an actual thought and feeling. They will learn to be aware of the ways that thoughts can influence their emotions and how it is sometimes unhelpful. In addition, they will be able to evaluate critically whether their automatic thoughts are accurate and have evidence, or if they are simply just biased. At the end of their therapy, they should have developed the skills to notice these negative thoughts, interrupt them, and correct the thoughts properly.

How Does CBT Work?

Cognitive Behavioral Therapy works by emphasizing the relationship between our thoughts, feelings, and behaviors. When you begin to change any of these components, you start to initiate change in the others. The goal of CBT is to help lower the amount you worry and increase the overall quality of your life. Here are the 8 basic principles of how Cognitive Behavioral Therapy works:

1. CBT will help provide a new perspective of understanding your problems.

A lot of the times, when an individual has been living with a problem for a long time in their life, they may have developed unique ways of understanding it and dealing with it. Usually, this just maintains the problem or makes it worse. CBT is effective in helping you look at your problem from a new perspective, and this will help you learn other ways of understanding your problem and learning a new way of dealing with it.

1. CBT will help you generate new skills to work out your problem.

You probably know that understanding a problem is one matter, and dealing with it is entirely another can of worms. To help start changing your problem, you will need to develop new skills that will help you change your thoughts, behaviors, and emotions that are affecting your anxiety and mental health. For instance, CBT will help you achieve new ideas about your problem and begin to use and test them in your daily life. Therefore, you will be more capable of making up your own mind regarding the root issue that is causing these negative symptoms.

    1. CBT relies on teamwork and collaboration between the client and therapist (or program).

CBT will require you to be actively involved in the entire process, and your thoughts and ideas are extremely valuable right from the beginning of the therapy. You are the expert when it comes to your thoughts and problems. The therapist is the expert when it comes to acknowledging the emotional issues. By working as a team, you will be able to identify your problems and have your therapist better address them. Historically, the more the therapy advances, the more the client takes the lead in finding techniques to deal with the symptoms.

    1. The goal of CBT is to help the client become their own therapist.

Therapy is expensive; we all know that. One of the goals of CBT is to not have you become overly dependent on your therapist because it is not feasible to have therapy forever. When therapy comes to an end, and you do not become your own therapist, you will be at high risk for a relapse. However, if you are able to become your own therapist, you will be in a good spot to face the hurdles that life throws at you. In addition, it is proven that having confidence in your own ability to face hardship is one of the best predictors of maintaining the valuable information you got from therapy. By playing an active role during your sessions, you will be able to gain the confidence needed to face your problems when the sessions are over.

1. CBT is succinct and time-limited.

As a rule of thumb, CBT therapy sessions typically last over the course of 10 to 20 sessions. Statistically, when therapy goes on for many months, there is a higher risk of the client becoming dependent on the therapist. Once you have gained a new perspective and understanding of your problem, and are equipped with the right skills, you are able to use them to solve future problems. It is crucial in CBT for you to try out your new skills in the real world. By actually dealing with your own problem hands-on without the security of recurring therapy sessions, you will be able to build confidence in your ability to become your own therapist.

1. CBT is direction based and structured.

CBT typically relies on a fundamental strategy called 'guided recovery.' By setting up some experiments with your therapist, you will be able to experiment with new ideas to see if they reflect your reality accurately. In other words, your therapist is your guide while you are making discoveries in CBT. The therapist will not tell you whether you are right or wrong but instead, they will help develop ideas and experiments to help you test these ideas.

1. CBT is based on the present, "here and now."

Although we know that our childhood and developmental history play a big role in who we are today, one of the principles of CBT actually distinguishes between what caused the problem and what is maintaining the problem presently. In a lot of cases, the reasons that maintain a problem are different than the ones that originally caused it. For example, if you fall off while riding a horse, you may become afraid of horses. Your fear will continue to be maintained if you begin to start avoiding all horses and refuse to ride one again. In this example, the fear was called by the fall, but by avoiding your fear, you are continuing to maintain it. Unfortunately, you cannot change the fact that you had fallen off the horse but you can change your behaviors when it comes to avoidance. CBT primarily focuses on the factors that are maintaining the problem because these factors are susceptible to change.

1. Worksheet exercises are significant elements of CBT therapy.

Unfortunately, reading about CBT or going to one session of therapy a week is not enough to change our ingrained patterns of thinking and behaving. During CBT, the client is always encouraged to apply their new skills into their daily lives. Although most people find CBT therapy sessions to be very intriguing, it does not lead to change in reality if you do not exercise the skills you have learned.

These eight principles will be your guiding light throughout your Cognitive Behavioral Therapy. By learning, understanding, and applying these eight principles, you will be in a good position to invest your time and energy into becoming your own therapist and achieving your personal goals. Based on research, individuals who are highly motivated to try exercises outside of sessions tend to find more value in therapy than those who don't. Keep in mind that other external factors still have an effect on your success, but your motivation is one of the most significant factors. By following CBT using the principles above, you should be able to remain highly motivated throughout CBT.

When Can CBT be Used?

The common uses for CBT typically revolve around helping people cope with their problems that are related to anxiety or depression. However, in a more general sense, CBT is used when an individual decides to pursue therapy in order to help with the problems they are facing. A lot of the time, these problems are disorders such as depression, anxiety, or more serious ones like

OCD and PTSD. They can also be less serious problems and can be as simple as someone that just wants to change their life for the better.

To dive a little more in-depth, the most common uses for CBT is actually depression and generalized anxiety disorder. However, CBT is also used and is very effective for other disorders such as:

- Body Dysmorphic Disorder
- Eating Disorders
- Chronic Low Back Pain
- Personality Disorders
- Psychosis
- Schizophrenia
- Substance Used Disorders

Since CBT focuses on the relationship between thoughts, emotions, and behavior, those who suffer from disorders that stem from mental health may find it helpful to try CBT. Most modern-day therapists opt for CBT as the best technique to handle the problems that the client may be facing as it covers numerous disorders, and the client can learn it and continue to use it without the therapist's help.

On a simpler note, CBT can just be used for general therapy. This may be a situation where somebody is attending therapy sessions in order to remain in touch with their thoughts and feelings. Although this person may not be suffering from any particular disorder, CBT is a helpful tool for someone who wants to organize their thoughts.

Identifying Your Unhealthy Thinking Patterns

To effectively use CBT, you must understand the different types of cognitive distortions or otherwise known as 'unhealthy thinking patterns. By understanding each of these styles, you can determine when these patterns are happening and you can challenge these thoughts to prevent yourself from exhibiting unhealthy behaviors. In our case, unhealthy behaviors would be falling into bad habits like procrastination.

1. Mental filter: You choose one single undesirable detail, and you exclusively dwell on it. Your perception of reality becomes negative based on it. You only notice your failures but you don't look at your successes.
2. Disqualifying the positive: You discount your positive experiences or success by saying, "that doesn't count." By discounting all your positive experiences, you can maintain a negative perspective even if it is contradicted in your daily life.
3. All or nothing thinking: This is otherwise known as 'black and white thinking.' You tend to see things in either black or white or success or failure. If your performance is not perfect, you will see it as a failure.
4. Jumping to conclusions: You make a negative assumption even when you don't have supporting evidence. There are two types of jumping to conclusions:
5. Mind reading: You imagine that you already know what other people are thinking negatively of you, and therefore you don't bother to ask.

6. Fortune-telling: You predict that things will end up badly, and you convince yourself that your prediction is a fact.

7. Overgeneralization: You see one single negative situation as a pattern that never ends. You draw conclusions of future situations based on one single event.

8. Magnification/Minimization: You blow things out of proportion or inappropriately shrink something to make it seem unimportant. For example, you beef up somebody else's achievement (magnification) and shrug off your own (minimization).

9. Emotional reasoning: You make the assumption that your negative emotions reflect the reality. For example, "I feel it so, therefore, it is true."

10. Catastrophizing: You associate terrible and extreme consequences to the outcome of situations and events. For example, if you are rejected for a date, it means that you are alone forever, and making an error at work means you will be fired.

11. Labeling and mislabeling: This is overgeneralization to the extreme. Instead of describing your mistake, you automatically associate a negative label to yourself, "I'm a loser." You also do this to others; if someone else's behavior is undesirable, you attach "they are a loser" to them as well.

12. "Should" statements: You motivate yourself using "shoulds" and "shouldn'ts" as if you associate a reward or punishment before you do anything. Since you associate reward/punishment with shoulds and shouldn'ts for yourself, when other people don't follow it, you feel anger or frustration.

13. All at once bias: This is when you think risks and threats are right at your front door, and the amount of it is increasing as well. When this occurs, you tend to:

14. Think that negative situations are evolving quicker than you can come up with solutions

15. Think that situations are moving so quickly that you feel overwhelmed

16. Think that there is no time between now and the impending threat

17. Numerous risks and threats seem to all appear at the same time

18. Personalization: You take responsibility for something that wasn't your fault. You see yourself as the cause of an external situation.

By understanding these cognitive distortions and unhelpful thinking styles, you will have the opportunity to interrupt the process and say, for example, "I'm catastrophizing again." When you are able to interrupt your own unhelping thinking styles, you are able to readjust it to something that is more helpful. In the next chapter, we will be discussing some tips and tricks to help you challenge your own cognitive distortions. This is one of the main strategies within CBT.

Challenging Your Unhealthy Thinking Patterns

Once you are able to identify your own unhealthy thinking patterns, you can begin to reshape those thoughts into something more realistic and factual. I have categorized all the different unhealthy thinking patterns and what questions you should be asking yourself to develop different thoughts.

· · ·

Similar to self-discipline and habit building, it takes a lot of effort and dedication to change our own thoughts, so don't get frustrated if you are not succeeding right away. You probably have had these thoughts for a while, so don't expect it to change overnight.

Probability Overestimation

If you find that you have thoughts about a possible negative outcome, but you are noticing that you often overestimate the probability, try asking yourself the questions below to reevaluate your thoughts.

- Based on my experience, what is the probability that this thought will come true realistically?
- What are the other possible results from this situation? Is the outcome that I am thinking of now the only possible one? Does my feared outcome have the highest possibility out of the other outcomes?
- Have I ever experienced this type of situation before? If so, what happened? What have I learned from these past experiences that would be helpful to me now?
- If a friend or loved one is having these thoughts, what would I say to them?

Negative Core Beliefs

- Do I have any evidence that supports my negative beliefs?

- Is this thought true in every situation?
- Would a loved one or friend agree with my self-belief?

Selective Attention/Memory

- What are the positive elements of the situation? Am I ignoring those?
- Would a different person see this situation differently?
- What strengths do I have? Am I ignoring those?

All or Nothing Thinking

- Is there a middle ground or grey area that I am not considering?
- Would I judge a friend or loved one in the same way?
- Was the entire situation 100% negative? Was there any part of the situation that I handled well?
- Is having/showing some anxiety such a horrible thing?

Catastrophizing

- If the prediction that I am afraid of really did come true, how bad would it really be?
- If I am feeling embarrassed, how long will this last? How long will other people remember/talk about it?

What are all the different things they could be saying?
Is it 100% that they will talk only bad things?

- I am feeling uncomfortable right now, but is this really a horrible or unbearable outcome?
- What are the other alternatives for how this situation could turn out?
- If a friend or loved one was having these thoughts, what would I say to them?

Should Statements

- Would I be holding the same standards to a loved one or a friend?
- Are there any exceptions?
- Will someone else do this differently?

Mind Reading

- Is it possible that I really know what other people's thoughts are? What are the other things they could be thinking about?
- Do I have any evidence to support my own assumptions?
- In the scenario that my assumption is true, what is so bad about it?

Personalization

- What other elements might be playing a role in the situation? Could it be the other person's stress, deadlines, or mood?
- Does somebody always have to be at blame?
- A conversation is never just one person's responsibility.
- Were any of these circumstances out of my control?

CONCLUSION

At the end of this book, I'd first like to congratulate you for already showcasing the self-discipline to learn about techniques and strate gies to help you build better habits. You have already taken the first step in the right direction. The next step in all of this is to apply everything you have learned into your real life. Start imple- menting little things one by one and stick with it. You will start to see results, I promise.

Be sure to be doing easy but effective tricks like removing tempta- tion wherever you can and learning to identify when you are making procrastination excuses. Removing temptations in the first place is a great way to save on your willpower as it generally requires a person to use a large amount of it to resist temptation. If you find yourself making excuses as to why you can't do something related to a habit you're trying to build or a goal you're trying to reach, ask yourself if the excuse your making is actually legitimate or are you just saying that as you don't 'feel' like doing that task right now? By questioning your own thoughts and motives, you will better be able to distinguish real reasons from excuses.

The last thing I want to emphasize for you is to start small with your habits. Don't try to build a new habit that is extremely large and involved, such as running every day for 1 – 2 hours. Although you may have a goal in mind that requires you to run for long periods of time, burning yourself out at the beginning will only make you fearful of committing to this habit. Remember to break down large goals into smaller tasks and turn those smaller tasks into healthier habits. Start with building a habit to run for 10 minutes each day. Increase it slowly over the next several weeks until you are running every single day without needing to think about it. This is where you want to be at with your habits. You want to almost feel uncomfortable if you aren't doing them.

I wish you the best of luck in your journey of habit. I have faith in you, and I believe everyone and anyone has the ability to change their life for the better simply by changing their mindset. Practice self-discipline and fight procrastination. That is how you will get there.

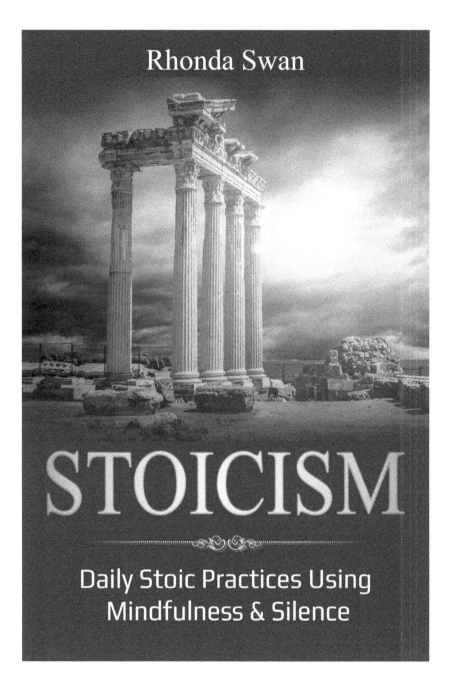

Rhonda Swan

STOICISM

Daily Stoic Practices Using Mindfulness & Silence

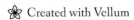

Congratulations on purchasing *Stoicism*, and thank you for doing so! This book has been designed to introduce you to the ancient philosophy of stoicism in a way that allows you to understand what this school of thought is, and how you can implement it in your modern life.

While society may have evolved and the way we live our lives has drastically changed, one thing remains consistent: the amount of control we have over our lives. These days, it seems as though we have an abundance of freedom and that, while society could stand to improve in many ways, we are much better off than we once were. With that being said, the concept of freedom is an illusion because, in many ways, we only control two things. No matter how society grows, changes, or adapts to anything we face as a collective, we will continue to only control two things on an individual level. When we learn how to control those things meaningfully, then we begin to experience true happiness, fulfillment, and peace. Which, by the way, was the primary pursuit of the ancient stoics.

Stoicism has withstood the test of time because it was developed on a school of thought that works. No matter what human you are or what era you are born in, if you can learn how to control these two aspects of yourself, you can achieve massive things in your life. Really, you can achieve anything in your life. All of the "greats" we look toward for inspiration, hope, guidance, and order have successfully mastered controlling these two things, and they have also successfully let go of their emotional attachments to virtually everything else. As a result, they have become incredibly powerful leaders of our society.

You might not be looking to become a societal leader, but that does not mean that you cannot benefit from knowing how to become a leader in your own life. In doing so, you will discover how you can begin to create a life that you desire, that fulfills you in every way possible, and that feels genuinely worthy of your time and attention. There is absolutely no reason for you to continue living a life of struggle, distress, discomfort, or complacency. If you are ready to leave all of that behind, you have come to the right place.

I hope you are ready to embrace the journey of learning about stoicism, and about your ability to control these two things in your life. As soon as you learn how to control your thoughts and your voluntary actions, *everything* will change for you. These two things are the only thing that you have absolute control over, and while it may seem so simple, the truth is that it is not. If it were, we would all be doing it without the need to research *how*. Fortunately, you have come to the perfect spot to have that question answered, and to discover just how you can use what is within your control to influence your life, your community, and the globe, should you desire to.

Before you begin reading, I want to thank you one more time.

There is an abundance of books out there on this topic, so I am grateful that you chose to read *Stoicism*. I hope you discover everything that you were looking for and that, by the end, you feel confident in your ability to control your own life and create your own destiny. Please, enjoy!

1 / WHAT IS STOICISM?

STOICISM, in a nutshell, is an ancient school of philosophy that taught people how to take absolute control over themselves and, therefore, gain greater levels of control over their fates. At the time that stoicism was invented, war was a particularly prominent and gruesome thing in most continents, and as such, people needed a way to learn how to control themselves and increase their likelihood of survival. This school of thought did not work just for those who were facing wartimes, though. It has worked for people across all parts of society in countless ways. In fact, it has been so useful that even people in modern times are continuing to benefit from the powers of stoicism and the potential this can unlock for you, within your mind, your actions, and your life.

In order to truly appreciate the power of stoicism and deepen your capacity to use this skill to your advantage, you are going to need to create a foundational understanding of what stoicism really is, where it came from, and what has shaped this school of thought. When you can truly understand and appreciate what stoicism is, where it comes from, and why it was developed in the first place, you will find that it becomes much easier for you to integrate it into your own life.

The Philosophy of Stoicism

Stoicism is such a unique, vast topic that it actually holds its own entire branch in the teachings of philosophy. Unlike other forms of philosophy, stoicism does not concern itself with what is going on in the world, what has turned the world into what it is now, why we are here, or where we are going after we die. In fact, stoicism does very little to question anything about the lives we are experiencing, why we are experiencing them, or what we might experiencing following these lives. Instead, stoicism focuses largely on the answers we do have access to, and the control we can have in our current lives. In other words, rather than creating more answers and following complex trails of thinking, which can lead to massive confusion or inconclusive search results, stoicism gives us answers.

Stoicism, itself, is very clear and simple. It is largely designed to help you master yourself and your mind through learning to focus exclusively on controlling your thoughts and your voluntary actions. Your involuntary actions and everything outside of your-self are not within your control, and so everything is labeled within two separate categories: that which you have influence over, and that which you do not. If you do have influence over something, you might use your voluntary actions and thoughts to use that influence to your advantage, if you feel the need to do so or if you can see the clear advantage that would come from doing so. If, however, you have little to no influence over something, or you have no need to use your influence to change something, then you let it go.

Rather than keeping people entrapped in emotional bondages or attempting to control things that they will truly never be able to control, stoicism releases you from those bonds and allows you to create a sense of freedom within yourself. When you are able to create a sense of control within yourself, and within what you truly can control, your entire perception of and experience toward the outer world changes. Through this, you will find an increased sense of confidence, happiness, fulfillment, peace, and joy. You will also find your sense of logic, ration, and reason expanding as you refrain from giving into emotional perils and instead navigate life in a more meaningful and fulfilling manner.

The History of Stoicism

The history of stoicism is fascinating, yet much like the entire school of philosophy itself, it is quite straightforward and simple to share. That is, it was developed on the porch where the early followers used to congregate to talk about stoicism. In fact, *"Stoa"* means porch, which is where the name came from. Stoicism itself originated as a form of Hellenistic philosophy but grew so much that, over time, it became its own school of philosophy entirely. It was founded in Athens in 300 B.C.E, and was influenced by Socrates and the Cynics. Back then, stoicism itself was cultivated through many people congregating on a porch and debating what stoicism even was, how the logical brain worked, and how man could use the power of his logical brain to override his emotional one. Through that, he could then gain more power over himself and, in time, create the destiny he wanted with the levels of happiness, fulfillment, and meaning that he desired.

Over time, stoicism began to spread across the globe, creating powerful lessons and studies for people from all around the world. In fact, early stoicism actually helped influence Christianity, as well as many other philosophical thinkers and schools of thought that were born following the introduction of stoicism itself. In the early 21st century, stoicism was reborn, in a sense, as modern people began looking back into this school of thought and questioning how they could use it to shape their own lives. Since it has grown massively in popularity and has helped countless people regain control over themselves and enjoy lives that they truly desired.

The Father and Contributors of Stoicism

The original father of stoicism was Zeno of Citium, which is what is now known as modern day Cyprus. Zeno began as a student of philosophy, but over time began to come up with his own thoughts and beliefs and would show up to the porch in Athens to share those thoughts and beliefs. Through this sharing, many showed up to debate with him, and he deepened his understanding of what he believed and, thus, what he was teaching to others. Although Zeno is the original father of stoicism, you will never find anything created by him specifically, for he never wrote books or produced a way to share his school of thought with the masses. Instead, he sat on the porches and shared it with anyone who would listen, and it was his students who wrote everything down and later shared that information with other people.

Fascinatingly enough, stoicism was originally called Zenonism, but that name was dropped. Back then, Stoics did not believe their founders to be perfectly wise, and they wanted to avoid having stoicism turned into a cult of personality. Thus they chose not to associate it with a person and instead associate it with the place of its origination. While there are some pieces of work still circulating from the first two phases of Stoicism, there are no complete pieces from back then. These days, any complete works you might find would have been written in the third wave of stoicism.

In addition to Zeno, Marcus Aurelius, Epictetus, and Seneca contributed to stoicism. Marcus Aurelius was the emperor of the Roman Emperor and was said to be the most powerful man on earth at the time. He would sit down every single day and write himself notes regarding the philosophy of stoicism in an effort to teach himself more and encourage himself to remain as Stoic as possible. Epictetus was a slave, who then went on to found his own school where he taught about many of the greatest philosophies from the ancient Roman empire, including stoicism. Lastly, Seneca was demanded to commit suicide by Nero, and at that time, he wanted to help his wife and friends comfort themselves amid the devastation they were facing. Thus, he taught them about stoicism as a way to help them navigate their grief and remain strong with everything that they were enduring during that time.

It is important to realize that at no point in the history of stoicism was there ever the intention of teaching people to beat themselves up, or teaching people to repress their emotions. Instead, the school of thought taught people how to navigate their emotions in a logical, rational manner so that they could not be overruled by them and, thus, controlled by them. When people learn how to address their emotions in a rational and logical way, they can use them to their advantage, rather than being broken down and controlled by them. This was the main goal behind stoicism, no matter who the teacher was or how the school of thought has shifted over the years.

STOICISM MATTERS in the modern world for many reasons. It is safe to say that although 300 B.C.E was a long time ago, we still maintain a strong sense of logic and reason in our brains. In fact, that logic and reason is what sets us apart from most of the other species on the planet, as we are able to exercise these two mindsets and use them extensively as a means to collect information and create our lives accordingly. Thus, even though this school of thought may have ancient origins, it remains incredibly relevant and important for us to understand in our modern world. Regardless of how much we evolve or what changes, the same two truths will always remain: you can control your thoughts, and you can control your voluntary actions. Unless we develop some form of mind control, whereby we can control others or extensively manipulate our environments through the power of our minds, these will remain the two things that we can truly control. Everything else has variables that are beyond our control and, thus, are not things we can ever truly and completely control.

Understand that while control is the overarching purpose of stoicism, it is not the only reason why you should engage in stoicism. Rather, stoicism was largely developed so that people could experience fulfillment and true happiness regardless of what was going on around them, or what was going on to them or within them that may have been beyond their control. By learning to adjust your focus and to control only that which is truly within your control, you release your obsessions with things that you cannot change and instead place the root of your happiness, fulfillment, and peace within things you can control. Then, you can control those parts of yourself to create a perfect environment for happiness, fulfillment, and peace to exist.

Why Has Stoicism Grown in Popularity?

Stoicism has grown in popularity for countless reasons. At the root of all of them is the simple fact that, as a living species, we have an undying urge to develop and evolve over time. We want to continue to improve ourselves so that as our species continues to evolve we get better and better. Since our logic and reason set us apart from virtually every other species on this planet, it makes sense that we would want to learn how to control this intelligence so that we can begin to leverage this unique part of ourselves. When we learn how to embrace stoicism, we learn how to include logic and reasoning in our thought processes and behavioral patterns, and we also learn how to use them to help us navigate our emotions more efficiently. We know that, in many cases, our emotions are beyond our control as they exist as involuntary hormonal and chemical responses to the environment around us, and often the environment within us, too. However, our thoughts can be controlled, and so can our voluntary actions. This means that, when we learn how to control our thoughts and voluntary actions, we learn how to control the *expression* and *experience* of our emotions. In other words, they will still rise and be experienced by you, but how you choose to engage in that experience and express those emotions is entirely within your own control.

As society has continued to grow and reach new heights, especially in the 21st century, it rapidly became apparent that having such control could have a serious advantage in our wellbeing. While back in 300 B.C.E, this may have been optimal for soldiers and those fighting in the war; in the 21st century, this mindset is optimal for helping us create new systems upon which to grow our ever-evolving species into. For example, this capacity to control our emotions has allowed us to discover new ways to resolve conflict, new methods for protecting our property, and new means for acquiring things in our lives.

Some great modern examples of how being able to control your logic and reasoning brain so that you are not overridden by emotions can be found in the common family household, in society, and in business. In family households, we see that families are not being commanded by a single head figure anymore, but that each individual is growing increasingly more autonomous and creating the ability for them to lead their own unique lives. As we create this change, we are also seeing that there is no single person growing angry with us for making these choices, but rather we are being supported and maintaining close emotional bonds while each pursuing our own unique lives. In society, the increase in logic and reasoning has resulted in us having just laws that prevent people from being harmed or even murdered for displeasing other people. For example, if someone were to be mad at another individual, they would not simply shoot him like they may have back in the days of the Wild West. Instead, they would resolve the conflict or walk away and avoid engaging in further conflict with that individual, thus ensuring that no one was harmed over a conflict. In business, leading with logic and reason ensures that you are making just choices that will not threaten your livelihood or the livelihoods of other individuals because you are not acting out of fear, but instead, you are acting out of logic. For example, let's say you traded stocks as your profession. If you made choices out of fear, likely you would lose a large amount of money, and thus, you would not be very good at that job. If, however, you were able to exercise logic and reason, you could make choices based on specific calculations and not emotions, and you would maximize your capacity to earn funds through your trades. In fact, when it comes to investing finances into any sort of portfolio, one of the first things they teach you is to refrain from bringing emotions into your finances. The same rule is often taught to entrepreneurs, CEOs, managers, and other leaders because this ensures that they are making logical, calculated decisions that will serve growth, rather than fear-based ones that could tank growth.

Developing True Happiness and Fulfillment

Outside of the family, society, and professional structures, stoicism can create a large amount of benefit for you, too. When you learn to engage in stoicism, you learn to create your own true sense of happiness and fulfillment. These days, people from all around the world are searching out how to become truly happy and fulfilled. There are many reasons why people may not already be feeling this way, but the reality is that there is a massive portion of the population that continues to feel incredibly unfulfilled no matter what they do.

When individuals go on feeling unfulfilled, they will often begin to look for fulfillment in places where it does not truly exist. That is because these places often offer a form of instant gratification, which serves as a temporary form of fulfillment but quickly runs out once the novelty of that instant gratification wears off. As soon as it wears off, they go in search of more instant gratification so they can get that quick, short-lived fulfillment, which in turn becomes almost like a sort of addiction. Over time, those individuals can become so desensitized to that instant gratification that the feeling of fulfillment is shorter and shorter lived until they realize it is not really fulfilling them at all, and then it stops working. Once they reach that point, they realize they were never truly experiencing fulfillment at all and that they need to find a new way to experience real fulfillment so that they can stop feeling like a bottomless pit.

There are many ways that you may be able to create a real sense of fulfillment and happiness within yourself, though you might be surprised to learn that most ways fall back on the basic teachings of stoicism. For that reason, it can be incredibly helpful to start with stoicism in the first place, or intentionally deepen your understanding of stoicism, so that you can expand your sense of fulfillment and happiness. Often, when you get into the root of the practical actions that you can take to increase your sense of happiness and fulfillment, you find yourself experiencing a clearer capacity to create those two feelings within yourself. Thus, it becomes far more straightforward for you to create them, and you feel far better off in the long run.

The Emotional and Mental Advantage of Letting Go

Our modern world seems to have a very twisted view of how to let go. When it comes to our physical belongings, it often seems easy to just let go of things. You may find yourself effortlessly ditching old things anytime something new catches your attention. Anytime something newer comes out, you might get rid of your old items without thinking twice, favoring the newer and "cooler" technology over the older ones that were serving you fine up until the point that something new was offered. Then, rather than that old item actually needing to be replaced, you simply lost interest in it and wanted something different. This particular scenario occurs constantly around virtually everything that you bring into your home, at least for the average person. It is known as the "consumer mentality" and largely revolves around throwing things away any time they no longer serve you.

The ironic thing is, our "throw away" mentality often starts and ends with the physical, and our material belongings. Strangely enough, throwing away so many physical items is actually proven to be bad for us, and yet we find it so easy to do. Keeping our items until they were truly broken and then replacing them would drastically reduce our waste and take greater care of our planet, thus serving us in the long run. However, this approach does not allow us to achieve that instant gratification or need for short-lived fulfillment. Alternatively, holding onto emotional and mental "things" can actually be incredibly bad for us, creating resentment, emotional and mood-related problems, disempowered thinking, and all sorts of other problems. Yet, we find it so hard to "throw away" that which does not serve our emotional or mental wellbeing.

There truly is power in embracing and perfecting the art of letting go, and stoicism teaches you how to actually let go of the things that you cannot control. This is not about debating the importance of letting things go, or discussing the great difficulties it may take or the various outcomes you might face when it comes to letting go of things. Instead, this is about taking practical, logical action toward releasing things that are not serving you so that you can begin to embrace things that will serve you. Through this, you begin to place your focus and attention on that which your own control, which means that you increase your power to create your own fulfillment and happiness and decrease the outside world's power to take that away from you.

The Power That You Really Have

The power that you really have is massive, and what may be surprising to you is that everything you have wanted has been available for you all along. The only reason you have not been experiencing it yet is because you have been looking to fulfill it in ways that were beyond your control, and therefore unsustainable and ultimately inadequate for what you wanted and needed. When you realize that you have the ultimate power to offer yourself happiness and fulfillment, you realize that no one can take that away from you, especially when you root your happiness and fulfillment in a far more intimate way than external attachments.

As you learn to control your thoughts and voluntary actions, you can begin to think and behave in a way that is in integrity with your desire for fulfillment and happiness. This means that you can choose to think thoughts that serve peace, happiness, solutions, advancement, growth, and fulfillment, and choose voluntary thoughts that serve those parts of your life, as well. You can also choose to reject thoughts and voluntary actions that are taking away from your peace, happiness, solutions, advancement, growth, and fulfillment. As you continue to make choices for what you desire and against what you do not desire, you will see that your entire life begins to change. Thus, you create a reality that offers you everything you ever desired.

You are far more powerful than you ever thought; however, your power does not lie in controlling your environment, your relationships, or anything that is going on outside of you. Your power lies in taking everything around you that you cannot control and choosing how you will think and respond to it so that you can think and respond in ways that are genuinely fulfilling. Therein lies everything you have been searching for all along, and it is served in a way that is sustainable and far more meaningful than anything you could receive from the outside world. Arguably, this form of internal fulfillment and happiness is what we all truly desire, and it is why any level of fulfillment or happiness that you create outside of yourself will never truly give you everything you are looking for.

THERE IS a popular saying that goes, "Anything that is real cannot be threatened, broken, or taken away, and anything that can be threatened, broken, or taken away is not real." This particular thought may be a lot to digest, but it serves to show that there is plenty in this world that is not worth placing your energy into. In fact, most of the things we might find ourselves worrying about or struggling to "keep together" are likely not real, and therefore their inevitable falling apart or falling away is something you cannot prevent. You may be able to prolong it, but eventually, it will go away.

There are many, many things in your life that are temporary. Belongings, careers, relationships, people, circumstances, ages, phases of health, physical growth, things you like and do not like, all of these things and plenty more are only temporary. No matter what you attempt to do to protect it or keep it in your life, there is always a chance that it will change or be taken away. And, in most cases, it *will* change or be taken away. The real question is not "if," but "when."

Stoics know that there is no true power in rooting your sense of happiness or fulfillment in something that is not real. In doing so, you set yourself up for the inevitable fear and anxiety that comes with trying to protect said thing, and the massive amount of suffering you experience when it inevitably leaves your life. You are born in this world naked and alone, and you will die naked and alone. Everything that happens in between, except that which happens in your mind or that you do through your voluntary actions, is just temporary. Embracing this allows you to eliminate the fear around having and losing things so that you can begin to focus on what truly matters, and create a solid foundation of happiness and fulfillment within yourself. At the end of the day, what Stoics truly want is happiness, purpose, and fulfillment that cannot be taken away.

The Personal Creation of Happiness

Happiness is one of the few things in the world that you can truly experience from the outside world, no matter what is going on within yourself. This is why people who are severely depressed will have periods of being truly happy, as well. The problem is when your happiness is rooted exclusively in the outside world, it comes and goes and the frequency of it's coming and going lies entirely beyond your control. When your experiences of happiness lie beyond your control, you might find yourself feeling especially low and powerless every time something occurs that makes you feel happy. You might also find yourself struggling to experience the full extent of that happiness because there is a looming shadow that the happiness will inevitably be taken away from you, and that you will no longer experience it. The reality of it is that happiness *will* be taken away from you at some point if it is rooted in external sources, because that is simply the way the world works. Living in this constant cycle of experiencing happiness at times, and a complete lack of happiness at times, and having that looming shadow over the happiness you do feel can create massive feelings of sadness, as well as desperation inside of you. You may find yourself rejecting happy experiences because of your fear that they will end, and/or clinging onto feelings of happiness and attempting to force them to stay around so that they cannot be taken away from you. Then, when the external circumstances change, and the temporary happiness passes, you find yourself feeling deeper senses of sadness, and possibly feelings of unworthiness and unfulfillment because you cannot seem to make the things that make you happy *stay*.

While it is perfectly reasonable to experience happiness from outside of yourself, it is important that you do not set yourself up for failure with this. In other words, you want to make sure that you set yourself up to experience *more* happiness from the world around you, not your *only* sense of happiness from the world around you. When the world around you is intended to enrich your already thriving inner sense of happiness, then all of the happiness you experience from the world around you is merely a bonus to what you have already created within yourself. Stoics realize that the foundation of real, lasting happiness lies within their control and so they seek to use their thoughts and voluntary actions to create lasting happiness within themselves. Through this, they realize their power to create happiness, and they trust that no matter what is going on around them, they will know how to create more. Then, they experience lasting, sustainable happiness, and bonus rounds of happiness from the world outside of themselves.

While experiencing sustainable, self-made happiness, it is important to note that you will still feel all of your other feelings. Sadness, sorrow, anger, frustration, fear, anxiety, and a variety of other emotions can all exist alongside happiness. The difference is that these other emotions do not feel bottomless because you know that, ultimately, you are in charge of your lasting emotions, and you are choosing happiness as being your lasting emotion. Many people who embrace stoicism notice that even when they are angry or sad, these emotions do not sit as deeply because they can still find plenty of reasons to be happy no matter what is going on in their lives, or in their emotions. Thus, they have truly embraced the power of control that they have over their thoughts and voluntary actions, and they have discovered the real secret to living a truly great life.

The Experience of Self-Fulfillment

If external fulfillment is fleeting and unsustainable, then it makes sense that people would want to search for a deeper, more sustainable sense of fulfillment. That is exactly what those who turn to stoicism are looking for, as stoicism offers many opportunities for you to create a sense of fulfillment from within yourself.

Fascinatingly enough, many people do not realize that there is such a thing as an internal source of fulfillment. Many believe that fulfillment comes from getting the things that you desire, having what you want, and creating the level of status and prestige that you feel will bring you the fulfillment you seek. This is why so many people will start creating goals for them and achieving those goals, thus creating a sense of fulfillment. While goals are certainly an important thing to have, they are another form of temporary fulfillment, as you feel good in the moments after you achieve the goal, but eventually, that wears off, and so you have to set another goal for yourself to create fulfillment from. Thus, no amount of money, personal possessions, property, physical strength, numbers on a scale, or anything else achieved is going to truly bring you the fulfillment you desire.

Fulfillment comes from a place within you, and it exists no matter what is going on around you. In many ways, having a sustainable sense of fulfillment feels as though you have everything you could possibly want and need, and that you are always in a state of abundance no matter what is going on in your life. Much like with happiness, when you already have a sense of fulfillment existing within yourself, you no longer worry about what is going on outside of yourself. Thus, external sources of fulfillment like achieving your goals or getting something that you really wanted feels like a bonus, rather than the only thing bringing you fulfillment in your life. As well, when you go through periods where you are struggling to reach your goals or where you are not getting what you wanted, you do not suddenly feel incredibly unfulfilled. Instead, you feel entirely fulfilled anyway, and you trust that more things will come your way when the time is right.

Because creating a sense of fulfillment from within yourself is such a foreign concept for the average person in our modern world, and because this source of fulfillment is created in an entirely different way and, thus, feels entirely different, too, it can take quite a bit of practice to create your own sense of fulfillment. As you begin to understand what true fulfillment is, though, and how it is created, you will discover that this is actually an easy source of fulfillment to create and that it actually feels far more fulfilling than any other source of fulfillment. Further, your other sources of fulfillment will actually feel more fulfilling in the long run because you already have such a deep sense of fulfillment.

Discovering a Sense of Purpose

Countless people are in search of their purpose in life. Arguably, every single one of us wants to know what purpose we have in life, and wants to fulfill that purpose. As with most things, many people create a sense of purpose from outside of themselves by believing that their purpose is directly linked to their career, the role they play in their families or friendships, or the role they play in their society. They believe that they must maintain and continually better each of these roles in order to develop a sense of purpose, and that as they continue to do so, they continue to hold a greater level of purpose.

Contributing to your career, your family, your friends, and your community are all noble and important things to do, and it stands to reason that these are necessary elements to a healthy and well-rounded life. However, making the mistake of making any of these things your purpose means that, as with anything you have placed outside of yourself, your purpose can be taken away from you. As soon as your circumstances change, or someone comes or goes from your life, or you find yourself unable to fulfill something that you used to be able to do with ease, you will find yourself feeling as though you lack purpose. This can also lead to a lack of fulfillment and a lack of happiness in your life, as these three experiences are often deeply interconnected and play similar roles in your life.

With stoicism, you discover how to take your sense of purpose out of your external circumstances and place it within yourself. In doing so, you identify a purpose that is clearly meaningful to you, and you discover that you truly do have the capacity to pour that sense of purpose into your life, no matter what your circumstances might look like.

It is important to realize that your purpose is rarely associated with any fixed circumstances. For example, a surgeons overall life purpose is not to perform surgery, a parent's overall life purpose is not to raise children, and a partner's overall life purpose is not to be a life partner to another individual. Instead, your life purpose may be to bring healing to people, to nurture and care for others, or to show compassion and love toward others. When you get into these types of defined purposes, you begin to realize that you can easily perform that purpose no matter what happens in your life. The day you find yourself in different circumstances, you do not find yourself without purpose. Instead, you find yourself looking for a new way to apply your purpose to your new circumstances. Thus, you are able to continually serve your purpose and gain a sense of fulfillment and pride through that.

When you are able to root your happiness, fulfillment, and sense of purpose to something inside of yourself, you stop finding yourself living at the mercy of everyone around you. No longer will things like aging, moving, fluctuating finances, evolving friendships, terminating circumstances, or a change in your abilities affect your capacity to experience happiness, fulfillment, and a sense of purpose. Instead, no matter what happens to you or to your circumstances, you will always find a way to continue to experience happiness, fulfillment, and a sense of purpose. In that, you discover that you can thrive no matter what your circumstances are, and arguably you feel these experiences to a much deeper and more sustainable capacity than you ever would have had you not learned how to root these feelings to your own inner experiences and abilities.

THE CORE BELIEFS of stoicism largely lie within what you can control. As you already know, you have the power to control your thoughts and your voluntary actions, and nothing else. With that being said, stoicism is often broken down into multiple core beliefs that allow you to gain a better understanding as to what people mean when they say you cannot control something. It also helps you begin to understand the exact type of mindset you should be holding onto around these areas of your life so that you are able to experience happiness, fulfillment, and a sense of purpose in a truly healthy and sustainable way.

As you read through these core beliefs, I encourage you to see how they might apply to your own life. The more you can begin to relate these beliefs and teachings into your own personal life, the easier it will be for you to integrate them into your experience as you will have a sense of awareness around exactly where they fit in for you.

You Must Learn Your Level of Influence, and Use It

One of the biggest lessons is stoicism is surrounding your level of influence, and what you can do with that influence. Before you can really dig into doing anything with your power, you need to have a clear sense of understanding around where your power lies, and defined boundaries around where it does not lie. Anyone who tries to control something beyond their power is going to find themselves feeling powerless, because they will realize that their power is of no use in that area. If they discover where their power truly lies, though, they can use their realm of power to create many incredible things for themselves in their lives, often including everything they were once looking for in the things that made them feel powerless.

In general, there are four specific levels of influence that you have over things in your life: no influence, low influence, some influence, and a lot of influence. Knowing where these areas of your life lie are important, so you can prioritize your power into the areas that you really can control. Fortunately, our power is largely the same for all humans, so where my power lies in my life will be the same as where your power lies in your life. With that being said, here is a guideline for where your levels of influence lie and where you should be focusing the majority of your power.

Some things, you have absolutely no influence over. You cannot control the weather, natural disasters, or what nations of people in the world do, for example. You also cannot control whether or not people you love get sick or get injured, and in many cases, you cannot control whether you get sick or injured, either. There are many scenarios where illness or injury may present themselves that could be largely unpreventable or unavoidable by you or anyone in your life. Anything that you truly could not have humanly prevented or fixed is not within your level of influence. While these are things you should be mindful of and aware of, they are not things you should try to control or influence because you will ultimately find yourself feeling powerless and helpless.

Some things, you have a low amount of influence over. For example, government, certain other types of injury or illness, or smaller groups of people. When groups of people who have low levels of influence get together and speak up, that influence all comes together to create a larger sense of influence. However, on your own, it is unlikely that you would be able to do anything such as, say, change what is going on in the government or influence your workplace to implement new rules that you feel would better serve the company. There are also certain illnesses or injuries that you may be able to take some action toward preventing. However, your action may only have a very small capacity to prevent that illness or injury from occurring. Thus, you have a low level of influence.

Some things, you have a moderate level of influence over. For example, your overall day to day health, your emotions, the relationships you share with other people, or various experiences you have with things or people that you interact with on a day to day basis. You may not be able to entirely control these things, but you can do a fair bit to influence them. It is well within your power to, for example, eat healthy, exercise, take care of yourself, contribute to healthy relationships in your life, take care of your belongings, so they do not break down or need to be replaced prematurely, and otherwise contribute to creating a better quality of life for you. While you may not be able to entirely control these situations, you can influence them in a big way, which will allow you to do what you can to create positive experiences in your life.

Two things you have a high level of influence over, including your thoughts and your voluntary actions. These include what you choose to focus on, how you choose to express your thoughts or emotions, what actions you choose to take in situations you find yourself in, and generally how you choose to engage with life around you. At the end of the day, no one can choose your thoughts or your voluntary actions, except you.

The World Around You Is Not Yours to Control

In understanding your levels of influence, you must immediately begin to realize and accept the fact that the world around you is not yours to control. This can leave you feeling completely powerless and at the mercy of the world around you for a period of time. Until you learn how to feel in control of yourself, and you trust in your ability to use that control to help you thrive. However, until you are able to achieve that, you might find yourself feeling particularly small and vulnerable to everything going on.

Still, you *must* understand that the world around you is not yours to control. You cannot control the people around you or the circumstances you are a part of. People are going to get sick, get hurt, do things you do not approve of, feel emotions that you cannot control, and think thoughts that you have no power over. They are going to get involved in experiences that you cannot prevent, and that you are not responsible for, and you are not always going to be able to do something to stop those situations from happening. The world around you is going to experience things that are beyond your control. Sicknesses may plague society; accidents may happen, wars may begin, natural disasters may occur, and other things will happen that you cannot control.

When things lie beyond your control, it is crucial that you learn to accept this because, in accepting it, you can stop worrying about it. Worrying about such things leads you to believe that, in some way, you have the power to prevent them from happening or to protect the people involved with what is happening and, unfortunately, you do not. While certain voluntary actions you can do may contribute to improving certain things, in most scenarios, you are going to have to accept that you *are* powerless. Learning to accept that you are truly powerless allows you to stop trying to control everything so that you can step back from a position of control and, instead, focus on what you can navigate: your thoughts, and your voluntary actions. From there, you can focus on taking care of yourself and, when it is possible, contributing in a reasonable way that allows you to help other people or certain circumstances. In others, you may not be able to do anything at all so the best choice you may be able to make is to go about life as usual so that you can maintain a sense of normalcy and, as such, continue to create your own happiness and fulfillment no matter what situation you are in.

The People Around You Are Not Yours to Control

One obsession we seem to have in our modern society surrounds concerning ourselves with what other people are doing, and trying to control other people. This can happen in many different ways, ranging from trying to control how an entire society is run to trying to control how people treat you, or how they live their lives. Many people attempt to control those around them in an effort to create the types of relationships they want and the type of society they want, failing to realize that they cannot truly control these things. You cannot force a person into being your friend, or into sharing a specific type of friendship or relationship with you, no matter how much you might want to. You can, however, choose to respectfully end a relationship or distance yourself from a person while pursuing a relationship with someone else who is willing to have that type of relationship with you. This does not just go for friendships, either. This goes for family relationships, co-worker relationships, romantic relationships, and virtually any other type of relationship you desire. You cannot force someone to be the type of person you want them to be, simply because that would be better for you. If your parents are not who you need them to be, you cannot change that. If your sisters, brothers, aunts, uncles, grandparents, extended family, and other family members are not who you need or want them to be, you cannot change that. You cannot turn your co-workers into better people to work around, nor can you change the person who sells you groceries or pumps your gas. As well, you cannot change your lover, no matter how close you are with them or how intimate or vulnerable you are with them.

Trying to change people or forcing them to be someone they are not so that you can be happy is a very selfish, manipulative, and toxic behavior to get into. Sadly, many people in our society are engaged in this behavior because they either believe that what they are trying to accomplish is in the best interest of the other individual, or they believe that there is no other way for them to be happy except to change that individual. For example, if you try to change your co-workers because they are hard to work around, you might do this because you believe that there is absolutely no way for you to be fulfilled at work unless the other people you work with change.

Any mindset that has you attempting to change or control people is a mindset that you need to eliminate immediately. You cannot and will not ever be able to control anyone, period. Even if you have successfully manipulated and controlled people in the past, this was not because you had *true* control over them, but because on one level, they allowed you to have control over them by believing that they had no control. When that person does eventually figure out that you have no true control over them, they will leave. This is exactly how people get out of abusive, threatening, manipulative, dangerous, and otherwise toxic relationships. Eventually, they realize that they have the power to choose differently and so they do. Suddenly, the person who had been pulling strings and falsely believing that they were in control has no more power over that individual, and it is all because that person managed to remember where their true power lay. Thus, it was not true power over another individual, it was merely an illusion, and its time ran out.

If you truly love and care for other individuals, your thoughts and actions should reflect that by wishing the best for them and always believing in their ability to choose what is right for themselves. You can offer advice, guidance, and loving support, but you should never try to force them to make choices based on what you think is best or force them to behave in ways that you feel they should be behaving. When you are loving and accepting of people, you experience a sort of detachment in your relationship that allows both of you to experience true happiness and fulfillment within that relationship. If you do feel as though someone's behaviors are genuinely affecting you, then you can choose to prevent that from happening by distancing yourself from that person and using boundaries to prevent them from harming you. Just like you cannot control others' thoughts and voluntary actions, others cannot control yours.

You Can Control Your Thoughts and Influence Your Emotions

This is a part of self-control that many people get confused, and that can lead to an array of issues down the line if you are not careful. It is important to understand that you *can* control your thoughts, but you *cannot* control your emotions. You can, however, influence your emotions with both your thoughts and your chosen behaviors. Otherwise, your emotions are merely chemical and hormonal reactions that you experience to the world around you, and the world within you, and so they are going to exist regardless of what you attempt to do about it.

Emotions are one of those things that you have a high level of control over. You can choose to engage in voluntary actions that create certain emotions, for example. Though, this may not always create the exact emotions you desire, but it can help you encourage the creation of them. For example, if you are looking to feel happy, you might engage in a favorite hobby, talk to someone you love, or do something that generally makes you feel happy. Thus, you have influenced yourself to feel happy. Using this high level of influence is a great way to create the types of emotions you want to experience, while also transforming your emotions into the ones you want to experience if you have experienced one that you are not particularly interested in feeling. For example, let's say you have been feeling sad, and you are ready to stop feeling sad, you might do something that makes you feel happy in an effort to influence your emotions to change.

Another way you can influence your emotions is through what you choose to think. In cognitive behavioral therapy (CBT), you learn that your emotions are often the result of your subconscious or conscious thoughts. Thus, what you think stimulates what you feel. While you cannot easily control your subconscious thoughts, you can control your conscious thoughts, and that will help you choose thoughts that promote your ability to feel happy, fulfilled, and purposeful, rather than thoughts that may make you feel otherwise.

Beyond using your thoughts to control your emotions, your thoughts can be used for many other things, too. You get to decide what you focus on, what you spend mental energy on, and how your mind serves you. Your mind is an incredibly powerful tool and when you choose to decide how you are going to use it, you get the opportunity to use it for virtually anything you want. You can use it to entertain yourself, to problem-solve, to stimulate various emotions, to create new things, to accomplish various goals, or to do anything you want. Truly, your mind is yours to control, and you can use it in whatever way you see fit for any given situation that you find yourself in.

You Can Control How You Choose to Live Your Life... to a Point

In life, you can control your voluntary actions. You cannot directly or consistently control things like your heartbeat, your immune system, your health, your aging, the color of your hair or skin, the size of different parts of your body, or anything else like that. However, you can influence these aspects of yourself through your thoughts and voluntary actions.

When it comes to voluntary actions, think about how you choose to respond to or behave in different situations. For example, you can choose how you express your anger or dissatisfaction, or how you express your sadness or frustration. You can choose how you take care of your physical health and what types of voluntary actions you take that allows you to, say, eat a better diet or engage in physical exercise. You can choose how you manage any illnesses or ailments that you may face, how you act at work or around your friends and family, or what type of behaviors you engage in during different situations.

There are many, many things that you can choose in your life. In fact, every day you are faced with thousands of possibilities for behaviors you can choose to engage in and actions you can choose to take. Are you going to call that person, or no? Are you going to apply for that job, or no? Will you try out that new hobby, or no? Will you take that trip, or no? When they bully you, will you allow it? When they criticize you, will you act on it? You get to decide many different actions you take on a day to day basis, and each of those actions will contribute to the different experiences you have and the situations you find yourself a part of. Learning how to properly control your voluntary actions means that you will begin to make choices that align with what you truly desire in your life, and stop allowing your voluntary actions to be overruled by your emotions. This way, you will stop acting out of anger, fear, curiosity, love, obsession, addiction, compulsiveness, or other feelings, and you will begin to act logically, rationally, reasonably, and in a way that actually serves what you truly desire.

When you learn how to genuinely control your thoughts and voluntary actions, you begin to realize that what you wanted was available to you all along. You always had the power to think thoughts and take actions that would serve your ability to feel happy, fulfilled, and purposeful. All you had to do was stop looking for external sources and start looking for ways to create it within yourself.

STOICISM HOLDS strong roots in using the logical and rational side of your brain, and one of the greatest things you can do with this part of your brain is learning how to navigate your emotions in a more evolved manner. In other schools of thought, using logic to navigate your emotions in a more meaningful manner is also known as emotional intelligence. The foundation of this entire practice lies in realizing that emotions are inevitable, natural, and normal parts of life, while also realizing that you can navigate your emotions better from a place of logic than you can from a place of pure emotion.

When you navigate your emotions from a place of pure emotion, you find yourself experiencing primal, overwhelming, and oftentimes uncontrollable feelings that ultimately drive all of your behaviors and actions. This is where you find people feeling victimized by their emotional state and feeling as though there is no way they can possibly navigate their emotions in any other way. For example, you might believe that anytime you feel anger you must express that anger to the person you are angry toward, or that anytime you feel threatened you *have* been threatened and so you must protect yourself. Often, you find yourself acting on emotions in an overreactive manner, or even acting on emotions that are entirely irrelevant or ill fit to the situation that you are currently a part of.

When you allow yourself to step away from this pure emotional experience, also known as emotional hijacking, you create the opportunity for you to intentionally navigate your emotions. Through this, you can achieve your intended goals and desires with your emotions and properly express them in a way that prevents you from repressing all of those emotions. In the end, this method of expression and emotional navigation is far more matured and effective, allowing you to experience your emotions in a more meaningful and fulfilling manner.

Taking Personal Responsibility for Your Emotions

The very first step of navigating your emotions in a stoic manner is taking responsibility for the emotions that you experience. Even though you might not be the one responsible for creating those emotions, as they are an involuntary experience, they do belong to you as they were created in your body, and they are experienced by you. Further, they are acted on by you, and those actions are accounted for by your voluntary actions. Thus, you are the one who gets to decide what actions you are going to take to intentionally respond to your emotions.

When you do not first mentally take responsibility for your emotions, intentionally taking actions on your emotions feels much more challenging as you are in a space of believing that your emotions are beyond your control. Being in this state means that you are ultimately giving away your power, and that you are taking on all of the burdens and consequences that come with the methods you use to express your emotions. The sooner you can take responsibility for your emotions, the sooner you will be able to reclaim that power so that you can take control of your actions and use them to your advantage.

It is important to remember that no matter how you perceive your emotions, or how you feel during your emotional expression, they are *always* your responsibility. This means that even if you genuinely believe they are out of your control and that you are a victim of your emotions, they are still your responsibility. Even if you believe someone else is at fault for causing your emotions, or you attempt to blame someone else for how you feel or how you acted, they are still your responsibility. Once again, you, and you alone, are responsible for how you think and how you act with your voluntary actions, and so anything you do is entirely your responsibility.

Rather than attempting to mentally evade responsibility, then the best choice is to realize that they are your responsibility and to choose to navigate them in a better way. This way, you can stop digging yourself in deeper and start taking practical measures to change the way you respond to your emotions, thus allowing you the opportunity to officially change the way you navigate your emotions.

If you are having a hard time taking responsibility for your own emotions, chances are you are still giving your power away or reducing the control over your power. Again, the only person to be held responsible for this, and at fault for this, is you. While you may be able to attribute the cause of this to previous experiences or the way people have treated you in the past, you must be willing to now take responsibility for the aftermath and fix it for yourself. You can do this by affirming to yourself that what happened in the past was in the past, but starting today you are going to take responsibility for and ownership over any emotions you experience. This way, you can begin to take responsibility for and ownership over any thoughts and voluntary actions you choose to associate with your emotions going forward. From now on, you should be consciously recognizing that every action you take, even if it was unintentional, was a choice you made, and therefore, it is your responsibility, and your fault. Taking radical responsibility in this way will help you truly begin to determine whether your actions are in integrity with who you want to be and how you want to be, or if they are not. If not, you know that you need to quickly take action to change the way you are responding, and the way you respond in the future.

Intentionally Choosing How to Navigate Your Emotions

Not realizing that you can intentionally choose how to navigate your emotions can largely stem from a lack of understanding around how emotions are made, what their purpose is, and what they require in order to be adequately expressed. In many ways, the expressions you are currently using are habitual and, mentally, you have learned that they give you some form of fulfillment that allows you to feel a sense of relief from those emotions. For example, if you are angry and you scream or become aggressive, as soon as you finish screaming or releasing your aggression, you will find yourself feeling that the sense of anger is completely out of your system. Unfortunately, you will also likely find that shame, embarrassment, and frustration set in next as you are disappointed in yourself and the way that you responded to your feelings. However, the next time you get angry you may go ahead and respond in the same reactive manner, because you know that this allows you to feel a sense of relief.

Every single emotion you experience likely has a pattern around how you think about and express that emotion, which allows you to experience that form of relief or release from that emotion. While habits are rooted in your subconscious brain, they get there through voluntary actions you have chosen at different points throughout your life, and you are continuing to voluntarily choose to engage in that habit every time you experience that trigger. Thus, it is your responsibility to uproot those habits and begin to embrace a different method for voluntary emotional expression.

When you begin to intentionally navigate your emotions, there are four things you need to do: you need to identify the emotion, identify the goal of that emotion, identify what will give you a sense of relief from that emotion, and then take action on that emotion. When you begin to analyze your emotions in this way, you take the entirety of your power out of your emotions and split it up between your logical mind and your emotional mind. This way, you can allow yourself to feel your feelings, but you can also navigate them in a more intentional and meaningful way.

As you begin to identify your emotions, make sure you do this with a logical mind and that you identify your emotions as accurately as you can. For example, if you are angry do not just say that you are angry, look to see if you can identify what specific type of anger you are feeling. Are you frustrated? Jealous? Insecure? Threatened? Afraid? Enraged? If you are feeling sad, identify what specific type of sadness you are feeling. Are you disappointed? Depressed? Longing? Grieving? Lonely? Knowing exactly what you are feeling is going to help you identify the goal of your emotion and the best course of action because this allows you to accurately understand what is going on. When you can create this intentional and specific course of action that is relevant to exactly what flavor of emotion you are feeling, you will find that you are able to create a resolution that is far more fulfilling and relieving than anything else.

Once you have identified the emotion you are feeling, you need to understand where that emotion came from and what the goal of that emotion is. If you are feeling jealous, for example, what are you specifically jealous of? What do you wish you had that someone else has, and why does it seem like you cannot have this in your life? If you are feeling grief, why are you grieving? What have you lost that you wish you could have back? Knowing exactly what you are feeling, and why, will give you the opportunity to create a resolution for yourself because you will be focused on resolutions that are focused on the specific reward you are looking for in your mind. While you might not be able to have exactly what you want, you will be able to start to shift your perspective and take voluntary actions that help you release the feelings you are feeling.

The last step before taking action on your emotions is to decide what actions are going to get you the results you most desire. For example, if you feel jealous because you want something someone else has, rather than being angry, feeling bad, or behaving rudely, you might comprise a plan for how you will get something similar in your own life. Or, if you are grieving, you may not be able to get back what you lost, but maybe you can do something that helps bring you closure, or spend some time soothing yourself so that you can navigate those feelings of grief in a more peaceful and compassionate manner. Choosing the actions that you will take from a place of logic and reasoning ensures that the actions you take have a specific purpose and that you are likely to fulfill your emotional desires through those actions, without having any negative consequences. This way, you are not acting irrationally or impulsively, but instead, you are acting in a way that gets you what you need and allows you to deal with your emotions properly.

Finally, you need to go ahead and take your actions. At this point, you need to commit to taking them, and you need to see them all the way through. In doing so, you should also be choosing to think from a perspective of realizing that what you are doing is fulfilling, and that it is helping you get exactly what you want and need out of the situation you are facing. This way, you are far more likely to experience a sense of emotional release and reward, allowing you to get exactly what you were looking for out of that particular chosen action.

At first, the feeling of relief may seem minuscule compared to the feelings of relief you may have gotten out of your habitual expressions, largely due to the fact that your brain is used to habitually rewarding you for your original expressions. Over time, though, your new expressions will feel more and more fulfilling, especially as you begin to see the positive side effects of choosing them. For example, you, and your brain, will start to realize the lack of shame, guilt, and embarrassment you feel around anger because you have been expressing it in a reasonable way, or the lack of fear you feel around sadness because you have been releasing it in an effective manner. As this begins to happen, you will realize that your intentional expressions are far more useful and fulfilling, and therefore far more worth your effort than the habitual ones that were causing more problems than they were solving.

Never Over-Express an Emotion You Are Experiencing

One of the absolute most important rules of navigating emotions when it comes to stoicism is never over-expressing emotions that you are experiencing. Reacting to emotions without first logically sorting through them and choosing your response to those emotions will nearly always lead to you behaving in ways that result in you feeling poorly about the choices you made. This may not be the case for positive emotions; since they generally always bring about more positive emotions, but anytime you find yourself feeling a more charged or negative emotion, you might find yourself feeling particularly ashamed of your behaviors. You will also always end up accumulating a large amount of consequences for the ways you behaved, which can lead to worse problems over time.

You should always strive to think first and act second when it comes to navigating your emotions, no matter what is going on. The more you can think first, then act second, the better because you will find yourself dealing with your emotions and, in the long run, the better you will find yourself feeling overall.

Not engaging in the think first, act second rule can not only lead to you overreacting on your emotions, but it can also lead to you feeling as though you cannot trust your emotions because you genuinely believe that you cannot control yourself with them. This is an awful position to be in when you know that you are ultimately responsible for your emotions and that you are going to take responsibility for the consequences, because it may seem like you cannot help yourself, and the consequences are inevitable. You may even begin to self-sabotage as a way to avoid situations where you might be exposed to certain emotions so that you can avoid them altogether. Of course, this can lead to its own set of consequences as you begin to find yourself living in fear of you and your emotions, which are an inevitable experience of life. Rather than continually giving into overreactions, learn to manage your emotions in a more intentional manner and be as consistent in this as you possibly can be. Over time, you will find yourself effortlessly reacting in far more meaningful ways and using any accidental overreactions as a method for teaching yourself, rather than shaming yourself and worsening the situation.

One of the most powerful things you can do when it comes to increasing your trust around your emotions and lessening your overreactions is to start being more compassionate toward yourself when you experience emotions. Rather than bullying yourself for making a mistake and then driving yourself to want to repress the experience that you feel ashamed of, view that mistake as being a learning opportunity. Intentionally take responsibility for how you behaved, allow yourself the space to intentionally wind down from those feelings, then begin to review the situation so that you can better understand how that situation played out and why you over-reacted. This way, you can begin to educate yourself on your own patterns and tendencies, and you can be more mindful and aware of them going forward. Through that, you will find yourself making much better choices and experiencing more growth every single time you come up against challenging emotions, thus proving that you are doing better every single time.

Always Favor Logical Responses Over Emotional Reactions

According to the philosophy of stoicism, one should always favor logical responses over emotional reactions, largely due to all of the reasons surrounding emotional and material consequences you could face if you do not. Beyond that, though, favoring logical responses over emotional reactions put you directly in control over yourself, your emotions, and the experiences that you have in life. This way, you can use your emotions as your power, rather than have them working against you and holding you back in life.

When you first begin to transition to moving from a place of logic over moving from a place of emotion, you might feel as though you are not capable of getting enough out of your emotional expressions. Or, you might make the mistake of believing that only *part* of your emotional expression is in your power, and the rest of it is out of your power. These two false beliefs will lead to you experiencing an immense amount of disempowerment around your emotions and will not support you in moving into a place of logic, intention, and power.

It is also important that as you learn to favor logic over emotion, you also learn to favor *your* logic over anyone else's. Now is not the time to seek external validation by discovering what other people think or feel about your emotions, or how they believe you should act on them or behave in response to your emotions. Only you will know what sorts of responses are in integrity with who you are, what you desire, and what you are looking to fulfill through each emotion you experience. At times, you might feel the need to make choices that other people do not agree with, and other times you might find yourself needing to refrain from responding with any actions at all, even though that may feel impossible at times. The key is to understand that what *you* logically believe to be the right decision, and what *you* feel to be in integrity with who you are and what you want for yourself is more important than anything else. This is where you begin to create a sense of personal happiness, fulfillment, and purpose, and where you start to build your trust in yourself and your ability to navigate different situations, including challenging ones. As you continue to build this strength and trust up within yourself, you will find yourself trusting even more in your own logic and power, and moving even more strongly from a place of stoicism and intention.

Navigating especially charged emotions with stoicism can feel even more challenging than navigating your average emotions with stoicism. When you are feeling something intense like anger, you might find yourself feeling as though leaning back on your stoic practices is not enough, and like your emotions are really starting to take over. This is because, in a way, they are. However, that does not mean that you cannot take back control and start navigating your emotions in a more intentional manner.

When it comes to navigating your more charged emotions with stoicism, the best way is to give yourself food for thought, as this helps you put your emotions and actions into greater perspective for yourself. Otherwise, the general method for approaching these emotions will be the same, though you will need to put more effort into standing strong in your intentional responses, as this can feel rather challenging and even impossible when you are overly charged.

Putting Your Emotions Into Perspective

First things first, you need to put your emotions into some serious perspective. As I have already mentioned, your emotions are natural, hormonal, and chemical responses that occur within your body or brain. But what does that mean exactly? It means that your emotions are a part of your built-in survival tactics, and that they, like your instinct, are deeply engrained in your human experience. And, much like your instinct, they can be used to your advantage if you understand them and know how to use them for your benefit.

Anytime you are exposed to stimuli in life, which is all the time, your body is "reading" that stimuli and deciding how to respond to it. This starts with subconscious thoughts about what the stimuli is; then it turns into feelings and thoughts about that stimuli. This can trigger anything from fear or anger to contentment or joy, depending on what you are experiencing. Every single emotion is developed in this way, and many of your thoughts are developed in this way, too. Though, of course, you have more conscious control over your thoughts than you do over your creation of emotions.

When you experience emotions, in particular, your body is flooded with the creation of certain hormones and chemicals that create those emotions. These hormones and chemicals are designed to drive you to engage with your environment in a specific way, always intended to promote your survival. For example, if you are angry, your feelings of anger are designed to help you have enough energy and strength to fight or flight from the situation that you are currently in. Or, if you are happy, your feelings are designed to reward your brain with positive chemicals and hormones so that it *wants* to do more of what has driven this sense of happiness. This way, your brain will naturally encourage habits and behaviors that feel good, and discourage ones that don't. Plus, it will learn to remember said things, and you will be able to use this to fuel your overall wellbeing in the long run.

Realizing that your emotions are literally a chemical or hormonal response to stimuli, and not substance that indicates the absolute truth, means that you can stop treating your emotions like they are accurate and worthy guides when they are triggered. This way, you can start questioning your emotions and giving space for your logical mind to take over, rather than succumbing to the primal behaviors of your emotional mind.

It Is Your Opinion Making You Angry

If you find yourself being the type of person who has ever blamed other people for making you angry, either in what they are saying or what they are doing, then you are not taking proper responsibility for your emotions. Anytime you believe that someone else's actions or words have the power to make you angry, or act on that anger, you are holding yourself back by choosing to hold onto this opinion. What is *actually* making you angry, however, is the opinion you have of the situation or the circumstance that is making you feel angry in the first place. You are the one who is choosing to hold onto thoughts that are fueling your anger, rather than choosing to let go of those thoughts so that you can release them and move on with feeling happy, fulfilled, and purposeful.

Remember that even if someone else says something about you or does something directly to you, what they have said or done is solely their opinion, and their responsibility. You do not have to agree with or own their opinions as your own. In choosing to actually reject that person's opinions, you allow yourself the opportunity to create your own opinion separate of theirs, which can be far more productive in helping you eliminate any need for anger in the first place.

For example, let's say someone calls you a rude name. *If you* choose to hold the opinion that their opinion is true, or that their opinion of you is in any way harmful to you, then you are going to feel angry and hurt by what they have said. If, however, you choose to hold the opinion that their opinion is wrong and that you do not agree, then their opinion has no power because you have already invalidated it. You could take it one step further by applying this reasoning to any other situation. For example, if someone called you a red sports car, you would know for a fact that you are not a red sports car, and therefore, what they said would seem irrelevant and pointless to you. So, then, why would you choose to get angry over them holding any other opinion about you? At the end of the day, if you choose not to own someone else's opinion, then they can think whatever they want and you will continue to remain strong and calm within yourself. You have no reason to be angry when you do not agree with the person who could otherwise be causing anger within you.

Recognize the Consequences of Your Anger

Before you ever act on your anger, always, *always* remind yourself that anger has consequences. It might feel good to experience anger and to release it, because venting your anger creates a sense of elation and righteousness within you. You might find yourself feeling powerful, successful, and good after expressing your anger because it seems as though it did what it was intended to do. At least, at first.

Once you step back and truly look at it, though, you realize that your anger has consequences, and those consequences can be challenging to deal with. You could damage your reputation, get in trouble with the law, disrespect your own morals, or even cause damage to something material that costs you big in the long run. It may seem thrilling and fulfilling to express your anger the moment it hits, but just remember that it will always have its consequences and you will be the one left paying the price. Rather than paying those consequences, take a moment and decide whether or not they are worth it. I guarantee you that every single time you will realize that they are not.

You Are Only Hurting Yourself

When you get angry, and you face your own consequences, you begin to realize how much your anger costs you and how much you are hurting yourself every time you express anger in an illogical manner. For example, let's say you get angry at someone for a seemingly rude text they sent you and you throw your phone and it breaks. Who pays the price for this situation? You, as you have to replace your phone and incur the expense of that new device. Or, let's say someone decides they want to remove themselves from your life and you get angry because you feel rejected. Who ends up feeling worse in the end? You, because no amount of anger would have prevented that person from leaving *and* now you may have additional consequences to face based on how you have behaved.

Even if you do not express your anger and you hold it in, you will continue to be the one who pays for it. Every time you choose to hold onto anger, you put yourself in a position where you can spontaneously become angry over merely thinking about said subject, which can lead to you ruining your own day. Some people even hold onto grudges, or many grudges, and ruin many of their own days over something that was never worth holding onto in the first place. While they continue to hold onto that anger and suffer, the other person is off living their life and has likely forgotten all about the situation.

Anytime you choose to hold onto anger, and you do not rationally and reasonably release it in an intentional manner, you are choosing to hurt yourself. It is never worth it to hold onto anger.

Identify it, understand its purpose, logically express it and release it, and allow yourself to completely move on from that anger so that you are no longer creating unnecessary consequences for yourself.

The Person You Are Angry With Is Like You

Getting angry with people can often create a sense of divisiveness between you and that other individual. You might find yourself feeling as though they have wronged you, and therefore, they are bad and you are somehow better than them or different from them because of the situation you are in. The reality is, though, that we are not all that different from each other. When you find yourself angry with someone else, stop and honestly consider who that person is, what they were doing, and why. Human beings often behave in similar ways, and chances are if you were in that person's shoes you would have behaved exactly the same way that they did at the time. Even if that person did not behave in a way that you would have, you may be able to develop an understanding of why they behaved the way they did, and it is highly likely that their behavior actually had nothing to do with you in the first place. Instead, it likely came from a place of how they were feeling and how they believed they could protect themselves from that feeling or create a sense of relief from it.

When you realize that the person you are angry with is not all that different from you, it becomes easier for you to accept them for their behavior and have compassion for them and the decisions they made. Even if they, themselves, do not recognize their behaviors or take responsibility for them, you can choose to witness this in yourself and have compassion for them. You can also choose to believe that they were doing the best they could with the situation they had and the mental and emotional tools they have, and through that, you can realize that it is okay for you to let them off the hook for what they have done. This does not mean that you should give everyone a free pass to behave in unkind or unreasonable ways toward you. However, it does allow you to mentally let them off the hook so that you do not hold onto that anger any longer.

Compassion Trumps Anger

When it comes to navigating situations where anger is present, it can be easy to want to go all-in with your anger. You might find yourself truly believing that you have every right to be angry, and that may lead you to want to feed into that anger and live there. The truth is, you might be right. Maybe you do have every reason to be angry. Maybe you have perceived the situation correctly, understood what was going on well, and have truly been wronged or exposed to an unfair and unkind situation. Perhaps your anger is totally worthy, and so there is no reason to deny yourself your feelings of anger.

Even when this happens, though, you do not have to succumb to *just* anger. You can experience anger *and* compassion. You can acknowledge that what happened to you was incredibly wrong, have compassion for yourself and what you went through, and have compassion for what led the other person or people to do what they did. Realize that you do not fully understand why someone behaved the way they did, and that even if they could explain it to you, you would never truly, intimately understand why. Give people the benefit of the doubt and have compassion for them. Chances are, they, too, are paying the consequences for their mistakes. If you need to, assert boundaries, create more space, and protect yourself against further issues. Yet, also be sure to create the space for you to have compassion for that person so that you can refrain from letting the anger bury roots in your heart and stay there longer than it needs to. When you disallow hate a place in your heart, you give yourself plenty of space to heal.

Never Shoulder Someone Else's Consequences

When someone has wronged you, sometimes the pain you feel can lead you to want to take responsibility for fixing the broken situation. For example, let's say your best friend or spouse betrays you, and the discomfort of having been hurt leads you to pick up the broken pieces and put the relationship back together, whether or not they are helping fix the situation. You might find yourself trying to force them to feel remorse, change, and commit to the relationship more effectively so that you can experience the positive, comfortable relationship that you now feel you are missing due to the betrayal. This is a normal knee-jerk reaction to pain because, in your mind, you simply want everything to feel okay again. However, this behavior directly results in you taking responsibility for someone else's consequences, and it can turn into a vicious cycle of you constantly doing this in an effort to keep your own life as close to normal and comfortable as possible. Some people will even go so far as to shoulder consequences to situations they are not a part of and that they have no responsibility for, such as apologizing on behalf of someone else or carrying the financial burdens of someone else's poor behaviors. All of these types of situations can lead to a surplus of anger, as well as a great deal of strain and burden being placed directly on your shoulders.

It is important that you understand where the boundaries lie as far as what is your responsibility and what is not your responsibility, especially when it comes to consequences. In situations where you are not directly involved in the wrongdoing, it is not your responsibility to apologize, or take on the burden of the consequences that belong to someone else. No amount of additional chores, financial burdens, or any tasks should end up on your to-do list because someone else has done something wrong. Make sure you always keep yourself *out* of the direct conflict in situations that you are not a part of, as this keeps you free from dealing with consequences that are not your own.

In situations where you are a part of the conflict, it is important that you realize that the consequences that are caused by someone else is not your responsibility. You should not be the one going out of your way to fix a relationship someone else broke, to repair bonds that were damaged by another person, or to otherwise fix things someone else is damaging, *especially* if they are doing nothing to fix the situation. Rather than focusing on fixing what someone else broke between the two of you, focus on helping yourself and healing yourself. If someone else makes a mistake, let them be the one to extend the olive branch and put effort into repairing the situation before you decide whether or not you want to put work into it, too. If they do not make any effort to repair the situation, you know they are not worth your effort, either. Your time would be better spent enjoying healthier situations, than constantly shouldering the consequences of someone else's choices.

See Your Anger as an Opportunity for Growth

Anger has been speculated on by psychologists for years, with many believing it is a secondary emotion or one that occurs when we had not respected our own boundaries or recognized our own needs before it was "too late." In other words, we continually let things go on in a way we do not like until we finally get angry enough to lash out, and then we use that angry energy to make changes. Rather than waiting until you are angry, look for opportunities to recognize low levels of anger early on and give yourself a chance to make adjustments right away. Or, if you find that you have reached higher levels of anger where it feels more challenging to hold back or bite your tongue, use that as an opportunity to ask yourself how you can use this as a moment for growth. What was it that indicated that something was going wrong, before the anger struck, and what could you have done *then* to avoid the situation you got into?

In addition to thinking about how you could have avoided the situation you are in now, consider how you have handled your anger and how you might be able to better handle your anger in the future. The truth is, no matter how good you get at recognizing and managing the triggers that make you angry, you are still going to feel anger in your life. This means that knowing how to navigate the anger itself is just as important as knowing how to reduce the amount of anger you experience overall. That way, when your anger is inevitably triggered, you navigate it in a more stoic and peaceful manner, rather than in an explosive or reactive one. Your goal should always be to navigate anger in the most intentional, meaningful, and effective manner possible, as this is what will lead to the results you are looking for.

7 / HOW STOICISM WILL HELP YOU NAVIGATE CONFLICT

Navigating conflict using stoicism is slightly different from navigating anger in that not all conflict includes anger. Sometimes, conflict can be uncomfortable, confrontational, overwhelming, it can induce fear or anxiety, or it can invoke any other number of feelings that may seem challenging for you to navigate. It is important that you understand that these feelings are normal, and that you recognize that there is a way to navigate them stoically. The guidance in this chapter will support you in this process regardless of whether you are the one who has the start the conflict, or if you were invited into a situation of conflict by someone else.

Own All of Your Emotions

The very first thing you should focus on doing when you find yourself facing conflict is recognizing and owning all of the emotions you are experiencing in relation to that conflict. Knowing what you are feeling will help you have more compassion toward yourself, navigate the situation in a way that is meaningful and effective, and look for potential opportunities to engage in personal growth or healing following the conflict.

You want to identify your emotions as clearly as possible, as this will ensure that you are able to fully understand what it is that you are going through. The best way to begin identifying your emotions is to expand your vocabulary surrounding emotions themselves so that you can start describing your emotions more effectively. For example, rather than saying you are mad say you are angry, frustrated, or enraged. Rather than saying you are fearful, say you are uncertain, insecure, confused, or anxious. Instead of saying that you are sad, say that you are depressed, grieving, or feeling powerless.

When you can clearly identify what you are feeling, you can begin to pinpoint the exact root causes for that feeling. These specific feelings are far easier to trace than vague, generic feelings that you may not fully understand yet. For example, if you are having an upset reaction to something and you say that you are feeling angry about it, you could wind up believing that this incident alone is the root cause of your anger and that would make it easy to feel wronged and deeply attached to your anger about that situation. If, however, you acknowledged that you felt angry because you felt disrespected, then you could begin to understand why you felt disrespected and what specific incidents lead up to that feeling. You could also begin to create healthy boundaries for yourself that would prevent people from disrespecting you in the future, and discuss your specific feelings with the person you are in conflict with so that they understand exactly where you are coming from. With this exact recognition of what you are feeling, you can also create the opportunity for you to find a resolution that serves in resolving that specific feeling, which will lead to you being able to move on from that feeling completely, rather than carry lingering feelings of anger and resentment long after the conflict ends.

As you begin to identify your emotions it is crucial that you own them and take responsibility for them. Remember, emotions that you do not take responsibility for are incredibly challenging to change because you are not allowing yourself to possess the personal power to change those emotions. Instead, you mistakenly believe that it is someone else's responsibility to fix those issues, despite the fact that even if someone else tried they could not create any reasonable change for you. The best thing you can do is take responsibility for said things so that you can create the change for yourself and grow beyond the emotions that you are experiencing. This way, you will experience real resolutions from those emotions, and therefore a real capacity for healing and moving on.

Give Yourself a Reason to Stay Honest

In situations involving conflict, it can be easy to change your mind to favor a more comfortable position in the situation you are a part of. For most of us, conflict is inherently uncomfortable, and it can stimulate feelings of danger for us, making it seem as though we must immediately do whatever we can to resolve the conflict, even if that means being dishonest with ourselves and others. This is why so many people resolve conflict by disrespecting their own boundaries or pressing the disrespecting of someone else's boundaries, to create comfort as quickly as possible. Unfortunately, this short term comfort often comes at the expense of long term comfort, which means the conflict has not truly been resolved and will continue to fester until it flares up again.

Rather than putting patches over the conflict you are in by allowing there to be mistruths and disrespected boundaries, focus on finding a powerful way to be honest with yourself and to stand your ground respectfully. You may not be able to clearly identify and encourage other people to uphold their boundaries, but you can work on making it safe for them to do so, while you do the same thing. This way, you are both much less likely to lean on faulty systems of dishonesty as a way to quickly resolve the conflict, only to have to face it again later on. Remember, you cannot control how another person behaves so ultimately, the only thing you can control is your willingness to acknowledge, assert, and remain unwavering in your own boundaries and wellbeing. Do not let anyone drive you away from your position of remaining honest and in integrity with yourself, as you will grow to regret your choices and resent the situation later on, and by then, it could be much more challenging for you to resolve the situation.

The best way to give yourself a way to stay honest is to find someone that you respect and then use them as a way to encourage yourself to stay honest. Giving yourself someone to look up to is a great way to encourage yourself, as it reminds you that there is something bigger than this moment that you are working toward and that staying honest is the best way for you to get there. You can use anyone as your source of inspiration, simply choose someone that you are inspired by, and that you respect and turn that person into your role model for remaining honest to yourself and in integrity with your truth. Anytime you find yourself feeling called to disrespect your own boundaries or walk away from your own sense of honesty and integrity, remember your idol and stay honest to yourself for them, and for you.

Know That There Is Life After Conflict

When you are caught up in a conflict, it can be easy to feel as though there will never be anything else beyond the conflict that you are experiencing. Of course, this is not rational, logical, or true, but it is the way it feels. Many times, the triggering of our subconscious minds and our fight-or-flight response leads to us feeling as though we are in a do-or-die situation, and that can be rather scary. Ultimately, your brain becomes so engrossed in the situation that you really do forget that the situation is not as all-consuming as you believe it to be, and that there will be an end to it, eventually.

Putting it into perspective and remembering that nothing lasts forever can help you break away from the intense and intimidating energy of the conflict and move into a more open minded space. This way, you can start to put everything into perspective and make decisions based on ration and reasoning, rather than decisions based on the emotional state of your flight-or-fight response.

Remember that no matter what happens in a conflict, even if things do not turn out as you had hoped, that is not the end. You can, and you will, rebuild from there and create favorable circumstances for yourself with what you have. You always have the opportunity to help yourself fix any situation you find yourself in by creating new circumstances for yourself based on the cards you are dealt. Since you are entirely in control over your thoughts and voluntary actions, there is always plenty that you can do to experience positivity even after the worst perceived failure.

Always Focus on a Meaningful Resolution

Anytime you are in conflict, you should always shift the attention away from deciding who is right and who is wrong and focus instead on finding a meaningful resolution to the conflict that you are experiencing. Focusing on who is right and who is wrong may seem like the most important thing in the moment, especially if you both strongly believe in your opinion and want to protect yourselves against the possible pain of someone else's opposing opinion. However, very rarely is it effective to worry about who is right and who is wrong, as the real answer is that there is both truth and untruth in both opinions. Rather than worrying about that, then, you should worry about what resolution is going to be the most effective and impactful for that particular conflict.

A meaningful resolution should be one that respects both parties involved, which has reasonable expectations of both parties involved, and that feels manageable by both parties involved. The most important things to each party should be included in the resolution whenever possible, too, to ensure that no one experiences resentment for not being properly represented by the resolution.

Sometimes, it can take a fair bit of creativity, consistency, and critical thinking to find a resolution that is going to be most effective in any given situation. I recommend taking your time and focusing your energy into this process more than the argument or the conflict itself, however, as this is how you are going to bring a peaceful and respectful end to the conflict.

You Are In Control of You

Lastly, I encourage you to remember that you are not required to show up to every conflict that you are invited to, and that you can choose to respond in a peaceful way. Rather than arguing, stooping to anyone else's level, getting angry, or getting into a fight with someone else, you can choose to peacefully disengage from any fights you are invited to and instead opt to have a conversation when the other person is willing to respect your right to peace. You are never obligated to yell, argue, debate, defend yourself, or tell your side of the story if you do not feel that you want to. You can always respectfully walk away, and that does not make you wrong, nor does it make you the "loser" of the argument, it simply makes you someone who is unwilling to engage in chaotic and disrespectful engagements.

If, and when, the other person is willing to engage in respectful correspondence, then you can try having the conversation again and perhaps using this more respectful and peaceful space to come up with a meaningful resolution.

STOICISM IS NOT JUST about learning how to navigate conflict and difficult feelings with greater ease, it is also about learning how to create a higher quality of life for yourself on a day to day basis. Learning how to use stoicism to create calmness within your daily life gives you a great opportunity to start enjoying a higher quality of life. One of the biggest benefits of learning how to increase your daily calmness, aside from the improved quality of life, is that it also brings down your overall stress levels and improves your overall mood. When you manage to achieve this, navigating things like stress, anger, and conflict become easier because you are dealing with a more calm baseline of energy. To better understand what I mean, think of it this way: if you were already stressed out every single day, and then someone gave you some news that increased your stress levels, you would likely be over the top by that point. After all, you were already carrying so much, putting anything else on top of your existing stress might feel like the straw that broke the camel's back. If, however, you were not typically carrying any stress at all, then the introduction of new stress in your day to day life would not seem like such a big deal because you were not already overwhelmed and overburdened. Instead, you would be in a calm and comfortable space emotionally, so this would simply feel like something new that you could navigate and release, thus making it easier and healthier for you to navigate difficult feelings.

Choose to Stay Present in the Moment

Chinese philosopher Lao Tzu famously said that "If you are depressed you are living in the past, and if you are anxious you are living in the future. If you are at peace, you are living in the present." This particular line is an incredibly important one for anyone to ponder, as it holds a great deal of truth to it, and it can also help you realize the importance of releasing both the emotional burden of the past and the future so that you can live in the peaceful present.

In our modern world, the majority of people spend their lives worried about what is yet to come, and upset about what has already happened. In many cases, the reality of their past and future can combine to create incredibly overwhelming and intense emotions that make it seem like even their present is doomed. Thus, they find themselves living with a great lack of peace.

Learning to recognize that the past has already happened and that the best you can do is learn from it, and that the future is not guaranteed and the best thing you can do is hope on it is important. For your past, you cannot go back and rewrite history, change your consequences, or fix things that you feel you did wrong. If you hold yourself hostage by dwelling on what you did, or on what happened to you, you will find yourself always feeling hurt, ashamed, and wronged by the life you have lived. You may find it challenging for you to move on because you feel you do not deserve to, which is not true, or like you cannot until someone else fixes what they did wrong to you, which is not possible. Even if that person could fix it, the lingering pain would continue to exist which would ultimately mean that it was up to you to fix it.

The future has yet to happen, and so many believe that if they worry about it and plan for it enough, they will be able to control how it turns out. While you can certainly influence the future by the choices you make today, you cannot control the future, nor should you try to. You should make plans for yourself and aim toward goals. However, you should also refrain from worrying about the future as even you have no idea how it will play out or what will happen in the long run. The best thing you can do is have hope for the future and hold faith that it will all turn out as it should, and that you will be physically, mentally, emotionally, and spiritually strong enough to handle whatever comes your way. That way, you can place your focus on the present moment instead, and grant yourself freedom from the set-in-stone past and the undetermined future.

Allow Yourself to Experience Gratitude

Gratitude is as much an expression of emotion as it is a chosen state of mind. When you allow yourself to experience and express gratitude, you experience an abundance of positive benefits, including a brain that literally rewires itself to be more positive and optimistic. Unfortunately, many people experience unrecognized or unexpressed gratitude, which leads to them not receiving the positive emotional and mental benefits of recognized and expressed gratitude. Unrecognized or unexpressed gratitude is often left on the table because "it was implied" or because "I already said thank you." Gratitude is about so much more than an implied state or a word. Gratitude is about allowing yourself to truly feel into the joy and gratitude that you experience when something positive or nice happens, or has happened, and to allow yourself to mentally receive said thing. When you experience gratitude in this way, you begin to experience far more positive emotions, and you truly start looking for more reasons to be grateful. In the end, you experience a calmer quality of life because rather than being wound up and worried about bad things happen, you are relaxed and looking forward to good things happening in your life.

Be Willing to Experience Healthy Detachment

In life, there are differing levels of attachment that are appropriate for different situations. You might think that there is a simple way to generalize which areas of your life are deserving of stronger attachments and which aren't, but the reality is that there is no sweeping generalization that can be made in regards to where attachments should and should not be made. Instead, you need to think about what is going to be ideal or most healthy for you in any given situation, and you need to be flexible enough to adjust those levels of attachment anytime you realize that a previously chosen level of attachment is no longer suitable.

Generally speaking, detachment is something that you should use as a practice to help prevent you from experiencing unnecessary pain in various situations. For example, in your relationships you may hold no attachment for a specific person to fulfill your emotions in specific ways, knowing that if you were to hold an attachment it would only hurt you in the long run. Instead, you could be detached and trust, then, that you could have your varying emotional needs fulfilled by yourself and met by different people in different relationships. You could also hold detachment toward different outcomes, the way life itself will go, the past, or around things that were previously bringing you any level of unnecessary stress in your life.

Remember That Your Time Is Precious

All too often, people waste their time. I don't believe they do this on purpose; I believe this happens because they get into the habit of wasting their time, and this makes it much easier for them to do so without even realizing it. For example, if you are used to watching TV in all your down time, you might feel like you never have enough time to engage in your hobbies because you are constantly busy. Of course, watching TV is not a high priority situation, but it has become such a major part of your routine that you fail to realize that this is something that could be adjusted to make more time for other things that you care about in life.

Regularly taking inventory for how you are spending your time and allotting plenty of time for you to engage in all areas of your life is important. You should give yourself plenty of time to engage in your career, manage your wealth, take care of your health, enjoy your favorite hobbies, spend time with your loved ones, spend time with yourself, and devote to your spirituality or faith if you are religious. Taking responsibility for your schedule and treating your time as being a precious part of your life is a great way to improve your overall sense of calmness.

Learn to Stop Procrastinating

Like you can lose plenty of time on habits that you do not realize are wasting your time, you can also lose plenty of time procrastinating. Procrastinating is a form of habit that wastes your time; however, it is not one that you engage in unknowingly. When you engage in procrastination, you know you are procrastinating because you frequently think about the fact that you should be doing it, but instead consciously choose not to. This can create a situation where you do not get things done when you need or want to, and where you begin to feel ashamed or frustrated with yourself because you are consistently and knowingly putting things off. Procrastinating also frequently leads to heightened stress levels because you end up feeling overwhelmed by the amount of work you have put off that you later have to catch up on.

Learning how to control your thoughts and voluntary actions enough to eliminate procrastinating from your habitual experiences is important, as it will allow you to begin to eliminate the stress that comes with procrastinating, too. When you learn to consistently work away at things that are important to you or that are important to your future, you find yourself experiencing greater levels of success over time. Get into the habit of doing a little, consistently, rather than doing nothing and rushing to get everything done at the last minute.

Discover Methods for Prioritizing Your Life

Learning how to identify the order of priorities in your life is important, as it allows you to deal with things in a way that will minimize your stress and maximize your results. While you may think prioritizing is exclusively for work-related activities or chores, the reality is that learning how to prioritize your entire life is important as it will give you the opportunity to always focus on what is most important to you in each moment.

Your priorities should be made based on what is going to feel best for you at that moment *and* what is going to give you the best results in the long run. For example, let's say you have an important work project to get done, but you are feeling particularly demotivated and would rather spend time relaxing and giving yourself a break because you have been feeling stressed lately. In this case, the obvious choice might be to work on the project you have for work, but the reality is that in the long run you are going to feel better if you address your stress first. You could, then, make a plan to spend a small amount of time focusing on doing something that minimizes your stress first then get into action after, you could find a way to minimize the stress associated with your project, or you could do both of these things.

You should focus on prioritizing everything in your life ranging from your physical, mental, emotional, and spiritual needs, to your practical needs in all eight areas of your life, including your career, wealth, health, relationships, love life, relationship with yourself, hobbies, and faith. Likely, you will find that your priorities change based on how you are feeling or what you need on a day to day basis, but as you learn to tune in and listen, you will find it effortless to recognize these priorities and schedule accordingly. As a result, you will find *all* of your needs being met, and not just the things that managed to be dubbed a priority.

Always Live in Integrity With Your Truth

One of the biggest disservices you can do for yourself is living out of integrity with the truth. When you live out of integrity with your truth, you end up doing things that feel wrong to you either physically, mentally, or emotionally because you have chosen to live in accordance with someone else's truth rather than your own. You can live out of integrity with your truth by not doing or saying the things that feel right for you in each moment. After you engage in these behaviors that are not aligned with your truth, you will likely find yourself experiencing shame, frustration, and feelings of disappointment within yourself based on the choices that you made, or did not make.

Rather than allowing yourself to stray further and further away from your truth, focus on doing what you can to lean into your own inner sense of truth in all ways, at all times. Say what you truly mean, and never say something that you would not be willing to genuinely stand behind. Do not do things that you believe are misaligned with your truth, no matter how much you think you have to or you should have to. Honor your truth in every way possible and live as closely in alignment with it as you can over the course of your life. You will feel much calmer and at peace after any situation where you spoke and behaved in alignment with your truth than you will after any situation where you did not.

Be Willing to Take Meaningful Action on Things

Anytime there is something that needs to get done in your life, or something that you want to get done in your life, you should always be willing to take meaningful action on said things. Meaningful action means that you are taking the actions that are going to actually help you move toward your goal, rather than actions that waste your time but make you feel like you are doing something meaningful. If you are taking actions that make it feel like you are doing something meaningful, but, in reality, nothing is really getting accomplished, then you are ultimately wasting your time.

Having daily routines that encourage stoicism in your life is a great opportunity for you to begin to embrace the true benefits that stoicism has to offer. As with anything, the more you practice stoicism the better you get at it and, therefore, the more you gain out of your efforts. This particular school of thought is not something that is going to truly change your life simply by knowing the knowledge about it, but rather is something that will begin to change your life by actually taking action on that knowledge and making it work for you.

The way you choose to embrace stoicism into your daily routine is entirely up to you, though there are some great practices you can consider to help you begin to create a morning, afternoon, and nighttime routine that will promote stoicism in your life. I encourage you to read through these sample routines and then adjust them based on your life and your needs. That way, you are able to have a routine that fits in your life and feels good for you, while pushing you to become the best person that you can possibly be.

A Stoic Morning Routine

The purpose of a stoic morning routine is to prepare you for your day by reminding you as to what is important and worthy of your attention and efforts, and what is not. Remember, the only things you can control are your thoughts and actions, so the best thing you can do for yourself is controlling them in a way that allows you to use them on things that truly matter and are worthy of your time and attention.

Each morning, you should remind yourself as to what it is that you truly desire and what you are working toward so that you have that focus clear in your mind. This way, throughout your daily experiences, you can assess what is important and what is not important based on the bigger picture of what matters to you. Allow yourself time to align with your values, create a vision for what you want to achieve for yourself, and to express gratitude for the life that you have been given and the opportunities that you have received, and will receive, to make the life you desire.

According to science, the first things you do in the morning set the tone for the rest of your day, so getting into a stoic frame of mind first thing in the morning can be a powerful way to maintain this mindset for the rest of your day. If you take even just fifteen minutes out of your morning to recall what it is that you are working toward, and then to actually work toward it, you will give yourself a great opportunity to create the results you desire.

A Stoic Afternoon Routine

Starting your day off with the right frame of mind is important, but we all know that day to day experiences can quickly draw you out of that frame of mind if you are not careful. Taking a few minutes out of your afternoon to adjust your frame of mind and get back into a stoic state is a great opportunity to help yourself continue to approach your day with a stoic mentality.

A good way to quickly refresh yourself in the afternoon is to take inventory of your day so far, and to use that to help you learn a couple of quick lessons that will help you get back on track. For example, let's say you take fifteen minutes in the afternoon to acknowledge that you have remained stoic for the entire morning. In this case, you could celebrate yourself for your success, acknowledge areas where your efforts worked, and resolve to continue practicing those stoic behaviors. If, on the other hand, you realize you have been drawn out of your stoic state, you can use this as an opportunity to recognize where and how you have been drawn out of it, and to determine how you can improve it. Then, you can resolve to make those changes to the rest of your day. In doing this, you increase your state of mindfulness around yourself and your behaviors and increase your likelihood of behaving in a stoic manner for the rest of your day, and in any similar situations you might experience in the future.

A Stoic Nighttime Routine

Every night, you can use stoicism as a way to help you review the day you had. In doing so, you should ask yourself three important questions: "What good did I do today?" "What could I do better?" and "How could I be the best version of myself?" You can either answer these three questions quietly to yourself, or you can write them down in a journal if you prefer writing things out. In answering these questions, you allow yourself the opportunity to create a stronger sense of awareness around yourself and your daily behaviors. You might find certain patterns where you can improve, or areas where you can become an even better person simply through reflecting and resolving to do better in the future. As you answer these questions, you will increase your self-awareness and mindfulness, while also allowing yourself to step away from emotional thoughts and into rational and logical thoughts that can help you experience a better life.

MINDFULNESS AND STOICISM GO HAND-IN-HAND, as mindfulness gives you the opportunity to recognize areas of your life where you are being drawn into emotional thoughts so that you can begin to intentionally balance them out with logical thoughts. It is important that you develop mindfulness alongside stoicism if you are going to create the opportunity to develop a strong sense of self-awareness that will help you guide and integrate your stoicism. Without self-awareness and mindfulness, you will likely find yourself understanding what stoicism is and half-heartedly embracing it, but ultimately struggling to really see all of the opportunities you have to integrate it into your life. When you have self-awareness, though, you see key areas of need and opportunity in your life, and you are able to then use this to your advantage.

Developing mindfulness is, like stoicism, a practice that takes many years and plenty of consistency to truly become amazing. In many ways, you will never fully master mindfulness just as you will never fully master stoicism, as you are only human, and there is only so much you can do. However, if you resolve to continually work toward recognizing and embracing lessons of mindfulness, you will find yourself getting better at it and integrating things like stoicism into your life in an even more powerful manner.

The Power of Mindfulness

Mindfulness practices are designed to help you learn how to intentionally regulate your emotions, reduce the amount of stress, anxiety, and depression you experience, and to focus your attention on what truly matters for you. Based on what mindfulness is, you can see why this particular skill works so seamlessly with stoicism. Essentially, stoicism helps you learn how to control your thoughts and voluntary actions, while mindfulness helps you regulate your emotions and reduce your emotional interruptions in your life. Creating a healthy balance between both means that you can recognize, experience, and express your emotions in a way that is truly healthy and supportive of your long term wellbeing.

Even if you only learned how to use mindfulness alone, your logic and reason would be drastically improved by default, based on the principles of mindfulness. That is how powerful this particular skill is, and why it is so important that you learn how to embrace it in your everyday life.

Using Mindfulness to Cultivate Self-Awareness

The first way that you should begin to develop your mindfulness skills is through cultivating a sense of self-awareness. Self-awareness is a level of awareness that allows you to recognize yourself and create a deeper sense of understanding and connection within yourself. Through self-awareness, you begin to recognize who you are, what your needs are, how you are feeling, and what you can do to better take care of yourself and, in turn, regulate and express yourself.

To begin to create a greater sense of self-awareness, you simply need to keep asking yourself, "How am I feeling?" "What do I need?" and "What do I want?" all day long. As many times as you can think to, ask yourself these questions and check in with yourself to find out what the honest answers to these questions are. Soon, you will find yourself asking these questions without even realizing it and recognizing the answers in a conscious manner.

It is important that anytime you consciously draw forth information from these questions, you express gratitude for receiving the answer and that you begin to take action on the answers you are given. In doing so, you reinforce the importance of self-awareness, and you begin to create a strong sense of trust within yourself and toward yourself. This will further increase your level of self-awareness, while also increasing your capacity to experience stoicism, as well as other great benefits such as greater self-confidence, self-esteem, and fulfillment.

Choosing Stoic Alternatives

As you begin to embrace self-awareness and develop a capacity to recognize your thoughts and emotions, you can create the space for you to recognize what your automatic behaviors look like, and to choose stoic alternatives. Your automatic behaviors are the habitual behaviors that you engage in based on whichever thoughts or emotions you are experiencing. Often, these behaviors are rooted in an emotional background, which means they may not necessarily be the best direction for you to choose as they may lack sound reasoning behind them. Even if you do decide that your automatic behaviors are ideal, you should always engage in them intentionally and from a conscious state of mind and voluntary behavior, as this ensures that you are creating outcomes on purpose, rather than by habit.

Choosing stoic alternatives ultimately means that you are going to choose to address each and every situation you come into from a logical and rational point of view, regardless of how you feel or how you feel pushed to behave. You should always focus on choosing voluntary thoughts and behaviors that will ultimately serve your fulfillment, happiness, and a sense of purpose, as this is, after all, the entire point of stoicism. Once you have consciously chosen an ideal solution for yourself, you can begin to act on that solution and create more success for yourself in terms of developing your stoic behavior and improving your life through stoicism.

SILENCE IS another behavior that goes hand-in-hand with stoicism. In fact, many people confuse stoicism as simply being an act of being quiet and reserved, because silence and stillness are where stoics are able to tap into their thoughts and choose logic over emotions. It is often in those moments of pause that they are able to recognize where their emotions exist and what their emotions are attempting to achieve, while also being able to recognize what the logical expression is for those emotional experiences.

In life, you will find that there are many natural points of silence or pause that you can use to your advantage, and that there are plenty of points where you can create your own sense of silence to use to your advantage. These are all great opportunities for you to momentarily pause from the busyness of the world so that you can focus on what is going on inside of you and create logical and rational responses for how you feel, and what you want and what you need.

Learning how to identify these points of stillness or pause and use them to your advantage takes time and practice, as we do live in a world that promotes busyness and noise. If you are used to being on the go all the time, and suddenly you try to recognize points to pause and take inventory of yourself, this can be uncomfortable or even strange. This may feel even more challenging if you are used to experiencing instant gratification in certain experiences, such as when you are expressing your emotions, and suddenly you try to change those experiences, such as by pausing to choose an intentional response.

Why Stoicism Often Looks Like Stillness

Stoicism looks a lot like stillness because of the nature of stoicism. This particular way of life is not about rushing into action and acting in ways that nurture your emotional need for instant gratification. Instead, stoicism is about using the power of your brain intentionally, which looks rather slow compared to the way we live our modern lives. When you use your brain properly, amplifying all of the power it has, there are many steps that need to happen before you can take action on anything, even actions as simple as speaking your opinion.

First, you have to observe the situation and take in as much information as you can so that you can create as honest and clear of a perspective as possible. The common way of doing things is to assume that your initial impression is right, while the stoic way of doing things is to recognize that your initial impression is probably wrong. Then, once you have collected enough information, you can begin to decide what it all means and choose how you are going to think in relation to this information. This particular part of the process can take some time as you will need to think about your impression of the information, too, to ensure that your impression is rooted in logic and not in an emotional response you are having to said information. Once you have accurately identified what everything means and what your chosen perspective is, you have to decide what your voluntary actions will, or will not be. Again, you then have to address your choices to ensure that you have chosen actions that are rooted in logic and that are going to have your desired outcome, not actions that are rooted in an emotional drive.

Going through all of these steps can be time consuming, and it is definitely not for the faint of heart. It takes a lot of practice to break away from the habit of responding or reacting to things immediately, and instead doing so intentionally and in a way that helps you achieve the results you desire. It is important, however, that you learn to do this as in doing so, you will find ways for you to begin experiencing far more aligned outcomes that get you much closer to your goals, as well as much closer to feelings of happiness, fulfillment, and purpose.

How to Cultivate a State of Quietness in Your Life

There are many ways that you can cultivate a state of quietness in your life. The best way to get started, however, is to recognize areas where natural quiet already exists in your life and use that to begin to build the foundation for quietness in your life. Generally speaking, each and every one of us experiences a moment of pause before we experience a reaction in our lives, no matter how intense that reaction may be. Particularly intense reactions, or reactions that are rooted in habit, may feel challenging to identify that pause for because they can come on fast and strong. However, there is *always* a moment of pause where your brain works to interpret the information you have received and then select a response to it. If you can begin to identify that moment of pause, you can start leaning into it, rather than rushing into a reaction over everything you experience in your life.

Leaning into a pause simply means that you recognize the moment where you are processing information and choose to intentionally begin to consciously process that information. You will likely still experience the subconscious reaction to that information, but you can consciously choose to factor that in as a piece of information, rather than use it as the chosen response. Then, you can begin to consciously choose what other pieces of information to factor in before making a choice as to what specific thoughts and behaviors you will use to respond to that information, too.

Another form of quietness you can incorporate into your life includes routine quietness. This would include 1-2 quietness "sessions" where you simply sit around and reflect as a part of your daily routine. You can incorporate these into your morning, afternoon, and/or nighttime stoicism routines; however, it is important that these are not structured periods of quiet. Instead, these should be around 10-15 minutes where you allow yourself to simply sit and recognize whatever comes up and then logically process it. This way, rather than forcing yourself to focus on something specific, you are allowing your mind to draw awareness to things that you feel still require time and attention. Then, you can work with your brain to naturally bring intentional resolutions to these things.

What to Do With Your Quietness

Once you have managed to identify areas where silence can exist within your life, you need to decide what you are going to do to maximize that silence. Remember, the purpose of silence is not for it to merely exist, but for you to have space to decide on a logical interpretation of what you are experiencing, formulate your personal opinion, and choose a reasonable response to the experience. This can be completed both in the moment that you are experiencing something, and after the fact.

During those moments of silence that occur immediately before you naturally want to react to a situation that is currently unfolding, you want to use that silence to make sure you have a clear understanding of what is going on. In these active moments, it can seem more challenging to go through the process quickly, so remember that your primary goal is to avoid experiencing an over-reaction of your emotions. With that in mind, you might make best use of your time by ensuring that you have all of the unbiased information, and that you thoroughly understand what the best decision is for you to make. In particularly heated situations, or ones where the stakes are rather high, you might consider specifi-cally asking for time to think through what your response will be. In doing so, you cultivate more time for you to reasonably respond to the situation you are experiencing. Otherwise, you can mini-mize the time it takes to respond to active situations by spending time getting to know yourself better. When you know yourself better in general, it becomes easier to understand your own opinion on and stance around various situations, and to identify what it would be in situations that are completely new to you. This way, you can think quickly and respond faster, and in a way that is still in integrity with your truth, during actively unfolding situations.

If you are using silence to reflect on things that are still affecting you, the end goal is to find resolve for those situations so that they stop taking up space in your mind. The fact that they are continuing to come up for you shows that you have yet to find closure, and so they are continuing to affect your thinking patterns. Giving yourself this space of silence means you can think about what really happened, do your best to gain retroactive perspective around the situation, identify your opinion then and now, and use the information you have gathered to find closure. That closure could be changing your mindset around the situation, or it could be releasing your emotions or taking voluntary action to bring offi-cial closure to the situation. If you do choose to take action, be sure that it is rooted in logic and not built-up, unexpressed emotions.

That way, the official closure truly does allow you to lay the situation to rest, rather than create more emotional and mental discomfort for you.

Turning Quietness Into Your Routine

Turning quietness into a part of your regular routine is a powerful way to give yourself the opportunity to take care of your mind, so much so that it allows you to create a deepened sense of calmness. When you regularly engage in silence, you give yourself frequent opportunities to let go of anything that has been bothering you and to create space for true silence in your mind. By that I mean, rather than cultivating silence so that you have room to bring closure to situations that may still be bothering you, you will be cultivating silence that allows you to simply sit in stillness and peace.

Even if you think you do not need to experience silence and stillness, give yourself space for it. You might be surprised to discover what types of problems may be lingering beyond your conscious awareness, ready to come forth when you create enough space for yourself to sit with them. The more often you can do this, the more you will be able to work through such things and truly calm what is going on beneath the surface of your conscious mind, thus giving you access to true peace, fulfillment, happiness, and purpose in your life. If you do find that you sit in stillness and silence and absolutely nothing comes up, enjoy this as a moment of quiet, which can be just as valuable to your wellbeing as a moment of processing.

Stoicism itself is a very simple, straightforward school of thought that is not meant to be debated. Therefore there is very little to do with stoicism that is up for discussion. With that being said, having things to consider and questions to ask yourself is an important way for you to understand yourself and your personal philosophy on life more, which can help keep you more grounded and connected with your sense of wellbeing. If you want to incorporate one interesting practice into your daily stoic routines, consider sitting down and writing your own food for thought surrounding logic, emotion, and stoicism. Otherwise, here are five great pieces from my personal journal that might help you get started.

Live Every Day as If It Were Your Last

Seneca, a Roman Stoic philosopher, once said: *"You live as if you were destined to live forever, no thought of your frailty ever enters your head, of how much time has already gone by you take no heed. You squander time as if you drew from a full and abundant supply, though all the while that day which you bestow on some person or thing is perhaps your last."*

For centuries, people have falsely believed that death makes life pointless and that there is no reason for us to try to make a happy, fulfilling, and meaningful life because we are all going to die one day, anyway. After all, why bother putting all that energy in when it will all end eventually? Seneca saw it differently, and so should you.

The truth is, death gives life purpose. Death makes life worth living, because it allows you to realize that your life is a precious and limited resource, and that you should make the most of it while you have it. Going through the world with an arrogant attitude, either refusing to improve your life because it will end one day, or refusing to improve your life because you have plenty left, only robs you of the time you have right now. The reality is, you have no idea when your time will end, and when the day comes that your time is drawing near, you will wish you had spent your time more wisely and that you had valued your life more greatly.

If you live every day as if this were to be your last day, you give yourself the opportunity to recognize what truly matters to you, and to act on that. Here, you discover what your values are, and then you create the opportunity for you to live through those values to ensure that you are living in alignment with your integrity. You also allow yourself to hold such great value over your own life, and the things that matter to you. With this mindset, you hold close to those you care about, you cherish and value their happiness, and you cherish and value your own.

Perhaps one of the greatest benefits you will gain from living this way is realizing that you care about a lot more than you thought you did, and you don't care about many of the things you thought you did, too. For example, you might discover that the sunrise and the sunset look more stunning when you think they may be your last, and that it does not really matter to you that your friend showed up 15 minutes late for lunch again because you are still glad to see them. This way, you stop fretting over the things that don't matter, and you start considering the things that truly do. Through this, you maximize the peace you experience in your life, and you grant yourself a beautiful earthly experience so long as yours lasts.

Food Is a Great Tool to Test Your Self-Control

Food is a necessity, but it is also something that many people vastly struggle with. Overeating, undereating, eating at the wrong times, eating the wrong things, and otherwise having issues with eating is a problem that runs rampant in our society. Very few people truly eat a diet that is natural and healthy for their body, and that allows them to experience the best health possible. The likely reason behind that is because there is an abundance of food of all varieties, and food truly does have the power to create sensations of reward in our brains. You can reward yourself through food at any hour of the day, through any food item you desire, and in any quantity that you desire. This is likely why so many people struggle with things like stress eating, or eating for comfort or emotional purposes. In our most natural form, prior to the abundant availability of food, we would have eaten when food was available to us, not when we simply felt bored or uncomfortable and wanted to busy ourselves or comfort ourselves through food.

Testing your sense of self-control can best be done by paying attention to your diet and noticing how you behave around the food itself. The pleasure of food is felt in the tongue, but the purpose of food is to assimilate with and nourish the body. So, are you giving into food for the purpose of pleasure, or working with food for the purpose of nourishment? Or, are you managing to create an instance where you can enjoy both of these outcomes from food in a positive and healthy manner?

A person who knows how to withhold from eating food when food is not truly needed, or from eating foods that are not truly good for them is a person with a great sense of personal strength. This is an individual who can recognize the logical importance of nourishing their body, and of refraining from foods that could be harmful to their body so that they can experience great health. In the end, they are taking optimal care of themselves and their body. Further, healthy foods can often be made in such a way that it is delicious for the person eating them. As food itself is supposed to be enjoyed, someone who can truly enjoy their food *and* make choices to nourish their body is someone who is truly engaging in the maximum amount of self-control around food.

Before you eat, at any time, ask yourself: am I eating this for pleasure, or for purpose? If the answer is for pleasure, consider using this as an opportunity to understand what it is that you are truly seeking, and to discover new ways to fulfill your desires. If your answer is for purpose, or for both of these reasons, then you are likely to eat for a great reason, and you should go ahead and continue on with your meal!

Failure Is a Natural Experience; Regret Is a Foolish Choice

No matter who you talk to, everyone has failed at one point or another. Failure, in some cases, may be subjective, while in others, it may be obvious. Either way, we have all experienced both forms of failure in the past, and likely we have all had trouble letting go of some of those failures we have experienced at different points in the past. It is important to note that failure is, without a doubt, an inevitable experience in life. Some of your failures are going to be small and will be easy to get over, while other failures are going to be massive and are going to feel like you have truly made possibly the worst mistake of your life. And, maybe you have. At least one of your mistakes has to be the worst one, after all, right?

No matter what failure you are facing, though, or the magnitude of consequences you are dealing with as a result of that failure, you must realize that failure is inevitable, and regret is a choice you do not have to make. To quote one of the major Stoic contributors Marcus Aurelius, the emperor of Rome, *"The impediment to action advances action. What stands in the way becomes the way."* This quote reminds us that failure is inevitable, but that no amount of failure has to stop you from continuing forward with whatever it is that you desire. If you truly desire something, you can easily move forward with pursuing that desire no matter what comes up or attempts to derail you from success. As long as you are willing to continue to put in the effort and make strides toward your success, you will see success in your lifetime.

Rather than being surprised by failure, expect it. And, do not allow the expectation of failure to prevent you from taking action for fear of what that failure will look like or feel like. Instead, embrace the fact that failure is inevitable and decide that should it strike, you will regroup and continue moving on, anyway. There *is* life after failure.

One more interesting food for thought surrounding failure is that the ancient Stoics believed that if you chose to engage in negative visualizations of what was yet to come, you were preparing yourself for the worst. In this way, you would be sure to be level-headed and prepared for the worst-case scenario, because you had already imagined it and decided to go on in spite of its possibility. For example, let's say you are about to give a speech on presentation for your boss. If the worst case scenario was that you made yourself look silly by stumbling over something and hurting yourself, you could visualize this happening, then visualize what would happen *after* that experience. This way, you are already ready for what could happen if everything went wrong, and so you are less afraid of it because you realize it is beyond your control, but what is within your control

In regards to your past, visualizing something bad or unwanted that happened over and over again will only create feelings of regret within yourself. Since the past is out of your control, and there is no practical or logical reason for you experiencing regret or anger in reference to your past, you are wasting your time and behaving in a way that is certainly not stoic. Instead, use the past and your failures to learn lessons and to help you grow so that you can do better in the future, then bring closure to your past experiences. This way, you can stop using these failures to hold you back.

Be Sure to Focus on the Small Things

Frequently, we are told to "focus on the bigger picture" and consider the end goal in our lives. In stoicism, you are taught to do this as a way to ensure that everything you concern yourself with is, in fact, worth concerning yourself with. While considering the bigger picture is important, it is also important that you take time out of your day to focus on the small things in your life. Especially in a society where we are rushed and always focusing on the next thing, it can be easy to forget about the little things that make life worth living, and that adds to the color and experience of life itself.

Never underestimate small conversations, beautiful scenery, little actions you take, or things that you would generally consider to be "too small to care about." Everything in your life is worth paying attention to, as each of the actions you take and the experiences you have are contributing to the outcome of your life. Little random things on a day to day basis matter, and little things changed over the course of several days matter.

For the random little things, you never know which random conversation might spark a new opportunity for you, or change the course of your life forever. Perhaps you say hello to someone in a grocery store, and they offer you an abundance of wisdom, or you say hello to someone at the bus stop, and they offer you the job opportunity you have been dreaming of your entire life. Or, perhaps your decision to eat at one restaurant or another saves you from getting food poisoning on that particular day, which means that you are healthy enough to accept a new job opportunity at work on the days you did not miss because you were not sick. You never know how your little choices and all of the little things you do are affecting your life, so pay close attention and make the choices that feel right for you.

For daily changes, consider the fact that one small change to your day, repeated over several days, can lead to massive change. For example, imagine if you switched out your daily soda for a glass of water, or your daily elevator ride for a chance to walk up the stairs instead. Or even if you just chose to walk up part of the stairs instead of all of them. Imagine how much your health would change from these tiny, simple choices. It may not seem like a lot, but your risk for developing health issues would be reduced, your wellness would be improved, and your quality of life would likely increase greatly. Plus, who knows, maybe when you go refill your cup of water in the break room, you gain a new opportunity, or when you are taking the stairs instead of the elevator, you come across your new best friend. You truly never know how the little things are all coming together to create the rest of your life, but know that they *always* are.

Ditch the Idea of Vanity

Finally, one of the most important things you can do for yourself is ditching the concept of vanity. Now, when I say this, understand that I strongly believe it is important to feel good about yourself, and when you look good, you feel good. You should take pride in how you look, and you should make the choices that *you* want to make, that will help you look good in *your* eyes. However, beyond this aspect of vanity, you need to throw the entire concept of vanity away.

Making choices that will make you look good to other people, whether it is based on the life choices you are making or the way you are physically presenting yourself, is a terrible idea. It may seem like a good idea in the short term when you find yourself possibly getting a certain opportunity because you chose to misrepresent yourself, but in the long run, it leads to you having to hold up a series of exhausting masks in your life. Nothing could be crueler to yourself than forcing yourself to use the two things you can control, your thoughts and your voluntary actions, to pretend to be someone that you are not. Saying you are someone you are not because it makes you sound better, doing things you hate doing because it makes you look better, or changing the way you look because it makes other people look at you better, is never a good idea. No amount of short term gratification from these choices is worth the long term disappointment, regret, and possibly even guilt and shame that you might face after having made these decisions.

You need to make decisions that are in integrity with who you are, and that includes how you represent yourself in terms of the way you speak, the things you do, and the way you arrange your physical appearance. This way, you are able to gain the opportunities that are meant *for you,* and you are able to get access to the types of situations that *you* would actually want to be a part of. Remember, this is your life and you have a hand in making it, and you should make one that you would be proud of and that you would genuinely enjoy being a part of. Otherwise, you are wasting your time and wasting your personal sense of power.

WITH STOICISM BEING FOUNDED in 3rd century BC, it makes sense that some of the teachings may seem outdated for our modern world. As you continue to learn about stoicism and embrace it in your life, it can help to understand specific ways that stoicism can actually be integrated into your modern life in a way that is relevant to our modern way of living, and overall culture. The following chapter has been designed to help you integrate stoicism into your life in a deep, meaningful way so that you can make the most of it in your modern life. As always, these are speculations, and you can integrate them in whatever way that you see fit. You may benefit from writing these down in your own journal and speculating on your own understanding or beliefs around how you can integrate stoicism into your modern life, too, to help you further improve your sense of stoicism and find ways to integrate it that work best for you.

Manage Your Attitude

Sass, arrogance, and entitlement seem to be words that are strongly rooted in our modern culture. As we continue to see a rise in personal freedoms, we also see a rise in people using fierceness and attitude as a way to liberate themselves from the confines that society may have placed on them at some point in their history. While certain levels of arrogance and entitlement can help you develop the confidence and esteem to live the type of life you desire, too much can turn you into someone that is rather rude, and who constantly feels as though they are a victim of the world around them.

Think of it this way, if you constantly believe that the world owes you something, and yet you cannot control the world around you, how are you going to cash in on that "debt?" You aren't. Further, the world doesn't, in fact, owe you anything. Yet, still, people seem to hold this belief, and will victimize themselves anytime the debt is not fulfilled. This can create a constant sense of frustration, disappointment, anger, and feelings of being betrayed or let down by the world around you. Of course, this is not the case: you were not owed anything in the first place, and you were never able to control you receiving said things you believed you were owed, anyway. Ultimately, you set yourself up for failure.

Rather than clinging to arrogance and entitlement and landing yourself in constant disappointments and let downs, consider instead paying attention to your own attitude and seeing what you can adjust within yourself. Where do you believe you are owed something, when you are not? What lead you to believe you were owed such things? What lead you to believe that other people were responsible for fulfilling said things in your life? Use reflection as a way to begin to understand the feelings you are experiencing, and to understand why you have landed yourself in this original attitude in the first place. Then, humble yourself.

Recognize that the only person who can reliably do anything for you, is you. That is not because other people do not care about you, do not wish the best for you, or do not want to help you. It is, however, because only you truly understand what you need, and only you can understand what can specifically be done to help you fulfill those needs. Others can help, but they cannot actually do it for you. Even if they could, it would not be nearly as fulfilling because you are *meant* to be the one to do it for yourself. That is the whole point.

Once you adjust your attitude and humble yourself, start focusing on what it is that you were really looking for in your entitlement, and begin to identify ways that you can create that for yourself in your own life. For example, if you believed you were entitled to have your basic needs of survival met by others, you may be feeling a need for more ease and more security in your life. So, create a circumstance for yourself where you can fulfill your own needs abundantly and with as much ease as possible. As you learn to begin taking responsibility for yourself and adjusting your attitude to place you in a position of power, you will find yourself navigating our modern world in a far more effortless manner.

Avoid Materialism

Our throw-away culture is dangerous, not only for our environment but for our wellbeing. So many negative mental, emotional, and physical repercussions can come from you engaging in materialism, to the point where it is truly not worthy for you to fall into its trap and remain caught there. Realizing the dangers that lurk in materialism can help you recognize why you must stay away from it, and can help motivate you to experience life in a different manner.

First and foremost, the mental impact of materialism is dangerous because it stimulates constant feelings of stress, fading fulfillment, a need to keep up, and feelings of overwhelm in your life. When you engage in materialism, you find yourself constantly wanting more, to the point where you believe that you need it, which means you are always going to be working as hard as you can to get more. Then, when you get it, you may feel a moment of fulfillment, only to fall back into feeling like you need more again right away. In fact, many people do not even feel that moment of fulfillment anymore because what they want exceeds what they can afford at any given time, thus leaving them in a perpetual state of wanting and working toward fulfilling their never ending wish list. This behavior is incredibly overwhelming, and completely unnecessary.

The mental repercussions can lead to the emotional repercussions of never feeling happy or fulfilled, feeling feelings of regret and buyer's remorse, or feeling feelings of being unworthy and undeserving because you are never "good enough" to have it all. You might find yourself feeling sad, isolated, forsaken, forgotten, and let down by society because it seems as though everyone has what you want, except for you. You might also find yourself feeling overwhelmed, tired, and frustrated by the amount of stress you accrue from the mental load of trying to keep up with your never ending desires that seem to lack any reasonable level of fulfillment or reward.

Physically, your world can become overrun by your material items, and that can leave you experiencing even more stress, too. Having a house full of clutter can impose many issues in your life, and can also result in you contributing to the throw-away culture that is so dangerous and damaging to our planet and all of the inhabitants of it, including ourselves.

Rather than getting caught up in consumerism, learn to buy only what you need and appreciate what you have. Then, spend all of that extra time in your life enjoying other things, like the world around you, the relationships you share with the people you love, or the hobbies that you enjoy. When you do things that are truly meaningful and that bring higher levels of fulfillment in the long run, you live a life that is far more worthy of your time and effort. In the end, you experience far less stress, happier and healthier emotions, greater rewards and fulfillment, a true sense of purpose, a greater sense of confidence and self-esteem, and a more positive impact on the environment around you.

Use Lack to Stimulate Appreciation

In our modern world, everything is available on demand. You can communicate with your friends in an instant, eat anything you want whenever you want, buy anything from anywhere, have things overnight shipped to you, and ultimately do whatever you want, whenever you want. Of course, there are various restrictions and limitations on that, but our access to various resources is greater than it has ever been, and easier than it has ever been. The result of that is something wonderful, but it can be easy to lose sight of how wonderful when you do not regularly take time to appreciate what your life is like with all of these wonderful benefits.

While you cannot eliminate your access in life, nor would you want to or even need to, you should regularly take time to consider what life would be like without access to all of these wonderful things. Consider what it would be like if it were challenging for you to connect with your friends, or if you did not get to see them as often as you do now. Think about how life might be different if you could not easily go to your fridge and grab food, or even go to the grocery store and get something to eat. Imagine what it would be like if you did not have access to many of the wonderful people and resources you have access to today, and allow yourself to use this as a way to recognize how enriched your life is as a result of all of these things.

Knowing how to recognize, experience, and express true gratitude for everything in your life is crucial. It is important to realize that your life, even amid any struggles you may have, is filled with many wonderful things, and that you have plenty to be grateful for. This does not mean that you do not deserve the right to be upset about injustices, misfortunes, or setbacks, but it does help you realize that your life is not exclusively filled with said things. Likewise, your life is not exclusively filled with positive, wonderful wins, and effortless experiences. Instead, your life is a series of many different positive and negative experiences, and amid it all, you have plenty of reasons to be grateful.

If you want to take this particular lesson a step further, give yourself time to ponder and navigate any feelings you have at the idea of any of these things not being present in your life. For example, imagine if you no longer had your friends in your life. This may feel depressing and uncomfortable at first, which goes to show you how enriching they are to your life and how much joy they bring you. However, you can also take this as an opportunity to consider how you might be able to enrich and empower yourself to continue having a good life even if your friends were not present in your life. This way, you can experience gratitude and joy with your friends in your life, without feeling unhealthy levels of attachment. Since everything in life is temporary, including life itself, this ensures that you are able to manage the emotional and mental impact of eventually losing your friends one day, when your relationship is ready to come to a close. While it will not make it any less sad, or minimize your grief in any way, it will remind you that your friend was not responsible for your happiness or fulfillment, you were. And, even though it may feel painful to do it without them, you are still fully capable of living a fulfilling life without that person in your life.

Create Genuine Cheer in Your Life

In another famous writing by Seneca, he quoted "*A man thus grounded must, whether he wills or not, necessarily be attended by a constant cheerfulness and a joy that is deep and issues from deep within, since he finds delight in his own resources, and desires no joys greater than his inner joys."* What Seneca meant by that was, no matter what is going on in your life, when you know that you are responsible for your own inner fulfillment and you are success-fully fulfilling it, there is a constant inner sense of joy that you experience because of that.

This constant sense of inner joy means that, whether you mean to or not, you will bring a sense of cheer with you into every situation, no matter what it is, because you know in the deepest way possible that, no matter what happens, you will be okay. Many people live their lives devoid of this true inner sense of joy, and therefore live in constant fear that everything they care for and work for in life could be taken away from them. If you live in a constant state of fear that everything could be taken away from you, this means that you have not created a sense of fulfillment within yourself. The fulfillment of inner joy is something that no one and nothing can take away from you, except for yourself. If something outside of you can take it away, you have yet to truly create that sense of fulfillment, which simply means that you need to keep working toward fulfilling it.

When you create this sense of inner joy, do not be afraid to embrace it and relish in it. Use it as an opportunity to create even more joy for yourself, and allow yourself to create that joy no matter what situation you are in. Find your own silver linings, in a way that genuinely feels good for you and brings you joy. Even if that silver lining is that you are responsible for connecting with your own resources, and therefore you have the capacity to create a safe space for you to navigate challenging emotions or situations away from a constant influx of chaos.

One of the most meaningful things to a stoic is the desire to have human experiences, and human experiences include both positive and negative experiences. With that in mind, even if the only thing you can feel cheerful about is the realization that you are having a human experience, have cheer for that. People around you might see you as being annoying or even frustrating to be around because you are so attached to your cheer, but that is not your problem. If you make it your problem, you are giving up your inner joy for the outside world. Instead, resolve to remain true to yourself and to remain true to your faculties, and continue to experience that inner sense of fulfillment and cheer no matter what.

Practice What You Value

One of the most tragic aspects of our modern society is that gaining information has become so easy that very few people digest and integrate information into their lives. Instead, people are constantly in the pursuit of consuming more information, without ever truly valuing or integrating the information that they already have. It sounds an awful lot like our modern issues with materialism, no?

Rather than being among the part of society that always wants to know better but never wants to do better, stop. Knowledge is not something to collect so that you can feel proud lingering your knowledge over the heads of others, nor is it something to collect. While knowledge is powerful, knowing without implementing is simply overwhelming your mind with more knowledge than you need. Thus begins the cycle of information overload, which can make it increasingly more challenging for you to truly digest and integrate the knowledge you are learning as you begin to become overwhelmed with the facts and you struggle to integrate any of it.

Whenever you find yourself collecting knowledge in life that helps you better understand what your own values are and how you can live in integrity with them, and yourself, use that knowledge. Integrate that knowledge, practice what you preach, and give yourself the opportunity to truly experience all of the fulfilling benefits of everything that you have been learning about. This way, you are actually gaining benefits from your knowledge, rather than merely filling your head and overwhelming yourself with facts that you know you will never use in your life.

Further, stop preaching your values and trying to promote yourself based on values that you are not actively integrating in your life. For example, if you value experiences over materialism, but you are constantly shopping and never devoting time to having meaningful experiences in your life, do not preach about your values. Doing so may help you feel proud and may feed your ego, but at the end of the day, it only makes you look silly and it leads to you suffering, as you are not actually living in alignment with your values *and* you are moving away from integrity and honesty. Instead of worrying about what other people think or promoting your values to everyone around you, simply live in alignment with them. Let your actions and your life be a clear representation of your values, and use that to help you create experiences that are honest and in integrity with who you are.

CONCLUSION

Congratulations on reading *Stoicism!* This book was written to introduce you to the school of philosophy that is known as stoicism, including the history of stoicism, the philosophy of stoicism, and the implementation of stoicism. Each chapter was designed to give you some insight into what this school of thought is, where it came from, why it exists, and how you can use it to help you create a much higher quality of life for yourself.

I hope that after reading this book, you find yourself recognizing where your true power lies, and how you can use that power to support yourself in having a higher quality of life overall. So many people believe that happiness, fulfillment, and a sense of purpose comes from the external world. They seek these experiences through their careers, purchases, relationships, and circumstances, and subject themselves to massive amounts of suffering when they do not find what they are looking for. Or, worse, when they find a false sense of what they are looking for and then lose it because everything in life is temporary, including life itself.

As you now know, the only true source of fulfillment, happiness, and purpose comes from within you. There is no other constant source of any of these experiences, and no source that will give you as deep or as fulfilling of an experience as the one that comes from inside of yourself. When you learn to create these things within yourself, you will live with a constant state of cheer in your heart and soul because you realize that nothing you experience in life, no matter how great or how awful, can change your inner state. While it may enrich your experience or teach you how to have an even better one, nothing can take away from that constant inner state of happiness, fulfillment, and purpose, and that is ultimately what we all seek in life.

Stoicism itself is not something that is meant to be debated; it simply is. It is developed and rooted in the process of taking action, recognizing where your power lies, and using that power to your advantage in life. Even so, there are plenty of ways that we can elaborate on what that looks like, how it feels, and what you can do to use that sense of power to integrate yourself into the life experiences that you truly desire.

After reading this book, the best thing you can possibly do for yourself is begin to develop a daily routine for stoicism in your life. Develop your morning, afternoon, and nighttime stoic routines so that you can begin to create plenty of time for you to reflect, practice mindfulness, and live life in reasonable alignment with your truth, rather than by the irrational choices of your emotions. This way, you are able to begin creating a life you truly desire. Also, remember that while your emotions are valuable and inevitable, they are not always honest or necessary to act on. Use logic and reasoning to understand every emotion you have, to identify its purpose, and to choose resolutions for yourself and every situation you are a part of that will allow you to create the results you truly desire. The more you can act from a place of logic and reasoning, the more happiness, fulfillment, and purpose you will achieve. Of course, just like the original Stoics, don't hold yourself up in a light of perfectionism, either. Everyone makes mistakes, and failure is inevitable. Rather than hiding from failure or attempting to be perfect, accept yourself and any mistakes you make and resolve to learn from them and move on. You are, after all, only human, and mistakes and failure are a part of the human experience.

Lastly, before you go, I want to ask a favor. Would you please take a moment to review the book *Stoicism* on Amazon Kindle? Your honest feedback would be greatly appreciated, as it helps others discover this wonderful title, and helps me create more great books for you.

Thank you!

EMOTIONAL INTELLIGENCE

Improve Self-Awareness, Self-Regulation,
Emotional Agility, with Empathy

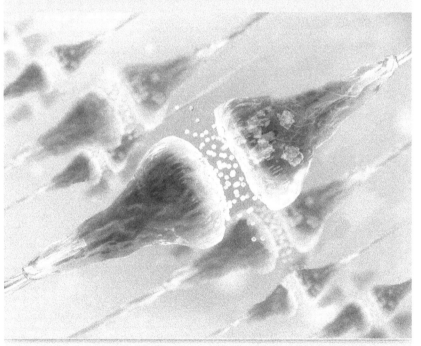

R H O N D A   S W A N

Emotional intelligence is incredibly important. It is necessary for people to be able to ensure that they can respond appropriately to those around them. It can be the difference between blowing up at someone and being able to keep your cool. When you lack emotional intelligence, your relationships will suffer. You will struggle in life. You will struggle to solve conflict or go through anything else that matters. You will struggle in many ways when it comes to interacting with other people, and that can make the difference between being able to be successful in your endeavors and failing.

When it comes down to it, your social skills will either make or break you. If you do not have good social skills, people will not want to be around you. They will not want to put up with you. They will prefer to avoid you whenever possible, and for good reason—if you cannot cope with stress or interact meaningfully with others, you put unnecessary strain and burden on those around you. You make it harder for yourself to do just about anything.

Emotional intelligence is the measure of your social skills. It is the measure of how you can do with other people. It is a way of determining how well you can function in social settings. It involves several different competencies that consist of several smaller skills that come together. These are skills that will aid in being able to better manage just about every aspect of your relationships with other people. This is crucially important to your ability to successfully interact with others.

Within this book, we are going to address what emotional intelligence is. We are going to go through all the pertinent information that you will need to know to better understand what it means to be emotionally intelligent, how you can become emotionally intelligent, and more. We will spend some time looking at empathy and emotional intelligence. We will understand why and how this skillset matters so much. We will take a look at people that may be struggling with their emotional intelligence at the moment as well as how to begin to strengthen it as well.

By reading this book, you will be able to learn how to arm yourself. You will learn how you can better develop these skills so you can be successful in your own endeavors. You will learn to be able to develop the skills that are going to work together to make you successful. You will learn about everything that you will need to know, and you will learn how you can put it to good use.

There are plenty of books on this subject on the market, thanks again for choosing this one! Every effort was made to ensure it is full of as much useful information as possible; please enjoy!

1 / WHAT IS EMOTIONAL INTELLIGENCE?

IMAGINE that you are at a party with friends. You and your friends are all sitting together at the table, talking. You voice some sort of personal preference toward something, and suddenly, someone else at the table gets immediately enraged. Instead of stopping to spend some time talking to you about their own disagreement, they screamed and berated you for being wrong at the end of the day. Rather than coming to an adult agreement that everyone could live with, these guidelines aid in ensuring that you do better. These guidelines ensure that at the end of the day, you are able to halt the behaviors that are likely to exacerbate the problem.

Within this chapter, we are going to take a closer look at emotional intelligence. In reading through this chapter, you will get a much clearer idea as to what emotional intelligence is and how you can use it yourself. As a crucial skill, you may feel like emotional intelligence would be limited somehow. You may assume that people cannot strengthen their own abilities to become emotionally intelligent people that they know that they can be. However, this particular trait is comprised of skillsets, and as such, it is quite simple to bolster it in all sorts of manners that will make this more noticeable. Think about it this way; however—the better that you get along with other people, the more emotionally intelligent you likely are.

Emotional Intelligence

To make sure that you understand what emotional intelligence is, you must be able to identify the definition of it. You must be able to understand what comprises this skillset so you can begin to recognize it, no matter the situation. You may think that this is something that would be difficult to identify and define, but it is actually quite simple. Ultimately, it comes with two distinct concepts that combine to create one overarching trait.

Firstly, you must be able to recognize, understand, and manage your own emotions. This is very simple—this is the ability to take a look at yourself and know your own emotional state. In order to become emotionally intelligent, you must be able to understand the ways that your emotions are going to impact you as an individual. Your emotions, especially when tensions run high, or you are feeling stressed out, will directly influence your behaviors. This is very important to remember—with stress or tension, you may find that your behaviors are more stress-driven. You may find that you are going to struggle to cope with the stress at hand. You may feel like being able to succeed is an impossibility and that could not be further from the truth.

Secondly, you must be able to consider the emotions of other people as well. You must be able to recognize the way that other people are feeling, oftentimes through taking a look at the behaviors that they exhibit, or their own body language. You must make sure that you understand their emotions—this is being able to relate to the way in which other people are feeling and is commonly linked to empathy. You must also understand how to influence other people's own emotional states as well.

This means, then, that emotional intelligence is the art of being able to understand and influence both the emotions of yourself and the emotions of others. It is your ability to navigate through the emotional behaviors that people have. It is the ability to understand the emotions of other people; also, you can ensure that you meet them. It is being able to see the way that the emotional current within a room changes so readily and suddenly.

In theory, these are skills that will be facilitative of relationships. It is nice to think that you will be able to understand or influence someone else to be able to change their behaviors. However, in practice, this becomes a skill set that is imperative to success. If you are going to work with other people, how can you do so if you do not see when they are upset? How can you work on a team with other people if you cannot possibly understand their perspectives or see the ways in which their emotions influence them?

At the end of the day, the emotional intelligence that you have will be apparent just about everywhere in your life. It will present repeatedly, no matter what it is that you do with yourself. It will show up in just about every way that you interact with other people, and because of that, you must make sure that you understand it. If you understand emotional intelligence and then recognize that you struggle with it, you are able to make the necessary changes to ensure that you are able to better it.

The skills in particular that you will see will have four facets to them. They involve perceiving, using, understanding, and managing emotions. Each of these involve slightly different actions on your own part that come together to create the act of being emotionally intelligent in the first place. Perceiving emotions is all about being capable of recognizing and identifying your own emotions, or the emotions of other people, whether you are looking at someone's body language, their words, or looking at some other form of expression. You are able to simply see and understand what the other person is feeling. Using emotions refers to the fact that you can make use of your emotions to be able to influence your responses. This is very important as well—it involves you being able to make use of the way that you think or the way that you approach a situation to encourage you to influence your own reaction to it. Understanding emotions allows you to be able to recognize the body language that someone else is showing and understand what it means. It is being able to recognize the nuances between what it means to be frustrated or annoyed by someone or something. It is very important in understanding these smaller differences and understanding that, at the end of the day, emotions are incredibly nuanced. You need to be able to recognize these nuances. Finally, managing these emotions is being able to regulate your own emotions, or to influence the emotions of other people as well.

. . .

Emotional intelligence is, ultimately, measured, much like how intelligence itself is—with a quotient defined by a test that is done. The difference between the two is that intelligence quotients (IQ) typically test to see how well you are able to rationalize something. Emotional intelligence quotients (EQ) focus on the ways that you respond; you would react to certain situations to determine how likely you are to be emotionally intelligent in the first place.

Before we move on to the rest of the book, we are going to see this play out with itself. We are going to take a look at an example of someone responding to the same situation with low, average, and high levels of emotional intelligence. Imagine for a moment that you have had a freak snowstorm in your area at home. Your entire town has shut down, and roads are closed. You are stuck at home with your children, who likewise are quite stressed out considering the current situation. Your children continue to bicker with each other and fight with each other about just about anything that happens. If one of them gets the purple plate, the other child throws a tantrum. If one child takes over to play video games, the other feels left out and frustrated. However, the last straw for you is that entirely accidentally and without malice, your child accidentally broke your living room television in a freak accident involving one of the controllers for your video game system.

We are now going to take a look at a typical response from a lower emotional intelligence level, an average level of emotional intelligence, and a high level of emotional intelligence. As you read, you will see that all three present incredibly different from each other, and this is to be expected, as each one is going to have a different degree of self-control.

Low Emotional Intelligence

Someone with low emotional intelligence may find that they do not take this well at all. They find that they do not recognize their own anger at all, and that means that their own anger is able to fester and potentially lead to worse problems. In this instance, you may not realize that you are angry when you are—as a direct result, you run into all sorts of other implications. You may find that you yell at your child for breaking a television, which likely is not cheap at all.

You may find that you do not recognize your anger and, therefore, do not understand the ways in which your anger hurts both yourself and those around you. You yell at your children for what they were doing with little regard to how that will make them feel because, if you do not recognize your own emotions, you cannot hope to find some way to manage them as well. You may find that your emotions are entirely out of control, and as a result, you behave impulsively.

Beyond that, however, you show no regard for how your emotions are influencing those around you. While you may not realize it in the moment, your own response to your anger absolutely will impact your children. It becomes that lens that your children see their own anger through—they are more likely to respond in kind because they saw you doing it. You set them up to emulate your behavioral tendencies and responses just by virtue of exposing them to it.

Average Emotional Intelligence

Someone with average emotional intelligence, on the other

hand, may get highly angry , especially at first upon realizing that a very expensive item was just damaged that will likely need to be replaced at some point. This is reasonable—no one, even those that are highly emotionally intelligent, are not saying that you are not allowed to be angry. You are more than welcome to be angry about the situation at hand. However, you should also be able to respond appropriately. In this instance, an appropriate response is likely telling your child that there will be a real consequence for their behaviors.

You may walk your child through the problem and talk to your child. You will likely be frustrated, and you may snap, especially at first, but you are able to stop yourself and remind yourself that you need to calm down and respond emotionally intelligently.

Average emotional intelligence is where the vast majority of people fall—their tempers or emotions may flare temporarily some-times, but they are not going to actually harm the way that you are able to interact with others. You are usually able to work out how best to manage yourself so you know how to interact with others. You are able to sort of recognize when those emotions are begin-ning to get out of hand so you can stop them, and that matters immensely. You need to be able to stop that temper when it flares. You need to be able to recognize when your temper becomes a problem and when it becomes a detriment to not only you but also those around you as well.

High Emotional Intelligence

Finally, when it comes down to having a higher emotional intelligence, you are usually able to not only see your own emotions and how they are impacting you, you can see how your own emotions are impacting your child as well. You may be able to tune in to the fact that your emotions are going to influence how those around you think and feel as well. You may recognize the ways in which you see other people reacting to you. You may see that your own emotions are leading to high emotions in the other person and you can use that fact, the fact that those around you will respond to your emotions, to influence how you present yourself.

You can essentially take control of the emotions of other people by ensuring that you respond appropriately and accordingly. You are able to prevent yourself from lashing out at people, knowing that if your own emotions get the better of you, you cannot hope to quell the emotions of those around you. In this instance, you know that your emotions and your response to your children will directly alter the way in which they respond to you. You see that when your temper gets the best of you, then your children respond in kind. However, you also see that when you respond calmly and rationally, your children return the favor. They see that ultimately, you are responding in a way that shows that you are empathizing with them. They recognize that you see the way in which they are trying their hardest to really respond well to them. They feel like they can trust you, and they feel better about the situation as well.

Your emotions will be highly influential on other people. They are able to get other people to think and act differently than ever. Your response to something can directly alter the response that everyone else has as well. If your response to something going wrong is to respond kindly and with compassion, you will naturally put other people at ease, and when you are highly emotionally intelligent, you not only know that, you count on that as well. You allow yourself to alter the way that other people respond to you just by virtue of recognizing that they will strongly be influenced by the way in which you are acting.

EMOTIONS ARE difficult to cope with on the best of days. Having highly rampant emotions can feel like a detriment more often than not when you are the one trying to cope with them, and that is not necessarily for lack of trying. Some of the highest tensions that can arise often come from uncontrolled emotions that have run rampant. Emotions, despite being incredibly important in your life, are also incredibly primitive on an evolutionary level. This is because they have been evolving over millions of years in order to help the body survive. In fact, the vagus nerve, a nerve believed to be a major regulator of emotional response to stress among other things, has been found to be present to some degree even in evolutionarily primitive animals, such as lizards.

Emotions themselves can be tricky to deal with. They can be good or bad. They can drive you toward acting in ways that you will regret or in encouraging you to change up what you are doing in hopes that, at the end of the day, you respond to them. They can lead to problems with relationships. They can lead to impulsive behaviors that are not helping anyone. They can cause you to act in ways that you regret.

However, before you begin to develop the ability to control your emotions, you must first be able to understand what they are in the first place You need to be able to understand what their evolutionary purpose is to understand better what it is that you are seeking to control and influence when it comes time to develop your own emotional intelligence. Recognizing those purposes will help you greatly in being able to take back control.

What Are Emotions?

Emotions themselves are quite difficult to really define in a concrete manner that everyone can agree to. It is one of those ideas that people understand but struggles to articulate when they are asked what it is. In this instance, emotions are an instinctive state of mind that are typically reactions to either internal or external stimuli. That may seem like a lot all right up front, but it is actually quite readily broken down into easier to understand bits.

It is instinctive—this is the state in which something is automatic for you. You instinctively know how to suck, swallow, and breathe, in that order, when you are a newborn baby to allow you to feed. That is an instinctive behavior that you have. You have other instinctive states and actions as well—such as your emotions. Your emotions happen automatically without you thinking about them. You do not hear a joke, think about it, consciously decide, "That's funny, so I should feel happy," and then laugh. Rather the state of happiness comes naturally without trying to force it and without trying to make it happen. This is important—it happens without effort on your part.

· · ·

Of course, if they are automatic, you may be wondering what the point of any of this is—if your emotions are automatic, can you really learn to control and influence them? The answer here is yes; you can learn that. However, we will be addressing that fact shortly. However, keep in mind that rather than influencing your emotions directly, you are often learning to have the restraint to hold yourself back from lashing out at someone or doing something that you will regret. You are controlling the actions more so than the emotions.

Emotions are also reactionary. This means that they are occurring in response to something else. You may feel angry when you see someone doing something that you disagree with. You may be sad when you see someone with a sign begging for food is sitting there with a child or a dog. It is important to note that, at the end of the day, your emotions directly come from the way in which you think about something that you have seen. It is understandable to feel sad when you hear about someone else losing their job or suffering from a loss in the family. It is normal to feel frightened when you are suddenly being chased by a bear. It is normal to feel angry if you feel like you are being threatened in some way.

Your emotions come from all of that. They are reactionary in the sense that you are feeling them after having been exposed to something, either internal or external. It could be that someone showed you a picture that made you sad. It could be that you had a frustrating thought. No matter what the root cause of your emotion is, one thing is for sure—it is usually in direct response to something else, and it is rarely ever consistent.

Your emotions are going to be influenced by just about anything around you. If you did not like the way that the wind blew, you could potentially be quite angry over it. They are not required to be rational, and oftentimes, they are not rational at all, and this is precisely why you need emotional intelligence. You need to be able to rely on the fact that you will sometimes feel in ways that do not make sense. You need to recognize that you will sometimes feel or want things that are not practical, and that is okay. You can learn to cope with it and move on.

Universal Emotions

Despite how complex emotions are, there is one way that they actually become simpler—they are universal. There are six, in fact, that are believed to be entirely universal. These are emotions that are meant to be shared with other people for all sorts of reasons. However, we are a social species, and there are great benefits to being socially skilled. It makes sense that we would have emotions that are universal—as social species, we need to be able to communicate clearly and effectively with those around us.

These emotions, which we will take a look at shortly, are believed to be entirely universal. This means that no matter where you go in the world, they will be recognized thanks to the universal expression of the body language. You could even find a remote tribe of humans that has not been in any contact with the outside world, and they would be able to read these expressions or express these emotions. This is very important to remember—you need to ensure that you understand that these emotions, in being universal, are those that you will face on a regular basis. You will feel them yourself. You will see other people showing signs of these emotions, and that matters greatly.

Keep in mind that each and every one of these emotions has their own purpose. They each serve you to keep you alive just a little bit longer in any way that they can. The universal emotions are:

- **Happiness:** This is a feeling that is meant to influence you into feeling like you should repeat what you did to trigger happiness. It is your reward emotion that is felt to remind you that your behaviors were good and beneficial to survival. You see this oftentimes with people and their children- they feel good with their children most of the time and they feel happy when they look at them.

- **Sadness:** This is sort of the antithesis to happiness in a lot of ways—your sadness is meant to make you recognize that whatever you did was a mistake. It is meant to make you feel bad, so you do not repeat whatever behaviors had just occurred, allowing you to learn from what had happened so you can avoid making that mistake again.

- **Fear:** This is an emotion that is meant to keep you alive. You feel fear when you are faced with something that you cannot fight off. You feel fear when you are in danger, and you know that you are being threatened. You recognize that your very life could be in peril. It is meant to put your body on high alert to protect yourself.

- **Anger:** Anger is a subsidiary to fear—it is a secondary emotion. You feel anger in response to a threat that first makes you feel fear. This is meant to help you feel like you can fight off the threat to defend yourself.

- **Disgust:** Disgust is something that you feel in response to seeing something repulsive. It may be that something smells really bad, and you feel disgusted, or you have seen some sort of behavior that you are not okay with. Either of these are common causes for disgust and the disgust that you feel is predominantly to keep you away. It is meant to be a sort of deterrent for you.

- **Surprise:** Finally, the last of the universal emotions is surprise. When it comes to surprise, you are responding to someone or something in a very strong manner. Typically, surprise is felt in response to something not lining up with what you expected to see. When the expectation and reality did not align, you found that ultimately, you needed to pay closer attention to see what it was.

The Cause of Emotions

When it comes right down to it, emotions vary greatly, and scientists and psychologists have not been able to come to an agreement on how emotions are generated within the body. The cause of emotions is difficult to really contend with, and so we have three common theories that are widely used. These three theories are the James-Lange theory, the Cannon-Bard theory, and the Schachter-Singer model. Each of these are slightly different, but they all attempt to explain the origins of emotions.

. . .

James-Lange theory

The first of the theories that we will discuss here is the James-Lange theory. This theory states that emotions begin as a physiological reaction to something external. That physiological reaction becomes interpreted in some way, and your mind then creates the proper response in return. Essentially, there is a stimulus that is felt or observed or experienced. Then, you have a physical response, known as arousal. That arousal is then interpreted to be an emotion.

Imagine for a moment that you are deathly afraid of geese. Geese, for some reason, had always terrified you because you were chased and pecked by one at a farm when you were young. Ever since then, you have had a phobia of geese.

Now, imagine that you are walking in the park with your dog. Then, you happen to see it—there is a goose staring at you. In response to the goose staring at you, your body prepares to run away if necessary. Your body pumps blood quicker, allowing you to be able to move quickly if necessary. Your body begins to breathe quicker to pull in enough oxygen to support that movement if it is necessary. You feel a spike in energy as adrenaline prepares you to be able to run if you need to. Your mind recognizes that all of this is happening. It sees the changes to your physiological state and it then begins to interpret them. You are then able to translate those physiological signs into the emotion of fear.

. . .

Cannon-Bard theory

The next primary understanding of emotions comes from the Cannon-Brad theory. This theory looks at the emotional response and the physiological response as simultaneous. One does not precede the other—rather, in response to the stimulus that you are responding to, your brain sends out signals to create the emotion while also creating the physical symptoms of that emotion at the same time. In particular, the hypothalamus controls the physical reaction while the cortex then creates the emotional aspect.

Think of it this way—as you are walking along the park path with your dog, you suddenly see a goose. In response to the goose, you feel your own pulse pick up, and your breathing patterns change. Simultaneously, you also feel fear. These go and in hand in this instance.

Schacter-Singer model

Finally, the last theory that we are looking at is slightly different. In this case, your emotion is created through a series of steps. While the previous examples have focused on a linear, one-step model, this one pushes two, and it actually makes perfect sense. With this model, you will ultimately have the stimulus appear. In this instance, you will be walking down the path just in time to see that big goose staring at you. The goose triggers a two-pronged reaction. The stimulus produces the arousal—that physical response to what you have experienced. On top of that physical response, however, you also have a cognitive experience as well.

Your emotion, then, is the creation of the combination between your physical arousal toward something as well as a core thought or belief about it. In this instance, you will experience that pounding of your heart and the flood of adrenaline in your body. This will combine with a thought that you have developed from your own trauma of having a negative experience with geese in the first place. Your physical response and your cognitive belief of geese are scary then combine to create the fear that you feel. However, that cognitive belief there could change things significantly. If you had a positive cognition instead, that fear would likely instead be translated into something else. Rather than fear, you would feel excitement instead. The underlying belief of the situation is ultimately what is going to directly influence the response that you have to whatever is happening.

Emotions as a Motivator

Emotions, then, serve their own very important roles in human behavior. In particular, they are designed to be major motivators. They are designed to encourage you to think or behave in a certain way in hopes of trying to keep you alive for as long as possible. This is primarily unconscious—your unconscious mind, the part that you cannot access on your own, is responsible for a wide range of the behaviors that you have to complete. Your unconscious mind controls how you feel as well. While your conscious and unconscious mind cannot directly communicate, your unconscious mind can influence your emotions in hope of influencing your behaviors as well.

. . .

Your emotions are there to help regulate out your responses, then —they are meant to trigger those instinctive behaviors that you will need to follow in hopes of keeping you alive. Think of it this way— you feel fear as an instinctive response, so you will instead stop and run from something rather than charging forward. The fear makes you feel like you should freeze up. Can you defeat the fear? Sure—but it is not particularly easy. Your body wants you to stop and be cautious, and overcoming it, while possible, could potentially uproot that entirely.

Essentially, your emotions exist as a part of a cycle that will become very relevant as you continue to understand emotional intelligence and everything that it can do for you. In particular, you must keep in mind that your thoughts, feelings, and behaviors are intricately linked together. This is something that is widely recognized and utilized in many therapy sessions. Your thoughts will directly influence your emotions. We already saw that suggested earlier when looking at potential causes for emotions. Those emotions then influence your behaviors. The behaviors and the end results from those behaviors then reinforce that thought process, allowing for a complete cycle between these three concepts. This cycle is important to remember—it will strongly influence you and impact the ways in which you are able to behave.

3 / EMPATHY, EMOTION, AND EMOTIONAL INTELLIGENCE

As a social species, people are strongly dependent upon others. We naturally seek and crave that attachment from person to person. We naturally want to see that connection between ourselves and others. We want to have friends and family. We crave that connection more than anything else to the point that depriving humans of that connection and the ability to socialize is actually deemed a form of cruel punishment more and more in recent days.

We need some sort of interaction with people, and not getting that for longer periods of time can start to have negative, and sometimes irreversible side effects. People need to be able to interact with other people because it allows them to meet those needs for connection. It can literally impact the body negatively if you are to be entirely cut off from the outside world against your own will. It can be found to create anxiety, insomnia, nightmares, and more. People need to be able to interact.

· · ·

This need to interact is driven strongly by the fact that we are a social species. We have evolved to keep a group of people close to us at all times. We need that group of people with us to ensure that we do, in fact, feel supported. We need our villages, so to speak—those people that we have deemed our best friends and most important family members so they can all work together. We need that connection.

That connection is driven strongly by empathy. Without empathy, you cannot truly have that meaningful connection that you are likely looking for in life. You must be able to empathize with other people if you hope to be able to develop meaningful relationships —this is just common sense. Without empathy, you likely do not have the interest that you would need to care enough about developing that relationship for genuine means in the first place.

Within this chapter, we are going to address this process. We are going to take a closer look at what empathy is, how empathy works, and why empathy matters. It is a trait that makes us fundamentally human—without this trait, it would be nearly impossible for people to survive nearly as long as we have as a species. We will be addressing why empathy is so important and how it directly relates to emotional intelligence as well.

Empathy

Empathy is the component of human connection that allows for relating to one another. When it comes to feeling empathy for someone else, you are able to essentially put yourself in someone's shoes and walk a mile—in an instant. You are able to understand what is going on within someone else's mind, and within their world. You know the emotions that they are feeling. You may even have a pretty good idea about what they are thinking about as well. This is important to remember—when you look at this, you are able to recognize that, at the end of the day, this is the principle at the heart of everything that you need to know to relate to others.

Empathy allows for two major purposes—it allows you to relate to other people and it allows you to communicate with other people as well. These are both slightly different, though they overlap to some degree. Empathy is that feeling where you look at someone else and know how they are feeling or what they are thinking at that moment. It is crucial to understanding body language and the individual in general and without it, you are not going to be able to ensure that you can, in fact, properly relate.

Empathy can be broken down into five sorts of skills or components. These components are precisely how empathy is able to work to allow for the benefits to manifest in the first place. These five components include understanding others, developing others, service orientation, leveraging diversity, and political awareness. Together, they combine to create empathy for other people—a skill that everyone should be able to develop.

- **Understanding others:** This is the ability to recognize and sense how other people are feeling in the moment. You may be able to tell when someone is stressed out, for example, or you may be able to sense more nuanced emotions as well. You may be able to tell when someone around you is frustrated or exhausted. You may be able to tell when someone around you is struggling in some way, shape, or form. You are essentially tapping into what someone else needs.

- **Developing others:** When you are able to develop others, you act in ways that will benefit others. You are usually doing so by attempting to meet their needs or helping to attend to their emotions that they are currently suffering from. If, for example, you hear that your partner is very stressed out, you may be able to help them manage that stress your own way through the use of other tools. You may be able to help them discover ways that they can benefit themselves.

- **Service orientation:** This is the attitude of other people who should always be cared for before you care for yourself. It is attempting to go out of your way to ensure that you have met the needs of someone else. Even if it is an inconvenience to you, you find that you would much rather do that than leave the other person to suffer.

- **Leveraging diversity:** This is taking a look at the way in which the differences within a group matter. You are able to recognize that the uniqueness of everyone in your group is different and that those differences can absolutely be taken advantage of. You choose to take advantage of their differences and recognize the value of each and every one.

- **Political awareness:** This is the ability to understand the group's underlying needs, allowing you to understand what is going on beneath the surface, so to speak. You are essentially allowing yourself to figure out precisely how you should be talking to other people. You recognize that at the end of the day, you will need to be able to understand those group dynamics to ensure that ultimately, you can survive.

The Importance of Empathy

Being able to understand the emotional states of other people is incredibly important. When you can understand those emotional states, you know that ultimately, you are better equipped to ensuring that you can understand what those around you are also suffering from. This is very important, especially in tribal times in which we had a small tribe to rely on. Those earlier human groups were quite dependent upon the people in their group settings. This primarily manifested likely through the use of empathy as a sort of communication method.

With empathy, you know what someone else is feeling at a glance. You can tell what someone else needs because you can read them. You know that someone needs your help because you can see it or sense it. This is very powerful—this is like super powered intuition that will tell you precisely what it is that you will need to hear.

Empathy and being able to read body language cues matters greatly. If you can read that the person next to you is in dire need of care and you can provide it, the neighborly thing to do is follow up and ask if you can do anything. Your empathy encourages you to move forward and attempt to help the other party. Because you then go and attempt to help the other party, you are helping them to thrive. You may be helping someone get up off of rock bottom to stand into the role that the other person needs. You may be providing all of that support that they are desperately in need of.

The communication provided by empathy is still relevant today, even if we no longer live in a life where we need to worry about a lot of the factors that used to be a regular cause for concern in life. Rather than being afraid of what you will do alone, if you have high levels of empathy and other people around you need something. The empathy levels provided are crucially important.

Empathy and Emotional Intelligence

When you feel empathy for other people, you are able to essentially foster a bond with them that would otherwise never be present. You are able to recognize the emotions of those around you, allowing you to understand that connection. It establishes you and your partner as a team together. It allows you to stop and consider their needs alongside yours, and you will likely weigh them relatively evenly because you think that they deserve that equal consideration. You will be able to understand them, and in understanding how they feel, you will also be able to essentially use this to your advantage. You will be able to ensure that you are motivating yourself and others to ensure that you all get your needs met.

Empathy, though it can be difficult to learn at first, can be a great way to help foster a new relationship with someone that you have ever met. Ultimately, we will all meet new people from time to time. We all wind up making new friends or coworkers at some point in time, and that matters greatly.

. . .

When it comes to empathy with your own emotional intelligence, it is important for you to be able to recognize what happens when you do foster these bonds with other people. When you do start to interact with other people thanks to your empathy that you have for them, you can then begin to properly develop those relationships that you wish to have. You may see someone ringing you out at the grocery store who seems to stumble over the job still. They may apologize to you for taking so long—but they are taking so long because they are new and they do not know what they are doing.

If you are an empathetic individual, you will recognize the situation. You will recognize the pain that comes along with it. You will see how your own actions can be directly related to this and that you can either make the situation worse by complaining and refusing to be understanding, or you can choose to help alleviate some of that stress by recognizing the truth—that the person is new and still learning. You are essentially showing compassion to someone else thanks to the empathy that you feel. Is it an inconvenience to be slowed down? Absolutely—but it is also a human being on the other side of the transaction and you do not see the purpose in attempting to force the point or attempting to hurt someone else. Rather, you decide that you would prefer to show that degree of compassion that you know that he or she deserves. In showing that compassion, you allow yourself to better regulate. You allow yourself and those around you to recognize that a basic little courtesy is a great way to help remain empathetic, emotionally intelligent, and help someone feel better.

4 / DOES EMOTIONAL
INTELLIGENCE REALLY MATTER?

Now, at this point, you may be questioning whether or not emotional intelligence even matters in the first place. You may be wondering if it is truly worth all of the effort that you must push into emotional intelligence. You may want to know if it is truly worth the effort to ensure that, at the end of the day, you behave emotionally intelligently. The short answer is yes—it is always important for you to be behaving in ways that are conducive to being emotionally intelligent. Emotional intelligence is crucial in just about every aspect of your life, as you will be introduced to shortly.

Emotional intelligence is essential. There will not be a single day that will go by that will not require the use of emotional intelligence to some degree or another. The principles that you will see shortly are incredibly important and they provide benefits just about everywhere. You will see precisely how emotional intelligence really matters in this chapter. We will discuss the difference between EQ and IQ and how, more and more, people are beginning to prefer those that have a higher level of EQ, regardless of IQ level thanks to them making a better employee long term. Finally, we will go over several different contexts in which emotional intelligence is a driving factor.

EQ vs. IQ

Before we go over what makes emotional intelligence so incredibly important, however, you must address the differences between EQ and IQ, as well as why EQ is the preferred method of judging the potential compatibility between people and their jobs. Firstly, let's take a look at EQ—this is the emotional intelligence quotient that was designed to quantify the emotional intelligence value. It is widely compared to IQ, which is the number that is designed to quantify cognitive intelligence. The EQ is designed to allow someone to be evaluated to determine just how likely it is that someone is going to be capable of navigating complex social situations. However, you must also remember that EQ is designed to be self-reported. EQ is all about test questions that you will have to answer subjectively. You will need to report how you think that you do in each category—meaning that it is not always the most accurate method through which you can determine how fit someone is for a specific job.

What you ought to remember, however, is that more and more, the higher EQ individual is believed to be more likely to succeed. This is primarily due to the fact that, at the end of the day, what matters when you are working in close proximity with someone else? It is far easier to train someone that does not have the work experience to do a job than it is to train them how to get along with other people.

. . .

EQ is fluid—it can be altered, but that requires a desire to change. That requires the other part to want to do better. It requires them to want to figure out how they can change what they are doing to better fit in with the situation at hand. When you take a close look at how someone is socially, however, you are able to find someone with the right personality. Personality is much harder to alter than skills training, so people are beginning to prefer the higher EQ individual to the higher IQ individual.

You are even beginning to see questions about EQ when you go to job applications or when they ask you to submit an application in the first place. They will ask you questions that are designed to fish for a response that will enable them to judge just how well you deal with these difficult situations. You will be asked how likely you are to do something a certain way. You will be asked to consider just how willing or able you are to make sure that, at the end of the day, you can solve a problem with a coworker. You will be asked how you intend to approach other people in general. As you emphasize that you plan on facilitating the relationships that you have, even in the workplace, and as you emphasize your emotional intelligence skills, you will find that you become far more hirable than you were before.

This does not mean, however, that there is no place for people with higher IQs. Rather, many places will prefer good or at least decent personal skills over someone who has that high IQ but is incredibly socially awkward. At the end of the day, the social awkwardness can be a huge deal breaker when you are exposed to it day in and day out. You get to a point where you need to make a change of some sort—and that change may very well be the point at which you are going to have to force it.

Emotional Intelligence and the Workplace

In the workplace, emotional intelligence reigns supreme. You need it to help you navigate nearly any situation. Now, unless you work at home, producing something and rarely ever have any outside points of contact with clients or employees, your emotional intelligence becomes crucial. Consider this—a police officer that has been busy is likely to be under plenty of stress. Now, that stress could manifest in a few different ways—it could manifest into a situation in which the individual is able to cope with the stress relatively productively and relatively simply. However, the stress could also become overwhelming if the individual does not already know how they should be compensating for that stress, they can begin to lash out at people that do not deserve that sort of backlash. It is very important to remember that, at the end of the day, your emotional intelligence determines whether or not you are able to cope or stress out others.

If you are in any sort of high-stress, high stakes job, such as medical care, paramedics, firefighting, police, military, or anything else that runs a very serious risk of injury, then you need to consider this. You need to consider that ultimately, being able to better cope with that stress thanks to your own emotional intelligence can potentially make the difference between enjoying your job and your job coming entirely overwhelming.

Emotional Intelligence and Relationships

Emotional relationships are another point in which you can really clearly see the impacts of emotional intelligence. If you do not have emotional intelligence, your relationships will suffer greatly. You will struggle to make sure that your partner is able to feel like they get that support that they need and deserve. You may fail entirely to ensure that they feel that you value them, and if you can fail at that, you run the serious risk of your relationship ending entirely. People do not want to stay with someone that makes them feel unvalued. People do not want to stay with partners that make them feel worthless or unworthy. You failing to provide that for your own partner can actually become a big sign that there are problems with your own emotional intelligence. Lacking emotional intelligence in a relationship can actually be incredibly destructive. It can actually lead to the creation of all sorts of negativity. It can lead to toxicity and abuse, and because it can destroy a relationship, your own emotional intelligence should always become an important priority.

With high emotional intelligence, however, you are able to navigate these conflicts that will, inevitably, arise. Remember, relationships do not have to be perfect. They do not have to be without any conflict. Conflict is a normal, natural part of life, especially when you have so many people so close together at the same time. You need to be able to manage your conflicts that do arise in a way that is meaningful and polite to both sides. This allows you to settle issues without much of a problem. It allows you to hold discussions that matter most, and the empathy felt can be a great way to really help keep everyone on the same page.

Emotional Intelligence for Leaders

Another aspect of life that involves success for those that can master emotional intelligence is leadership. EQ is essentially the precursor for leadership. If you hope to be a good, strong leader, you must be able to become emotionally intelligent. The best way to be an effective, fair leader is to be highly emotionally intelligent and then to use that knowledge to your benefit. You will see this often—you get someone that is highly charismatic working together to help solve some sort of problem. That charisma is almost undeniably attractive for many people- they struggle to stay away from it and as a direct result, they end up following that leader. They cannot help it—they feel compelled to do so.

However, truly emotionally intelligent leaders have what it really takes to ensure that they succeed. They know how to make sure that they are meeting the needs of their people, essentially ensuring that the people want to continue to go back to them for help, time and again. They know how to support those around them, and they likely genuinely mean what they are attempting to do. These people are driven by their empathy and their drive to get what is right. They know what they want and they know that to get it, they will need to make changes and make the appropriate sacrifices. The leaders that struggle with EQ usually get over-thrown at some point because they are not very desirable. Because they do cause problems for those around them, people do not want to keep them around. They do not want to follow the individual that struggles with EQ. They do not want to feel like they are under feeble or flimsy environments.

5 / THE BENEFITS OF EMOTIONAL INTELLIGENCE

EMOTIONAL INTELLIGENCE MATTERS GREATLY. It matters to those that have it and it matters to those on the receiving end as well. It is necessary for people to have emotional intelligence if they hope to be successful. It is a subject that has been popular for a long while, even though, at the end of the day, it is one that is only recently drawing attention from others. Emotional intelligence itself is a skillset that bestows many, many benefits to those that are able to draw from it. It is a skill set that leads to many improvements and benefits throughout one's life in nearly every aspect. It can benefit your relationships. It can benefit your work performance. It benefits your attitude and self-esteem. It will help you essentially anywhere that you can implement it and that matters greatly.

Within this chapter, we are going to go over some of the most important benefits that emotional intelligence has to offer. These are benefits that you, too can reap if you are able to begin implementing this particular skillset into your daily life. If you are dedicated and diligent, you should also be able to better develop these skills into one that matters for you.

You Work Well in Teams

The first major benefit that you will take a look at here is that you will be adept at teamwork. This is precisely because you learn how you can navigate through all of those difficult situations. You learn how you can better manage your relationships. You learn how to better work with other people—you learn how you can ensure that you communicate well with those around you and because you can communicate so well, you know that at the end of the day, you can make sure that the team flows well.

Oftentimes, when you work in a team setting, you have to come up with some way in which you can properly juggle how other people prefer to interact and how they interact with each other as well. You need to figure out what those group dynamics are and see how they are so intertwined with each other, and it is only when you can figure out how they intertwine that you then begin to see other aspects. You begin to see how people interact with each other and how you can facilitate and encourage that. You begin to see the underlying undertones that show you who is good with what, and that matters.

Beyond just that, however, when you are on a team with other people, you will usually do everything in your power to work well with them. You will want to ensure that those on your team are successful just as much as you want to be successful. You just want to do your best—and you likely have the skillset that you will need precisely for that reason.

· · ·

You Cope Better With Change

When you are emotionally intelligent, you often find that change is not nearly as scary as it used to be. You have the emotional self-regulation skills that you need to prevent the changes that will occur from becoming overwhelming. You essentially remind yourself that you have the ways in which you can manage your emotions, no matter what the difficult situation that you are facing is. If you are facing, for example, a sudden loss of a job, you are able to face the fact that in losing your job, you have other opportunities that will open up for you as well.

Essentially, when it comes to emotional intelligence, you have the skillsets required to ensure that, at the end of the day, you are capable of coping. You are able to ensure that you know what it is that you will need at the end of the day. You ensure that you develop healthy coping mechanisms and you can recognize when you have a need for them in the first place. This sort of self-regulation allows you to ensure that you are better able to deal with yourself and succeed more often.

You Can Navigate Difficult Conversations

No one enjoys having a difficult conversation. Whether your conversation is about how someone stinks and needs to take showers, or it is telling someone that they are fired, or anything else, difficult situations are no fun to get through. No one gets their job because they want to spend all of that time trying to disappoint people. They get those jobs because they want to ensure that they can help. However, sometimes, when you help people, you also have to be able to have that difficult conversation as well.

· · ·

Think about doctors and nurses for a moment—they do their job because they feel entirely compelled to help other people. They know that what they want more than anything is to ensure that everyone around them is well taken care of, and they do anything in their power to do so. However, these people who save lives will, sometimes, fail to be able to do so. They will sometimes fail to be able to stop someone from hurting. They may sometimes fail a surgery. They sometimes send out a wrong diagnosis or ask for invasive tests that were not necessarily required at that point in time.

Sometimes, difficult conversations arise, and those with the highest levels of emotional intelligence tend to be the ones that can cope with it. They are the ones that are able to navigate those difficult conversations with tact and grace, ensuring that people do, in fact, begin to feel better. They are able to help those around them. They are able to practice helping other people, even in their darkest or most difficult moments and that is very meaningful.

You Do Better With People

When you are emotionally intelligent, you generally do better with people. You are better able to navigate those tough social skills and situations that matter. You are able to ensure that you, for example, are able to deescalate a conflict. Sometimes, you need to calm someone down. Sometimes, you have bad experiences that need to be worked out. Sometimes, you have done something wrong that has hurt other people.

No matter what, however, being emotionally intelligent works to help bolster against it. With your emotional intelligence, you can start to sort of fend off the degradation of relationships that will otherwise develop over time. You can work harder to ensure that at the end of the day, you and those around you succeed. You ensure that you and those around you are more than capable of developing the relationships that you need. You ensure that you and those around you are able to fix anything that comes up.

It Makes You a Strong Leader

Emotional intelligence is largely considered to be a methodology that lends itself toward leadership—and this makes perfect sense. When it comes down to being a good, strong leader, you have several tools at your disposal when you make use of emotional intelligence. In particular, you will have skills that will help you navigate just about any situation. You will be able to look at a group and understand the underlying dynamics. You will be able to see the ways in which you can facilitate the changes that you want to see or that you need to see happening around you. You will be able to ensure that, at the end of the day, those people working around you are succeeding. You will see how they are able to work harder and ensure that they do better.

Those with higher EQs are typically more prone to becoming leaders in general—especially beloved ones. It may be that you never intended to find that position as a leader, or you always wanted it, but one thing is for sure. When you are emotionally intelligent, you can succeed—you *will* succeed. You will be able to negotiate with ease because you will be able to tune into the other person's mindset. You will be able to recognize what matters the most and where the strengths of those around you are.

You Are More Self-Controlled

People need self-control. Self-control allows them to avoid making risky, dangerous, or simply unintelligent decisions. Sometimes, people have impulses to go out and do something tough or do something that does not make sense. Perhaps one of your team-mates is entirely convinced that they are going to buy a pet cat and bring it into to office as the office pet to produce higher production levels. Perhaps you get into a fight with someone around you. Maybe you argue with your partner at home. No matter what, however, when you have emotional intelligence, these aspects will not faze you—you will be able to respond accordingly. You will be able to protect yourself and those around you. You will avoid lashing out simply because you will have those necessary skills to make sure that you are controlling yourself.

Self-control is difficult to muster for the vast majority of people. They may find that they prefer the impulsivity that they have primarily used, and ultimately, that is their decision. However, with your own emotional intelligence, you should always prioritize ensuring that you are self-controlled. It will take you far in life. You should be able to have a tough conversation with someone that caused you problems without ever actually becoming emotional about it. You should be able to remain calm if something bad happens. It is important to remember that if you do behave nega-tively or irrationally in a situation, then you want to stay calm. It is only when you stay calm and focus on what needs to be done that you can be sure that you are making the right decisions.

You Are Compassionate

Perhaps one of the most positive and pleasant benefits of emotional intelligence is that it makes people compassionate. When you are able to behave with compassion, showing that degree of caring about what is going to happen to those around you, you are able to deepen your connection with other people. As you deepen that connection with them, you ensure that you up to your own reputation. You teach the other person, whether a client, an employee, or a complete and total stranger that you simply allowed to use the restroom before heading back off to do whatever it was that they were doing, you are able to ensure that everyone does learn something—they learn that they can trust you.

With compassion, you are able to foster connections. You can connect the group around you and you can help improve the general attitude. Your own compassion can literally change the entire dynamic within the entire group. This benefit comes along with empathy, a very crucial skill when it comes to emotional intelligence, and we will be talking a bit more about empathy later on in the book.

You Are Motivated

People with high emotional intelligence are typically incredibly optimistic. They are typically always working because they feel that drive within themselves. They feel like they want to keep bettering themselves—this is known as a growth mindset. They have this mindset that pushes them to continually work as hard as they can to ensure that, at the end of the day, they can succeed. It is there to help them learn how they can become motivated by ambition instead of external sources.

People who are emotionally intelligent are typically working hard because they think that working hard has its own inherent value. They love to get pay raises, but they are not likely to push for it or say that they are deserving of it because of what they did. They are oftentimes well within their rights to go above and beyond to really help and support those around them to see precisely what they can do.

. . .

If you are emotionally intelligent, you likely work hard and refuse to give up. You are willing to do everything that you have to do in order to ensure that ultimately, you do the best work that you possibly can. You feel like you are motivated entirely by merit rather than anything else, and that is a good thing.

You Manage Time Better

Finally, the last benefit that we will address (but this is not the last benefit overall) is better time management. Whether you are managing a business or simply trying to improve yourself, one of the best resources that you can master the use of is time. When you are able to master the use of time, you are able to ensure that you are not wasting a precious resource that you cannot get back at any point in time. You have a finite amount of time, and no attempts to mitigate that can change it. Everyone dies eventually— it is just a matter of knowing when it will happen. Because of this, it is greatly important to recognize that time management matters.

When it comes down to being emotionally intelligent, time management is a skill that you develop. You are able to see the dynamics within the office and see which ones work while others need to be tweaked or changed some other way. It allows you to manage your own time better as well—being emotionally intelligent; you can usually figure out precisely how you can better manage a business. You can learn to hire only those that also show higher degrees of emotional intelligence, for example. You can also help to keep people working productively with your own group as well.

Now, with those perks of emotional intelligence in mind, it is time to go over some of the most common signs that you may be lacking in emotional intelligence. Keep in mind that if you do discover that you lack emotional intelligence, it is not the end of the world. You can learn to overcome this. You can actually develop emotional intelligence, and while it may be a long road to make it happen, you can learn how to bolster your own emotional intelligence, and the last half of this book will really emphasize those points.

You Stress a Lot

Stress is the bane of just about everyone's existence. No one enjoys that feeling of their blood pressure spiking and their hearts racing. However, it is very common when you struggle with your EQ. Because emotionally intelligent people have the ability to self-regulate, they are usually able to better cope with what is going on in the world around them. They are usually a bit more confident with themselves and being willing to stress or struggle. However, when you lack emotional intelligence, you may struggle to manage the situation in the first place.

· · ·

Studies have shown that when you fail to use your emotional intelligence skills, you are more likely to use a method to manage your mood that is less than stellar. It could be that you experience depression or anxiety, and you try to self-medicate it with drugs or alcohol. You could even fall prey to self-harming behaviors. You simply cannot cope healthily with what is happening around you and that leads you to feel like you are stuck or unable to better yourself or those around you.

You Struggle to Assert Yourself

When you lack EQ, you struggle to know when it is appropriate to speak up about something bothering you and when it is better to let something go. You do not have that ability to understand when you are choosing to do something that is likely to be seen as a problem. You do not recognize that line between assertion and starting a fight, and because of this, you struggle to properly assert yourself.

Instead of using assertion, which would allow you to be clear about what is bothering you, you may instead find that you are going to be stuck feeling like you cannot voice your complaints at all. Or, alternatively, you will spend far too much energy or time trying to assert yourself only to wind up being aggressive or even passive aggressive at times.

On the other hand, if you make use of emotionally intelligent methods, you are able to keep yourself balanced and focused. You are able to focus on how to talk about a problem without making the problem the other person. You are able to essentially recognize when the problem is the person or when the problem is another problem altogether.

. . .

You Do Not Know What Triggers You

We all have some sort of trigger to our moods. This is something that, when it happens to you, is immediately going to set you off. It may make you scared or angry, or something in between. However, when it happens, you lose control—you start to act out or lash out and you lose your grip on your own emotions. They are very powerful aspects of people's personalities, and everyone has one of some sort. It could be something related to a trauma—people with post-traumatic stress disorder oftentimes find that they are triggered, for example, by loud sounds reminiscent of their time in warzones.

You, too, have some sort of trigger. If you are shaking your head no right now as you read this, however, that is a sign that you do not know what your trigger is. You do not know what it is that will set you off—and something will—it is just a matter of figuring out what it is. When you do not know what your triggers are, you know that you are going to struggle more. You know that you are ultimately going to find that you cannot deal with them when they do pop up at some point in time. People with emotional triggers usually lash out at people to some degree.

When you develop emotional intelligence, however, you develop the skillset that you will need to understand what your triggers are. You will learn to recognize them for what they are, and in knowing what they are, you can take precautions when you know that you are in a situation that is likely to trigger you in the first place.

You Struggle to Articulate Your Emotions

Articulating your emotions is a very important job. You need to know what bothers you and what makes you happier or sadder if you hope to be able to navigate the world effectively. You need to know precisely what it is about the world that bothers you, and you need to be able to clearly say it.

Even if you are not emotionally intelligent, you will still experience those emotions. You will still feel them—but you will not be able to tell other people what is going on. Think of the stereotypical child tantrum—a toddler flailing and screaming and pounding on the wall. That is his way of dealing with not being able to articulate emotions. You need to be able to thoroughly and accurately tell others what you feel so they can begin to understand and help.

You Make Assumptions

Oftentimes, people who struggle with their EQ also tend to create opinions very quickly without support or research, and then they decide that they are never going to accept anything other than that particular viewpoint. They will not stop defending that belief system that they develop and they will repeatedly assert and insist that their own particular belief is the right one. They refuse to change their mind, no matter how much evidence may be presented that is contradictory. This is a huge problem for them— they struggle to ensure that they are better able to correct for mistakes along the way. Remember, change is necessary. Change happens and sometimes people are wrong. However, when it comes down to people who are not emotionally intelligent, they have a hard time recognizing when it is time to change their beliefs to something that is going to be a bit more fitting to the situation.

You Feel Misunderstood

Without emotional intelligence, you assume that other people do not understand you in the same way that you do not understand them. You do not understand how you are coming across to those around you, and when they take what you were saying the wrong way, you feel upset, frustrated, and misunderstood. However, this feeling of being misunderstood is a symptom of an even greater problem—you are unable to articulate yourself properly. You are unable to figure out how to speak to other people to ensure that they understand you and get what you are trying to say.

This is something that everyone struggles with sometimes. Perfect communication, every single time, does not exist anywhere. People struggle to communicate sometimes and that is just fine. However, if you are unable to make yourself understandable on a regular basis, it is time to consider whether or not you need to make the changes to your own approach and your own communication methods that you have. When you can make those changes, you are able to better deal with the problem at hand. You can begin to tweak your communication with others. You can focus on how to better articulate yourself as well. In doing so, you can improve the entirety of your ability to communicate with others.

You Hold Grudges

When you struggle with your EQ, you are much more likely to hold onto those negative emotions than others are. Really, though, that attempt to cling to your grudges is little more than a response to your stress—you are likely to repeatedly trigger your body to respond to more stress. When you hold onto your grudge, you are clinging to your stress, and that is a major problem. You need to be able to let go of that stress to move on.

· · ·

When you develop the propensity to use emotional intelligence, however, you learn to eliminate that stress altogether. You learn what you can do to help yourself change what you are doing. You can learn to let go of all of the negativity that will otherwise plague your life and keep you down. You can let it go to not only be healthier in mind, but in the body as well.

You Blame Others for Your Emotions

People lacking in emotional intelligence struggle greatly to understand how they feel. They struggle to talk about how they feel and why they feel it. They struggle to figure out what it is that is going on around them to make them feel bad. They also assume that, when they do feel some way, or when they behave according to their emotions in the first place, that it is someone else's fault. They assume that the blame for their emotions does not sit on their own shoulders, but rather on those around them instead. If they get angry, they will blame it on the person that they are angry at rather than accepting that ultimately, other people are not responsible for their emotions. At the end of the day, only you are responsible for your own feelings. Only you have the power to control them—other people do not make you feel angry. *You* and your mindset make you feel angry, and there is a major difference between the two that you need to consider. When you become emotionally intelligent, you learn to recognize the difference and you stop blaming others for your own feelings.

You Hold Onto Mistakes

Similarly to holding onto grudges, many people that are not emotionally intelligent find that they get caught up with the mistakes. They make mistakes, as all people do, but rather than learning from them, many people that struggle with their EQs simply try to forget their mistakes instead. They try to ensure that they are able to better avoid the problem, and they refuse to let it go.

· · ·

The problem, however, is that, then, you do not let go of the mistake and you continue to stress yourself out. Alternatively, you could choose to let it go without forgetting them. The emotionally intelligent individual masters this act—they are able to distance themselves from any failures and mistakes without worrying about them. They essentially refer to the fact that they made a mistake and learned from it and move on. They do not want to dwell on the past because other than learning to not make that same mistake again; there is no benefit in dwelling or beating themselves up over it. They do not see the value in rehashing out the failure over and over again when, in reality, they already did everything that they needed to do.

You essentially need to find that right balance between remembering the mistake but not being afraid of it—when you are able to figure out how to forgive but not forget your mistakes without falling down, you are usually able to ensure that your mistakes become learning experiences rather than something that is going to tear you down.

You Don't Get Angry

Sometimes, people who are not emotionally intelligent but want to have this misconception of the process. They assume that they cannot be angry at all—they assume that they are going to need to hide their emotions altogether. These people will essentially fake their emotions—they will know that they are feeling a negative feeling, so they try to hide it behind feelings of happiness or joy. They do this because they do not want to fall into the trap of not being able to show that they are emotionally intelligent—but pretending to be happy when you are not is actually a sign of the exact opposite.

. . .

No matter what you feel, you are better off being able to express it. Think of it this way—when you are constantly covering your emotions, you are not being genuine. You are not showing people the truth and without the truth, how can you create the necessary change that you are looking for? The answer is, you cannot. Remember, people who are emotionally intelligent will allow their negative feelings to come out sometimes. It is okay to feel mad sometimes. It is okay to express your anger or your sadness sometimes. It is okay to be honest about your feelings, no matter what they are.

You Get Offended

Finally, perhaps one of the most recognizable signs of a problem with someone else's EQ is becoming offended easily. Most people who have lower EQs are not entirely in touch with who they are as people. They are not entirely confident in themselves—in fact, usually, they are the exact opposite of confident. They do not feel good about themselves at all, and because they lack those good feelings, all they do is feel like they are being picked on. Even small pokes and jokes at these people can set them off because they do not feel confident or comfortable in their skin.

People who are emotionally intelligent are self-confident and they are also typically quite open-minded. Together, this results in someone that is not particularly easily offended. Rather than being easy to anger or annoy, people with higher EQs typically have no problem being at the butt of a joke. They do not mind being teased or made fun of and they do not find it offensive at all. In fact, they make jokes about themselves on their own to tease themselves sometimes as well!

7 / THE PILLARS OF EMOTIONAL INTELLIGENCE

WHEN IT COMES to how to think about emotional intelligence, the best way to do so is to break it up into considering several pillars. Each pillar is like its own foundation, supporting the entirety of emotional intelligence atop its peak. Without one of them, the rest would crumble. Each pillar is its own individual way of looking at the world, but at the same time, they stand apart. Your ability to be able to control the way that you interact with your own emotions is entirely dependent upon many different aspects of your life and of many different skills that you must be able to develop. When it comes right down to it, emotional intelligence is widely expanding and is comprised of building blocks that make each pillar and each pillar holds up the entirety of the concept.

Each pillar is called a competency. Each competency is a skill set that you can have that embraces the entirety of emotional intelligence. Every single skillset is important in its own way, and they tend to compound upon each other as well. Generally speaking, you can see the ways in which your own emotional intelligence can play out to impact all aspects of your life, and even each other as well. Your ability to be self-aware controls your ability to self-regulate and so on. These all work with each other to create the concept, and when you can recognize that, you can recognize that your own emotional intelligence, despite being labeled in several concepts, is actually incredibly interrelated.

Within this chapter of the book, we are going to take a quick look at the pillars and what they are. We will be briefly defining what these pillars are and how you can expect them to play out. When you see these pillars and how they interact with each other, you can be sure to begin getting that understanding of them that you need. We will go over each pillar now briefly, but keep in mind that, beyond this chapter, you will be getting much closer looks at what these concepts are. You will see the ways in which you can begin to understand the principles here, and as you continue to read later, you will learn what the proper skill sets are, how they work, and what you can except within them. You will also later be given all sorts of different activities and tips to being able to improve your emotional intelligence for each skillset as well.

Competencies of Emotional Intelligence

The competencies of emotional intelligence are essentially the ways that you can better interact with the world around you. They are the ways that you can better cope with the world and how you can begin to properly understand everything that emotional intelligence entails. Essentially, they are labels for the skillsets that you will be using. They are the labels that you will use so you can group together the several skills that come together. When you hear competency, think pillar. It is that family group. Competencies are typically grouped further—you have personal and social competencies, which will be the talking point of the next chapter as well. You must understand this and how you can interact with the entirety of the situation to be able to understand what is going on within them.

Self-Awareness

The first principle of emotional intelligence is self-awareness. This is the most basic of the principles. It is there, so you know what you are doing, how you are doing it, and why you behave the way that you do. Your ability to be self-aware is highly dependent upon your ability to be able to pay attention to yourself in the moment. If you want to be self-aware, you must be able to touch base with yourself.

This particular skill is crucial—without it, you cannot hope to be able to go any further with your own emotional intelligence. If you struggle with being emotionally intelligent, you need to keep in mind that at the end of the day, this skillset sets the stage for everything. How can you self-regulate without self-awareness? How can you hope to be socially aware if you cannot be self-aware? How can you actively and skillfully help yourself manage relationships if you cannot pay attention to yourself and how you behave?

Self-awareness is one of those that many people, unfortunately, struggle with greatly, despite the importance of this principle. If you are able to take better control of yourself with your self-awareness, however, you can begin to defeat the problems that you have. If you are struggling with emotional intelligence, this is the most likely culprit and you will want to start here to fix your problem.

Self-Regulation

Next, you must consider self-regulation as well. This principle is your ability to control yourself—physically and mentally. It does not concern itself with stopping yourself from feeling strong negative emotions. You are more than welcome to feel your strong negative emotions, but at the end of the day, you must also ensure that you are able to better recognize how to keep yourself from behaving negatively as well. Your ability to self-regulate becomes a sort of filter that prevents you from behaving in ways that are dangerous or too negative to be used regularly or safely. If you have problems with self-regulation, you are oftentimes impulsive, typically due to your emotions, and you find that you really struggle to cope with many of the situations that you get yourself stuck into.

This particular competency is oftentimes also referred to as self-management—you may find it under that name in other books or throughout the internet. They are really two words for the same competency—the ability to control yourself. The skills within this are all about becoming a dependable, stable person, and they are greatly influential. These skills are those that begin to make you someone that may become a strong leader or someone who may, at the end of the day, be able to continue to advance. You must be able to interact with yourself if you want to be able to interact with other people. You must be able to influence yourself before you can influence other people. If you can do this, you can usually ensure that you are better able to interact with people in general.

Social Awareness

Social awareness becomes incredibly important as well, and without it, you are going to struggle to be able to keep up with other people that you are interacting with. If you struggle to interact with other people on a regular basis for any reason at all, it will likely be because of the ways that you behave and the ways that you can understand the people around you. If your personal competencies are just fine, there is a good chance that the problem that you are having is actually with your ability to be socially aware.

Being socially aware is being able to understand the way in which people around you are behaving. To be socially aware is to understand that at the end of the day, people will behave in predictable ways. To be socially aware is to be able to better cope with the ways that you behave because you can tell where other people are coming from. To be socially aware is to be able to recognize that at the end of the day, other people have their own feelings and thoughts, and it is of great benefit to you to be able to continue to emphasize those. When you are able to recognize the ways that other people behave, you can begin to take control of them as well.

If you are ever going to interact with other people at all, you must have this social awareness. You must be able to better become socially aware to ensure that at the end of the day, you can better cope with the problems at hand. When you are able to interact with other people better than ever before, you know that you are better able to do anything.

Relationship Management

Finally, relationship management represents the level that all people that want to lead aspire to. This is being able to become a great, brave leader that everyone is proud of. This is to be able to better influence people. It is everything that emotional intelligence culminates into and it defines how you are better able to interact with everyone else. As you are able to better process everything, you become better at understanding the nuances of relationships. You see how to influence and how to lead. To be strong in this competency is to be able to really roll with the ways in which you live. To be strong in this competency is to know that, at the end of the day, you can better control the ways that you see the world. To be strong in this competency is to be capable of changing the world and to make sure that you leave it in a way that is far better than it ever was before you arrived into it.

Each of these pillars are incredibly important in their own ways and at the end of the day, even if you do not aspire to be a CEO of a company or otherwise lead people, you will find that to develop emotional intelligence is to be able to become the person that you have always wanted to be. These are the people skills that you have—if you do not have the people skills, you will find that you cannot make sure that everything works properly. You will find that you bungle relationships. You will struggle to interact with people. You may even be left feeling depressed or brought down by the fact that you do struggle. It is incredibly important to have these skills developed no matter how much you think that you will use them and no matter how hard you may have to try to make them happen at the end of the day. If you can learn these skills, you can learn to change the world. You can become the best you that you can possibly be.

8 / PERSONAL VS. SOCIAL COMPETENCIES

AT THE END of the day, it becomes simple to divide up your skills in regards to emotional intelligence into two different camps, so to speak. They get bunched up into what are personal and social competencies. These competencies are divided up like this so you are better able to understand what is going on at the end of the day. Dividing them up helps you to recognize the ways that you must be able to change your own behaviors in hopes of being able to control your own emotional intelligence. Essentially, being able to look at your competencies in this manner allows you to see where empathy comes into play. Empathy is like the bridge that holds this all together, and without the empathy factor, you are likely to find that you cannot better your own abilities within this skillset.

At the end of the day, being able to sort of divide this out gives you a better way to see the parallels between all of the competencies. It allows you to see where the similarities lie so you can better understand how they connect together. You can better see the ways in which you can draw from the different competencies and how they can better allow you to understand the way that your skills at a fundamental level can impact the way that you interact with everyone else as well.

Within this chapter, we have a few key points to consider. We will address what it means to be a personal competency and a social competency. Then, we will consider how empathy acts as the bridge for it all. When you are able to bring in empathy as well, you know that you are better equipped to be able to interact with other people as well.

Personal Competencies

The personal competencies, as you likely would guess, are those that are directly related to you. These are the competencies that you must be able to embrace to allow yourself to better understand interacting with other people. When you are able to better interact with yourself and understand yourself, you get that foundation that you will need to help yourself. You will get that foundation that you will require to help yourself to ensure that you can better interact with people, no matter what the situation and no matter who you are with. You will essentially learn how you can better interact with and control yourself to allow yourself the ability to make sure that you can keep yourself under control. The whole goal of the personal competencies is to be able to keep yourself within your own grasp, ensuring that you do not give in or blow up at other people. When you consider it this way, you are able to essentially guarantee that you know how to manage yourself. This starts with being able to take a closer look at the individual and your own personal behaviors.

. . .

Effectively, if you wanted to summarize it up, you would consider this to be the way in which you are competent on an individual level. It is how well you do when it comes down to being able to control yourself and your own behaviors. It is how you can regulate yourself and how you can make sure that you are not a loose wire. To be personally competent means that you are someone that other people can enjoy being around. It means that you are, generally speaking, a stable individual that is capable of controlling your emotions. When you look at this in this manner, you will find that you are better suited to being able to be a good person. You can be within your relationships with ease without bothering people. You do not let your own emotional problems hold you back or cause problems for others.

Social Competencies

Social competencies, then, are how you interact with other people. These are the ways that you are able to interact with people that you know. They are the ways that you can manage how you act with other people and how you can begin to change the way that other people feel. To be socially competent is to be able to understand other people and to be able to navigate those interactions. You must be able to be personally competent before you can hope to achieve this as well, but when you do achieve this, you can know that at the end of the day, you are better able to interact with people. You can remind yourself that you do have the skills that you will need to ensure that you have good relationships with other people as well, so you can better cope with everything that you are doing at any point in time.

Empathy

Between the personal and social competencies is empathy. Empathy is defined as the way in which you are able to understand the thoughts and feelings of someone else. To empathize with someone else is to be able to relate to them. It is to be able to understand where they are coming from and how you should interact with them. To empathize with other people is to ensure that you are better able to understand them. You put yourself in their own shoes, so to speak. You begin to see how they are feeling.

To be empathetic, you are able to understand other people around you. You are able to understand, almost intuitively, the thoughts, feelings, and needs of those people. To be empathetic, you must be able to do five key things:

- Understand other people: This is necessary, so you are able to see and feel what other people are feeling. This is your ability to be able to see the emotional cues to better understand what is going on when it is happening. To be able to understand other people emotionally is to be able to read their emotional and nonverbal cues.
- You must also be willing to develop others—this means that you are able to act upon the needs of other people. You are able to help them become what they need, or you are able to get them what they need if you can. You are willing to help people learn and help them begin to get access to what matters. Especially in a leadership position, this also encompasses being willing to provide rewards and praise for those around you. When you do all of this, you know that you are better prepared to cope with those around you.
- You must develop a service orientation—this is the way that you are better able to help other people. It is the attitude of wanting to help give people what they want and need. It is that willingness to go further to make

sure that the other person is satisfied. It is meant to allow yourself to genuinely help other people and improve relationships by taking those cares.

- You must leverage and recognize diversity. This means that you are able to see the differences within a group, but in a way that you are able to see how you can bring it all together to help everyone help each other. When you are able to achieve this, you are essentially figuring out how best to put everyone where they can do the best good. This means that you are able to see the opportunities as they present, and you are able to see that that means that some people will have different jobs and different needs. It is the idea that you do not need exact equality—you need fairness. Every person has their own skills. One person who does not need support at something should not have it forced on them for the sake of equality. Rather, if they do not need the support, it should be given to someone who does need it.

- Finally, empathy requires that you develop a political awareness—this is the ability to see the way that the relationships within a group are playing out. When you take a look at the ways that people interact with each other, you then get to better see the ways in which they interact with each other in the first place. When you can see that, you are better able to recognize the ways that they are connected, and you can better tell how you can navigate the group waters.

When you are focusing on empathy and developing it for emotional intelligence, you are developing a way in which you will be better able to interact with those around you. You will be able to interact with people because you are better able to see the ways that they relate. You will be able to make sure that at the end of the day, you are better capable of ensuring that everyone around you can be better understood.

Empathy itself can usually be considered in three different forms: You can identify it to be cognitive, emotional, or compassionate. Each has its own place at the end of the day, but you will ultimately want to aim for compassion, which is kind of the middle of the road. When you engage in cognitive empathy, you are able to recognize what is going on in someone's mind. You are paying attention to their thoughts and feelings. You are looking at it from a rational perspective—you tell yourself, "He feels sad," but you do not feel moved at all on your own to feel any emotions at all. To feel emotional empathy is to feel the emotions of someone else. It is essentially catching their emotions, something commonly referred to as the emotional contagion. This is something that you can see when you see someone that you love or care about going through a rough time—you usually feel bad for them just as they do. You pick up on their emotions and you share them.

Compassionate empathy, however, is what you really want to get. This is the form of empathy in which you are better able to understand the feelings of someone else. You are better able to tell the emotions that someone else has and you can feel and recognize them, but you take it further—when you have compassionate empathy, you also feel a need to help them. You feel a reason to act —you feel compelled to do whatever you can to make sure that they are getting the support that they need as well. You are attempting to figure out any way that you will be able to aid someone else to ensure that, at the end of the day, they do get everything that they need and they are cared for properly. When this happens, you know that you are in a position that allows you to better deal with the other person's emotions and you leave them in a better spot than they were before.

As THE MOST fundamental of the competencies, self-awareness becomes one that you must build and bolster before you can really hope to tackle anything else. This s the skill that you will need to create any of the other improvements that you would like to see. To be self-aware is to ensure that you can better interact with other people by being aware of yourself. At the end of the day, it is your own mental self-portrait—the more accurate that your self-portrait is, the more likely you are to be self-aware.

Defining Self-Awareness

Self-awareness, at its simplest, is your ability to understand how you feel as well as how your feelings impact your behaviors. It is your ability to touch bases with yourself, acknowledge how you are feeling, and then also being able to figure out why. You are able to identify the source for the emotions that you are feeling, and you can usually also ensure that you better recognize how they will either help or hurt you. When you see that, you know that you will better be able to cope with the feelings of your own to better figure out how to cope.

. . .

To be self-aware is to understand your own personal abilities. It is your ability to see how you should be able to value yourself and how to evaluate your own strengths and weaknesses. Without self-awareness, you are likely to over-commit and be unable to deliver on a regular basis. You may not realize when you are upset or why you are upset. You may struggle to understand why, at the end of the day, you cannot better cope with the problems that you are facing, or how you can defeat them. To be self-aware, on the other hand, allows you to better deal with all of that. To be self-aware is to know what you are feeling and how your job is. It is to be able to understand yourself intricately. It is to recognize the ways that you can better change and where you struggle.

The Skills of Self-Awareness

Self-awareness, at the end of the day, is associated with three primary skills that you must be able to develop. If you do not have these three skills, you will find that you cannot possibly develop that self-awareness that you do need and because that is a very real risk, you must take the care to not only understand these skills, but also to make sure that you take the time to support and develop them.

Emotional awareness

To be emotionally aware is to understand what your emotional state is at any point in time. It is to be able to stop, remind yourself that you need to check in on yourself, and then understand the way that you are feeling right at that moment. This is a crucial ability that many people struggle with. All too many people find that they cannot check in with themselves. They find that they really struggle to better deal with the emotions that they have, and because they cannot tap into that understanding of what their emotional state is, they find that they really struggle to ensure that it is the right one. At the end of the day, you must remember that your ability to understand your emotions determines so much about yourself. It determines whether or not you are better equipped to handling the problems that you face. It determines whether you can even identify if there is a problem to begin with. Being able to be emotionally aware also allows you to recognize that your emotions are valid under any situation—it allows you to understand how better to deal with your emotional states so you can better cope with the ones that you have at any given moment. You recognize that at the end of the day, emotions are emotions and you can recognize that they are all valid in their own ways, no matter what they are and no matter how you have them.

Accurate self-assessment

Accurate self-assessment is all about understanding both what you are good at and where you struggle. It is your ability to have an accurate idea of what your abilities are at any point in time and how you can use those abilities to ensure that you are capable of success. You are able to see the ways in which you are better able to cope with the problems that you have, and because of that, you are better able to manage yourself.

You must understand what your strengths are accurate. This means that you cannot hyperinflate what you think that they may be. You cannot try to give yourself the idea that your thoughts are actually much more than they actually are. You must be willing to stop and see that at the end of the day, your strengths must be properly understood and evaluated. When you assume that your strengths are better than they are, you get yourself in over your head. When you assume that they are worse, on the other hand, you under-commit.

Likewise, you must also understand your weaknesses and where you struggle. You must be able to see the ways in which you may need help. When you cannot identify your weaknesses, you often-times get yourself into all sorts of trouble that could have otherwise been avoided. This means that you can see issues in other places. If you do not think that you actually struggle with organization, but you really do, you probably should not be in charge of figuring out the organization system at your place of employment, for example. It is important that you are able to better define your abilities accurately, and if you cannot do that, then you are going to have problems later down the line.

Self-confidence

Finally, the last key skill in this competency is self-confidence. Usually, this is sort of the result after you have been able to better develop your abilities. It is your ability to be self-confident—to recognize that you are capable of doing what is within your realm of possibility because you know that you are able to do it. Your confidence comes from trusting and knowing yourself. You feel more equipped to handle just about anything because you know that at the end of the day, you will not overcommit yourself. You know that you can trust yourself because you have a good idea of what is going on for yourself and you know that that is usually enough to keep track of what you are doing or how you do it.

Now, at this point, were are going to look at some of the skills that you can make it a point to develop when it comes to trying to build up your self-awareness. At the end of the day, you can always focus on self-awareness in other aspects—you can ensure that you are paying attention, for example, to the way that you can properly master the skills that you were introduced to earlier in the book. However, you can also attempt to bolster your self-awareness with all sorts of different activities. Here, you are going to be introduced to six activities that are incredibly simple to implement but will greatly improve the chance that you are going to be able to develop yourself.

Develop Your Emotional Vocabulary

One of the biggest problems that people can run into with their self-awareness is simply not having enough words to describe their emotional states. When you are not self-aware, you will find that you struggle greatly in understanding what it is that you must be able to do to ensure that you can better respond to the emotions that you are dealing with at any point in time. This can be a huge problem—if you do not have the word to describe how you feel, how do you hope to fix the problem? If you do not have the ability to tell those around you how you feel, how can you possibly ensure that you are better able to relate to people?

There are many different ways that you can begin to develop and improve your emotional vocabulary. In fact, there are many resources out there for children and for writers to help them come up with better vocabulary for their emotional states. When you stop and begin to learn more of the words for more of the emotions that you can develop, you can begin to better cope with a lot of the problems that you would otherwise be hindered by. Developing these skills will help you immensely when it comes down to discovering how best you can properly address the problem.

Spend Every Evening Reflecting

Every evening, you should set aside five minutes. It does not have to be long at all—all you have to do is sit down and listen to yourself. To do this, all you need to do is find a quiet place and spend a few minutes understanding what it is that you have felt throughout the day. When you can do this, you can stop and consider what it was during that day that bothered you. What upset you today? What made you feel better? What made you happy? What made you angry? We all have different reactions to different situations and being able to identify that is incredibly important at the end of the day.

By spending each day reflecting on your emotions, you can begin to better address what is going on around you. You can better begin to understand the ways that you feel and how you can later the ways that you feel in hopes of also being able to catch other information as well. Your evening reflections should become that sort of check in time that will allow you to begin to identify that.

Journal About Your Emotions

After you have reflected on your day and identified how you felt, it is time for you to stop and journal. When you spend every day journaling about a problem that you have faced, you can find that you will actually run into other situations as well. This journaling time can help you greatly when it comes down to figuring out your mindset and what it is that bothers you. When you journal about the way that the day has made you feel or how you have spent the day, you should quietly consider what you could have done instead of what you did. This can help you to figure out what it ist hat you can do better next time so you can defend yourself and ensure that you have fixed the problem.

Practice a Mindfulness Body Scan

Another method that you can use to help yourself become self-aware is the use of a mindfulness body scan. The way that you can do this is to stop, focus at the top of your body, and then slowly but surely go down the entire body. You are looking for the sensations that are within yourself. You are looking for the way that you are currently holding your body as well as the ways in which you can let go of how you are holding your body. When you are able to pay attention to this, you can better understand how your body reacts in the moment when you are emotional.

For best results, try doing this when you know that you are in different moods. Try it when you are happy—you will see that you can notice different sensations when you are. Try it when you are angry and sad. When you make use of this technique on a regular basis, you can see that at the end of the day, you will be able to better process everything and identify the ways that you are feeling at any point in time. The more that you do this, the better you can get at it with time. You will slowly, but surely come to recognize the ways that you can impact your body, and in doing so, you will be able to better identify your moods in the moment.

Accept Negativity

At the end of the day, we cannot fix certain things in life. We cannot defeat negativity. We cannot avoid negativity. However, negativity, if left to fester, can defeat use. Instead of letting it fester, however, you can make it a point to change the way that you behave. You can choose to ensure that, at the end of the day, you will better make sure that you are able to better interact with yourself and your emotions. The trick to doing this is by making sure that you accept the negativity in your life.

This does not mean that you have to like it. Rather, you must make it a point to recognize that it is not going anywhere. See that it is a regular part of life and that you must be able to cope with it. When you can acknowledge that negativity is normal and begin to see the ways that it will play out around you, you can prevent yourself from continuing to struggle in the future.

Learn to Identify Patterns

Finally, one last skill that you can use to help yourself develop that self-awareness that you may be lacking is through the use of learning to identify patterns in your behaviors. Look out for the times and the behaviors that tend to make you feel certain ways. Pay attention to them. Perhaps you go through your journal every now and then to begin looking for the patterns that you are likely to experience. These patterns can be huge problems at the end of the day. If you have patterns that show that you are regularly angry and cannot cope with the anger that you have, you will run into a huge problem. You must be able to find these patterns so you can control them and ensure that, at the end of the day, negativity does not rule you.

THE SECOND COMPETENCY and the second part of personal competencies include self-regulation. This skillset has several other skills alongside the ones that you have already been introduced to. When you are able to develop the self-regulation that you need, you know that you are better able to control yourself. You know that you can trust yourself no matter what is going on and that is a good sign for you.

This skill directly compounds upon self-awareness and if you struggle with self-awareness, you will be best served going back to work there for a while before returning here. You must be able to develop those skills if you hope to be capable of dealing with your ability to self-regulate.

Defining Self-Regulation

Self-regulation is your ability to manage yourself. It is your ability to filter yourself from doing something that you may regret. Think about it this way—if you were to be currently very angry, you might be feeling aggressive. You may have just lost at the video game that you were playing for the tenth time in the same place and you desperately wanted to simply move on and be done. However, you knew that you needed to keep trying. You felt like you needed to keep on attempting to solve the problem, so you kept trying to play the game. However, after that tenth loss, you could not control it anymore and you threw the controller that you were using into your television. Now, you have your frustration, a broken television, a worthless controller, and you are now even further than ever from being able to continue with your game so you can beat it. You just made the problem worse for yourself because you lacked the self-regulation that you need.

To be able to self-regulate, you must be aware of your emotions in the moment. You are then able to help yourself manage those emotions when you can self-regulate. This skill works almost like a shepherd to the emotions—it allows them to be felt while still keeping them out of danger and still keeping them from getting out of hand or making problems. When you can self-regulate, you know that you are better able to cope with the world around you. You know that you are better able to do just about anything because you are better able to cope with what you have to do.

Your self-control becomes a fundamental way that you are able to keep yourself on track. It ensures that, at the end of the day, you can help yourself. You can help make sure that your behaviors are those that make sense rather than those that may become major problems for you later down the line. When you are able to better take control of your emotions, you are typically better able to control yourself as well.

. . .

The Skills of Self-Regulation

Self-regulation usually brings with it five more skills that you must be able to master for yourself. These skills are all crucial in being able to understand how to interact with yourself and how you can ensure that, at the end of the day, you can better cope with yourself. You will need to master each of these skills within this competency if you want to be able to self-regulate effectively. As a reminder, if you are currently struggling with other aspects of self-awareness, you may want to return there temporarily to ensure that you can better get a handle on everything that you will need.

Self-control

To be able to control yourself is the most fundamental part of this entire skill. If you cannot be in control of yourself, you cannot be certain that, at the end of the day, you will be able to better control yourself at all. Your emotions are major influences on your behaviors and if you are not careful, you will find that you cannot manage what you are doing at any point in time and that is dangerous. You must be able to control yourself if you want to be able to interact with other people.

Self-control is what was missing in the example by throwing a video game controller through the television. When you cannot control yourself, you run the very real risk of having other problems in your life. If you are not careful, you can wind up hurting other people. If you cannot control your emotions, you cannot hope to have meaningful interactions with other people in your life or in your relationships and that is a major problem that you must be able to face if necessary. When you are stuck in this sort of position where you cannot control your emotions, you run into other problems as well.

Trustworthiness

With your ability to self-control comes the ability to become trust-worthy as well. When you are regulating yourself out, you must be able to better control all aspects of yourself, and that includes being able to deliver when you are asked to do something or when you commit. When you are committed to something and you do not follow through, then you probably have problems regulating yourself. You must be able to do this, especially considering the fact that your self-regulation is a foundation if you want to be emotionally intelligent in general. If you cannot regulate every-thing out, then you are going to see other problems that you will need to solve as well.

Conscientiousness

Along with the other abilities comes conscientiousness. This is your ability to consider everyone else and to pay special attention to details. You make it a point to be as thorough as possible so you will be able to better deal with the problem at hand. If you are conscientious, then you are likely to put everything right back where you got it. You will keep things organized so you can better deal with everything that you are doing. You will ensure that, at the end of the day, you can better cope with everything that you are doing so you do know that you can better regulate yourself out.

Adaptability

Adaptability refers to how well you can cope with the changes that may come your way. It is your ability to roll with the punches, so to speak. When you are able to self-regulate, you can usually develop this ability relatively simply—you are able to ensure that you do properly adapt to what must be done. If you find that you fail at something, you will likely bounce right back and keep on trying to make it work for you. This ability is one that becomes incredibly powerful—it is the ability to keep moving forward, even in the face of failure. It is the ability to keep on trying, even when something goes wrong. You must be able to do this if you want to be able to function normally.

Being adaptable is not always easy—oftentimes; it is actually something that is incredibly difficult. It is not always easy to push yourself to keep trying when things go wrong, and many people can get stuck here. It can be difficult to keep going when things suddenly take a turn, but at the end of the day, you must be willing and able to keep trying. Things go wrong in life all the time and the sooner that you learn to cope with that, the better. The sooner that you learn how to best deal with these problems, the sooner you are able to function.

Innovation

. . .

Finally, the last of the skills within self-regulation refers to innovation. To be innovative is to be able to do whatever it is that you need to do with whatever you have. It is to be creative—it is to think outside of the box when it comes down to it. If you are able to be innovative, you know that sometimes, you really need to be able to change the way that you think when it comes down to understanding what to expect or how you should choose to behave. When you can be innovative, you can make just about any situation work for yourself in just about any way that you can. You will do anything within your power to ensure that you can be successful with what you have rather than attempting to buckle down and refuse to budge because something did not go according to plan.

WHEN IT COMES RIGHT DOWN to it, being able to self-regulate is crucial. You need to be able to ensure that, at the end of the day. You know how to keep yourself under control. It may be that your emotions usually run rampant. It could be that you have other problems in your life instead. No matter what the problem is, however, you are going to find that the best way to fix the problem is by making sure that you better cope with the emotions that you have as you have them. You can learn to do this so long as you follow certain techniques. These techniques will help you to learn how best to keep control over yourself, even when you are feeling emotionally volatile. We are going to look at five ways that you can help yourself improve at emotional self-regulation within this chapter.

Deep Breathing

One of the best tools that you have in your body is your ability to breathe. This keeps you alive. It literally provides you with life-saving oxygen. However, it also allows you to control your actions. When it comes right down to it, you have a very special ability— you are able to breathe deeply to control your emotions. When you have this ability in tow, you can usually keep yourself calm in even some very stressful situations. All you have to do is breathe deeply.

Place a hand on your stomach. Take in a deep breath from your nose. Breathe in and count to five as you do so. Then, hold the breath for two seconds. Finally, slowly and gently breathe out through your mouth, with your lips pursed like you are blowing out a candle. How does this feel?

This method should work to calm you down, no matter what you are feeling. Just make sure that you repeat it a few times for the best result.

Is This Emotional or Rational?

Next, you should try to consider the point of whether what you are doing is emotional or rational. While emotions have a very important role in your life and ensuring that you are able to do everything that you know that you need to do, they can also be a huge problem for you if you cannot properly control them. You must be able to recognize that at the end of the day, you need to act rationally the vast majority of the time. The next time that you find that you are getting antsy to make a decision or to do some-thing and you are feeling like emotions are running high, stop yourself. Ask yourself if what you are doing makes any sense at all right at that moment. Is this actually something that you should be doing? Is it going to be a problem in the future? What are you doing? Why are you doing it? If it is not rational, you may find that you are better off resisting entirely.

Hold Yourself Accountable With Other People

When it comes to self-regulation, another way that you can ensure that you keep yourself on task is by making yourself accountable. You can do this with one simple task—tell yourself that you will tell other people what you are doing. If you are going to be interacting with people around you, tell them that you have a goal that you are going to achieve. It could be something silly—you could declare that you are going to learn how to sing a trendy song in another language just to be funny. It could be something serious, like deciding that you will pay off a certain amount of debt this month. No matter what it is, make it a point to remind yourself to do so by telling other people about your plans.

When you tell other people what it is that you are going to do, you essentially set yourself up, so you have to follow through, or you risk the embarrassment of someone else knowing that you failed to do what you needed to do or what you promised to do. This is usually enough of a fire under you to keep you moving and to keep you on track for your goal, no matter what it is.

Pause Before Reacting

When you are going to react to something around you, always stop for a moment. You should never allow yourself to respond or react to someone or something impulsively or instinctively. This can be a huge problem—for example, if someone were to give you bad news, you would not want to suddenly punch them. Instead, make it a point to pause, realize that you have a problem, and then override those intentions. Make sure to step back and prevent yourself from making this mistake by pausing.

When it comes right down to it, you can take a deep breath to help you here. You can stop yourself, take a deep breath, and then ask yourself if it really makes seen to do what you are thinking about doing right that moment. Is that really a good idea? If not, hold off.

You will probably be better off if you resist the impulse. This can help ensure that you do not make any big mistakes that are going to be a problem for you.

Never Make Big Decisions Without a Night to Wait

Finally, the last piece of advice to help develop your self-regulation is to make sure that you do not make big decisions impulsively. No matter how good of an idea as it sounds to get that new car that looks great and is just the right color, try waiting to see if it still sounds like a good deal in the morning. You should always make sure that you take a moment to stop and consider what is going on in your mind. Is this an emotional impulse? It may very well be one. Stop and make yourself consider whether or not you should make that decision for an entire day before you actually make it.

For the most part, there are very few decisions that have to be made immediately. You can take the time to stop and consider which car works best for you. You can stop and wait the day when it comes to signing the papers for a loan for a home. You can spend the day considering which job you should take over the other. All you have to do is be willing to take the break and then consider after having a chance to sleep on it. Oftentimes, we find that we do not actually want to do that in the first place

THE THIRD OF the competencies to understand is social awareness. This is the first skill in which you have made the jump from
thinking about yourself to starting to consider how you will
interact with other people, and just like the other skills that you are
trying to develop, it is crucial to have. You will need to work hard
to ensure that you are better able to cope with your interactions
with others. You will need to spend time really working at this if
you hope to be able to self-regulate. You must recognize that at the
end of the day, you are better able to deal with yourself in a social
setting if you work on your social awareness.

Understanding Social Awareness

Imagine for a moment that you are talking to someone new.
You do not yet know them, but you know of them, and you know
that you have heard that they tend to be difficult to deal with
because of the ways that they tend to interact with other people.
This means that you need to be able to better interact with them
because you do not want to cause problems. You know that if you
are not careful, you are likely to set them off, and that can be a
huge problem at work. However, when it comes right down to it

when you meet the new person and start to talk to them, you discover something—you discover that you are unable to better interact with them at all. You realize that you cannot better cope with the situation at all because at the end of the day, you cannot read the situation. When the other person is standing there with crossed arms and a scowl, you do not see that they appear to be frustrated. You do not see that they appear to have a problem with what is going on and you continue on without considering what the aftermath may end up being.

That is a lack of social awareness—you cannot see what is truly going on. You simply see what you want to see without being able to recognize that at the end of the day, there may be a problem there. You do not see the way in which what you are doing may actually become a problem for yourself. You do not see when you begin to cause problems for someone—in fact, you do not seem to understand the other person at all, and that is a huge problem for you. When you do not understand how they are acting or how you should be interacting with them, you start to struggle.

Someone who is socially aware, however, is able to be supportive. Someone with this skill set is able to recognize what needs to happen at the end of the day. They are able to see the way in which they may go that extra mile to help someone else and they see how at the end of the day, the way that they behave with everyone actually has a major influence on what is going on. This skillset is crucial to have for any interactions with other people. If you cannot develop this skill set, you will likely permanently have all sorts of problems with the relationships that you have. You will find that you do struggle to interact because you do not get what you should be doing or how you should be doing it. This is a *huge* problem People do not like to interact with people lacking social awareness. People do not like the constant seeming of being entirely unaware the other person is. It can be frustrating for people to deal with. They hate it and yet, it is something that is commonly not even considered.

The Skills of Social Awareness

When it comes right down to it, the skills of social awareness are those that you will desperately need if you want to be able to better cope with the relationships that you have. If you want to be able to interact with people, you must be able to do three key things. These three skills are crucial for you to develop:

Empathy

Remember, empathy is the bridge between self and social competencies. You must be able to have empathy if you want everything else to follow and without that empathy, you are not going to be able to interact very well with other people.

Remember that at the end of the day, your empathy is the ability that you have that guides you into being able to understand other people. It is the ability to better cope with the reactions and the relationships that you have so you can better see the way in which you can interact with people. You need to be able to do this so you can better see how, at the end of the day, you can interact with people. If you cannot empathize with someone else, how can you possibly hope to be able to relate to them at all?

· · ·

To be socially aware is to be able to understand the state that someone else is currently in. It is to be able to discover what it is that really matters at the end of the day. To be socially aware is to see the politics that come into play in relationships with other people, and they are always there. That requires empathy. If you cannot empathize and understand people, you cannot possibly be able to become socially aware.

Organizational Awareness

The second skill of social awareness that you must remember is being able to function within an organizational state. You must be able to see the way that a group, or an organization, will run and how everyone else interacts with each other. Essentially, you need to be able to see the connections between people and put them to good use. You should be able to tell when people do what and how they interact. You should be able to see the relationships out in front of you, enabling you to tell how people are able to better interact with each other. If you can do that, you know that you are better able to interact with people because you will not be surprised when things go a certain way.

Service

Finally, to be able to be socially aware, there is one last skill: You must be happy to provide services for other people. This is being totally content to ensure that you do things for people that meet their needs. This is the ability to be a caregiver in a sense—you are able to tend to the needs of other people so you can better understand what is going on with them. You need to do this so you can better interact with people—you must be able to properly process the way in which you interact with people and you must be willing and able to ensure that you do help them as well.

Social awareness gives you a certain degree of insight to people that many people lack, and in lacking this, people usually miss the opportunities of being able to help other people. When you develop this social awareness, however, you discover the ability to be so much more to so many more people around you. You develop the ability to be able to understand what people need. You develop the ability to provide people with what matters to them and what is going to help them the most. You learn how to develop and foster relationships that you may not have had otherwise.

Most importantly, however, when you are able to repeatedly meet those needs and the emotional states of other people, you develop trust. You gain that ability to be deemed as trusted by those around you and because of that, you develop that ability to be seen as deserving of trust and deserving of a position that could help you.

I℉ ᴠᴏᴜ, like many other people out there, believe that you struggle with your social awareness, you are not alone. You can begin making use of these different exercises to help yourself begin to slowly foster your ability to use this fundamental skillset so you, too, can discover the ways in which you can better facilitate relationships.

Listening Practice

When it comes right down to it, most people do not actually understand how they should be listening to other people. They get into trouble because they do not stop to remind themselves that, at the end of the day, they need to also make sure that they are listening to others actively. Many people listen with the intention to *answer* rather than to *understand*. This means that they are constantly distracted, trying to come up with how they can also answer the question, or refute a point. Instead of doing this, however, what if it were the case that you chose to listen to understand instead?

· · ·

When someone else is talking, give them your undivided attention. Ensure that you are watching them, and you do not have any distractions, such as your phone or a television. Make sure that you give them that attention and then quietly pay attention to what they have to say. Do not speak and only offer nods or "Mhm"s of encouragement to show that you are listening. When they finish speaking, take a moment to summarize what they said and then ask if you understood them. If so, then go ahead and think of your answer.

Practice Identifying the Emotions of Others

Another great way to pick up on emotional states is by creating a game out of taking the time to identify how people are feeling at any point in time. This is done through many different means—you can usually do so by making sure that you properly pay attention when you go out and about. Turn it into a challenge—attempt to name the emotions that other people are showing. Do this while you are out in public, or intentionally go out and people watch just for this purpose. It can help greatly when it comes to being able to better manage your own ability of emotional intelligence.

You can also do this in movies or when watching television. Spend some time watching the background characters—the people that do not do anything but add ambiance and try to identify their own feelings as well. The more that you do this, the better you become at being able to identify people's emotions. You are essentially giving yourself that practice that will aid them greatly and if you can take it and take advantage of that practice, you can become great at being able to regulate and recognize the way that other people feel at a glance.

. . .

Practice Naming People

Another point to consider is the act of naming everyone when you meet them. If they have offered you a name, make sure that you use it during the conversation. Also, always greet people by name and say thank you to them by name. This is important for two reasons. Firstly, it is good practice for you to remember that everyone around you is a person too, no matter how you see them. You must remember that they are also people that deserve their own attention and their own respect. You also make it a point to make them feel better as well. When you name them, and they get to hear that some stranger has used their name, they feel like you value them more—and to an extent, you *do*. This process is great to use, both in theory and in practice. Even when you feel like you have the skills that you need, this should be used regularly anyway. Let this become a habitual skill for you.

Come Up With Icebreakers

Nothing is worse than going to a meeting or being stuck in groups awkwardly with nothing to discuss and no real clear way that you can begin to deal with the people around you. If you get stuck in this situation, and you are also struggling with your own social skills, you may just be asking for a disaster. This is a huge problem for people—they get stuck, and when they get stuck, they get nervous. With nervousness comes all sorts of other problems and before you know it, you have embarrassed someone or otherwise caused problems for yourself.

Instead of getting caught in this trap, however, you can come up with a few icebreakers that you take everywhere that you go. These icebreakers allow you to defeat the problems that you have. They allow you to better manage yourself and your time. And even better, when you already know what you will do when you get stuck in this situation, you will be able to also make sure that you are able to help everyone in your group. You essentially allow for everyone to have a way to break the ice, break the awkwardness, and then get on with everything that you had planned.

Practice Mindfulness

Mindfulness is a very important skill that you can use to make sure that you are present in the moment. Mindfulness itself is just the art of doing something mindfully—that is to say, they are doing something with their full focus on it. To e mindful is to make sure that you do focus entirely. It is that ability that you develop to ensure that, at the end of the day, you can better understand the world around you. You essentially get the option to better control the way that you respond to everyone around you by making sure that you can, in fact, control the way that you interact with yourself.

By being mindful in public, you can focus on the way that other people respond. You can quietly and mindfully be in the moment with other people. You can make sure that, at the end of the day, you do spend that time developing and fostering the relationships that you have around you so you can better process what you are doing.

Make Gentle Eye Contact

Finally, to boost your social awareness with other people, you can make sure that you make eye contact. This is something that can be uncomfortable for a lot of people, but at the end of the day, it is incredibly useful for people to do. When you make use of gentle eye contact, you are able to make yourself feel connected to the other person. Remember, gentle eye contact means that it naturally breaks on occasion—you are not staring down the other person, nor are you attempting to make them uncomfortable. It is natural eye contact that will split sometimes.

If you find that making eye contact is too uncomfortable for you, however, there are methods that you can use to sort of feigning it. At the end of the day, making eye contact with other people is valuable. People value having their gaze met and if you cannot do that for them, you will likely be deemed to be untrustworthy or otherwise someone that should be avoided.

To feign it, however, you can simply look right between someone's eyes. Look at that place right underneath where their brows come together. Chances are, they will not notice that you are not actually making eye contact, and you get to avoid the discomfort that would otherwise come with it.

FINALLY, the last competency that you will need within the emotional intelligence framework is relationship management. This particular competency is where everything all comes together to create that well-rounded, emotionally intelligent framework that you desire. When you are able to complete this competency, you are able to begin discovering the ways in which you can better interact with the world around you. When you develop this skill set, you begin to see that, at the end of the day, you do better manage the problems that you have. You discover that you are better than ever at being able to interact with people. You are able to lead and to influence. You are motivational. You are liked. You are able to do all of this because other people deem you to be a confident and fair leader thanks to what this skill entails.

Understanding Relationship Management

When it comes right down to it, relationship management allows for a connection to be fostered between yourself and those around you that leads to the other people feeling validated. They feel like you understand them well and that you are there to support them—and they are right. When you are able to manage your relationships, you are able to complete the necessary skills that you will need to be able to lead groups of people with ease. You will be able to better deal with those around you with grace and tact because you will know what really matters at the end of the day.

Keep in mind that this is so much more than simply being kind to people or being seen as a friendly person. This requires effort. It requires you to be intentionally attempting to do what you do. It requires you to be dedicated to ensuring that, at the end of the day, you will get the best out of what is going on around you. You will be able to help influence the way other people feel and you will be able to influence the way that they respond as well.

Relationships are difficult even in the best of situations, and unfortunately, it can be very easy to run into problems with them. It can be difficult to work with people, especially if you clash with the other person somehow. It could be that you have different values, or you could simply not like the same things. Even if this is the case, however, you have a duty to trying to figure out how best to interact with those around you. You have a duty to ensuring that you are better able to cope with everything that you do and making sure that, at the end of the day, you can better relate to those around you, no matter who you are with.

When you develop this skill, however, you are always able to find that common ground. You are always able to locate that one thing that brings you and those around you together so you can better deal with the problems that you have faced. When you can do this on a regular basis, you discover something important—you discover that, at the end of the day, you *can* control your relationships and ensure that you can influence what is going on around you, even if you feel like you and the people that you are surrounded with are incompatible fundamentally in some way, shape or form.

To be effective at managing relationships, you must be able to go through four steps. These will help you to figure out how you can interact with people in a way that is conducive to this relationship management in the first place. These criteria are:

- **Decisions:** These are always based on the best way that you can act in the moment. You take a look at the situation that you are in, the ways that you can act, and the people that you are around in order to figure out how best to interact with everyone. You are able to understand how people feel, and then you take that understanding so you can then decide how you will interact, knowing that how you choose to interact will directly impact everyone in the group.
- **Interactions:** After making your decision, you must then interact with the people around you. This may be done in person, with you directly interacting with them, or it could be done through other methods as well, such as writing a letter, being in a group, or anything else.
- **The outcome:** This comes when you see how, at the end of the day, you were able to alter the behaviors of everyone around you. This is what you are attempting to achieve by acting in the way that you are. You are always trying to find that proper outcome to ensure

that, at the end of the day, you do get what you are
looking for. Because you are always shooting for an
outcome that you want, you are making sure that this
is intentional. You are purposefully aiming for
something specific that you can use.

- **The needs:** This is what will influence the outcome
that you are seeking. When you have a need that must
be met, you are able to change your attempts at
interacting with those around you so you can get them.
You are essentially looking at the way in which you
can better interact in hopes that you can get those
needs met.

The Skills of Relationship Management

Of course, none of those things happen in a vacuum. There
are several skills that align with the ability to make sure that you do
get the outcomes that you are attempting to achieve. These skills
are crucial to employ—they determine the ways in which you are
actively interacting with other people to ensure that you are able to
manage the relationships that you have. The skills that you will
require for this particular competency include:

Influence

You cannot be a good leader if you are not influential. If you are
trying to be able to manage relationships, then at the bare minimum, you must be able to influence those around you to make that
happen. Influence is the skill that allows for changing the
thoughts or behaviors of people around you. You are able to take
different methods and allow yourself to create those changes. In

particular, this makes use of persuasion. It is typically highly frowned upon to be manipulative in emotional intelligence—you want to ensure that the people that you are interacting with genuinely want to interact with you and they are not doing it out of force. When you can see that, you are generally at least getting off on the right foot.

You must be able to be charismatic to be influential—you must be able to make sure that, generally, people want to engage with you and that they want to follow you. You want to be able to use this ability so you can begin to develop those relationships that matter to you.

Inspirational leadership

As the leader in a group, you must be able to convince people to follow you. This means that you must be able to properly ensure that everyone around you is more inclined to follow you. To be an inspirational leader, you must be someone that people naturally want to follow; you must be someone that people generally see as being valuable and being someone that they do want to see succeed. To be this person, you must be willing and able to do what you can to ensure that you are willing to help people, to listen, and to do what you can to be the leader that they need.

To become an inspirational leader, you must develop that ability to better inspire people. That means that you must learn how you can talk to people. You must learn how you can better cope with people. You must learn how to motivate others into doing what it is that you are doing and how you can influence them.

Developing others

To develop others is to help them grow as a person. It is to be able to see the strengths and weaknesses that they have and recognize that you can change them. It is to be able to give the other people everything that they will need to be able to better control what they are doing at any given point in time, allowing you to better see what really matters at the end of the day. When you can do that, you know that what you are doing is really important.

When it comes down to how you can develop everyone else in your life, you learn that there is one important factor: Being able to see where people truly shine. You are great at figuring out what people thrive at and what they may need to work a little bit harder at may be. When you can develop this skill set, you know that you are better able to point out the way that people around you thrive and ways that they may actually struggle somewhat. This is normal—it is normal for people to have wide differences in their capabilities—but you find that you are great at being able to find them and then aid in finding a solution to the problem. You are able to guide people through everything that they would need to do and what they would need to know to better help themselves.

Change catalyst

· · ·

A change catalyst is a person that is responsible for being the trigger that causes the change. When you are able to develop your relationship management skills, you begin to recognize that sometimes, that person should be you. You begin to see the ways that you can come together to be that person so you can be the one that ensures that everyone gets along. When you are able to become this person with ease, you know that you are able to get the change to happen, whether other people agree with it or not.

You generally are driven entirely by the fact that you want to be able to keep things running the way that they should be. You can see where change is warranted and where it is needed, and you push for it to happen so you can guarantee that you get it. You are able to see that things are often better if you can push the change rather than assuming that you will keep the situation exactly as is rather than attempting to stick to what is familiar. You know that sometimes, you need to shake things up.

Conflict management and team building

When you are able to see the way that people are interacting on a regular basis, you become capable of understanding the fundamentals in their relationship. You begin to understand that you can, in fact, ensure that they are better able to interact in ways that are meaningful and that they are also able to ensure that, at the end of the day, they do matter. You are able to choose to interact with people and to encourage them to interact with people in ways that make the most sense, both personally and to help the team out as well.

. . .

This usually comes down to you being able to stop a conflict in its tracks—you are usually able to remind yourself to settle down, stop, and ensure that at the end of the day, you can better interact with people around you. You are able to understand the way that you can influence the arguments that people are having. You understand that you can better guide them in coming up with solutions that make the most sense for them. You are essentially able to come up with a common ground for them—you can find somewhere that they can both agree to agree and guide them through being able to agree to disagree sometimes, too.

You are skilled at also bringing relationships together—you are great at ensuring that the people who are placed together are able to better interact with themselves and with those around them as well, all thanks to the ways that they think. You can see where the people have the potential to get along really well and you take advantage of that. You will be willing to facilitate new relationships together anywhere that you can, knowing that at the end of the day, through doing so, you can better manage what is happening around you.

To IMPROVE relationship management does not actually have to be that difficult. You can learn to be more relationship oriented in many ways, mostly involving the skills that you have been provided thus far. However, there are other exercises that you can use that will help you to better manage your relationships as well. Let's go over six more methods that you can use to better your emotional intelligence—with these six addressing your relationship management skills.

Learn to Give Feedback Properly

At the end of the day, you must be able to interact with people properly if you hope to be able to manage relationships at all. One of the biggest places that people make mistakes in doing so is in their attempt to give feedback. All too often, people find that they cannot properly acknowledge the way that they should be offering their feedback. They mess it up, and they cause problems. With that in mind, let's go over how to give feedback properly so you can make it constructive and helpful, ensuring that, at the end of the day, everyone that needs to get their feedback will without it being a problem.

. . .

To begin, make sure that you ensure that the feedback has a good purpose. Is it actually constructive? If so, continue. If not, you probably do not actually need the feedback anyway.

Make sure that when you do give your feedback, you provide it in a way that is focused on it being your own perception of it. This means that you should be using "I" statements rather than attempting to tell them that they messed everything up or that they need to fix everything because they are wrong. When you focus on the "I" instead, they do not feel like they are being attacked, which is precisely what happens when you start with "You" instead.

Learn to Accept Feedback Properly

Along those same lines, you must also be willing and ready to accept feedback yourself as well. This means that if someone comes to you with feedback, you must be happy to accept it. Give it your complete attention and do not try to get defensive. It can be difficult to be faced with criticism, especially if you think that it is not fair, but you should make it a point to at least try to.

This means that you must hear it out without interruption. Listen to what the other person has to say—really listen. As they speak, try to understand things from their side and acknowledge that. After they are done talking, it is time for you to stop and consider the way that they decide to approach the situation as well. Thank them for what they had to say, and then really reflect on the criticism that they gave you. If you want to be a good relationship manager, you have to ensure that lines of communication are always open and that you do not intimidate people into feeling like they cannot approach you with the problems that they find or that they face.

Always Follow Through

You should always make sure that you follow through when you say something. When you promise to do something, you owe it to that other person to get it done. You owe it to them to ensure that, at the end of the day, they are better managing everything that is going on. You owe it to them to ensure that, at the end of the day, you can do everything in your power to follow through. If you promised something that is taking you too long, then you may need to figure out some other way to approach the situation. You may need to figure out some other way to help those around you feel like you are taking it seriously. If you cannot follow through at all, you must communicate that at the soonest point that you can. You must make sure that the other party feels like they can, in fact, trust you. It is only when you are deemed trustworthy that you will be able to properly manage the relationship.

Use Tokens of Appreciation

When it comes to managing your relationship, it can help greatly to also use little tokens of appreciation sometimes. This is not to bribe people—rather, you are attempting to make it clear that you appreciate what the other person is doing. You are making it clear that, at the end of the day, you can recognize the efforts that when into things and that you wish to show the other party that you do appreciate them. When you do appreciate them in this manner, you show them that you were thinking about them.

This does not have to be anything grand, either—you can make sure that you leave a little thank you note when someone goes above and beyond. You can ensure that you leave a note for someone saying that you saw them working hard and that you wanted to let them know. You could stop and get someone coffee on your way to work. You could offer to help them in return for the way that they have helped you. No matter the method that you choose, you can begin to better manage your relationships because the people around you will feel like you are more respectable when you are actively helping them on a regular basis.

Take Control and Make Decisions

When it comes right down to it, relationship management is about leading and influencing. It is about being able to take charge and ensure that you can see how you can better manage the relationships around you. To do this, however, you must also be able to recognize that sometimes, you need to simply force the point and make a decision. You need to take control of how you respond so you can better deal with the people around you. You need to be willing to make decisions, even when they are difficult ones.

The life of a leader is not as glamorous as people tend to think and oftentimes, you need to find ways that you can really show other people that you take things seriously. One way to do this is by making sure that you take charge when you deem it necessary. Doing so is not only imperative—it is necessary. Take charge the next time that you are faced with a difficult decision. Make sure that you spend the time trying to make it work.

Under-Promise and Over-Deliver

Finally, one last way that you can really help yourself with relationship management is to make sure that you are always paying close attention to your promises that you make. If your job is to be as reliable as possible, it is crucial for you to figure out how best to manage the situation at hand. If you realize that you have the problem of regularly promising the moon, but entirely missing the mark, you can fix that. The trick to doing so is through making sure that you never overpromise. You can do this by consistently and intentionally always estimating that it will take you longer to make something happen. Make sure that you always make it a point to spend some time looking at the ways in which you are attempting to do things for others actually make sense. This means that you need to under promise instead of overpromising. When you under-promise instead, you make sure that you can then over-deliver. When you over-deliver, you make people happier because they get things sooner than expected, and you have the added benefit of having been able to have that extra leeway if you needed it.

17 / PUTTING IT ALL TOGETHER

FINALLY, you have reached the end of this book. At this point, you understand what it is that emotional intelligence entails. You understand the skills that come together to create the person that you want to become. You understand the ways that you can begin to improve the problems as well, allowing you to better deal with the way that you can talk to people. You know what it is that you want to be and how to get there, but you may find that you do not yet know where to start. How can you begin to finally understand what matters? What do you have to do? How can you really begin to get started now?

The answer is, there are still a few more steps that you can take to begin to understand how you can actually take the plunge. You have been provided with everything that you will need to know and understand at this point in time. You see how you can better begin to become that person that you want to be—and this book will finally guide you through the process of becoming that person.

. . .

When it comes right down to it, there are a few steps that you can take from here. You can begin to understand where you are now so you can progress to where you need to be. You can learn to master your negative thoughts. You can learn to become cognizant of your current emotional states. You can begin focusing on how best you can be capable of managing your own positive environment. You can begin to develop your own resilience, as well. As this book draws to an end, take a look at some of these last ways to think about how you can change what you are doing to help yourself become the emotionally intelligent person that you know that you can become. Consider this your foundation—the launching point for everything that you need to do.

Get Your Baseline

The first step for you to take is to discover what your baseline reading is. This is the reading that you know will guide you. When you know how emotionally intelligent you are now, you can then discover the ways that you can change for the future. Let's face it— if you currently struggle with your emotional intelligence, there is a very good chance that, at the end of the day, you will already assume that your skills were fine. The most basic skill was self-awareness—remember? If you struggle with your emotional intelligence, there is a great chance that, at the end of the day, you will struggle to actually understand where you fall here. This means that you may think that you are actually far more emotionally intelligent than you actually are.

Take a look online. There are many resources out there that will be able to help you. You will be able to find tests for free that will help estimate how well you perform within the four competencies so you can get a baseline for how you will need to change to be able to be better stable yourself. When you are able to see how your own emotional intelligence falls, you then discover the ability that you can use to begin better processing yourself. You then know where you should be focusing on helping yourself discover the person that you are meant to be. You will need to spend the time discovering what it is that you need to do so you can better focus your efforts and that baseline will be that point for you.

Learn to Read Yourself

Another crucial starting point for you is to make sure that you learn to read yourself. You need to learn to see what your baseline behaviors are. You need to discover what it is to be the you that you are and then begin to discover the way that you can better deal with yourself. When you are able to recognize the behaviors and tendencies that you tend to fall into, you can then begin to protect yourself from them. You can learn how you can better avoid falling into these traps. You can learn how you can better begin to process things yourself. You can learn how you can begin to better predict when you are having problems by stopping and understanding where you are at.

This is essentially an extension of self-awareness—but self-awareness is so fundamentally important that it is worth having it rephrased here as a starting point. You must learn to embrace that if you wish to be able to better change the way that you are seen in the world around you.

Master Negativity

Another great starting point for you to consider and master is the use of controlling your own negativity. When you are able to master your control over negativity, you can ensure that it does not become a problem that you cannot cope with. It does not become something that you cannot defeat. Negativity, in particular, can have a huge effect in just about every area in your life, so the sooner that you manage to eliminate it entirely from your life, the better that you will do. You may find that at first, you struggle to eliminate it. However, in the future, you may find that it is actually not that hard to defeat the negativity if you know what you are doing.

Remember that negativity includes a negative environment. If you want to be able to become emotionally intelligent, you need the best foundation that you can get, and ultimately, that comes from your ability to better manage your emotions, which requires that you are able to eliminate that negativity from your life whenever possible and practical.

Remain Resilient

Finally, above all else, make sure that you maintain your resilience. Make sure that, at the end of the day, you can better process your emotions by ensuring that they do not make you feel like you are better off giving up on everything. This is a hard process. It is a long process. However, at the end of the day, it is absolutely worth it to follow through with. Do not let this process hold you down. Do not let it make you feel like you do not need to bother. Even when you begin to feel weak or like you would rather do anything else other than dealing with this, make sure that you keep moving forward. Resilience is necessary. It will help you. Persevere. Keep moving forward. The beginning is the hardest part, but if you can get past it, you will see great results.

CONCLUSION

Congratulations! You have made it to the end of *Emotional Intelligence*. At this point in time, you have learned all sorts of information that would be necessary for you to be able to better cope with the emotions that you currently suffer from so you can become more emotionally intelligent. Whether you already knew that you struggled with your emotional intelligence, whether you had a pretty good idea that you were not as emotionally intelligent as you would like, or if you found that other people told you to take a look at these processes and how you could become more emotionally intelligent, you have made it to the end. You have gotten all of that crucial information that you will need to be able to better manage yourself, and in managing yourself, you will be able to better manage those around you as well.

Within this book, you were given several different topics to consider. You were introduced to the idea of emotional intelligence, and you learned all about it. You were guided through how it is a method that you can use to better yourself; you learned about how it can better guide you through how you interact with other people. It taught you everything that you would need to know about how best to process yourself, your emotions, and your relationships.

From here, it is time for you to begin implementing the work that you have discovered. It is time to start working on how you can become an emotionally intelligent individual so you can begin to better take control of yourself, your emotions, and better your relationships. It is time to start pushing forward to better yourself, and if you put your mind to it, you will succeed. Remember, you must start by strengthening your emotional intelligence with self-awareness. Remember just how crucial it is to be able to see your own emotional states so you can then begin to better process the ways in which you must behave. Remember that, at the end of the day, you can better yourself. Remember that, at the end of the day, you can learn to build these skills for yourself so you know that you can succeed in your life. Remember that, at the end of the day, you can better cope with everything that comes to your face. All you have to do is get moving to make it happen. You can do it. You have the power to do it. You can become a more emotionally intelligent individual. You can learn to defeat everything. You can do it if you push yourself.

Good luck on your journey! Hopefully, it will bring you to a point in which you do feel like you are in control. Hopefully, you do get to that point in which you feel like you are successfully able to manage yourself. Hopefully, you do begin to feel more confident in yourself, and hopefully, this book played a role in that all! If it did, please head over to Amazon and leave a review detailing your experience with the book! Feedback is always greatly appreciated!